ABRAHAM

The Father of the Jews

Bible Biography Series
Number Nine

John G. Butler

Copyright © 1993 by John G. Butler

Published by
LBC Publications
325 30th Avenue North
Clinton, Iowa 52732

Printed in the United States of America

ISBN 1-889773-09-3

First printing 1993
Second printing 1996
Third printing 1998
Fourth printing 2001

Introduction

The Bible Biography Series is a series of twenty books written about Bible characters by John G. Butler. These books are expository studies of the Scripture. They are extensively organized and outlined, filled with Gospel lessons and practical applications of Scripture to every day life, written in easy to understand laymen's language, and theologically and morally they take a strong, old-fashioned, fundamentalist position which is increasingly unpopular but greatly needed in our day.

These books are very helpful to preachers in providing material for sermons and lessons on these Bible characters and texts. They will also be found to provide much instruction for the individual in his or her personal Bible study; and because of their organized structure, they are very adaptable to Sunday School classes and Bible study groups.

The twenty books of the Bible Biography Series consist of books on *Joseph, Jonah, Elijah, Elisha, Gideon, Samson, John the Baptist, Peter, Abraham, Lot, Paul, Moses, Joshua, Samuel, David, Nehemiah, Jacob, Hezekiah, Mordecai,* and *Ruth*.

The author, a native of Iowa, is a veteran, fundamentalist, Baptist preacher who has been teaching and preaching the Word of God for over forty years with nearly thirty-five years of pastoral experience in Ohio, Michigan, Illinois, and Iowa. He is also the author of the *Studies of the Savior,* a series of books about Jesus Christ.

Contents

PREFACE 9

I. SUMMONS FROM GOD 11
(Genesis 11:27 – 12:9)
A. The Receiver of the Summons
B. The Review of the Summons
C. The Response to the Summons

II. SOJOURNING IN EGYPT 36
(Genesis 12:10 – 13:4)
A. The Famine in the Land
B. The Forsaking of the Land
C. The Folly out of the Land
D. The Flight Back to the Land

III. SEPARATION FROM LOT 56
(Genesis 13:5–18)
A. The Contending by the Herdsmen
B. The Counselling by Abraham
C. The Choosing by Lot
D. The Confirming by God

IV. SOLDIERSHIP OF ABRAHAM 71
(Genesis 14:1–16)
A. The Raiding of Sodom
B. The Rescuing of Sodom

V. SOVEREIGNS AND ABRAHAM 83
(Genesis 14:17–24)
A. The King of Salem
B. The King of Sodom

VI.	SURETIES FOR PROMISES..................................98

(Genesis 15)
A. The Confirmation About the Heir
B. The Covenant About the Inheritance

VII.	SCHEME OF SARAH 122

(Genesis 16)
A. The Proposing of the Scheme
B. The Problems From the Scheme
C. The Policing of the Schemers

VIII.	SPEAKING WITH GOD 147

(Genesis 17)
A. The Prelude in the Speaking
B. The Particulars of the Speaking
C. The Postlude to the Speaking

IX.	STRANGERS FROM HEAVEN 172

(Genesis 18)
A. The Ministering of Abraham
B. The Messages for Abraham
C. The Mediation by Abraham

X.	SHAME IN GERAR..197

(Genesis 20)
A. The Resorting to Deceit
B. The Reprimanding of Evil
C. The Reconciling of Men

XI.	SON OF PROMISE 219

(Genesis 21:1–19)
A. The Birth of Isaac
B. The Belittling of Isaac

| XII. | SUMMIT WITH ABIMELECH | 244 |

(Genesis 21:22–24)
A. The Request in the Summit
B. The Reproving in the Summit
C. The Results of the Summit

| XIII. | SACRIFICING OF ISAAC | 260 |

(Genesis 22:1–19)
A. The Command for the Sacrificing
B. The Conduct in the Sacrificing
C. The Consequences From the Sacrificing

| XIV. | SEPULCHER FOR SARAH | 296 |

(Genesis 23)
A. The Occasion for a Sepulcher
B. The Obtaining of a Sepulcher

| XV. | SPOUSE FOR ISAAC | 316 |

(Genesis 24)
A. The Choosing of the Girl
B. The Communication for the Girl
C. The Choice by the Girl

| XVI. | SERVANT OF ABRAHAM | 349 |

(Genesis 24)
A. The Calling of the Servant
B. The Consecration of the Servant
C. The Comparison of the Servant

| XVII. | SUNSET OF LIFE | 367 |

(Genesis 25:1–10)
A. The Supplements to His Family
B. The Specifics of His Will
C. The Statements About His Death

QUOTATION SOURCES 381

Preface

The life of Abraham marks a new division in the Scriptures. In the first eleven chapters of Genesis, Scripture covers some two thousand years of history in a rather rapid pace. The creation, the fall, a genealogy, Noah and the flood, a listing of the descendants and nations from Noah, the tower of Babel, and another genealogy take care of the first two thousand years of civilization and most of the first eleven chapters of Genesis. Then beginning with the last few verses of chapter eleven, the pace slows down dramatically. It takes the rest of the Old Testament to cover another two thousand years; and it takes the next thirteen chapters of Genesis, which features Abraham, to cover the next one hundred years.

Why the change of pace and the focusing on one men for a large section of Scriptures? Primarily because now the message of the Gospel is going to commence in more detailed form. The nation through whom the Redeemer of mankind will come is beginning in Abraham. This is disclosed in the covenant which God established with Abraham—a covenant which is very prominent in the Biblical record of Abraham's life. The chief promise in the covenant is the promise of seed for Abraham. He is to be the father of the Jews. But the greatest fulfillment of the promise is in The Seed, Jesus Christ, Who will come through the Jewish race. Abraham saw this, not as clearly as we are able to see it, but clearly enough so that Christ could say to the Jews, "Your father, Abraham, rejoiced to see my day; and he saw it, and was glad" (John 8:56).

The study of Abraham's life will not only be an instructive and rewarding experience in seeing many Gospel truths, but it will also be a very helpful experience in learning how to walk the life of faith in God's Word; for the Gospel not only involves the saving of the soul, but it also involves a new walk of faith. Abraham's successes and failures in this life of faith will teach invaluable lessons to the diligent student of the Word of God.

I.

SUMMONS FROM GOD

GENESIS 11:27 – 12:9

AFTER AN IMPORTANT genealogy to establish Abraham's ancestry, Scripture begins the story of Abraham with a special call from heaven. This is the great pivotal experience in Abraham's life which dramatically changed his life. But this Divine summons is not only extremely important for Abraham; it is also extremely important for all mankind; for it is a great landmark of the nation of Israel, of world history, and of the Gospel.

Regarding the nation of Israel, it is the beginning of that nation of all nations around which all the world is ordered (Deuteronomy 32:8).

Regarding world history, it is necessary to have a good knowledge of this summons if you are going to correctly interpret or understand the history of the world. Even in our day this summons is right in the middle of the most important events going on in our world.

Regarding the Gospel, the most significant thing about this summons given to Abraham is that it has to do with God's plan of redemption for mankind. In fact, providing redemption for mankind was the primary purpose for the summons.

To further study Abraham's Divine summons, we will consider the receiver of the summons (11:27–30), the review of the summons (12:1–3), and the response to the summons (12:4–9).

A. THE RECEIVER OF THE SUMMONS

The first thing we want to do in this study of Abraham's summons is to take a look at the man who received this Divine summons. Though Scripture does not say a great deal about Abraham's early days, it does, however, say enough about his early life so that we have considerable help in understanding and appreciating this summons and also the other events of his life as recorded in Scripture.

Concerning his early days, Scripture tells us about his relatives, his region, and his religion.

1. His Relatives

To learn about the relatives of Abraham who significantly affected his life, we will note his ancestor, his father, his brothers, his nephew, and his wife.

His ancestor. After the flood, the world was populated by the descendants of Noah's three sons: Shem, Ham, and Japheth. Abraham came from the line of Shem. Genesis 11 gives us an invaluable genealogy which traces the line of Shem down to Abraham. From this genealogy we can discern that Abraham was born about 300 to 400 years after the flood and about 2000 years before the birth of Jesus Christ in Bethlehem. In the history of man, Abraham came on the scene about halfway between Adam and Christ.

Shem, along with Japheth, was of better character than Ham, the third son of Noah, who provoked the terrible curse by Noah (Genesis 9:24,25). When Noah pronounced the curse on the descendants of Ham, he pronounced blessings upon Shem and Japheth because of their better character (Genesis 9:26,27). Shem's blessing was the superior blessing of the two, and the involvement of the Gospel in the summons given Abraham underscores that fact.

His father. Abraham's father was named Terah (11:27). Terah was an idolater (Joshua 24:2) and led his family to be the same. Abraham was very attached to his father; in fact, he was too attached. This is seen by the fact that until his father died, Abraham did not fully obey the Divine summons—which we will note more about later. Terah was a poor father in that he was a stumbling block for his son Abraham. He did not encourage Abraham to fully obey God's commands, but he led him into disobedience. Unfortunately, many, many fathers are of the character of Terah. They do not encourage their sons to go all out for Jesus Christ; but rather they encourage compromise, worldliness, and disaffection for God. No thanks goes to Terah for Abraham's noble life of faith.

His brothers. Abraham had two brothers: Nahor and Haran (11:27). Both played a significant part in Abraham's life.

The significant part Haran played in Abraham's life had to do with Haran's son Lot. Haran died prematurely in Ur before the brothers' father Terah died (11:28) and before the summons was given to Abraham. In death Haran left a son Lot who needed parental help. So Terah took Lot under his care (11:31). When Terah died then Abraham took over the care of his brother's son (12:5). We will note more about Lot shortly and also in later chapters of this book.

The significant part which Nahor played in Abraham's life had to do with brides. Nahor's granddaughter Rebekah became the bride of Abraham's son Isaac (Genesis 24), which event we will study in detail in a later chapter of this book. And Nahor's great granddaughters Rachel and Leah became the wives of Abraham's grandson Jacob (Genesis 29).

His nephew. As noted above, Abraham's nephew Lot was very much involved in Abraham's life as a result of Abraham taking Lot under his care (12:5). And Lot became a great problem for Abraham. Lot did not have the spirituality that Abraham did. Though he went along with Abraham to Canaan, his heart interests were vastly different than Abraham's; and this produced such a big problem for Abraham that it was finally necessary for him to separate from Lot—we will note more about this in an upcoming chapter of this book (for a more thorough study of Lot, see author's book on Lot).

His wife. Abraham's wife was Sarah (11:29). She was a blood relative of Abraham, for she was a half sister to Abraham. She was the daughter of Abraham's father but not the daughter of Abraham's mother (Genesis 20:12). In those days marriage among near of kin was practiced and with God's blessings, but later it was rightly forbidden. The early history of man necessitated marriage of near of kin from the standpoint of the smallness of population. Bible critics get noisy about such questions as where did Cain get his wife, but they raise noise in vain. Cain obviously married a sister or a niece—where else would he get a wife? And Abraham married his half sister, for Scripture plainly tells us so. That does not justify such practices today, for they are not needed now. But in those days they were.

Sarah will play a very important part in the story of Abraham. In fact, no other relative will be so prominent in the story of Abraham as Sarah was. As we will note in later studies, she was a beautiful woman who, though demonstrating faith in the birth of Isaac (Hebrews 11:11) and being an example in her respect of her husband by calling Abraham "lord" (I Peter 3:5,6), was too often a headache rather than a help for Abraham.

2. His Region

Abraham's native land was "Ur of the Chaldees" (11:28). This place was located where the Euphrates River emptied into the Persian Gulf. Scholars inform us that as a result of the silting of the gulf area over the centuries, the entrance of the Euphrates into the Persian Gulf is now extended a hundred miles or so south of where Ur was located. Ur lies today in the southeast corner of Iraq about seventy-five miles north of the Kuwait border. Thus Ur's location was not far from the center of the Desert Storm War of 1991.

Ur was an important seaport for trade from India and Africa via the Persian Gulf. The region in Abraham's day was also fit for the raising of flocks, and so it is not surprising that Abraham from his early days was involved in this occupation which he continued to do with much success in Canaan.

3. His Religion

When God called Abraham, he was an idolater. That is not surprising; for Ur was then an important center of paganism; and as we noted above, Terah, Abraham's father, was an idolater who had led his family to also being idolaters. Scripture makes it clear that idolatry was practiced by the family of Terah (which included Abraham). "Thus saith the LORD God of Israel, Your fathers dwelt on the other side of the flood [Euphrates River] in old time, even Terah, the father of Abraham, and the father of Nachor [Nahor]; and they served other gods" (Joshua 24:2).

Star and moon worship were prominent forms of idolatry then. "In that clear transparent atmosphere, the heavenly bodies blazed with extraordinary effulgence, beguiling the early Chaldeans into a system of Nature-worship, which speedily became identified with rites of gross indulgence and impurity, such as those into which humanity always falls, when it refuses to retain God in its knowledge, and gives itself up to the dictates of its own carnal lust" (F. B. Meyer). Though Abraham was separated from it by God's summons to him, the idolatry clung to his brother Nahor and continued on down to Nahor's grandson Laban and to Laban's daughters (Jacob's wives) as is attested by Genesis 31:30–34.

In emphasizing this unsavory religious background of Abraham, Isaiah speaks to Abraham's descendants about the "hole of the pit whence ye are digged" (Isaiah 51:1). What a great change took place in Abraham because of God's summons to him. His whole life was transformed. His character, attitudes, position, and eternal destiny were all gloriously changed because he did not reject God's call to him. The same is true in the matter of soul salvation.

That Abraham was called out of idolatry underscores the fact that he received this Divine summons as a result of God's grace. And how fitting that a summons which was so significantly involved with God's plan of salvation should be given to one primarily because of grace. Some try to show that Abraham lived differently than those around him in Ur; and, therefore, that is why God chose him for the summons. But Scripture does not encourage that idea at all. What Scripture does encourage us to conclude, however, is that it was grace, God's marvelous grace, that reached down and pulled Abraham out of the pit of idolatry and changed his life so wondrously. Abraham, like all redeemed souls, is a trophy of God's grace.

B. THE REVIEW OF THE SUMMONS

The summons, though extremely significant, was quite short. But God has a habit of packing a tremendous amount of truth into a few words, and this summons given to Abraham is a good illustration of that fact.

The summons was composed of two parts: precepts and promises.

1. The Precepts

"Now the LORD had said unto Abram, Get thee out of thy country, and from thy kindred, and from thy father's house, unto a land that I will show thee" (12:1). The precepts were basically twofold. Abraham was to leave one place and go to another. To obey these precepts, four significant things were required of Abraham: separation, sacrifice, labor, and faith.

Separation. "Get thee out" is the command to separate. The call of Abraham was a call to separation. He was to separate from a place ("thy country") and a people ("thy kindred, and from thy father's house"); and, as Scripture makes plain in the story of Abraham, it also included separation from the practices of evil. If one is to do the will of God and live for and serve Him acceptably, he will oftentimes have to separate from places, people, and practices which go counter to obeying God.

Separation is not popular. Man much prefers to mix, not separate. Thus, preachers, churches, and denominations who emphasize separation are scorned and called legalistic, backward, and unloving. Opposition to separation is so strong in our churches today that the separatist practices of godly fundamentalism of past years is quickly fading into oblivion and being replaced by the popular, but corrupting, mixing philosophies of modern evangelicals. Our churches and our Christian schools are ever giving more and more evidence of this unholy and destructive change. But without separation from the world, we lose our holy influence on the world. "It is impossible to move our times, so long as we live beneath their spell; but when once we have risen up, and gone, at the call of God, outside their pale, we are able to react on them with an irresistible power. Archimedes vaunted that he could lift the world, if only he could obtain, outside of it, a pivot on which to rest his lever. Do not be surprised then, if God calls you out to be a people to Himself, that by you He may react with blessed power on the great world of men" (F. B. Meyer).

Some may argue here that Abraham left one idolatrous civilization (Ur) to dwell in another (Canaan). But when Abraham came to Canaan, he did not fraternize with the Canaanites! Yes, there were the necessary covenants (Genesis 14:13, 21:32) and business transactions (Genesis 23) with those who dwelt in land of Canaan. But aside from these necessary contacts, he remained a stranger and a pilgrim to the people of the land. In Canaan, Abraham was in the world, but not of the world.

Note that the separation commanded here of Abraham was twofold. He was to come out that he might go in. He was to leave one place that he might go to another place. Separation is to always be this way. We do not just leave something and stop. No, we leave something that we might go elsewhere. We do not separate from unholy places, people, and practices and then stop. No, we separate from these things so we can be qualified for and better give ourselves to God's service. We have some who would not go near a den of iniquity or be with unholy people but who seldom serve the Lord. They sit like mummies in church pews filled with pride because they don't do this and don't do that and they don't go to this place or that place of evil. But they are only in the "don't" category, for they never "do" anything. They have missed the important dual aspect of separation. They have missed the fact that "don't" is to help us "do."

Sacrifice. In order to obey the Divine summons, Abraham had to do much sacrificing. He had to give up the land of his nativity, his friends, and relatives; all of which would be very dear to him. "The summons of God will ever involve a wrench from much that nature holds dear. We must be prepared to take up our cross daily if we would follow where He points the way. Each step of real advance in the divine life will involve an altar on which some dear fragment of the self-life has been offered; or a cairn [pile of stones making a tomb] beneath which some cherished idol has been buried" (F. B. Meyer).

Failure to sacrifice is one of the greatest hindrances to Christian service. Many folk have greatly limited their service or even missed God's calling altogether because they were unwilling to sacrifice much of anything for God. They will not sacrifice position, possessions, family, friends, wealth, time, or comforts. But Abraham would never have gotten to Canaan and become the great patriarch of the Jews if he had not sacrificed. And there would be no way of salvation if God had not sacrificed His Son—the greatest sacrifice ever made. So think it over—is your service limited and God's work suffering because you are not doing well in the area of sacrifice?

Labor. To obey God's precepts required much labor for Abraham. He had to drive his large flocks, move tents, furnishings, and family members hundreds of miles (it was some 600 miles just from Ur to Haran) to get to Canaan. This was anything but an easy task, but it was necessary to do if he was to obey the Divine summons.

Anyone who sets out to obey the Lord will find that labor will be a very prominent feature of obedience. Much toil and sweat will be involved to fully obey the precepts of God. Therefore, lazy folk will never do well in obeying the Lord. They will never serve much at all. On the other hand, one of the reasons Apostle Paul served so well was that he was not afraid of work.

SUMMONS FROM GOD

In his epistles he speaks much about labor and says in one place, "I labored more abundantly than they all" (I Corinthians 15:10). When Christ chose His twelve disciples, He chose good workers. A number of the disciples were fishermen, and one of the early notations made of them in Scriptures is that they "toiled all the night" (Luke 5:5) in their fishing business. These men were not lazy men. They were not afraid of work. And, therefore, with the exception of Judas, these men all made good disciples; for to be a good disciple, one has to be a good worker.

Faith. That faith is very much involved in these precepts is seen in "unto a land that I will show thee." God ordered Abraham to go to a place that He did not reveal to Abraham at the time He gave Abraham the summons. The writer of the book of Hebrews emphasizes this faith aspect of the precepts when he says that Abraham "went out [from Ur], not knowing whither he went" (Hebrews 11:8). Hence, Abraham must by faith walk step by step and day by day trusting that God would reveal the directions to him as necessary. God did not tell Abraham everything at once. It was piece by piece.

To obey under this situation is scorned by natural man. He wants everything revealed at once. He wants the destination, route, and purpose all revealed before he takes one step towards the destination. However, that is not faith; and the precepts require faith if we are going to obey them. We must have the faith that God will show us what we need to know when we need to know it. We must have faith in God's wisdom and way. Without such faith we cannot honor God well and will not serve God well.

It is important that we distinguish between true and false faith here in the application of "I will show thee." A number of professing believers excuse their indecision and inactivity on the fact that God has not yet shown them His will. They talk much about the will of God and that someday God will show it to them. But they claim He has not yet revealed His will to them— so they sit. You will note, however, that Abraham did not sit just because "I will show thee" had not come to pass; for there was much Abraham could and should do without the "I will show thee" being fulfilled. And when we do those things which we already know to do, then someday we will indeed find out what the "I will show thee" is all about. Christians who sit in idleness in regards to the Lord's service or who seem to forever sit in a state of indecision cannot excuse their attitude and conduct by "I will show thee." Furthermore, if they sit in idleness, they will never see much fulfillment of the "I will show thee" promise.

2. The Promises

After telling Abraham what he was to do, God gave Abraham some promises to encourage and inspire him to obey the precepts. God said, "I will make of thee a great nation, and I will bless thee, and make thy name great; and thou shalt be a blessing. And I will bless them that bless thee, and curse him that curseth thee: and in thee shall all families of the earth be blessed" (12:2,3). Note it was promises and not reasons that God gave to encourage service. This is generally the practice of God. F. B. Meyer explains this practice of God about as well as anyone when he says, "God's commands are not always accompanied by reasons, but always by promises, expressed or understood. To give reasons would excite discussion; but to give a promise shows that the reason, though hidden, is all-sufficient. We can understand the promise, though the reason might baffle and confuse us. The reason is intellectual, metaphysical, spiritual; but a promise is practical, positive, literal."

We will look at six things concerning these promises: the future of the promises, the number of the promises, the location of the promises, the opposition to the promises, the fulfillment of the promises, and the Gospel in the promises.

The future of the promises. Considerable time must go by for the fulfillment of all the promises given to Abraham. In fact, many hundreds of years must go by before some of the promises are fulfilled. This will definitely not appeal to the flesh, but it will give faith an opportunity to thrive. The flesh wants everything now and has little patience for waiting God's time. Therefore, the flesh is seldom excited by the promises of God though they are great blessings indeed. Abraham was a different story, however. His faith was great, and so he valued the promises.

The number of the promises. There are at least seven promises in the summons. They are (1) "I will make of thee a great nation," (2) "I will bless thee," (3) "I will . . . make thy name great," (4) "thou shalt be a blessing," (5) "I will bless them that bless thee," (6) "I . . . will curse them that curseth thee," and (7) "in thee shall all families of the earth be blessed."

When we compare the number of precepts with the number of promises, we readily observe that what God will do for Abraham is much more than what Abraham is asked to do for God. Many complain that God's commandments are restrictive, killjoy, and burdensome. But you can never complain of God's commandments like that when you consider His promises. God's promises more than compensate for any effort you must give, for any cost you must pay, and for any distasteful thing you must do to obey His precepts. No one ever loses who honors God's precepts—God's promises will see to that!

The location of the promises. God usually gives the precepts before He gives the promises, so in Scripture you will generally find the promises located after the precepts. Such is the case in this summons. First come the precepts and then come the promises. God first tells what Abraham is to do; then God tells what He will do. God first impresses upon us our duties; then He speaks of our wages.

This is a healthy order and one that men need to practice a lot more than they are practicing. Men seem to be only interested in their pay—they evidence little interest in their duties. They are more concerned about their privileges than responsibilities. All of this is a selfish attitude, and such an attitude is one that does not perform one's duties well. It is the foundation of the "rights" emphasis; an emphasis which is more concerned about privileges than obligations and which says I am more concerned about how you treat me than how I treat you.

Abraham will realize all the promises of the summons if he gives due attention and respect to the precepts. The same holds true for anyone. Those who can think of nothing else but their rights, their privileges, and their pay will generally come up short in these areas because they do not give proper emphasis to responsibilities, duties, and obligations which bring about the rights, privileges, and pay. Much of the complaint by minorities about not getting their rights unfortunately lies right here. While we do not deny that minorities have been unfairly treated, yet their failure to enjoy the "rights" they talk so much about is too often because they do not give much attention to duty. Most of the minorities who have done very well in the privilege, pay, and promotion area are those who do not spend much time complaining about lack of rights but concentrate on their duty. The same goes for Christians who complain of lack of blessing from God. Emphasizing precepts first is, of course, not a popular emphasis; but it is an emphasis we verily need to practice and proclaim much more today!

The opposition to the promises. Circumstances oppose just about every promise God ever made. Every promise is, therefore, a test of our faith—do we give greater weight to the circumstances or to the promises? Faith will vote in favor of the promises; unbelief will vote in favor of the circumstances.

Abraham's circumstances seemed to be against the promises in this great summons. God promised that Abraham would be a great nation, but circumstances laughed at that promise, for Abraham had no seed, and he and Sarah were too old to have a child. God's promises said He would bless Abraham; but circumstances predicted loss, not gain. Two of God's promises said that Abraham would be a great benefactor to the world, but circumstances said that Abraham was only causing hardship to those around him in leaving Ur and making the arduous trip to

Canaan. God's promises said He would make Abraham's name great, but circumstances made Abraham look like a fool—not a great man—in leaving his native land and his family to go into a strange country. God's promises (especially the "curse them that curseth thee") said Abraham would be safe, but circumstances said that obeying God's precepts would put Abraham right in the midst of unfriendly people.

So Abraham's circumstances did nothing to encourage the fulfillment of the promises made to him in this summons. But as Scripture teaches repeatedly, circumstances are no match to God's promises. Every promise made to Abraham was victorious over the opposing circumstances. How that ought to lift our spirits and cause us to not let circumstances get us down when they seem so against the fulfillment of God's promises to us.

The fulfillment of the promises. We want to note some of the obvious ways in which these promises have been fulfilled. We will of necessity be brief here compared to the abundance of the fulfillments. But a few notations about the fulfillment of these promises will help remind us of God's great faithfulness in fulfilling His promises and help show us how wonderfully His promises are fulfilled even though circumstances seem to legislate against their fulfillment.

The fulfillment of the first promise (Abraham's seed would become a great nation) is a matter of history and is going to be realized in an even greater way in the future. The greatness of Israel under the leadership of David and Solomon show the fulfillment in the past of Israel being a great nation. When Christ comes back to sit on the throne of Israel in the millennium, the greatest fulfillment of this particular promise will occur.

To see the fulfillment of the second promise (God would bless Abraham), one has to read only a few chapters further on in Genesis. In those chapters one will see Abraham coming into great material prosperity; and, even more importantly, one will see the great spiritual blessings which came to Abraham. God truly fulfilled His promise about blessing Abraham.

The fulfillment of the third promise (Abraham's name to be great) is uncontestable. For some four thousand years, the name of Abraham has stood above most names in terms of fame. Not only is his name revered by the Jewish people, but he is also revered by many other people of the earth—from the followers of Mohammed to the followers of Christ.

The fourth promise (Abraham would be a blessing to others) like that of the second promise, begins to manifest fulfillment quickly in Scripture. Abraham's rescue of the inhabitants of Sodom is an excellent example of the fulfillment of that promise and is reported in Genesis 14 just two chapters further on from our text. An important lesson we learn from this promise and fulfillment is that when God blesses us it is so we can bless others. God's blessings are not to be enjoyed selfishly, but they are to be used to bless others. "I will bless thee" is to be followed by "thou shalt be a blessing."

The fifth and sixth promises (bless them that bless thee and curse them that curse thee) are two interrelated promises which mankind must not ignore, or they will miss great blessing and suffer great judgment. On the judgment side of the promise, Egypt, Babylon, Rome, and Germany are some of the well known nations who were at one time great world powers but because of their mistreatment of the Jews were destroyed or became second class nations. On the blessing side of this promise, the United States has been greatly benefited by its benevolent attitude to the Jews—an attitude, however, which is waning alarmingly fast in our country. Our benevolent attitude towards the Jews in World War II, as an example, resulted in a great influx of brain power when Jewish scientists fled Nazi Germany and came to the United States. Being the first nation of the world to recognize Israel's independence in 1948 has surely been a result of much mercy from God for our country.

The seventh promise (all the families of the earth to be blessed through Abraham) has many fulfillments. The most important fulfillment is the Gospel which we will deal with next in a separate section. Here we will note some of the other significant fulfillments of this promise. We start off by noting that one of the greatest fulfillments of this promise is the Bible. It is primarily a Jewish book. The Word of God was written by Jews with the exception of Luke (and some believe Luke was a Jew). A prominent Jewish scholar, Dr. S. Schechter, said, "Our great claim to the gratitude of mankind is that we gave the world the Word of God, the Bible"; and he is right. Another fulfillment of this promise is found in the existence of our country. The man who came to the rescue of our country during the Revolutionary War by providing the funds necessary to continue the war and, hence, bring freedom to our land, was a Jew, Haym Salomon.

We note more fulfillments of this promise which continue to bring additional blessing to mankind. The first to invent the means of producing, transmitting and detecting of wireless waves was Hermon Hertz, a Jew. The pioneer of aviation who was the first to fly heavier than air machines (gliders) was Otto Lilienthal, a Jew. He inspired the Wright brothers to their daring experiments which they acknowledged. The original inventor of dirigibles was David Schwartz, a Jew. The first automobile to run on liquid fuel was built by a Jew, Siefried Marcus. The great scientist Albert Einstein, who contributed much to the world in his work, was a Jew. The three element radio tube which did so much for the radio was invented by Robert Von Lieben, a Jew. Transmission of photos by wireless is credited to Arthur Korn, a Jew. Invention of the spider wheel which made the bicycle possible was done by a Jew, Nahun Salomon. The discovery of petroleum was by Abraham Schreiner, a Jew. Discovery of the process of color photography was by Gabriel Lippmann, a Jew. Founder of stainless steel was a Jew, Benno Strauss. Co-discoverer of insulin for diabetes was by a Jew, Minkowsky. The mother of William Booth, the founder of the Salvation Army, was a Jew. The American Red Cross was established at the home of a Jew, Adolphus Solomon. On and on we could go; but for lack of space we stop so we can go on to the next section which is about the greatest of all fulfillments of this promise, namely, the Gospel.

The Gospel in the promises. We have no doubt about the Gospel being in the promises God gave Abraham in this great summons. The Apostle Paul makes that clear when he says, "And the scripture . . . preached before the gospel unto Abraham, saying, In thee shall all nations be blessed" (Galatians 3:8). There it is—the greatest of blessings for mankind wrapped up in one of the promises of the summons given Abraham. Through the seed of Abraham came Jesus Christ to be the Redeemer of mankind which is what the Gospel is all about.

This truth about the Gospel being in one of the promises of the summons makes it clear that the primary purpose of the Divine summons given to Abraham here was redemptive. Therefore, we can say that Abraham's obedience to it was just like obeying the Great Commission; for the results are the same. Both commissions, summons, calls, or orders or whatever you want to call them are part and parcel of the same thing, namely, the redemption of mankind.

C. THE RESPONSE TO THE SUMMONS

After a poor start, Abraham's response to the summons was that of obedience. We will note the delay in his obedience, the dedication in his obedience, the difficulties for his obedience, the dividends of his obedience, and the devotion in his obedience.

1. The Delay in His Obedience

Abraham did not fully obey the summons when it first came to him. He delayed his full obedience until after his father Terah died. It was not a good start for Abraham; and had it not been for God's grace, Abraham would have been another casualty in the service of the Lord.

To further examine this delay in his obedience, we will note the confirmation of the delay, the cause of the delay, the compromise in the delay, and the correcting of the delay.

The confirmation of the delay. Some do not think there was any delinquency in Abraham's response to the summons. They feel that Abraham's summons (as recorded here in Genesis 12:1) came in Haran. However, Acts 7:2,3 makes it very clear that Abraham did indeed receive a call when he was in his native home of Ur. This text is part of Stephen's sermon before the Sanhedrin. Stephen said, "Men, brethren, and fathers, hearken; The God of glory appeared unto our father Abraham, when he was in Mesopotamia, before he dwelt in Charran [Haran], And said unto him, Get thee out of thy country, and from thy kindred, and come into the land which I shall show thee." Receiving the call in Ur meant Abraham's stay at Haran was an unauthorized delay in his obeying the summons from God (the fact that his kinfolks were with him also demonstrated delinquency in his obedience which we will see later). The recording of the call given here in Genesis 12:1 was either a second giving of the summons to Abraham in order to get him moving out of Haran, or it was review of the first summons in order to explain the action of Abraham departing from Haran to go to Canaan. Whatever the case (and that depends largely on whether "had" in Genesis 12:1 is justified by the Hebrew or not—scholars disagree), Abraham was delinquent in obeying his summons.

The cause of the delay. The delay in Abraham's full obedience was caused by his failure to do all that the summons told him to do. The summons told him to "Get thee out of thy country, and from thy kindred, and from thy father's house" (12:1). He obeyed the part of the summons about getting out of his country, but he did not obey the part about leaving his relatives. Some defend Abraham here by insisting the call was originally given to Terah which is why the Scripture reports that "Terah took Abram his son, and Lot the son of Haran his son's son, and Sarai, his daughter in law . . . and they went forth with them from Ur of the Chaldees, to go into the land of Canaan; and they came unto Haran, and dwelt there" (11:31). But the Acts 7:2 text, which we noted above, refutes the idea Terah received the call in Ur; for it says Abraham was the one who received the call in Ur. Also Isaiah 51:2 says God "called him [Abraham] alone." God did not call his father or brothers or nephew. Just Abraham was called (this of course included his wife, for a wife is to follow her husband). But Abraham allowed some of his relatives to go; and, furthermore, he even gave up the authority of the venture to his father—which is why Scripture reports Terah as being the leader. Terah had no business being the leader; that was Abraham's calling, not Terah's. Both Abraham and Terah are at fault here. Terah presumed and Abraham neglected. This presume/neglect problem is seen throughout society today. It is seen in the home (the wife presumes, the husband neglects), in the school (the counsellors presume, the parents neglect), and in the church (the dissidents presume, the good people neglect). It is behind ERA, NOW, and other unsavory movements in our land. It is simply plain opposition to God's order for mankind.

Abraham's failure to completely obey by not separating from all those whom God told him to separate from is a pungent lesson regarding whom we keep company with and whom we include in our ventures. F. B. Meyer says, "It becomes us to be very careful as to whom we take with us in our pilgrimage. We may make a fair start from our Ur; but if we take Terah with us, we shall not go far. Take care, young pilgrim to eternity, to whom you mate yourself in the marriage bond. Beware, man of business, lest you find your Terah in the man with whom you are entering into partnership."

The compromise in the delay. At first Abraham may have consoled himself in allowing some of his relatives to travel with him, for after all they were willing to leave Ur, and they gave the impression they would go to Canaan (11:31). But upon reaching Haran the troop stopped. That was far enough. Going to Canaan was too much.

How often compromise plays this tune. Full obedience is unacceptable to the carnal. They greet full obedience with a warning not to go too far. Extremism, impractical, unnecessary, and other like words are used by the carnal to describe full obedience to the Lord. But it is never extreme to fully follow the

Lord. It is never impractical to obey God in every detail. It is never unnecessary to go all the way with God.

The correcting of the delay. "Terah died in Haran" (11:32), and a New Testament text confirms that his death resulted in Abraham finally getting back on the right track. The text is from Stephen's sermon to the Sanhedrin. In that sermon Stephen said that Abraham "came . . . out of the land of the Chaldeans, and dwelt in Charran [Haran]; and from thence, when his father was dead, he removed him [Abraham] into this land [Canaan]" (Acts 7:4). It was only "when his father was dead" that Abraham got moving again. There are two important warnings in this death of Terah. The warning about delay in obedience and the warning about dissuading others from obedience

First, *delay in obedience* invites pain. How often God has to take something from us in order to get us back into His service. Abraham was obviously attached to his father. In fact, he was more attached to his father at this point than he was to God. That does not go over well with God—and justifiably so—and the day came when God took away Terah from Abraham. Again we quote from F. B. Meyer who says regarding the death of Terah, "Here we may get a solution for mysteries in God's dealings with us, which have long puzzled us; and understand why our hopes have withered, our schemes have miscarried, our income has dwindled, our children have turned against us. All these things were hindering our true development; and, out of mercy to our best interests, God has been compelled to take the knife in hand, and set us at liberty."

Second, *dissuading others from obedience* invites judgment. Terah was a hindrance to Abraham so finally God removed him. True, Terah was up in years; and it could be said that he simply died of old age. But his death, even though it may have been simply because of old age, is still too ominous in regards to Abraham's moving to miss the mention of this lesson. Sometimes ornery church members, who are obstructionists in the work of the church, are removed by God in order for the work to progress. Most churches have some in the congregation who, if they were removed, the work of the Lord could advance much more quickly and effectively. Beware that you are not one of these obstructionists. God may move up the date of your funeral or in some other painful way cut you off from the church so it can function as it ought. What a sad commentary it was about Terah that his death resulted in an obstacle being removed so the work of God could go forward as it ought. Let us all pray that our lives will be a great help to the Lord and that our removal will not be a removal of an obstacle in the Lord's work.

2. The Dedication in His Obedience

When Abraham, at the age of seventy-five (12:4), finally left Haran for Canaan, his dedication to obeying the call was so much better than it was when he left Ur and headed for Haran. We note here two things about his conduct in going to Canaan from Haran which demonstrated his great dedication to obeying the summons. They are his submission and his stamina.

Submission. "Abram departed, as the LORD had spoken unto him . . . And Abram took Sarai his wife, and Lot his brother's son, and all their substance that they had gathered, and the souls [servants] that they had gotten in Haran; and they went forth to go into the land of Canaan; and into the land of Canaan they came" (12:4,5). "As the LORD had spoken unto him" sums up Abraham's great submission to the Lord as he left Haran for Canaan. He obeyed God's Word fully. We note it particularly in three areas.

First, he did not take his relatives with him which would hinder his full obedience to the Lord (he did take Lot, of course; for Lot was part of Abraham's household in the same way an adopted son would be—but Lot did cause problems later which we will study in another chapter).

Second, he went where God told him to go ("went forth into the land of Canaan") and did not stop short of the goal as he had previously done.

Third, everything in Abraham's household (his family, his substance, and his servants) was made subservient to the will of God. Full dedication means just that—everything in our life yields to the priority of God's service. Few believers know much about this kind of dedication, however. They come to church when it's convenient, they give with reservation, and they leave their enthusiasm and emotions at the ball game which means they come to church listless and uninterested.

Stamina. Dedication will manifest itself in stamina. Quitters—those who are deficient in dedication—lack stamina. Abraham certainly was not a quitter in his performance as recorded in our text. He kept at his task until it was accomplished. He "departed" (12:4), "went forth" (12:5), "passed through" (12:6), "removed" (12:8), and "journeyed, going on still" (12:9). "Going on still" says it best regarding his great stamina to do the will of God. He was determined to do the job as superbly as he could. He did not enter Canaan and then stop at the northernmost border just as he crossed the border (he came from the north). No, Abraham passed through all the land. He would see it all.

"Going on still" reminds us of the dedication of Gideon's band of three hundred men. Scripture says that when they were pursuing the enemy, they were "faint, yet pursuing" (Judges 8:4). They, like Abraham, had stamina in the Lord's work.

A lot of believers need help in the stamina area. They lack the stamina aspect of dedication to do the work of God right. They go only as far as necessary but not one inch farther. Their goal is the bare minimum. They have no interest in excellence. The lowest passing grade satisfies them. "Going on still" does not appeal to them at all. They quickly lose interest in serving the Lord, and then they foolishly wonder why their spiritual lives and service are so unsatisfying.

3. The Difficulties for His Obedience

"And the Canaanite was then in the land" (12:6). The

Canaanites were the people who inhabited the land of Canaan where Abraham was sent by God. They were not a godly group. They represented hostility, danger, and other problems for Abraham. It would not be easy for Abraham to live in a land where these people lived. It would require much courage, patience, labor, and wisdom to live victoriously in Canaan.

God never promised an easy road for the path of obedience. The lazy, timid, careless, cowards, and unenthusiastic will not last long on this path. The world likes to picture the Christian as sort of a Casper Milquetoast weakling who is too afraid, too weak, and too dumb to do anything else. But nothing could be farther from the truth. Obedience to God is not easy; for you must stand up to scorners, have courage to go into dangerous places when He orders it, labor incessantly (there are no union hours in God's work), and fight with all your strength against the foes of your soul. Abraham was not on a vacation stroll coming from Ur to Haran to Canaan. Moving his flocks and family that distance was a great task. And then when he got to Canaan, the work was not over. Difficulties on every hand confronted him.

Do not mock the Christian life as a cop-out for those who do not want to face difficulties in life. It is just the opposite. It is a whole lot easier to live a godless life than to live a godly life. If you don't think so, just try living godly in front of the wicked; and you will change your mind in a hurry.

4. The Dividends of His Obedience

After Abraham had gotten to Canaan, "the LORD appeared unto Abram, and said, Unto thy seed will I give this land: and there builded he an altar unto the LORD, who appeared unto him" (12:7). Obedience to the Lord pays great dividends. As we noted earlier, obedience required much sacrifice. But no sacrifice will be made that is not eventually more than compensated for by the dividends God gives for obedience. Our text here mentions some choice blessings which Abraham received after he obeyed the summons by going all the way to Canaan. We note four of these blessings: fellowship, revelation, assurance, and inheritance.

Fellowship. "The LORD appeared unto Abram." Abraham had to give up friends and relatives to serve the Lord, but he still had the Lord with him. He could still fellowship with God. Never discount the blessing of having the presence of the Lord with you. It is a choice blessing, for "in thy presence is fulness of joy" (Psalm 16:11). The world is constantly seeking for happiness and having no success in finding true joy. Why? Because they leave out God. Abraham did not leave out God in his life. His life was concerned about doing God's will. Therefore, he enjoyed the great blessing of continued fellowship with God. In fact, Scripture records some special and lengthy times of fellowship between God and Abraham, and the fellowship was so good that Abraham had the distinction of being called God's friend (II Chronicles 20:7, Isaiah 41:8, and James 2:23). This is a great blessing that comes only by obedience to God.

Revelation. When Abraham reached Canaan, he received further revelation from God. The Lord said, "Unto thy seed will I give this land." Obedience has much to do with our spiritual learning. When we obey, God opens our eyes to understand His Word, to learning more from Him and about Him. When we disobey, He closes our eyes; and we walk in spiritual ignorance. School is fine and has its place, but obedience is a more important key to knowing and understanding the Word of God.

Assurance. "Unto thy seed will I give this land" was a promise which told Abraham very plainly that he had done the will of God. He had gone to the right land. He was where God wanted him to be. Obedience is accompanied by assurance. When Abraham arrived in Canaan, God gave him assurance that he had indeed done the will of God. The will of God will always be vindicated sooner or later. God does not leave you in uncertainty as to whether or not you have done as He has instructed.

By various ways and means, He gives you assurance. Obedience will discover that fact.

Inheritance. "Unto thy seed will I give this land." Obedience brought Abraham a great inheritance. It brought him the land of Canaan. This is the first time Abraham is told by God that the land of Canaan is his inheritance, that it will be given to his seed (which included him also, cp. 13:15,17 and 15:7). It is interesting to note that the word "give" in verse 7, which we quoted here, appears over one thousand times in the Bible. A good number of these appearances have to do with God giving the land of Palestine to His chosen people. Our text is the first place in Scripture where this promise is made. This promise will be made in nearly 150 passages in the Old Testament—from the time of the patriarchs to the time when a remnant returned from exile (Nehemiah 9:35,36). It even shows up in the giving of the ten commandments (Exodus 20:12).

As we go further in our study of Abraham, we will learn much more about this gift of land to Abraham's seed. It was a very important part of the covenant God had with Abraham and his seed. This gift of land needs to be understood well, for there is so much fighting in the Middle East about the land today. The Scripture makes it clear that the land belongs to Israel, for God gave it to them. The claims of all others are not valid claims.

5. The Devotion in His Obedience

When Abraham reached the land where God had sent him, "there builded he an altar unto the LORD" (12:7). How well this reveals his great devotion to the Lord. Why does this altar show great devotion on Abraham's part to the Lord? Because he built it in heathen Canaan. He was not afraid to own his faith and to worship God before the heathen. He publicly and unashamedly professed his faith in God before those not sympathetic to his faith. It takes great devotion to God to do that.

We are overloaded with secret disciples today. They are careful to do nothing that would give their faith away. They mix with the world and live like the world, and no one would ever suspect they are a Christian. When the world tells dirty stories, they laugh right along with the ungodly. When they go out with the world to eat, they make no effort to thank the Lord before they eat—they claim it is too embarrassing to pray before the unsaved. But Abraham was not that way. Let the heathen mock, laugh, turn up their noses at this newcomer in their land—but Abraham will still worship God anyway. May we do likewise.

II.

SOJOURNING IN EGYPT

GENESIS 12:10 – 13:4

WHEN ABRAHAM WAS settled down in Canaan and his traveling days from one country to another seem ended, "there was a famine in the land [Canaan]: and Abram went down into Egypt to sojourn there" (12:10). Unlike his moving from Ur to Haran and then on to Canaan, this going to Egypt was not an authorized trip even though the land of Canaan was experiencing a great famine. Hence, as one would expect, this traveling in disobedience to God got Abraham in deep trouble. But for the intervening grace of God which turned him around and got him back in Canaan, Abraham would have destroyed himself, lost his calling, and been unheard of in history.

To study this sojourning experience in Abraham's life, we will consider the famine in the land (12:10), the forsaking of the land (12:10), the folly out of the land (12:11–17), and the flight back to the land (12:18 – 13:4).

A. THE FAMINE IN THE LAND

"And there was a famine in the land . . . the famine was grievous in the land" (v. 10). We will note three things about this famine: the site of the famine, the season of the famine, and the severity of the famine.

1. The Site of the Famine

The famine came "in the land" where God had sent Abraham. Coming "in the land" will cause the will of God, the promises of God, and the dedication to God to be greatly challenged. Good times do not challenge these things very much, but bad times certainly do.

The will of God challenged. The location of this famine would challenge Abraham about whether or not it was really the will of God for him to come to Canaan. If he judges situations the way most people (and this includes most professing Christians) judge things today, he will conclude that the famine being "in the land" indicated he made a mistake in coming to Canaan.

Today it seems we judge just about everything on the basis of outward success. So we think that if a farmer does the will of God, he will have better crops; if the salesman does the will of God, he will have more sales; if the pastor does the will of God, he will see his church grow in attendance; if a church member does the will of God regarding giving, he will see his finances improve; and if Abraham goes to Canaan, he will enjoy good times. But if the farmer's crops fail, if the salesman loses sales, if the pastor sees his church attendance fall till the church wants to run him off, if the one who liberally gives to the Lord sees his income drop and his financial situation become very precarious, and if Abraham experiences a famine in the land, we tend to conclude that these folks have made a mistake and are out of the will of God.

But the will of God is not determined primarily by outward success but primarily by the Word of God. And nothing in the Word of God tells us that being in the will of God always means smooth sailing on life's voyage. Just because there was no famine in Ur and Haran does not mean that Abraham should have stayed in Ur or Haran. Abraham had the Word of God to vindicate his Canaan location as being the will of God. Upon reaching Canaan, Abraham was informed by God that "Unto thy seed will I give this land" (Genesis 12:7). As we noted in our previous chapter, this statement of promise was tantamount to saying Abraham was in the right place. Whether he experienced a famine or not had nothing to do with determining if he was in the will of God. It was the Word of God that determined that.

So it is with us. Therefore, we need to know the Word of God well so we will know the will of God well. Otherwise we will draw wrong conclusions about those famines we encounter on the path of obedience and will let them divert us onto the path of disobedience.

The promises of God challenged. The coming of the famine would also challenge Abraham about the validity of God's promises. God had said He would bless Abraham, but now there was a famine which seemed to curse instead of bless. Natural man will look at these circumstances and mock God and His promises. But wise men will act much differently. They will hold their peace, for they know that trials are often the only way some of the greatest blessings can come to man. Paul said, "For our light affliction, which is but for a moment, worketh for us a far more exceeding and eternal weight of glory" (II Corinthians 4:17). If our light afflictions do so much for us, think what heavy afflictions will do! Peter described the trials of our faith as "being much more precious than of gold" (I Peter 1:7). That does not sound like a curse but like a great blessing. Jesus spoke of the rugged trial of persecution as something that would prove to be a great blessing. He said, "Blessed are ye, when men shall revile you, and persecute you . . . Rejoice, and be exceeding glad; for great is your reward in heaven" (Matthew 5:11,12). Trial for God's obedient children may seem on the surface to mock the promise of blessing, but time will definitely prove otherwise. That fact should greatly encourage us when we are in the midst of trial and cannot perceive in our own human thinking any blessing whatever coming from it.

The dedication to God challenged. The famine experience in Canaan really challenged the dedication of Abraham to obeying God. In fact, it was a stronger challenge than Abraham could handle; for his dedication to obedience at that time was not strong enough to survive the famine. Nothing challenges our dedication to obeying God like hard times. Many folk are willing to obey God when it results in good times; but if obedience brings upon them rough experiences, they are ready to quit. If their obedience is praised and it results in promotion and popularity, they are zealous about God's commands. But let their obedience be criticized or cause them to lose friends or a job, and they will do some rethinking about God's commands and decide they no longer want to submit to them. We do not walk on the path of obedience long before our dedication will be tested to see if we are obeying the Lord because of delightful circumstances or because of Divine commands. How do you fare in these tests?

2. The Season of the Famine

One of the times or seasons in which trial often comes to us is right after we have had some great spiritual victory or mountain peak experience. So it was here with the timing of this trial in Abraham's life. The trial came right after Abraham had reached a new high spiritually in his life. He had obeyed the Lord and come to the land of Canaan. Then he had lived his faith unashamedly before the world, for he had built several altars unto the Lord right in public view of the heathen Canaanites. This was accompanied by new revelations from God. All these things spelled a great spiritual high for Abraham—then came the famine.

The time after great spiritual victories and experiences is a very critical time for the believer. It is a time when the believer has a tendency to become proud and also to become careless and let down his guard. So after our spiritual highs, two things will frequently occur. First, God will send trials to keep us humble. Paul spoke about this when, after receiving special revelations from God, he said, "And lest I should be exalted above measure through the abundance of the revelations, there was given to me a thorn in the flesh, the messenger of Satan to buffet me, lest I should be exalted above measure" (II Corinthians 12:7). Second, Satan will send temptation to harm us because he knows that if our guard is let down because of a spiritual high, he will be more effective in attacking us. Frequently he will try to use the trial which God sent to humble us to instead do such things as create in us doubt about God's way and disdain for God for allegedly not taking care of us.

The timing of Abraham's trial brings a strong and important lesson to us to beware of the peril of post-victory and post-blessing problems. Do not let victory or blessing puff you up with pride, for it was God Who gave you the victory and the blessing. And do not let down after these experiences either; for the enemy will spot your laxness and deliver a knockout punch, if you are not careful.

3. The Severity of the Famine

Our text says the famine was "grievous." This would indicate that the famine was long and had really devastated the food supply. Adding to the grievousness of the famine for Abraham would be his situation. To start with, he was a stranger in the land; and, as any traveler knows, trouble away from home is more grievous than trouble at home. Also, he was living amongst hostile people; and, therefore, he would not find much help from them. Furthermore, Abraham had many under his care which in time of famine would increase the burden of the famine. Besides his wife and Lot, Abraham also had many servants plus large flocks of animals who depended on him for their sustenance. All these things would add much to the weight of the already burdensome famine.

Some of our trials will indeed be grievous. But the severity of these trials will be more than compensated for in the fact that they give great opportunity for two important things to occur. These two important matters in life are the development of man's faith and the display of God's glory. We must perceive this perspective of severe trials lest we complain and dishonor God concerning the extreme heaviness of some of our trials. True, all trials provide opportunity for our faith to develop and God's glory to be displayed; but the more severe the trial, the greater the opportunity for these things to occur.

Sojourning in Egypt

The development of man's faith. As we make progress in our spiritual lives, trials will get harder. When a sports team enters a tournament, the further they advance in the tournament the tougher will be their competition. They will have to beat the best to be the champion. So it is with our faith. If you want to be a champion for God, you will have to conquer something more than trivial trials in life. God wants to build strong, healthy saints. He has enough weak-kneed, wishy-washy disciples and wants more of the strong, faithful variety. Faith cannot be developed on a peaches and cream diet, and you do not build muscles by weight lifting marshmallows. Grace grows and is developed through strenuous trials. Without these severe trials we do not develop strong faith.

The display of God's power. God wants to be glorified and should be glorified (unfortunately, in our age of man-exaltation, we have forgotten this very important fact and even selfishly begrudge having to share any limelight with God). One of the ways in which God is glorified is in the display of His power. The greater the power displayed by God, the more glory there is for God. So the more severe the situation for His people, the better the opportunity for Him to show His great power in delivering His people. Hence, He allows severe trials to come to His own that He might show His great power in delivering them.

Those who complain about God making us suffer so He will be glorified need to remember that God suffered at Calvary in the person of Jesus Christ so that we might be glorified as children of God—the greatest glory a man can ever have. So our suffering for His glory is not an unfair arrangement for us—but you must admit it is for God, for He suffered so much more at Calvary than we will ever suffer.

B. THE FORSAKING OF THE LAND

"And Abram went down into Egypt to sojourn there" (12:10). Abraham did not react well to the famine. Egypt was not where Abraham was to be. He was to be in Canaan. But when our faith fails and we walk by sight rather than by faith, we seldom stay in our Canaans.

We will look at three things about his move to Egypt. They are the rationalizing about his move, the reason for his move, and the reoccurrences of his move.

1. The Rationalizing About His Move

Some try to excuse this failure of Abraham by emphasizing that he was young in the faith and could not be expected to do otherwise than what he did. That argument sounds good to the carnal and to the spiritually naïve; but it will not pass muster with God, compare well to the exploits of many young believers, and take away the problems which Abraham incurred through this failure. Sin is sin and excusing it does not solve problems.

It is true that we do not expect new believers to immediately walk as mature believers, for we recognize that growth in grace is progressive. But Abraham had been progressing in faith over a number of months now; and this going to Egypt represented inexcusable backsliding, not a lack of maturity. In commenting on this failure of Abraham, Joseph Parker said, "It is a bad thing to rack our brains for excuses on behalf of the Bible worthies when they fall; if God did not excuse them, we need not stretch our charity into a covering for their sins."

Rather than trying to excuse Abraham for his failure, we need to take warning from it to help us keep from failing when our faith is tested by stressful situations. But today we seem interested in excusing as much sin as possible. Therefore, when someone sins, instead of condemning the sin and warning others and ourselves about it, we rush to console the sinner and excuse the sin. Then we stupidly wonder why mankind is failing more and more to walk uprightly. Let's stop looking for excuses to sin and start condemning sin.

2. The Reason for His Move

The reason Abraham moved to Egypt when the famine came

Sojourning in Egypt

to Canaan was that he ceased to use the Word of God for his guide and used other guides instead. Abraham had come from Ur all the way to Canaan with God's Word as his guide. But when the famine hit, he ceased walking by that guide of all guides. So he ceased to walk by faith which is the only way you can walk victoriously in life. Faith is rooted and grounded on the Word of God (Romans 10:17); and when you forsake the Word, your faith is bound to fail. It certainly was so with Abraham.

Abraham used two other guides instead of the Word of God: circumstances and self-preservation. These guides are very revered by the world today. They seem so much more attractive than the Word of God. But they will lead us to destruction if we replace the Word with them. We will examine these two guides Abraham used and see why they are so attractive and also why they are no substitute for the Word of God.

Circumstances. Abraham's circumstances in Canaan and the circumstances in Egypt really seemed to sanction Abraham's move from Canaan to Egypt. After all, Canaan was in the midst of a severe famine which would really make it difficult for Abraham to take care of his family, servants, and flocks. But Egypt was in much better condition; it looked very attractive to the eyes of the flesh. As Robert Candlish says, "The temptation [to go to Egypt] was a severe one. Egypt was at this time a flourishing nation; the fertile valley of the Nile supported a considerable population; and the country was already assuming the character which it afterwards bore as the granary of the world." Food and pasture—the things Abraham needed—were abundant in Egypt. Thus the flesh would conclude that surely this dictates a move to Egypt.

But though circumstances often seem so logical as a guide for our lives, they are not trustworthy. It is not wrong to include circumstances in guiding our decisions, but circumstances alone cannot be depended upon to show you the right way. Circumstances must always be interpreted by the Word of God, by

Divine revelation. Though they look so appealing, they can also be very deceiving in appearance. Every circumstance, no matter how favorable it seems to be, needs to be examined by what God says; or we will go astray. Abraham appeared to have an improved circumstance in Egypt, but it proved otherwise. Many are the drop-outs in life who made decisions based solely on what appeared to be improved material circumstances.

Self-preservation. Another popular guide, which Abraham obviously used, is self-preservation. The thinking would be that if he stayed in Canaan, he would not survive; but if he went to Egypt, he would survive. Self-preservation is indeed pretty important in life, but it is not so important that it can replace the Word of God as our guide in life.

The world, however, places a premium on self-preservation; and oftentimes many Christians do likewise. As an example, during the days of the early church, some believers worked in idol factories. The great church leader Tertullian rebuked them for this unsavory employment. Their reply was that they had to live. Tertullian responded, "Do you?" Tertullian was using the Word of God as his guide; the Christians who worked in the idol factories were using self-preservation as their guide.

Many professing Christians today would cease working where they do and stop doing many other things they do if their guide was the Word of God instead of self-preservation. Self-preservation must not replace the Word of God as our chief guide, or we will deviate far from the will of God and greatly defile ourselves. If Jesus Christ had used self-preservation instead of the Word of God as His guide, there would have been no Calvary. If the martyrs of early Christendom had used self-preservation instead of God's Word as their guide, there would be no martyrs; and the church would have died out long ago.

Abraham was called to go to Canaan, not Egypt. He was, therefore, safer in Canaan in the midst of the worst of famines than in Egypt in the midst of plenty. Going to Egypt appeared to enhance Abraham's self-preservation; but before he even arrived in Egypt, he realized his self-preservation was imperiled greater than it had been in Canaan—something we will note more about shortly. So self-preservation certainly failed him as a guide. It is the Word of God that does not fail in guiding us correctly.

3. The Reoccurrences of His Move

Abraham's trip to Egypt was not the last time Abraham's family would go to Egypt to sojourn in time of stress. Joseph would be sent to Egypt as a young man and would live there the rest of his life because of his brothers' cruel hatred (Genesis 37:28; 50:22–26); Jacob and his family would go to Egypt to sojourn in a time of famine, and his descendants would be there for some four hundred years before they came back to Canaan (Genesis 46:1–7; Exodus 12:40); an expedition of Israelites who escaped the Babylonian captivity would "go into the land of Egypt to sojourn there" and also die there in judgment (Jeremiah 44:12) during Jeremiah's day; and last but not least, the prized descendent of Abraham, Jesus Christ, would go with Joseph and Mary to sojourn in Egypt for several years following His birth to escape the murderous actions of Herod (Matthew 2:13–15).

Some of these sojournings were approved by God, some were not—including Abraham's sojourning. All of this points out what we have noted above about what our guide should be in regards to actions we take. Egypt was basically off-limits for God's people and for obvious reasons. But there were times when God plainly instructed some of the seed of Abraham to go to Egypt. The key, therefore, to knowing the will of God in the sojourning to Egypt or in anything else is to know the Word of God. All other guides must be subservient to the Word of God.

C. THE FOLLY OUT OF THE LAND

"And it came to pass, when he was come near to enter into Egypt, that he said unto Sarai his wife, Behold now, I know that thou art a fair woman to look upon; Therefore it shall come to pass, when the Egyptians shall see thee, that they shall say, This is his wife: and they will kill me, but they will save thee alive. Say, I pray thee, thou art my sister, that it may be well with me for thy sake; and my soul shall live because of thee" (12:11–13). What a very foolish thing Abraham did in Egypt regarding his wife. But Egypt was one place that really encouraged this evil conduct by Abraham. There are indeed some places in life that encourage us to sin. If we do not stay away from those places, as God commands, we will bring many headaches and heartaches into our lives. It is "Woe to them that go down to Egypt for help" (Isaiah 31:1) as the Prophet Isaiah said later, and this "Woe" can be said for many places in life.

Folly begets folly. The folly of forsaking the land leads to folly out of the land. One sin results in another sin. When we start sinning, we get in deeper and deeper if we do not stop and repent. But how often folk ignore this truth and think such foolish and fatal thoughts as: just one drink will not hurt, changing the laws to permit just one form of gambling will not hurt, and just one lie will not hurt. But "just one" leads to another and another and another. So it was with Abraham and so it will be with anyone.

We want to note here four evils involved in this folly of Abraham's action in Egypt regarding his wife. They are fearfulness, selfishness, deceitfulness, and injuriousness.

1. Fearfulness

"And it came to pass, when he was come near to enter into Egypt, that he said unto Sarai his wife, Behold now, I know that thou art a fair woman to look upon; Therefore it shall come to pass, when the Egyptians shall see thee, that they shall say, This is his wife: and they will kill me" (12:11,12). As soon as Abraham got to Egypt, fear possessed him. He was not filled with peace. Faith brings peace. But when we cease walking by faith, we lose peace and are filled with fear; so much so that we often fear our own shadow. Walking by faith brings us the sense of God's protection. Walking by the flesh does nothing of the sort, and so fear takes over.

The world may seem so bold and macho, but deep down inside they are afraid. Without God, without Christ as Savior, without faith in God's Word, they have nothing to quell their fear. How different it is, however, with those walking obediently by faith in God's Word. Peace, not fear, possesses their souls. It is a peace money cannot buy. Do not throw it out the window by ditching faith as Abraham did here.

2. Selfishness
"Say, I pray thee, thou art my sister, that it may be well with me for thy sake; and my soul shall live because of thee" (12:13). Spiritual decline promotes selfishness; and oh, what a selfish, base attitude Abraham had here. Abraham is looking out primarily for himself. Afraid they will take Sarah away from him and kill him in the process, he does nothing to protect Sarah from the low moral conduct of others but is only concerned about saving his own skin. He is so selfish that he imperils the purity of others that he might survive and enjoy life. How very low Abraham stooped because of his failure of faith.

Selfishness is a major theme of the world today. This should not surprise us, for the world rejects walking by faith in favor of walking by the flesh. Selfishness is what inspires the rights movement—these folk are concerned only about how others treat them, not about how they treat others (a problem we noted in the last chapter). It is behind gambling—those who push gambling see the gain they will make but do not give consideration to the millions upon millions of others who will lose. It is behind abortion—the welfare of the pregnant woman is all that is considered, not the welfare of the unborn child. "Pro-choice" is only for the pregnant woman; it is "no-choice" for the child. Those pushing abortion ought to call themselves "no-choice," for it is exactly where they stand in regards to the child in the womb. And "no choice" spells murderous selfishness!

3. Deceitfulness
Abraham's scheme to save himself from being killed by the

Egyptians—something he fears at this time more than he fears God—was to have Sarah lie. He told Sarah, "Say, I pray thee, thou art my sister, that it may be well with me" (12:13). Some try to excuse Abraham here by saying that it is the universal custom of Orientals to lie. Well, so what? That does not make lying acceptable, and Abraham has no justification for lying. He is serving a true God and his conduct ought to reflect truth!

Abraham's lie was a half truth lie. Sarah was his half-sister (Genesis 20:12), but she was first and foremost his wife now. So Abraham is not exonerated here by the fact that it was a half truth. A half truth is still a whole lie. But whether he lied or did not lie in his speech makes no difference as to whether or not he is guilty of deceitfulness, for Abraham definitely intended to deceive. No need to argue about the merits of Sarah's story. Abraham simply did not want Sarah to tell the truth about their husband-wife relationship.

Many folk console their consciences by the fact that they did not technically lie with the lips. But they are still guilty of lying; for though they may speak nothing but the truth, it is spoken in such a way as to give a deceitful appearance. You can speak the truth and still be lying because of the intended effect. On the other hand, you may not speak the truth and still be honest; for you may not be aware that you are not speaking the truth about something but think you are telling the truth about it. What is important are your intentions in your speech. Are you trying to give a true representation or a false one? God looks at our intentions when judging our speech.

If what you are doing requires deceit, you are doing the wrong thing. Walking on the path of faith does not require dishonesty. Jesus said He was the "Truth," and those who follow Him ought to reflect truth in their lives. The believer's strength is in truth, not lies. The world's way is the way of deceit, but that is not God's way.

4. Injuriousness

"And it came to pass, that, when Abram was come into

Egypt, the Egyptians beheld the woman that she was very fair. The princes also of Pharaoh saw her, and commended her before Pharaoh: and the woman was taken into Pharaoh's house . . . And the LORD plagued Pharaoh and his house with great plagues because of Sarai Abram's wife" (12:14,15,17). One of the big problems in sinning is that one not only hurts himself by his sin, but he also greatly imperils a host of other people. Abraham's sinful ways eventually brought suffering to his wife plus the head of the Egyptian government and countless others in the government of Egypt. In the great summons God gave Abraham, He told Abraham he was to be a blessing to the world (Genesis 12:2,3). But here he is being a curse. He has put Sarah in a situation that could do nothing but bring great anxiety to her plus ruin her morally if God does not intervene, and he is causing plagues to come upon Pharaoh and his household. That Abraham, one of God's own, should cause so much problem for others by his sin reminds us that sometimes a saint out of fellowship with God can rival the devil in causing trouble.

D. THE FLIGHT BACK TO THE LAND

Abraham needed to get out of Egypt and return to Canaan. He did not belong in Egypt and his sojourning there was causing many problems for others and was also getting himself into much trouble with man and God. How Abraham got out of Egypt and back to Canaan is a most interesting and instructive story. To examine this story of Abraham's return to Canaan, we will look at the reason, retribution, rebuke, riches, revival, and repeating involved in the return to Canaan.

1. The Reason

"And the LORD plagued Pharaoh and his house with great plagues because of Sarai Abram's wife" (v. 17). The main reason that Abraham was able to get out of Egypt and back to Canaan was God's grace. God's grace is always behind deliverances from troubles men get themselves into by disobeying God. Abraham certainly did not deserve to be extracted from the snare he got himself into in Egypt; for he had deliberately left the place where God wanted him to be, he had allowed his wife to be taken from him to become part of Pharaoh's harem, his personal conduct was characterized by fear and dishonesty and selfishness, he was a problem to society, and his worship of and witness for God were simply non-existent. His conduct had indeed been poor conduct. God would have been justified if He had left Abraham to die in his troubles in Egypt rather than seeing to it that he return to Canaan. But God did not do that. His grace ordered circumstances ("plagued Pharaoh and his house with great plagues") to come about that would free Sarah and send Abraham and all that he had back to Canaan. Abraham could say what the Psalmist said centuries later and what we can also say, "He hath not dealt with us after our sins, nor rewarded us according to our iniquities" (Psalm 103:10).

God's delivering of Abraham from Egypt and sending him back to Canaan is a good illustration of compelling grace. Pharaoh was moved providentially (the plagues) by God and, as a result, told Abraham to "get!" And Abraham got. This is like the grace that compelled folk into the Great Supper. "And the lord said unto the servant, Go out into the highways and hedges, and compel them to come in, that my house may be filled" (Luke 14:23). In applying this to soul salvation, someone (we do not know who) has said, "Twas the same grace that spread the feast that gently forced me in, else I had refused to enter and perished in my sin." But for God's compelling grace, none of us would be saved.

2. The Retribution

"And the LORD plagued Pharaoh and his house with great plagues because of Sarai Abram's wife" (v. 17). As we noted above, it was the plagues that God used to began to move things in the palace which eventually resulted in the rescue of Sarah from the evil situation in which Abraham's failure had put her. And these plagues were serious ("great"), or they would not have moved Pharaoh to act as he did. Some think Sarah sent word to Pharaoh as to why the plagues were coming. Others think God spoke to Pharaoh by a vision to inform him the reason for the plagues as He did to Abimelech (Genesis 20:3–7) when Abraham some years later tried the same lying act. Still others think his servants figured out the reason and told Pharaoh the reason. But it really makes no difference how Pharaoh became informed of the true situation of Sarah; the fact is, he was informed; and when he was informed, he acted with firmness; for judgment was what inspired his actions.

Pharaoh, unlike multitudes today, did not mock the idea that plagues on mankind were related to his immoral behavior. The disease of AIDS threatens to annihilate us, and the godly insist it is judgment upon mankind for man's vile, immoral ways. But most of mankind laughs at that idea. Pharaoh would not, however. He believed that moral defilement brings much trouble to society. And because he believed that fact, he was able to get the plagues stopped by correcting the moral problem God was upset about. It is such a simple thing; yet with all our boasted intelligence today, we still have not come to that obvious conclusion about the plagues that threaten mankind because of our immoral ways. We try condoms and other so called "protective" devices which do not work. We research feverishly to find some vaccine to kill VD germs when all the time we could stop the problem by simply changing our moral behavior to conform to God's way. Let the world learn a lesson from Pharaoh.

3. The Rebuke

Pharaoh gave Abraham a very humbling rebuke. "And Pharaoh called Abram, and said, What is this that thou hast done unto me? why didst thou not tell me that she was thy wife? Why saidst thou, She is my sister? so I might have taken her to me to wife: now therefore behold thy wife, take her, and go thy way" (12:18,19). Here is Abraham, a man who has been given a high calling from God, being justifiably rebuked by a heathen king. It ought to be the other way around. But, alas, when saints get out of the will of God, even the world acts better at times. Joseph

Parker said, "There are men today who make no profession of Christian faith, whose honor, straightforwardness, and generosity would put to shame many who claim a good standing in the Church." Many churches have no testimony in their community because their members live such shabby lives. One thing that has not helped this problem is that churches are too often obsessed with numbers rather than character.

Abraham's deliverance was humbling. But it is always humbling when God delivers us from our sin. God's deliverances never puff up the sinner with pride. Be it in salvation or in other rescues, we will be always be humbled.

4. The Riches

"And Pharaoh commanded his men concerning him: and they sent him away, and his wife, and all that he had. And Abram went up out of Egypt, he, and his wife, and all that he had, and Lot with him" (12:20 – 13:1). When Abraham returned to Canaan from Egypt, he brought with him "all that he had" (12:20) which was no small amount of wealth; for in Egypt Abraham's wealth had greatly increased. The increase was chiefly a result of the abundance of things Pharaoh had given Abraham when Pharaoh had Sarah in his house. Pharaoh treated "Abram well for her sake: and he had sheep, and oxen, and he asses, and menservants, and maidservants, and she asses, and camels" (12:16). Abraham had fared so well in Egypt that when he returned to Canaan, "Abram was very rich in cattle, in silver, and in gold" (13:2).

To the worldly mind, this seems to say that Abraham's unauthorized trip to Egypt was a very rewarding trip; for it paid handsome material dividends. He certainly would not have done that well in the famine in Canaan—so reasons the worldly mind. But before you get excited about the great increase in riches and conclude that going to Egypt really wasn't such a bad thing after all, you had better consider the problems that Abraham had with all his increased gain. All that glitters is not gold. The added gain he got in Egypt was nothing but trouble for Abraham for

SOJOURNING IN EGYPT

the rest of his life. The rewards of disobedience look so nice on the surface, but underneath they are not rewards but curses.

What were Abraham's troubles from his gains which he got in Egypt? We note three of these troubles. They had to do with his conscience, his clan, and his concubine.

First, his *conscience*. Abraham's conscience would bother him about how he got his increased gain. In Egypt, he could rejoice in his increased possessions and in how well he was faring in contrast to what his prospects were in Canaan with the famine there. But his rejoicing would be greatly diminished, if not killed altogether, by the fact that this gain came at the expense of losing Sarah and exposing her to much evil. A troubled conscience is a mighty big pain in the neck. It is not soothed by great possessions. Lack of peace is a terrible lack as anyone who has lacked peace will tell you. No amount of gain will make up for this lack. Many, if not most, of the wealthy have this conscience problem today. Getting Sarah back may have helped his conscience somewhat; although it still could be troubled at what Sarah experienced in order for him to get wealthy. But getting Sarah back did not stop his troubles.

Second, his *clan*. When Abraham got back from Egypt, his possessions caused much friction in his family—particularly between he and Lot. This resulted in he and Lot separating. Wealth gotten evilly does not make happy homes or bring families together! It is a great disrupter of the family.

Third, his *concubine*. One of the things Abraham increased in when in Egypt was in servants (12:16). And one of those servants was Hagar (Genesis 16:1). Hagar later became a temporary concubine (Sarai wanted to call her another wife of Abraham, but God never did), and this became a whopping big problem because of Ishmael (we will note this problem in a later study). This problem still plagues the Middle East.

The problems Abraham experienced from his gains from Egypt need to be considered more today. So often folk do evil to gain some coveted possession or position, and for a while it looks like they have been very successful. But be careful about drawing conclusions too soon. Those increases in gains will bring an increase in grief, not gladness. Those increases in possessions will bring an increase in problems, not pleasures. Furthermore, this problem of Abraham reminds us of the sobering truth that though we may be rescued from our sins, forgiven our sins, and sent back to Canaan, yet the effects of our sins will still dog us the rest of our lives. We have many folk today who seem to think that when they are forgiven that every thing in life will again be all sunny and nice and as though they had never sinned. Such a view leads to a lenient view of sin and a watered down view of the holiness of God. However, Psalm 99:8 says, "Thou wast a God that forgavest them, though thou tookest vengeance of their inventions [evil deeds]." You may be forgiven your sins but still bear in your body many consequences of your sin. You may be forgiven your sins but still be disqualified for some positions in God's service because your sin left you with some social scars intolerable for a public servant of God. You may be forgiven your sin but still have to deal periodically with mind problems created by your sins. Unauthorized trips to Egypt will leave you with troubles that will bother you the rest of your life, even though you have left Egypt and come back to Canaan. God's grace and forgiveness encourages the repentance of our sin but not the repeating of our sin.

5. The Revival

"And Abram went up out of Egypt . . . to Bethel, unto the place where his tent had been at the beginning . . . Unto the place of the altar, which he had made there at the first: and there Abram called on the name of the LORD" (13:1,3,4).

Going to Canaan from Egypt is always "up" (13:1) geographically, but here it was also "up" spiritually. The "up" here symbolizes the direction of Abraham's spirituality as a result of his coming "out" of Egypt. Canaan for Abraham represents God's place, God's precepts, and God's plan. Egypt represents the world with all its vices. Moving "out" of Egypt to Canaan is therefore always "up." The evidence that Abraham was going

Sojourning in Egypt

"up" spiritually instead of down as he did in Egypt is in the fact that when Abraham got back to Canaan, he got back to the altar and "called on the name of the LORD" (13:4). Thus he was getting back to worship, back to God. Truly a revival took place in his life in his return to Canaan. In Egypt there was no altar, no calling upon God. People's devotion to God does not do well when they are out of the place where God wants them. No backslider, no worldly Christian will do well in true devotion to the Lord.

6. The Repeating

Matthew Henry noted in his commentary that in this ordeal of Abraham's rescue, we have a preview of history to come. With Henry's help, we can observe at least four significant ways in which Abraham's deliverance from Egypt was repeated in Israel's deliverance from Egypt over four hundred years later. First, each went to Egypt because of a famine in Canaan (12:10, cp. Genesis 45:9–11). Second, each escaped Egypt because of great plagues (12:17, cp. Exodus 7–12). Third, each was told by Pharaoh to get out of Egypt (12:19, cp. Exodus 12:30–32). And, fourth, each left Egypt with much of Egypt's wealth (12:16, 20, cp. Exodus 12:36).

This preview of history to come underscores how wonderfully Scripture is put together. It is a marvelous book put together not at random or by accident, as some of the critics would have us believe, but by the direction of the Almighty.

III.

SEPARATION FROM LOT

GENESIS 13:5–18

RETURNING TO THE land of Canaan stopped some troubles for Abraham, but it did not stop all his troubles. Right after reporting Abraham's return to the land of Canaan and to the altar of devotion to Jehovah God, Scripture reports a family squabble. The herdsmen of Lot, Abraham's nephew, were contending with herdsmen of Abraham. The solution to the trouble was separation—separation of some of the family from the rest of the family. It was a painful remedy, but true peace frequently requires the taking of most unpleasant action.

In examining this experience in Abraham's life of separating from Lot, we will consider the contending by herdsmen (vv. 5–7), the counselling by Abraham (vv. 8,9), the choosing by Lot (vv. 10–13), and the confirming by God (vv. 14–18).

A. THE CONTENDING BY HERDSMEN

"And there was a strife between the herdsmen of Abram's cattle and the herdsmen of Lot's cattle: and the Canaanite and the Perizzite dwelt then in the land" (v. 7). We will note the reason for the contention and the risk in the contention.

1. The Reason for the Contention

The contention in our text was directly related to wealth. Because of the wealth of Abraham and Lot, "the land was not able to bear them, that they might dwell together; for their substance was great, so that they could not dwell together. And [so] there was a strife . . . " (vv. 6,7). Abraham had been raising his

Separation From Lot

nephew Lot, and now Lot has grown to manhood and is in business for himself. Like Abraham (and probably with Abraham's assistance), Lot has become wealthy. "And Lot also, which went with Abram, had flocks, and herds, and tents" (v. 5). It is not difficult to see that many problems could arise as a result of the abundance of the herds and flocks of these two men. Lack of pasture space, the problem of watering times and order, and the fear of rustling would all make the situation ripe for strife.

We hear so much today about the problems which poverty causes society that it is hard for us to believe that wealth can be a serious problem, too. Poverty does indeed cause problems; but Scripture reminds us, and experience will do likewise, that wealth can be a bigger troublemaker. We do not read far in Scripture before we learn of this truth. Here in our text Abraham and Lot had big trouble because of wealth. Later Abraham's two grandsons, Jacob and Esau, will have the same problem; "For their riches were more than that they might dwell together" (Genesis 36:7). We do not have to look far in society either before we see the problems that riches cause. As an example, people crave to win the lottery; for they think that will bring them bliss; but, as testimony shows, it will bring them so much trouble, they will eventually loath the day they won the lottery. Also most sports and other entertainment stars think they have really got it made when they finally get a big multi-million dollar contract. But when you read about their lives, you read mostly about troubles. And how often it is that even many peaceful Christian families suddenly begin to have strife among themselves and a parting of the ways because of their coming into money through an inheritance or some other way. When they were without, they got along well; but when wealth entered the scene, strife also entered.

Now some of our readers who have lived in poverty for a long time are probably thinking that they would like to deal with the problems of wealth for a change instead of all the problems they have because of lack of money. But once they experience the problems of wealth, they will change their minds quickly.

Pointing out the problems of wealth does not mean we are condemning wealth per se. Wealth is not inherently evil. The problem is that people have too much affection for wealth. F. W. Robertson said, "The enlargement of a man's possessions is very often the contracting of his heart." If you want to avoid the problems of wealth, do not set your heart on wealth. Furthermore, do not sulk in self pity if you are on the low side of material possessions. Instead of sulking, be thankful for the blessings you do have. Let contentment be your close companion—which is more likely to be your companion when you lack in material things than when you are filled to the full with them. Do not covet wealth to the extent that you lose the best things in life; such as here in the case of Abraham and Lot in which the family was broken up because of wealth. Do not envy the rich. If the truth were known, they may envy you a lot more than you think.

We must not ignore the fact that part of the problem of strife here stems from Abraham's unsavory gaining of wealth in Egypt. We noted towards the end of our last chapter that though Abraham was able to keep all the great gain in possessions he got in Egypt, it would haunt him when he got back in Canaan. And the first installment of "chickens coming home to roost" concerning his ill gotten gains from Egypt is this strife recorded in our text. Wealth gotten legitimately can bring problems if not treated properly, but wealth gotten evilly will always bring big problems eventually as Abraham is finding out in this strife experience.

2. The Risk in the Contention

The Holy Spirit inserts a sentence in the text regarding the strife between the herdsmen of Lot and Abraham that has a very ominous tone to it. Right after we read of the strife, we read that "the Canaanite and the Perizzite dwelt then in the land" (v. 7). With the Canaanite and the Perizzite in the land, the striving between the herdsmen of Lot and Abraham became a great risk to both the welfare of the flocks and to the witness of the faith. The striving could diminish the flocks and destroy the witness.

Separation From Lot

The welfare of the flocks. The striving of the herdsmen would give the Canaanites and the Perizzites opportunity to plunder the flocks. The herdsmen needed to be taking care of their flocks, not fighting with each other. Engaging in fights could leave their flocks seriously unprotected from the pirating of the Canaanites and Perizzites who would not hesitate to use this advantage to steal from the flocks of Abraham and Lot.

Churches especially have had many problems like this. Church fights give the devil free hand to destroy the church. Fights within have often caused the church flocks to be scattered. Yes, some members of the flock who are well versed in the faith will find another church to attend. But there are many other members of the flock who have not grown much spiritually who are either scattered into apostate churches or discouraged into not attending church at all. While the church people fought among themselves, the devil came in and plundered the congregation. This, unfortunately, is the history of the decline or demise of many churches.

The witness of the faith. Abraham had given a good witness about his faith when he built those altars in the land to worship Jehovah. The Canaanites and Perizzites would be most cognizant of those altars. This was a new religion to them, and so they would be watching Abraham very closely to see how this new religion affected him. They will judge his religion and his God by his behavior. Hence, if Abraham and Lot cannot get along as brethren ought, it will create great dishonor and disrespect for the faith they embrace and the God they exalt.

One of the problems of inner fighting amongst believers is that it gives a poor testimony to the world of our faith and of the God we worship. Joseph Parker said, "They [the world] know not our God; but if we fight and bicker, and if we assail and devour one another, they must think evil of our religion, and they may secretly despise our God. Let us not shame our call and our destiny before the worshipers of idols . . . Let us give none occasion to the enemy to blaspheme."

Of course, all of this does not mean that we must not contend with evil in the church. If evils in the church are not challenged, whether they be moral evils or doctrinal evils, they will overcome the church and destroy it. Contending in this case is to preserve the integrity of our witness, the purity of our standards, and the honor of our Savior.

B. THE COUNSELLING BY ABRAHAM

When Abraham heard of the strife between his and Lot's herdsmen, he took action. He got together with Lot and gave some wise counsel regarding the problem, and this counsel led to the solving of the problem.

We will note the concern, the command, and the courtesy in the counselling Abraham gave Lot.

1. The Concern in the Counselling

"And Abram said unto Lot, Let there be no strife, I pray thee, between me and thee, and between my herdsmen and thy herdsmen; for we are brethren" (v. 8). Abraham did not delight in strife. He was not pugnacious in nature. He was a peacemaker, not a troublemaker. However, a good many folk in society are just the opposite; and our churches seem to have an over abundance of that kind. Such people wear their feelings on their sleeves, cannot suffer any of their rights to be violated, are jealous about how much attention they receive, and, in summary, are much more concerned about themselves than they are about the honor of God and the blessings of others. Strife does not bother them. They almost seem to loath peace. Such folk make good news media reporters in society and effective tools of the devil in church. But Abraham is concerned about peace. Not peace at any price, but peace where there ought to be peace instead of strife.

Abraham was especially concerned about stopping this strife because "we are brethren." Brethren are to love each other. They are not to be on the outs with each other, or the land will not have peace. The first institution God ever established was

Separation From Lot

the family, and it is the foundational institution in the land. If the family does not get along, society will not get along, and the world will not get along. The disintegration of the family today has much to do with the disintegration of society. Scorning family values is destructive to society. Show me a family in church that gets along well with themselves, and I will show you a family that is a great help to the work of the church and will not be troublemakers in the church. Show me a family at church that is always bickering and fighting among themselves, and I will show you a family that is trouble at church. If you cannot get along at home, you will not get along outside the home. How much, therefore, we need to work hard at keeping the peace among the brethren if we want peace anywhere else in society.

2. The Command in the Counselling

"Is not the whole land before thee? separate thyself, I pray thee, from me" (v. 9). This is a tragic but necessary command. Lot's conduct made him undesirable. It is clear from the context that it was Lot, not Abraham, who was at fault in this strife. Lot made no attempt to bring peace. He, like many church members, was not interested in bringing peace. He was too selfish and self-centered to work for peace among the brethren. He was more interested in pasture than peace. He was more concerned about getting what he could to help himself rather than giving what he could to help others. Hence, Abraham must tell Lot to "separate thyself from me."

Society seems very slow to realize this need of separating those who behave poorly from the rest of the group if peace is to be obtained. If the belligerent is not removed from society, society will be continually troubled and finally be destroyed. If evil is not removed, the blessings of righteousness will not be experienced. If Lot is not removed from the camp, the Canaanites and Perizzites will eventually ruin both the herds of Lot and the herds Abraham, and they will also destroy their camp. Until wicked Queen Athaliah was removed, Jerusalem did not have peace, for "the city was quiet, *after* that they had slain Athaliah with the sword" (II Chronicles 23:21). Scripture says, "When the wicked perish, there is shouting [joyous shouting, for happiness has returned to society]" (Proverbs 11:10). When dissidents in a church continually upset the work of the church, they need to be removed from the membership of the church. And when folk are disrupting a church service, they too must be removed. It is all the same principle.

3. The Courtesy in the Counselling

"Is not the whole land before thee? . . . if thou wilt take the left hand, then I will go to the right; or if thou depart to the right hand, then I will go to the left" (v. 9). What a magnanimous offer by Abraham! What courtesy! He gives Lot first choice of the land—then Abraham will take what's left. Abraham's conduct here certainly reflects a great restoration of his faith since his sojourning days in Egypt. "Certainly his foot slipped in Egypt, but he is strong now, and he looks every inch a king as he stoops before Lot [to give him first choice]" (Joseph Parker).

Abraham could have insisted upon his rights. After all, he was the elder. Also he had graciously taken Lot under his care and raised him after Lot's grandfather had died (who had cared for him after Lot's father had died earlier). And Abraham had doubtless helped Lot to his present well being materially. If anyone deserved to get first choice, it certainly was Abraham who was the elder, the guardian, the benefactor, the wiser, and the peacemaker—the one who is seeking to stop the strife. But no, Abraham gives up his privilege and lets Lot take first choice. No wonder the strife ended quickly. To always give priority to your rights does not solve problems—it only aggravates them. Nothing demonstrates this more clearly than our own society which has for some time now continually fussed about their rights.

Abraham's courtesy reveals his priorities regarding material things. He was more concerned about peace than about making an extra buck. While he had considerable wealth, he was not primarily concerned here about improving his accumulation of wealth or in gaining an advantage over Lot in who would get

Separation From Lot

the best pasture and watering privileges for their flocks. He had higher goals in life; goals that are not embraced, unfortunately, by many. Carnal interests were not primary with Abraham; spiritual interests were. "Would to God that such indifference about carnal interests were more prevalent . . . among the professors of religion! This would show a becoming deadness to the world: it would give an evidence that our hearts were set on things above, and not on things below: it would illustrate more strongly and convincingly than ten thousand words, the efficacy of faith, and the excellence of true religion" (Charles Simeon).

C. THE CHOOSING BY LOT

We have been told little about Lot in previous Scripture. But in our text for this study, we begin to learn about the character of Lot; and what we learn about the character of Abraham's nephew is not good. The poor character of Lot is really evidenced in our text in the choice he made of which land he would take in moving from Abraham. We will note three things about his choice, and all three will show his poor character. They are the guide in his choosing, the gracelessness in his choosing, and the guile in his choice.

1. The Guide in His Choosing

"And Lot lifted up his eyes, and beheld all the plain of Jordan, that it was well watered every where, before the LORD destroyed Sodom and Gomorrah, even as the garden of the LORD , like the land of Egypt, as thou comest unto Zoar. Then Lot chose him all the plain of Jordan" (vv. 10,11). Material prosperity was the guide which Lot used to determine his choice of land. Now it is not necessarily wrong to buy your gas or groceries where the price is the lowest. It is not necessarily wrong to buy farm land which is the most fertile. Choosing something because it is more economical is not necessarily evil. That is not the condemnation we make here of Lot. The condemnation of Lot here is that material advantage was all that guided him. He never considered anything else. He never sought the counsel of

God, he never prayed for wisdom to make a right decision. Character was not a factor in his choice, spiritual opportunities and blessings were not in his choice, and family values never entered his choice. It was not food for the soul that guided his choice, but food for the sheep and cattle. It was not fellowship with the saints that guided his choice, but fortune in his pocket.

Many men down through the ages have been like Lot, and the end result is not pretty. The young ruler would not give up his fortune to follow Jesus, and it brought sorrow to him (Luke 18:23). Many people choose jobs, schools, friends, marriages, and housing mostly on the basis of material gain and advantage and prestige. They care not if their choice brings them into a place where there are not any good churches or where spiritual health is jeopardized. It is material gain which motivates their choice. Joseph Parker said, "Men do not care how poor the Church is, if the farm be good. They will give up the most inspiring ministry in the world for ten feet more garden, or a paddock to feed an ass in . . . They will take away six children into a moral desert for the sake of a garden to play in; they will leave Paul or Apollos for six feet of greenhouse."

2. The Gracelessness in His Choosing

When Abraham gave Lot first choice in selecting the land, Lot did not hesitate to immediately start choosing. With gracelessness (which is encouraged by greed) he quickly grabbed the opportunity of first choice and chose what he thought was the best land. He did not care if his good uncle Abraham had good land; Lot only cared about himself. Lot did not back away from taking the first choice by graciously telling Abraham that he was the elder and that he had for a number of years cared for his nephew and had helped his nephew get a good start in life; and, therefore, he ought to take the first choice. No, Lot made no such speech. Instead he unhesitatingly seized the opportunity he thought he had to make material gain and made the choice of what looked like the best land in sight. Abraham's benevolence inspired no reciprocal kindness in Lot.

Separation From Lot

A person too eager for material gain will not be known for grace. Men like this will run roughshod over anyone who gets in their way. They will push and shove without caring who they hurt so long as it puts more green stuff in their pockets. They will try to find a way to use every situation in their lives for material gain. Friendships, church relationships, family, the benevolence of others, and even the hardship of others will all be studied to see how they can be used to obtain extra gain. It is an ugly character, but one day it will meet up with the anathema of the Almighty.

3. The Guile in His Choice

Lot thought he was really getting a great possession when he chose "the plain of Jordan" (v. 10). No other land looked so nice. To the outward eye and to the man thinking only of material gain, the area looked exceedingly good. However, Lot was fooled and tricked by the devil. The attractiveness of the land only deceived the onlooker about the evil in the land. In the land was Sodom, and "the men of Sodom were wicked and sinners before the LORD exceedingly" (v. 13). Sodom was a terrible moral cesspool. The sin of homosexuality abounded. But the world, of course, would not speak disparagingly of Sodom. They would talk about the wealth, celebrities, food, entertainment, the night spots, etc. that Sodom had. To the world, Sodom had everything. But Sodom did not have everything. It lacked righteousness, the thing they needed the most. Lacking righteousness, they were, therefore, filled with wickedness.

So Lot was not getting the great place to live in that he thought he was getting. This would cost him dearly; for as a result of the character of the people in the land he chose, he did not get to enjoy his gains very long. Soon he lost it all plus what character he had left. The losses started when Sodom was plundered by a foreign power (Genesis 14). They continued when Sodom was destroyed in fire and brimstone (Genesis 19) for their great wickedness. Then, with material gains gone, Lot, in drunkenness and incestuous conduct, lost what remained of his character and respectability. Lot, like so many people, was beguiled by the glitter of material gain and, as a result, ended up barren of everything: cash, conscience, character, and companions—companions of the best kind, such as Abraham.

It is instructive to note the increasing involvement of Lot with Sodom. When Lot moved to the plains of the Jordan, he did not move into Sodom right away. He first "dwelled in the [other] cities of the plain" (v. 12); then he "pitched his tent toward Sodom" (Ibid.); later he "dwelt in Sodom" (Genesis 14:12); and then later still we read that "Lot sat in the gate of Sodom" (Genesis 19:1), which means he was so involved in Sodom that he was one of the rulers. We do not apostasize all at once. It is a series of steps that continually weaken us in our ability to stand against temptation. Someone has said that that which is repulsive if seen too often is first tolerated, then pitied, then embraced. How true this was in the case of Lot and Sodom. It is also true in the case of many professing saints today. One area you can readily observe this is in their watching of TV. They see so much evil on TV—and that which is repulsive (normal TV fare) if seen too often will first be tolerated, then pitied, then embraced. This explains the demise of the character of many professing believers.

D. THE CONFIRMING BY GOD

With Lot gaining the best land according to the perception of the human eye, the thinking of natural man would be to question the wisdom of Abraham's action of giving Lot first choice. It looks like Abraham got "ripped off" because of his giving Lot first choice. But nothing could be farther from the truth. Abraham was absolutely right in what he did; and shortly after Lot had separated himself from Abraham, God came to Abraham and confirmed the wisdom of Abraham's action.

Sometimes when a person does the will of God, it does not look at first like he did the right thing. The blessed results of doing the will of God do not always come quickly. The good seeds that have been planted do not always spring up as speedily

Separation From Lot

as other seeds oftentimes do. This frequently discourages the faithful soul, and there are plenty of critics around who will add to the discouragement by pointing out the apparent lack of success in the life of the obedient one compared to the worldling. But be patient; truth will be vindicated; righteousness will be exonerated; and doing the will of God will be confirmed in due season. Let every one who dares to follow God's way be encouraged by the fact that sooner or later God will confirm in substantial ways that you are on the right path. We noted this encouraging truth in chapter 1 of our book and will note it here again, for Scripture repeats the lesson.

In looking at this confirming by God of Abraham's action, we will consider the nature of the confirming and the response to the confirming.

1. The Nature of the Confirming

God confirms the rightness of our path in a number of ways. Two of the most frequent, encouraging, and blessed ways are in the presence of God and the promises of God. These are blessings which those outside the will of God do not have. Lot did not experience them, but Abraham did. Abraham was rich where it counted.

The presence of God. The statement "And the LORD said unto Abram, after that Lot was separated from him" (v. 14) not only leads into the promises, but it also tells us of the presence of God. God came to Abraham to speak with him. Thus Abraham was made aware of the blessed presence of God in his life—a blessing he experienced previously after moving to Canaan from Haran. Of course to the worldling, this blessing is of little value. The only value they are interested in is that which can be computed in dollars and cents. They are not interested in the presence of God. The farther away from God they can get, the better they feel. But that is the thinking of fools. Wise men know that the presence of God is more valuable than anything we can gain from this old world. "In thy presence is fulness of joy" (Psalms 16:11) surely says something about the great blessing of God's presence.

Lot did not enjoy the presence of God. He did not feel God near to him. No, when you walk in the world, you will feel distant from God. How often backslidden Christians complain that God seems so far off from them. But their disobedient life has resulted in that consequence. The Word says, "Draw nigh to God, and he will draw nigh to you" (James 4:8). It works the other way, too. Disobedience to God is not drawing nearer to God but getting farther and farther away from Him. Lot did not seem to care about being in the presence of God's people which reflected a greater problem; namely, he did not care about being in the presence of God—and God obliged. Abraham, however, was a decidedly different situation.

The promises of God. The obedient life is always a recipient of blessed promises. Therefore, wonderful promises came from God to Abraham for his obedience. And they served as a strong confirmation of his doing God's will. "And the LORD said . . . Lift up now thine eyes, and look from the place where thou art northward, and southward, and eastward, and westward: For all the land which thou seest, to thee will I give it, and to thy seed forever. And I will make thy seed as the dust of the earth; so that if a man can number the dust of the earth, then shall thy seed also be numbered" (vv. 14–16). Lots of land and lots of offspring were promised to Abraham. No one gets short changed who follows the Lord. Abraham did not get "ripped off" after all. Lot may have thought he was really getting a good deal, but there is not a man alive today who would want to trade it for the deal Abraham got from God. Abraham got more land than Lot and a promise of offspring Lot could not match. The descendants of Lot were small in number compared to Abraham's. Worse, Lot's descendants all came from an incestuous relationship with his daughters.

This promise-filled revelation of God regarding the seed and land for Abraham was an amplification of previous promises

God had given Abraham when he had first come into the land of Canaan (note Genesis 12:2 for the first promise regarding his seed and Genesis 12:7 for the first promise regarding the land). There will be more enlightenment of these promises for Abraham in the coming years of his life. All of this gives us a lesson on the progress of Divine illumination. The lesson is that God does not tell us everything all at once. It is line upon line and precept upon precept (cp. Isaiah 28:10). And progress in illumination will be inseparably associated with progress in obedience. This association of illumination with obedience explains why many folk do not get much from the Word and why they never seem to grow in wisdom and understanding of the Scripture. God does not give things of great value to those who do not appreciate their value. If we do not appreciate the value of something, we will not respect it or care for it or use it properly. This is so true regarding spiritual blessings such as illumination from the Word of God. God does not cast His pearls of great price before hogs (Matthew 7:6). And illumination of the Word of God is a pearl of extreme price. Therefore, you will never be illuminated much in the Word unless you walk faithfully before God. You will not learn much of the Scriptures unless you are willing to demonstrate in the decisions you make, in the stands you take, and in the priorities you embrace that you value the spiritual over the material as Abraham did in the case of Lot.

2. The Response to the Confirming

Abraham's response to the confirmation of God was a noble one. "Then Abram removed his tent, and came and dwelt in the plain of Mamre, which is in Hebron, and built there an altar unto the LORD" (v. 18). In his walk and worship, Abraham evidenced his excellent response to the confirmation from God.

Walk. God confirmed the rightness of Abraham's action with some wonderful promises. But He also gave a precept to go with the promises; for promises are not without precepts, as we noted earlier in this book. They are inseparably connected; and to realize the promises, you must obey the precepts. God had told Abraham to "walk through the land in the length of it and in the breadth of it" (v. 17), and Abraham began to do just that. The command to walk through the land was obviously not one that Abraham had to do all at once; but it was a command for Abraham to become acquainted with his possessions, to learn what the dimensions of the promise were so he could appreciate what God was giving him.

When God gives us blessings, we ought to respond in obedience to the duties He assigns us. When God tells us what He is going to do for us, we need to get busy with what we are supposed to do for God. Otherwise we will not become acquainted with the blessings God has for us.

Worship. God's presence and promises ought to inspire our worship. They certainly inspired Abraham to worship, for Scripture says he "built there an altar unto the LORD " (v. 18). The altar honored God; it praised God. As Matthew Henry said, "When God meets us with gracious promises, he expects that we should attend him with our humble praises." Today it seems that in order to get people in church to worship, we have to bring in some entertainment, offer door prizes, or have some attendance contests. The presence and promises of God do not seem to inspire the average church member. The minister can preach wonderful things from God's Word, but this does not inspire many in the congregation. Church members are so carnal that the only way you can get a majority of the members to attend church is to offer them some carnal inducement. It is a sad but true commentary on the spirituality of our churches. Abraham was a different sort, however. When he heard the promises of God, he was moved to build an altar of praise and honor to God. But in contrast, not much true praise and honor come to God from those who have to be moved by carnal inducements to show up at church.

IV.
Soldiership of Abraham

Genesis 14:1–16

THE MILITARY EXPERTISE of Abraham was outstanding. But this soldiership attribute of Abraham is something of which few people are aware. However, our text will acquaint us well with Abraham's skill in the military field. This account in Scripture of Abraham's soldiership involves Abraham's rescue of his nephew Lot from troubles which Lot got himself into by moving to Sodom. We noted in our last chapter that Lot, lacking character, had made a very bad choice in choosing the plain of Jordan (where Sodom was located) as the place for his family and flocks to live. When he moved to the plain of Jordan, he first "pitched his tent toward Sodom" (13:12) and then later "dwelt in Sodom" (14:12) whose inhabitants God said "were wicked and sinners before the LORD exceedingly" (13:13).

After moving to Sodom and experiencing some temporary success, Lot's situation deteriorated rapidly because of the Dead Sea War. The war resulted in Sodom being sacked by Chedorlaomer, king of Elam, and three other kings who were allies of Chedorlaomer in the Dead Sea War. In the sacking of Sodom, "they took Lot, Abram's brother's son, who dwelt in Sodom, and his goods, and departed" (v. 12). This brought Abraham on the scene; and in a demonstration of great soldiership, he rescued Lot and the other Sodomites and their possessions.

To study this experience in Abraham's life, we will note the raiding of Sodom (vv. 1–12), which will show the need of Abraham's soldiership, and the rescuing of Sodom (vv. 13–16), which will show the deeds of Abraham's soldiership.

A. THE RAIDING OF SODOM

The raiding of Sodom was part of the first war between nations recorded in the Bible. We call the war the Dead Sea War because it was all centered around the Dead Sea area. There were, of course, many wars in history before this war; but this war, which included the raiding of Sodom, was the first war to be recorded in the Scriptures.

In examining this raid upon Sodom, we will note the cause of the raid, the coalition of the raiders, the cleverness of the raid, and the conquering by the raiders.

1. The Cause of the Raid

Sodom was not a free city. The city Lot thought advantageous to live in was under bondage. Before Lot had moved to Sodom, Sodom, along with some neighboring city states (Gomorrah, Admah, Zeboiim, and Zoar) in the Dead Sea area, had been overcome by the powerful king named Chedorlaomer; and for "Twelve years they served Chedorlaomer" (v. 4). It was during those twelve years that Lot moved to Sodom. Sodom and the four other city states, in bondage to Chedorlaomer with Sodom, did not like the servitude; and after twelve years of it, they decided they had had enough. So "in the thirteenth year they rebelled" (v. 4). This, of course, did not go over well with Chedorlaomer; and so "in the fourteenth year came Chedorlaomer, and the kings that were with him" (v. 5), to take revenge. This is what led to the raiding of Sodom.

Sodom's inability to successfully free itself from Chedorlaomer is a forceful illustration of the difficulty of breaking the yoke of sin. It is not easy to throw off the yoke. Old habits do not die easily. Old temptations may seem dead for awhile; but unless the grace of God intervenes, the Chedorlaomers of evil will be back to enslave you again. What a needed warning this is regarding all flirtation with sin. Sodom looks so pleasant; evil look so exciting; but the enslavement is always there; and it is very, very hard to get rid of it. Once the enslavement comes upon you, you will never get rid of it unless God intervenes.

2. The Coalition of the Raiders

Like many wars today, the Dead Sea War was not between just two nations. It was between a number of nations allied together. Here the coalition of attackers included four nations. The kings and their respective nations of this coalition were "Amraphel king of Shinar [Babylon], Arioch king of Ellasar, Chedorlaomer king of Elam, and Tidal king of nations [a group of small city-states]" (v. 1). Chedorlaomer was the leader of the four nations (vv. 5,9,17). Interestingly, the lands of these nations were mostly in the land we know today as Iraq. At least one nation and perhaps another governed area also in the land known today as Iran. But Iraq was the primary area from which this coalition came. With some of the attack of this coalition from the Iraq territory being in the land governed by Israel today (Chedorlaomer's attack included land on the west side of the Dead Sea), we can say that times have not changed much—today it is still the land of Iraq fighting against the land of Israel. The matter of invasion may change—in the Dead Sea War of Abraham's day it was an army on foot; in the Desert Storm War of our day, it was Scud missiles—but the lands battling each other are the same.

3. The Cleverness of the Raid

"And in the fourteenth year came Chedorlaomer, and the kings that were with him, and smote the Rephaims in Ashteroth Karnaim, and the Zuzims in Ham, and the Emims in Shaveh Kiriathaim, And the Horites in their mount Seir, unto El-paran, which is by the wilderness. And they returned, and came to En-mishpat, which is Kadesh, and smote all the country of the Amalekites [not Amalekites then, for they did not yet exist, but land known as the Amalekites when Moses wrote Genesis], and also the Amorites, that dwelt in Hazazon-tamar. And [then] there went out the king of Sodom, and the king of Gomorrah, and the king of Admah, and the king of Zeboiim, and the king of Bela (the same is Zoar), and they joined battle with them in the vale [valley] of Siddim; With Chedorlaomer the king of Elam, and with Tidal king of nations, and Amraphel king of Shinar, and Arioch king of Ellasar; four kings with five" (vv. 5–9).

The four attacking kings used good strategy in the Dead Sea War. Instead of directly attacking the five cities of the Jordan plain in the Dead Sea area after they came down from the north, they made "a wide sweep to the east and south [Seir] and then around to the southwest [to "Kadesh" as in Kadesh-Barnea]; then northeast to the western side of the Dead Sea [Hazazon-tamar, which is better known to Bible students as Engedi, cp. II Chronicles 20:2], and then lastly the troops swarm down upon their final objective" (H. C. Leupold). This effectively took away nations who could aid Sodom and her allies, and it tightened the noose around their necks.

Some may be puzzled about which way Chedorlaomer's coalition came into the valley of Siddim after wiping out the nations on the west side of the Dead Sea; for Scripture only says that after they had taken care of those nations, then the cities of the valley of Siddim went out to meet the attacking coalition (v. 8). The solution to the puzzle is that they came straight across from the hills on the other side of the Dead Sea. How could they do that with the Dead Sea being in their way? The answer is that the Dead Sea was obviously not as big as it is today. The judgment upon Sodom and Gomorrah substantially changed the geography in that area including enlarging the sea. Leupold said, "That 'they drew up in battle array in the valley of Siddim' seems to be a further indication that this portion, which is now the southern third of the Dead Sea, was in those days not yet inundated by the waters of the sea." That would readily explain the coalition's design. For after defeating the nations on the west of the Dead Sea as we know it today, they charged down from the hills on the west and went straight east across what is known today as the southern portion of the Dead Sea, but what was then land, and commenced their attack upon the cities of the valley of Siddim. When the attackers headed for Sodom and her allies from the west, then the nations of the valley of Siddim went out to meet Chedorlaomer and his allies in battle.

4. The Conquering by the Raiders

Once the attack began upon Sodom and her allies, they fell quickly. "And the vale of Siddim was full of slimepits [asphalt]; and the kings of Sodom and Gomorrah fled, and fell there; and they that remained fled to the mountain. And they took all the goods of Sodom and Gomorrah, and all their victuals [food supplies], and went their way" (vv. 10,11). The defense put up by Sodom and her allies was pitiful. They seemingly had the advantage—they outnumbered their attackers five kings to four, they were fighting on their home turf (which meant they had knowledge of those asphalt pits which they could have used to their advantage), and they had their supplies right close at hand. But in spite of these advantages, they wilted quickly in the heat of battle; and so Chedorlaomer and his coalition easily conquered the area.

Why did Sodom and her allies fall so quickly in the Dead Sea War? The answer is not hard to discover. It was their debauched manner of life that rendered them weak for battle. They had neither the courage nor the desire to fight the battle. That kind never does. You cannot lay around in night clubs every night, live a life of luxury, and pamper the appetites of the body, and still develop good, robust soldier characteristics. Wine, women, and song in heavy illicit doses will defeat an army before it ever takes the battle field. But nations do not learn. Like our nation, governments provide the soldier boys with plenty of booze, night clubs, and moral degrading opportunities to destroy their character with dispatch and to make the soldier a very poor soldier though he has the best equipment money can buy. One night in my Navy career, I watched a fire destroy the officers' club (fancy name for beer hall) on a Navy base near Corpus Christi, Texas. Within a few weeks the education building on the base was converted into the officers' club while the education folk were shoved into cramped and insufficient quarters elsewhere. It was clear what the priorities were. And they were not good! When you see things like this going on, the surprising thing is that we still win wars. The fact that soldiers fought so well in the Desert Storm War of 1991 cannot be divorced from the fact that due to Arab traditions, our soldier boys did not get to booze it up like they normally do. But the bureaucrats in high places in Washington D.C. would never catch on to that important truth.

B. THE RESCUING OF SODOM

Chedorlaomer and his allies were in for a great surprise. They thought they had wiped out every force that could come to the aid of the peoples they had conquered and plundered. But they had not considered Abraham. They may not even have known of him; but if they did know about him, they would not consider him a viable force to reckon with. He did not look like any military threat. He was simply a man with flocks and servants. But shortly after their raid of Sodom and the other neighboring cities, they got the shock of their lives. Abraham came to the rescue of Sodom.

We will note the soliciting for the rescue, the selflessness in the rescue, the soldiers for the rescue, the sagacity of the rescue, and the success of the rescue.

1. The Soliciting for the Rescue

"There came one that had escaped, and told Abram" (v. 13). How interesting! The people of Sodom knew about Abraham. They had doubtless heard about him from Lot. However, they had nothing to do with him until they got in big trouble. The dwellers of Sodom liked their wicked city. Abraham could live up there in Hebron away from "where the action is" (according to Sodom) all he wants. But they were going to enjoy the show in Sodom. Abraham would not be honored in Sodom. His values and perspective of life were not Sodom's. Sodom would scorn his convictions, his lifestyle, and his interest in God. But suddenly the thinking about Abraham changed. Sodom was sacked, and the citizens were taken prisoner. They needed help. Where could the people of Sodom get help? From Sodom's military? No. From friendly Gomorrah? No. From ally Zoar? No. From

Soldiership of Abraham

another ally Admah? No. Where oh where could they get help? Ah, there is Abraham up on the hill on the other side of the Jordan. Run to Abraham for help.

Here is a great lesson for the individual Christian and the church: you do not have to be popular with the world to be of help to them and to win them to Christ. We are making a grave mistake in our age in thinking that to reach the world and rescue the world from their sin cursed condition we must become more like the world. Bring on the "Christian-rock," make our church services like TV entertainment, don't be so strict about standards at Christian camps and colleges or you will drive away the unsaved is the advice of many misguided souls. Yes, the philosophy of much of Christendom today is move to Sodom and mingle with the Sodomites and you will be better able to help them than sitting up on a hill in Hebron praying to God and staying aloof from Sodom. But this sort of thinking by the worldly saint does not have one single iota of support from the Scripture. Our text will nail it to the wall. It is the separated, clean saint that can help the sinner best. Though you may be scorned and despised for your separation from evil, it will in no way deter your ability or opportunity to help in the hour of need. Rather, it will enhance your ability and opportunity to help. The one who escaped knew there was help in Abraham, not in anyone from where he had just come.

2. The Selflessness in the Rescue

"And when Abram heard that his brother [not brother as we use the term, but brother as in 'we be brethren' in Genesis 13:8] was taken captive, he armed his trained servants . . . and pursued them unto Dan" (v. 14). When Abraham gave Lot first choice, it was a very unselfish act on the part of Abraham. Now we see this selflessness of Abraham again. Particularly we see his selflessness here in both his display of grace and in his disinterest of gain.

His display of grace. What grace it was for Abraham to

immediately respond to the report and go to the rescue of Lot. He could have sat back and scoffed and said Lot was only getting what he deserved because he had greedily taken first choice, had disrespected his uncle's position, and had shown no appreciation for his uncle's help and care over the years; and, therefore, why should his uncle risk his life and the lives of his people to rescue that no good nephew.

But Abraham did not say that. He acted in grace. Grace is never selfish. Grace always has the welfare of others more prominent in its mind than any personal grievances. It is the same kind of grace that provided for the salvation of sinful man. Man had disobeyed God, disrespected God, ran from God, and been ungrateful to God just like Lot had been to Abraham. But God still seeks the salvation of man because of grace.

His disinterest of gain. Abraham did not seek the rescue of Lot and his fellow citizens of Sodom for any personal gain. He did not ask the one who brought the report of the capture what the reward would be for rescuing Lot and the others. Later on in our next chapter, we will see this fact emphasized much more obviously in Abraham's encounter with the king of Sodom after bringing back the people from Sodom. The king of Sodom wanted to pay him, but Abraham would have none of it.

This noble attitude of disinterest in gain was just the opposite of Lot's attitude. Unlike Lot, Abraham did not look at every situation to see how he could get personal gain from it. He was not going to make the tragedy of others an opportunity to get personal gain. How unselfish Abraham was. He thought of others first.

3. The Soldiers for the Rescue

"He armed his trained servants, born in his own house, three hundred and eighteen, and pursued them unto Dan" (v. 14). The army Abraham had to pursue Chedorlaomer's coalition was certainly small, almost laughably small, compared to Chedorlaomer's army. But, as we will note shortly, it was a better army.

Though small for an army, the number of servants tells us Abraham had a very large camp—or ranch as we would call it today. Leupold says that having 318 servants ready for war "points to a body of servants easily numbering a thousand and gives us some idea of the size of the flocks as well as the influence of the man." The size of Abraham's camp amazes us. Abraham was a small town in himself. His camp would be spread out over a good sized area. Lot had chosen prime land, but Abraham certainly had done much better.

Having the servants "trained" is a sharp contrast to what Sodom's military situation was and shows us what a good steward of time Abraham was. Ezekiel 16:49 tells us that one of the sins of Sodom was an "abundance of idleness." No wonder their military was so quickly vanquished by Chedorlaomer and his allies. Abraham was a different story, however. Idleness did not characterize his camp. Besides the normal duties of servants, they were also trained for military action. That is impressive. What a good leader Abraham was. We could surely use some leaders of Abraham's caliber in our government. Such leaders would recognize that peace must not cause us to discontinue or dangerously reduce military ability. Being prepared at all times is a must for a nation's security!

The excellent preparation by Abraham of his servants for battle gives God's people a good lesson on being prepared for spiritual battles. And we especially need to be prepared for spiritual conflict. How do we prepare? Paul tells us how. He said, "Wherefore take unto you the whole armor of God, that ye may be able to withstand in the evil day, and having done all, to stand" (Ephesians 6:13); and then he describes each piece of the armor: truth, righteousness, gospel peace, faith, salvation, and the Word of God. Finally he adds that we should also be praying. If we were as prepared as Paul exhorts us to be, our spiritual enemies would taste defeat whenever they tried to attack us. But having your interests in Sodom will not help you get prepared properly. You must, like Abraham, have your interests in the will of God, the altar to God, and the fellowship with God.

Some may think in reading the end of Genesis 14 that Abraham had more than the 318 servants to go to battle for him. There it is reported that Abraham was also accompanied in this rescuing work by three of his neighbors: Mamre, Eshcol, and Aner (Genesis 14:24, cp. 14:13). These three neighbors were in some sort of confederacy with Abraham ("these were confederate with Abram" [v. 13]). But as Candlish says, "Though three confederates are mentioned . . . it does not appear that they furnished any men for this enterprise." The way the three men are mentioned in accompanying Abraham indicates they came alone, not with any of their servants.

4. The Sagacity of the Rescue

"And he divided himself [his men] against them, he and his servants, by night, and smote them" (v. 15). Abraham was a wise general. He made his rescue attack at night, and he divided his troops so he could make the attack from different places. The dividing of the servants and the cover of darkness would confuse the enemy and keep them from knowing just where the attack was centered and how large an army was attacking them. The enemy would not conclude that only 318 troops were attacking. They would be ready to conclude that they were being attacked by an army that was large enough to come from several directions. This strategy of Abraham was not unlike that of Gideon some centuries later (Judges 7). Gideon divided his group of 300 into three groups and came at the Midianites from three different directions and also did his attacking at night. The cover of night kept the Midianites from knowing the full extent of the attackers, and the attackers coming from more than one direction caused the Midianites to think they were being attacked by a much larger group than they were. Thus, the Midianites panicked and ran for their lives.

Abraham's strategy also took advantage of the degraded situation that exists after a godless army has defeated a foe, taken great spoils, and is headed for home. "One can visualize the manner in which the victorious army returning back home lay scattered about, secure in the thought of having none to attack them, flushed with victory and, perhaps, with drink; no sentinels posted, nothing farther from the thoughts of all than the idea of an attack" (H. C. Leupold). How often the world is just like Chedorlaomer's forces. Loaded with the things of the world, engrossed in satisfying intemperate appetites, living in darkness, and taking no thought of their eternal safety, their lives are suddenly confronted with death; and they are unprepared to meet it successfully.

5. The Success of the Rescue

Abraham "smote them, and pursued them unto Hobah, which is on the left hand of Damascus. And he brought back all the goods, and also brought again his brother Lot, and his goods, and the women also, and the people" (vv. 15,16). Several significant characteristics of Abraham's success are quite evident from the text; namely, his success was miraculous and it was complete.

It was miraculous. The success of Abraham was phenomenal. It was like the success of Gideon in that it was an obvious miracle accomplished by the power of God. That 318 men should rout and overcome Chedorlaomer and his allies is astounding. Chedorlaomer was no amateur. He was a powerful king and had defeated city after city in his invasion of Palestine. Yet, Abraham with only 318 men chased Chedorlaomer's forces for some 120 miles and took back all the people and booty Chedorlaomer and company had captured.

When one walks in the right paths, he has God for an ally. And God's power is great! Lot had no power to deliver himself let alone deliver Sodom. Yet, Abraham could deliver the whole bunch with just 318 trained servants. The difference between the ability of Abraham and Lot was righteousness. Righteousness secures God's great miracle power. Our greatest might as a nation lies in our character more than anything else. But little does our nation or any other nation talk about that. Give me a nation that is right with God, and I will show you a nation that can win her battles no matter how outnumbered she is, for it will have the miracle power of God working for it.

It was complete. The completeness of Abraham's victory is demonstrated in the fact that he brought back "all" the goods and chased Chedorlaomer and his allies all the way north of Hobah which is northeast of Damascus. Scholars tell us it was about 120 miles that Abraham pursued the foe up the Jordan route and then up northeast of Damascus—the route which folk travelled to go up the Jordan plain to the Euphrates River region. Abraham made sure the enemy was driven far from the area of those they had attacked.

Nothing beats complete victory. Anything less leaves a bad taste in your mouth. Smite the enemy until he is finished. Korea and Viet Nam are living memorials to the folly of not fighting for a complete victory. Many Christians' lives are the same— they never quite conquer evil habits, they never deal with finality in regards to sin. So sin continually messes up their lives. Elisha was justifiably upset with King Joash for not smiting the ground more with the arrows, for it revealed that Joash would not have complete victory over Syria (II Kings 13:18,19). In war, be it spiritual or otherwise, we must never ease up in battle. Drive the enemy out of the land. Smite him until he can no longer attack you. Anything less is a compromise that will corrupt and destroy you.

V.

SOVEREIGNS AND ABRAHAM

GENESIS 14:17–24

THE FOURTEENTH CHAPTER of Genesis speaks of ten kings. Abraham was involved directly or indirectly with them all because of the Dead Sea War. In the passage before us, he has audiences with two of the ten in the "valley of Shaveh [a location generally believed to be near what later became known as Jerusalem], which is the king's dale" (v. 17). The first audience is with the king of Salem; the second audience is with the king of Sodom. The two kings and the two audiences are as different as daylight and darkness. One king is the best king of the ten in character; the other king is the worst king (or no better than the worst king) of the ten in character. One audience is a time of spiritual blessing, and the other is a time of temptation. But despite the contrasting character of the kings and of the audiences, Abraham came out well in both cases.

We will look first at Abraham's audience with the king of Salem (vv. 18–20), and then we will look at his audience with the king of Sodom (vv. 17, 21–24).

A. THE KING OF SALEM

The introduction in Scripture to the king of Salem is a simple one but also an instructive one: "And Melchizedek king of Salem brought forth bread and wine [to Abraham]; and he was the priest of the most high God" (v. 18). Melchizedek, the king of Salem, is a most interesting person. Mystery seems to envelope him. But it is this majestic mystery which enhances the obvious primary purpose of him in Scripture, namely, that of being a foreshadowment of Jesus Christ. Wherever he is mentioned, he is a wonderful type of Jesus Christ. That Melchizedek is a type of Christ we have no doubt, for at least eight verses in the Bible state that fact very plainly (Psalm 110:4, Hebrews 5:6, 6:20; 7:3,11,15,17, and 21). Interestingly, one of those texts (Hebrew 7:3) shows Melchizedek as a type of Christ not by what is said of Melchizedek in the Old Testament but by what is not said of him—which underscores the majesty of the mystery that surrounds the man.

In the verses of our text which speak of Melchizedek and his meeting with Abraham, we will look at five things about Melchizedek. Much of what we will see in these five things about him will speak of some important truths about Jesus Christ. These five things are his name, his offices, his location, his ministering, and his receiving.

1. His Name

Here we look specifically at the meaning of his name. The name Melchizedek means "king of righteousness" (cp. Hebrews 7:2). With such a great meaning, what a great name for a king is the name Melchizedek! Would that all the rulers of our world administered as "king (or president or governor, etc.) of righteousness." Too many rulers seem to rule in favor of unrighteousness. Laws are passed to support evil, to punish good, and to push God out of the land and bring the devil in. We need rulers who will by their power honor righteousness.

Spiritually, king of righteousness speaks of none other than Jesus Christ. He is the One Who through His redemptive work can bring righteousness to man, and He is the One Who will reign as King during the millennium when righteousness will be established in the world.

2. His Offices

Melchizedek had two offices. Our text says he was both a king and a priest. "Melchizedek king of Salem . . . he was the priest of the most high God" (v. 18). The combination of offices readily reminds us of Jesus Christ Who also is both a king and a priest (Christ has the office of a prophet, too). The priest's office emphasizes the Lamb name of Christ (John 1:29, Revelation 5:12), and the king's office emphasizes the Lion name of Christ (Revelation 5:5).

In combining the meaning of Melchizedek's name with his office as king of Salem, Hebrews 7:2 teaches us an important truth. The verse says of Melchizedek that he was "first being by interpretation King of righteousness, and after that also King of Salem, which is, King of peace." The truth taught here is that righteousness comes *before* peace. First, it is "King of righteousness"; and then it is "King of peace." This is a great truth that needs to be taught to our sin-sick world. The world strives for peace—they have conferences, wars, programs, plans, and organizations for peace. But they all fail because they forget or are ignorant of a fundamental truth: namely, righteousness brings peace. "And the work of righteousness shall be peace" (Isaiah 32:17).

This truth will be seen in salvation—before you can have peace with God, you must first obtain righteousness through the blood of Jesus Christ. This truth will be seen in society—before there will be peace in the land, there must first be righteousness in the land. This truth also applies to our minds—before we can have peace of mind, we must first live a righteous life. We blame just about everything for our lack of peace today. But we seldom blame our wicked living.

3. His Location

Melchizedek was located in Salem, for he was king of Salem. Salem is the location of Jerusalem ("Jeru" was some years later added to the name "Salem," making the name "Jerusalem"). Some do not think this particular Salem became Jerusalem, but other Salems in Scripture present real problems when attempts are made to associate them with Melchizedek. Psalm 76:2, however, helps vindicate the Jerusalem location when it refers to Jerusalem as Salem: "In Salem also is his

[God's] tabernacle, and his dwelling place in Zion."

This location puts Melchizedek about twenty miles north of where Abraham was living in Hebron at the time. This would make it easy for the two to be acquainted with each other, and so the meeting here with Abraham would not be that of strangers. In fact, it is very evident that Abraham knew Melchizedek very well; for, as we will see later, he paid him tithes—something he would not be doing if Melchizedek was a stranger. Abraham and Melchizedek, being some of the few who worshipped the true God in the land, would easily form a close friendship. When you live in the midst of heathen people and find a fellow believer, close friendship generally is the result.

Being the king of Salem (the city which eventually became Jerusalem, the city of the kings of Israel) is another way in which Melchizedek foreshadows the Great King, the King of kings. When Jesus Christ reigns as King during the millennium, He will reign from Jerusalem (Psalm 2:6), the city of the kings of Israel. Christ claims the throne because of His lineage to David, who reigned thirty-three years from this great city of the past and future.

4. His Ministering

Melchizedek went to meet Abraham as Abraham was returning home from rescuing Lot and Sodom by routing Chedorlaomer and his allies. Melchizedek was the only one of the ten kings in Genesis fourteen who was not actually engaged in battle in the Dead Sea War. But while he was not involved directly in the war, he did benefit by the attack of Abraham upon Chedorlaomer and his coalition. Abraham's military work brought improved security to the area. All in the area would benefit from this security, including Melchizedek.

Benefitting from Abraham's work, Melchizedek went forth to minister to Abraham. First, he ministered in the bread and wine; and then he ministered in the benedictions.

Bread and wine. "And Melchizedek king of Salem brought

forth bread and wine" (v. 18). The bread and wine would be welcomed by Abraham's group, for it represented the fundamental food needs of the men. Armies in those days were dependent on the people of the places they passed through to give them food and drink. Bread and wine speaks of that here.

But the bread and wine here also speak of Christ's redemptive work. Right after the words "bread and wine" are mentioned in our text, it is stated that "he was the priest of the most high God" (v. 18). This close association of bread and wine with the priesthood ministry of Melchizedek points us to the redemptive work of Christ for mankind. The bread and the wine (or the cup as it is called) are the two elements used to observe the Lord's Supper which is an observance that points to the sacrifice of Christ's body and blood for our redemption.

So the bread and wine speak of two things in our text. They speak of *refreshment* and of *redemption*. Both of these things speak of Christ. Christ not only saves us, but He also strengthens us. In Exodus 12, the Passover Lamb not only provided protection from death (a picture of redemption); but it also was to be eaten as food to provide strength for the Israelites. Ephesians 1:7 emphasizes the saving part: "we have redemption through his blood." Philippians 4:13 emphasizes the strengthening part: "I can do all things through Christ, which strengtheneth me."

Benedictions. "And he blessed him, and said, Blessed be Abram of the most high God, possessor of heaven and earth: And blessed be the most high God, which hath delivered thine enemies into thy hand" (vv. 19, 20). The benedictions were two in number. The first was for Abraham, the second was for God.

First, Melchizedek blessed Abraham. "Blessed be Abram." Abraham did not receive any honors from Sodom and her allies. The ungodly world is not in the habit of honoring the saints of God. Rather they honor their own corrupt people. Abraham got his honors from that which represented God and righteousness. Check your honors. Where do they come from? Do they come from that which represents God and righteousness? Honors from that which does not represent God and righteousness are honors that are not worth much. However, it seems those are the honors we strive for the most. We are sacrificing everything, including church and other spiritual opportunities, to gain the honors of the world. But we give little time to gaining honors from God.

Second, Melchizedek blessed God. "Blessed be the most high God, which hath delivered thine enemies into thy hand." This benediction gave credit to God for bringing victory in the Dead Sea War. We need to give credit where credit is due. Abraham's success was a result of God's power. With only 318 men in his army, he was greatly outnumbered by Chedorlaomer and his allies. It took a miracle from God to do the work Abraham did. So God is honored here for the victory. And He needs to be honored for all our blessings. Abraham was honored in the first benediction, but Melchizedek did not stop there. He went to the source of the victory, God Himself, and honored Him. So many today only honor man. Nations battle and have great victory, but God is not thanked. Soldiers are decked with medals—which is not wrong—but God is left out. Unless we begin to honor God for our blessings, be it in battle or in other areas, we will lose our blessings.

5. His Receiving

"And he gave him tithes of all" (v. 20). Some get confused in this text about who is giving tithes to whom. But the book of Hebrews clears away any doubt by making it plain that it was Abraham who was giving tithes. Speaking of Melchizedek, the writer of Hebrews said, "To whom also Abraham gave a tenth part of all" (Hebrews 7:2). As a victorious warrior, Abraham had gained much spoil from those he had conquered. The goods Chedorlaomer's coalition had taken from Sodom were returned to Sodom, as we will see next; but there was much spoil which Chedorlaomer had gained from other recent conquests; and from this Abraham gave tithes to Melchizedek, who was the representative of God.

This is the first mention of "tithes" in the Scripture; and it means a tenth, as is confirmed in Hebrews 7:2. Giving of the tithe at this time tells us that the tithe was not something limited to Israel under the law, as many misers would like to believe. People were tithing long before the law was given to Israel.

The tithe is a good principle in giving. Abraham is to be commended for his faithful tithing. But the New Testament does not limit giving to the tithe. It calls for more liberal giving. When Paul exhorted the churches to give, he did not mention the tithe. He spoke about a higher level of giving. He laid down principles that will discourage limiting giving necessarily to a tithe. As an example, when speaking of giving in his second letter to the Corinthians, Paul said, "He which soweth sparingly shall reap also sparingly; and he which soweth bountifully shall reap also bountifully" (II Corinthians 9:6). Christ said a strong statement about giving something more than a tithe when He used the widow with the two mites to illustrate what dedicated giving involved (Luke 21:1–4). Many professing Christians are nothing but tightwads towards God. They have never learned the joy of giving sacrificially. Their love for Christ has never amounted to enough to give abundantly. In fact, many have so little love they do not even come close to tithing, let alone giving above the tithe as the New Testament exhorts them to do.

B. THE KING OF SODOM

Like Melchizedek, Bera, the king of Sodom, also "went out to meet him [Abraham] after his return from the slaughter of Chedorlaomer, and of the kings that were with him" (v. 17). But what a different meeting was Abraham's meeting with the king of Sodom than with the king of Salem. Abraham went from visiting with the godly to visiting with the guileful.

Upon entering into an audience with the king of Sodom, Abraham was greeted with these words, "Give me the persons, and take the goods to thyself" (v. 21). The king of Sodom offered Abraham all the goods of Sodom as his remuneration for rescuing Sodom. While this looks innocent on the surface, it constituted a strong temptation for Abraham; and it makes

Bera's meeting with Abraham predominantly a lesson about temptation. Therefore, we will look at this audience Abraham had with the king of Sodom with this lesson in mind. We will note the strength of the temptation, the snare of the temptation, the selfishness in the temptation, and the success over the temptation.

1. The Strength of the Temptation

The offer the king of Sodom made to Abraham was a very strong temptation. It was strong in at least three ways. It was strong in the size, source; and season of the offer.

Size. The king of Sodom made Abraham a huge offer. He told Abraham to simply turn over the citizens of Sodom to the king; and he, Abraham, could have all their goods which he had rescued from Chedorlaomer and company. What great substance was offered Abraham. Scripture told us that Chedorlaomer and his allies "took all the goods of Sodom" (Genesis 14:11). Therefore, if Abraham accepted the proposal of the king of Sodom, he would gain all the wealth of Sodom! We wonder if Lot was standing by when the offer was made. If he was, his covetous heart would nearly die with envy. He had moved to Sodom to get a piece of the goods there, but here his uncle was offered the goods of everyone in the city of Sodom!

With such an amount offered Abraham, the temptation had to be very strong. Offering a trivial amount would be much easier to turn down than the goods of an entire city. Turning down a few bucks is not as hard as turning down millions of dollars. It would take great dedication to resist such a huge material offer. But Abraham was up to it and refused it pronouncedly (which we will note more about later).

Source. Another thing which made this temptation so strong was the source from which it came. It did not come from a nobody. It came from the position of a king. This would give the temptation much respect and much legitimacy as far as natural man is concerned and would thus strengthen the temptation considerably. After all, royalty is impressive; and, furthermore, if the powers that be say it is all right, then surely it must be all right—so thinks natural man.

The devil loves to solicit from impressive positions because it really strengthens his solicitation. People take notice when a famous person endorses a product or philosophy or practice. When an ordinary person endorses something, it does not move us very much. But when an important person recommends a product or a practice or a philosophy, we pay attention and are much more likely to accept the recommendation than if some insignificant person made it. Much temptation today comes from the high places—high in position, prestige, popularity, etc. Professors, with an impressive string of degrees behind their names, tell us the Bible is untrustworthy. Popular and powerful legislators and rulers of government tell us gambling is okay. Famous entertainers exalt the most rotten of moral practices. Yes, the devil sees to it that his advertisers are dressed in the most attractive finery, have prestigious positions, are popular and respected. It makes temptation very strong. But Paul warned us about this when he said, "Satan himself is transformed into an angel of light" (II Corinthians 11:14). We will never deal well with temptation if we are so spiritually naïve that we are beguiled by evil when it is dressed up in glamorous, popular, and respectable trappings. Evil is evil no matter from whom it is advocated or from what position it solicits or how attractive in appearance it may seem. Offers must be judged on the basis of holiness, not on the basis of how impressive the presentation or presenter appears to the natural man.

Season. The temptation came when Abraham had just had a great victory in war. Flush with victory, the spoils of victory beckoned. It was a time when he seemed to deserve this offer of all the goods of Sodom. He had put forth courageous effort in rescuing the Sodomites; now it is only logical that he be rewarded and that the reward be great in order to be compatible with the greatness of his achievement. Most folk would say he deserved this reward. But Abraham saw differently. He was not fooled by the logic of man. He did not let men over-honor him. He saw the danger of it all and could discern between right and wrong in regard to what spoils you take and what spoils you do not take and what honors you accept and what honors you do not accept. Not many have that kind of discernment today, unfortunately.

Temptation can come at any time. But there are times when temptation is especially likely to appear. Those times include the time right after we have had a great victory. This is almost always a special season for temptation. After victory we have a tendency to let down or to get proud, as we have noted in a previous chapter. This makes us more prone to yield to temptation. But Abraham was ready here. He did not let his great victory cause him to let down his guard or get puffed up, and so he won a great victory over temptation that day. Let us also be ever ready and prepared to meet temptation at any hour and be especially ready when those special seasons of temptation come around.

2. The Snare of the Temptation

Abraham saw the snare immediately and spoke plainly about it. "I will not take any thing that is thine, lest thou shouldest say, I have made Abram rich" (v. 23). The king of Sodom would have a claim on Abraham if Abraham accepted this offer. If Abraham testified that living by faith is what brought him great blessings, the king of Sodom would laugh and remind everyone that he had helped to enrich Abraham and that all this business about God doing it was ridiculous. While God could indeed enrich Abraham through Sodom's goods, in this case it would not be seen that way by man. Hence, Abraham would have no part of it. He was concerned more about God's glory than about his wealth. Furthermore, as we will see in our next point, Abraham's taking all the goods would be cruel selfishness and not a mark of character. And don't think the king of

Sovereigns and Abraham

Sodom wouldn't hesitate to remind folk of that fact, too; even though he offered Abraham the goods. Yes, there was a snare in this temptation as there is in all temptations. It looks good on the surface, but there is a hook in the bait. There are evil consequences for yielding. You get nothing from temptation but what you will have to pay for later on.

Abraham saw a truth many institutions are learning today—but the hard way. Do not let some corrupt government come around and endow you with many goods. You will be hooked for sure if you do. You will eventually be a loser. If you let the government help your institution build nice buildings and buy nice equipment, you will discover that, as a result, the government can dictate to you how to use those buildings and that equipment. It is not a pleasant discovery, as many colleges and other institutions can attest.

We need to note here that Abraham did take some of the goods "which the young men have eaten, and the portion of the men which went with me, Aner, Eshcol, and Mamre" (v. 24). However, that was not the king of Sodom's anyway. That was the simple maintenance and upkeep necessary for the soldiers and those in the battle. That was not part of the offer by Bera king of Sodom. No one would make any false accusations of Abraham on that score. It was the rest of the goods that would create the problem.

3. The Selfishness in the Temptation

If Abraham accepts the offer of the king of Sodom, he will leave all the residents of Sodom with nothing. That certainly was not the purpose of Abraham in rescuing the captured from Chedorlaomer and his allies. He did not pursue this daring rescue with greed in mind. It was a totally unselfish act. But to take all the goods of Sodom would be a different story entirely. He would leave the residents of Sodom with nothing. It would be a very cruel bit of selfishness indeed. While they would be thankful Abraham saved their lives and living in poverty is better than being a slave of Chedorlaomer, yet on Abraham's part, it would be such terrible, unkind selfishness that one recoils at the thought of anyone doing such a thing. When folk are in such great need, nations normally run to their aid. But if Abraham accepted the offer of the king of Sodom, he would be fleecing their pockets instead of aiding them. It would be like rescuing a man that had been robbed of everything and kidnapped—but then keeping everything the robber took.

The evilness of a solicitation, proposal, recommendation, or a philosophy can be quickly discerned by the test of selfishness. If it promotes selfishness on your part, it is bad; and you should have nothing to do with it. This thought will not go over well today, however: for the big emphasis today is on the exalting of self. The rights' movement is mostly a selfish emphasis. It is not concerned about how they are treating others but about how others are treating them. It opens the door to great selfishness. It is me, my, and I; and I do not care about what happens to you. Strikers want more salary and more benefits regardless of the hardships it may impose on others. Homosexuals are notorious in their selfish emphasis. They get mighty uptight about how you treat them, but their behavior and demonstrations show they have little, if any, concern about how they treat you. Yes, once you spot that selfishness in a proposal, recommendation, or philosophy—shun it earnestly; for it is evil.

4. The Success Over the Temptation

Abraham defeated this temptation with flying colors. Great victories like this are not accidental. They do not come without reasons. We note at least three reasons why Abraham was so successful in defeating this temptation from the king of Sodom: he was earnest; he was prepared; he was reinforced.

He was earnest. Right after the offer was made by the king of Sodom, "Abram said to the king of Sodom, I have lift up mine hand unto the LORD, the most high God, the possessor of heaven and earth, That I will not take from a thread even to a shoelatchet, and that I will not take any thing that is thine" (vv.

Sovereigns and Abraham

22, 23). Some would say, "Whew! Isn't that too strong an answer?" No! You do not fight sin timidly and come away with victory. Abraham's earnest answer made it extremely plain to the king of Sodom that he totally rejected the offer. This stopped the king of Sodom from making another appeal. He knew Abraham was adamant in his conviction and backed off. You must be very earnest in fighting evil, or it will walk all over you.

One of our problems today is that we respond so timidly to temptation. This alerts the tempter to the fact that we are not really dedicated to our position, and so he repeats his offer again with maybe some few subtle but appealing changes to get us to yield. But anytime you leave the door open far enough for temptation to get its foot in, you will have trouble with it. Slam the door shut! Keep out evil forcefully, and you will have victory over it. If you know what is right, do not hesitate to say so. And when temptation beckons, do not hesitate to be like Abraham and make your statement of refusal strong, plain, and emphatic. Temptation will never back off a timid answer. But a strong forceful one gets results. We are not criticizing discreetness, but do not let the emphasis on discreetness dull the sword that deals with sin, or you will not win many battles against evil.

He was prepared. At the beginning of Abraham's answer to the king of Sodom, Abraham said, "I have lift up mine hand unto the LORD, the most high God." This indicates that in the past before the temptation came, he in a solemn act of dedication raised his hand to God (a gesture of taking an oath) that he would not take anything from Sodom. Before the temptation came, he had already earnestly vowed in his heart to refuse it. He had fixed his position before he was confronted with evil. He did not have to stop and ask whether or not it was right or wrong. He had that question already answered emphatically in his mind.

How can we prepare ourselves like that today? The answer is to get into the Word of God and find out what God says about things and get that ingrained in our hearts. Then when we face temptation, the conviction from the Word of God will be ready to deal with the temptation. We will not be floundering around wondering what is right and wrong.

This, therefore, tells us why so many folk today do not do well with temptation. They do not get into the Word of God and get its precepts and principles deeply implanted in their hearts. They do not get into the Word of God and get their convictions made sound and firm. So when temptation comes, the only thinking they seem to have is that which they have heard from the world. You do not have to guess what that causes them to do—they quickly yield.

He was reinforced. God meets our needs right when we need them. This is not only true in a material sense, but it is also true in a spiritual sense. When we need that extra strength spiritually to overcome some evil that jumps out in front of us on the pathway of life, God will have supplied that extra strength in plenty of time for the crisis. Here in Abraham's case, Abraham had that wonderful meeting with the king of Salem prior to his meeting with the king of Sodom. If anyone thinks that was not a help in dealing successfully with the king of Sodom, they have little understanding of life. Strengthened spiritually by the meeting with Melchizedek, Abraham would have extra strength to deal with Bera king of Sodom.

Though Abraham had prepared himself for facing evil victoriously, he could still use more help to overcome this temptation. We can never be too strong spiritually. Though Abraham's own preparation was a big factor in his victory, the reinforcement he got through his meeting with the king of Salem only made the victory more certain, more complete, and more honorable.

Abraham's timely meeting with Melchizedek was evidence of the providence of God. God provided Abraham this reinforcement at just the right time. And Abraham did not misuse this providential opportunity like so many do today. God gives us great opportunities for spiritual strengthening. But unlike Abraham, we do not take advantage of them. We tell Melchizedek we are too busy to meet with him and to attend his services. So we miss out on the great spiritual refreshment we could have experienced which would have given us extra strength right when we needed it. This underscores the great need of our regular attendance in church where we hear the Word faithfully preached week after week. How often a sermon or just something said in a sermon can be so timely, so providential. It will dovetail with our experiences, for God is directing things. But if we do not give attention and honor to these Melchizedek meetings, they will not help us. Abraham did give attention and honor to his meeting with Melchizedek, and it strengthened him for great victory over the forthcoming temptation.

VI.

SURETIES FOR PROMISES

GENESIS 15

ABRAHAM HAS ANOTHER audience with a sovereign. In our last chapter, we saw him in audience with two sovereigns—the King of Salem and the King of Sodom. In this chapter, we will see him having an audience with the greatest Sovereign of all—God Almighty.

This audience with the Sovereign of sovereigns was a most encouraging audience for Abraham, for it gave him surety ("Know of a surety" [v. 13]) about two very important matters in his life—his heir and his inheritance. God had earlier spoken to Abraham about these matters. Regarding the heir, God had said, "I will make of thee a great nation" (Genesis 12:2) and "I will make thy seed as the dust of the earth" (Genesis 13:16). Regarding the inheritance, God had said, "Unto thy seed will I give this land" (Genesis 12:7) and "For all the land which thou seest, to thee will I give it, and to thy seed for ever" (Genesis 13:15). But as time went by, the sureness of the promises began to fade for Abraham. The physical situation of him and Sarah caused Abraham to question whom the heir would be, and the lack of any legal agreement (such as a covenant) caused him concern about obtaining the inheritance. But this audience with God brought Abraham much surety about God's promises regarding both of these matters, for it gave confirmation about the heir (vv. 1–6) and a covenant about the inheritance (vv. 7–21).

A. THE CONFIRMATION ABOUT THE HEIR
To study the confirmation about Abraham's heir, we will look at

the revelation of God (v. 1), the reasoning of Abraham (vv. 2, 3), the reply of God (vv. 4, 5), and the response of Abraham (v. 6).

1. The Revelation of God

"After these things the word of the LORD came unto Abram in a vision, saying, Fear not, Abram: I am thy shield, and thy exceeding great reward" (v. 1). Abraham's audience with God began with the revelation of some great truths about God. It is instructive to note that the revelation is preceded by the phrase, "the word of the LORD came." This is the first time in the Scripture this phrase appears. It will appear again and again in the Scripture. It speaks of one of the greatest blessings man can ever have. Man may lose all his possessions; but if he still has the Word of God, he still has abundant blessing in his possession. Value the Word of God. If men are poor stewards of this blessing, God will take it away from them. Nothing will curse a land so much as that. In indicting Israel, the prophet Amos spoke about this curse when he said, "Behold, the days come, saith the Lord GOD, that I will send a famine in the land, not a famine of bread, nor a thirst for water, but of hearing the words of the LORD" (Amos 8:11).

In this revelation of God through His Word, Abraham learned three important truths that would bring much comfort and strength to his entire life. He learned about the peace of God ("Fear not"), the protection of God ("shield"), and the prize of God ("reward"). The emphasis by God upon these three truths at this time in Abraham's life reminds us that God provides us with what we need right at the time we need it. As we will see in the examination of each of these three great truths, Abraham was especially in need of them at that very moment in his life. Count on God to supply your need when you need it even if you are unaware of your need.

Peace. Only God can give true peace, and He gave Abraham that peace with His "Fear not." Others may say, "Fear not" in an effort to bring us peace; but their "Fear not" does not hold the weight that God's "Fear not" does. When God says, "Fear not," there is no reason to fear. But when man says, "Fear not," you cannot always be sure you have no reason to fear.

Abraham needed peace. He could be justifiably concerned about retaliation from the armies he had just defeated. "After these things" refers to the whole ordeal of the Dead Sea War and Abraham's defeat of Chedorlaomer and his allies, and it also included his audiences with the King of Salem and the King of Sodom. He would not need to fear the kings, but he could indeed be concerned that those five armies he had defeated might return with reinforcements to retaliate against him. Regarding this fear, Barnhouse said, "Cowards are afraid before a battle; heroes are afraid afterward . . . The man who administers a defeat to the world becomes a target for its hatred."

But while Abraham, after the thrill of victory, would experience concern about retaliation, God came to bring peace. Walk in God's ways as Abraham did (noticeably here by turning down the King of Sodom's offers and by his respect and paying of tithes to the King of Salem), and you will experience the blessed peace of God in difficult times. None of us are exempt from situations which trouble us to the depths of our soul; but if these come on the path of obedience, we can count on God to bring us the peace we need and when we need it.

This is the first time "fear not" shows up in Scripture; but it will show up repeatedly throughout the Bible all the way to the last book, the book of Revelation. When we get to the New Testament, we learn plainly that "fear not" is inseparably connected to Jesus Christ. At His birth, the first thing the angels said to the shepherds was, "Fear not" (Luke 2:10). Our world lives in fear; but Christ, God incarnated, can remove fear and bring peace.

Protection. "I am thy shield" shows Abraham what great protection he has from the enemy. God Himself is Abraham's shield of protection. Abraham could easily feel that he was "a sitting duck" living in Hebron without great armies standing guard all around his camp; a camp which would be more like a huge ranch. What would shield him from a destructive invasion of the enemy into his camp? The answer is God. God will be the protector around Abraham to shield him from the enemy.

What is true for Abraham can also be true for any nation. But few nations appreciate this great truth. Our nation certainly does not evidence appreciation of the truth that God can be our Shield. By our laws and actions, we indicate we do not want Him around, do not want Him honored, and do not even want Him mentioned in many places of the land. We can build up our military might as much as we want; but if God is not our Shield, we have lost our greatest protection; we have become extremely vulnerable to the attacks of our enemy.

Prize. "I am . . . thy exceeding great reward." Abraham had given up much in refusing to take anything from the King of Sodom. Always after turning down some great but evil offer, the heart of man begins to think about the blessing which such an action will bring from God—and this thinking is justified. God does indeed bless His own who stand true, faithful, and pure. That is one reason why we turn down the offers of the world. We turn them down so we can have God's rewards instead. But there is often a delay between the performance and the prize. The prize does not always come right after the performance. This tests our faith, and at times we wonder if God will ever come through. He always does, of course; and here He comes through for Abraham and assures him that his reward from God is great.

"I am . . . thy exceeding great reward" is a tremendous reward but is hard for anyone but a dedicated saint to appreciate. Most folk today are only interested in things of the earth. To talk of God as their reward is a foreign language. If it cannot be bought with dollars and cents at some store, they are not interested in it. But someday they will wish they had been interested! We may be without a lot of things in this world; but if we have God as our Friend, Christ as our Savior, and His Word in our possessions, we have the greatest things in life. There is no reward and no prize which the world can give that compares. Abraham had the best reward of all. He gave up all that Sodom could give him and got God instead.

2. The Reasoning of Abraham

The communiqué from God, especially the reward part, prompted Abraham to express a major concern of his. This expressed concern evidenced a bit of pessimistic reasoning on Abraham's part. "And Abram said, Lord GOD, what wilt thou give me, seeing I go childless, and the steward [heir] of my house is this Eliezer of Damascus [his chief servant]? And Abram said, Behold, to me thou hast given no seed: and, lo, one born in my house is mine heir" (vv. 2,3). Abraham poured out his heart about his concern of who was going to be his heir. God had before, as we have noted, promised Abraham seed. But since it had been some years since God had made that promise, Abraham was very discouraged and now thinks he will not have seed from his own body.

Abraham's situation was a test of Abraham's faith. Abraham was a man of great faith, but great faith is not untested faith. In fact, it is the tests of faith that help to strengthen our faith. Abraham's pessimistic reasoning here evidences he was being tested in at least three ways—by inaction, inequity, and inability.

Tested by inaction. "I go childless . . . thou hast given no seed." A number of years had passed since the first promise (it could have been as many as ten years, cp. Genesis 16:3), but nothing had happened yet. Therefore, Abraham had about given up. But as we know, God did indeed fulfill the promise in a wonderful way. God's present inaction about fulfilling the promise did not mean He would never take action or that He was negligent or indifferent. His delay did not mean denial. The devil, however, uses delays to mock God, discredit His promises, and (as we will see in Genesis 16) encourage us to accept the devil's shortcut. But delay, if properly respected, can put character and muscle into our faith. Delay increases the size of the blessing, for it adds interest and dividends to the promise. If God holds your blessing for awhile, He will not be cheap in the interest He pays while holding your possessions. If you have claimed a promise and it has not come about yet, do not quit God. Rejoice for the greater blessings to come.

Tested by inequity. Abraham reminded God that "to me" no seed had been given. Others had been given seed. But not "me." It is always a trying experience to observe others, who in spite of the fact that they are not living for God as we are, experience blessings which we do not experience. Lot had children—both sons and daughters; but he was certainly not living for God, to say the least. Abraham did not have children, specifically a son, even though he was living for God. The heathen living around Abraham were also having children. They worshipped their idols and lived unholy lives, but they still experienced the blessing of children which godly Abraham did not. He had obeyed God, turned his back on the world's offers, sacrificed to the Lord, and separated from the world; yet he lacked the blessing of a son. Furthermore, Abraham's servants were having children. Abraham would excel them in piety, and he was providing for them. Yet, he had no offspring as they did. And as the years passed, his prospects for having children got less and less.

But, of course, the day came when he was given seed; and it was better than the seed of all the others put together. Therefore, do not let the prosperity of others discourage you. Do not let the apparent inequities in life cause you to question God's justice. When others are not upright like you and yet seem to do well in this world, remember Abraham. Your day is coming. Your Isaac will be much better than all their boys put together. Others may seem to prosper, and it may seem so unfair. But when you get Isaac, you will realize that you received the greater blessing and there has been no inequity with God.

Tested by inability. The "seeing I go childless" became the inevitable conclusion of human reasoning. He and Sarah were getting older every day, and the possibility of their having children was getting more and more remote. Inability stared Abraham right in the face. So much so that he believed that the heir would be his chief servant "Eliezer of Damascus" (v. 2), not his own son. It was customary in those days for a man without an heir to adopt a servant as an heir. Abraham thought that was his situation now because of his inability to have children.

How often our inability seems to contradict the promises of God regarding our future achievements. But God does not want us to glory in our own ability or in our own strength when that future achievement occurs. He wants His power to be honored instead. Therefore, before He fulfills the promise in us, He often nearly disables us so that we feel totally helpless apart from His power. So it was with Abraham and Sarah. They were up in years when the first promise of the son came to them. But before the son was born, their ability was diminished to the place where Abraham and Sarah laughed at the thought of their having a son of their own (Genesis 17:17; 18:12). But all of this gives God more glory. Their extreme inability will show the greatness of God's power.

This should be a great encouragement to all of us. It should help us pass the test of inability. Our inability has nothing to do with God's ability. Therefore, we must not let our inability question a Divine promise and discourage us into thinking it cannot be fulfilled. Promises are fulfilled because of the ability of God, not because of our ability.

3. The Reply of God

"And, behold, the word of the LORD came unto him, saying, This shall not be thine heir; but he that shall come forth out of thine own bowels shall be thine heir. And he brought him forth abroad, and said, Look now toward heaven, and tell [count] the stars, if thou be able to number them: and he said unto him, So shall thy seed be" (vv. 4,5). Abraham took his problem to the Lord and the Lord solved it for him. You may have problems a plenty; but if you take them to the Lord, you will find genuine help. Many, however, take their problems to everybody but the Lord and, as a result, come away with more problems. We have a lot of self-appointed experts today who will, for a sizeable fee, listen to you pour out your troubles; but who will by their unholy counsel only worsen your troubles. The counsel we need when we have problems is the counsel of the Word of God. Abraham sought that counsel and received much help as a result. God's reply to Abraham brought both correction and comfort.

Correction. "This shall not be thine heir; but he that shall come forth out of thine own bowels shall be thine heir" (v. 4). Abraham, in his pessimism about having a child of his own, felt that the heir of his house would be his chief servant Eliezer of Damascus (v. 2). Abraham's thinking was wrong, of course, and so God corrected his thinking by telling him that the heir would be Abraham's son, not his servant.

One of the valuable things the Word of God does is correct our thinking. Circumstances, friends, and the world around us can cause our thinking to get all mixed up. It can distort our values and twist our logic so that we draw strange and unjustified conclusions about life and God. Today, we hear so much babbling around us which reflects this problem. The solution to such twisted thinking is to get into the Scriptures. All men will have trouble thinking correctly if they do not keep their mind sound and stable through faithful study and meditation upon the Word of God. Abraham would not have said the incorrect things he did had he concentrated on the promises of God rather than on his circumstances and the practices of society around him.

Comfort. God told Abraham to "Look now toward heaven, and tell [count] the stars, if thou be able to number them: and he said unto him, So shall thy seed be" (v. 5). Abraham was discomforted by his circumstances, but he is now comforted by the Word of God. God's Word greatly encouraged Abraham about the future of his seed. The Word is filled with encouragement for our faith. Paul spoke of this truth about the Scriptures when he said, "Whatsoever things were written aforetime were written for our learning, that we through patience and comfort of the scriptures might have hope" (Romans 15:4). When we go into the Scriptures and read what God has said and what He has done, our faith will be encouraged, our Spirits will be lifted, and our hope will be renewed.

4. The Response of Abraham

"And he believed in the LORD; and he [God] counted it to him for righteousness" (v. 6). Abraham's response to God's promise of the seed, particularly of the son, is recorded in just a few words; but what a wonderful and significant response! We will note the sagacity and the salvation in Abraham's response.

The sagacity in his response. "He believed in the LORD." The word "believe" is "The biggest word in the chapter, one of the greatest in the Old Testament!" (Leupold). It means to confirm, to trust. It means to say "Amen" to what God said; for "The original Hebrew for 'believed' comes from a root whence we derive our 'Amen,' and we might paraphrase it by saying that 'Abraham said Amen to the Lord'" (Griffith Thomas). Thomas adds that "'Amen' in Scripture never means a petition ('May it be so'), but is always a strong assertion of faith ('It shall be so,' or 'It is so')." Leupold says that the form of the word "believe" in our text "would indicate that the permanence of this attitude is to be stressed: not only [did] Abram believed just this once, but Abram proved constant in his faith."

How wise, how sagacious it is to believe God! Yet, man champions unbelief. Today it is doubt that is honored, not faith. Go into the school classroom and you will find faith in God and His Word ridiculed, scorned, and despised. But doubt will be honored, revered, and esteemed—so much so that the only textbooks allowed in many classrooms will be those that teach doubt, not faith, in God and His Word. Many churches are this way, too. Sermon after sermon (if you can call them sermons) challenge the accuracy, authority, and acclaim of the Word. Doubt in God and His Word is embraced and exhorted. We are told we cannot put confidence in the Word of God but rather must believe the unsound and unsupported theories and ideas of the agnostics, atheists, and apostates. Yes, doubt is honored; and faith is dishonored. But that is not wisdom. You play the fool when you do not believe God. If anyone can be believed, it is God. Man is often unbelievable, but never God!

The salvation in his response. "And he [God] counted it to him [Abraham] for righteousness." Faith in God pays great dividends! It results in the salvation of our souls. It results in God imputing righteousness to us who have no righteousness of our own. "He counted it to him for righteousness" means God "counts him innocent; He gives him a verdict of 'Not guilty'" (Leupold). That is the only way anyone will ever be saved, will ever gain eternal life, will ever spend a blissful eternity with God, and will ever escape eternal condemnation for sin. Without righteousness, we will perish in our sins. But when God gives us righteousness, we are saved for eternity.

This text is one of the important Old Testament texts which tell us that salvation is obtained by faith. Abraham was not saved by the law, for the law was not yet given, and he was not yet circumcised. So righteousness was imputed to him by faith alone, not by works. The Apostle Paul, in enforcing the truth that salvation is not by works, refers to this verse several times in writing to the Romans and to the Galatians. "What saith the scripture? Abraham believed God, and it was counted unto him for righteousness" (Romans 4:3). "And being fully persuaded that, what he had promised, he was able also to perform. And therefore it was imputed to him for righteousness" (Romans 4:21,22). "Even as Abraham believed God, and it was accounted to him for righteousness" (Galatians 3:6).

What is it that makes this text such a wonderful illustration of salvation by faith? The answer is that what Abraham believed was the message God gave about the son, the miracle birth son.

Abraham believed what God said about his seed but specifically and primarily about what God said concerning Abraham's son. Isaac, the son, the miracle birth son (God had to work a miracle in both Abraham and Sarah to give the son to them), is a wonderful type of Christ, The Son, Who was also a miracle birth Son in that He was born of a virgin. So Abraham, like anyone else who gets saved (has righteousness imputed to him), believed what God said about the miracle birth son. In his case it was Isaac—a type of Christ; in our case, it is Christ Himself. "Whereas Abraham believed God would give him a son through the quickening of his body, we believe that God has given us His Son, and through His death and quickening from the dead a Savior is ours through faith" (A. W. Pink).

Some question why the declaration of righteousness for Abraham came here and not earlier. Surely he was a believer before this time, for he demonstrated faith in God's Word many years earlier. Leupold said, "Naturally, the answer has to be that Abram was justified by faith as soon as this faith began to manifest itself, which must have been years before this time. Why first record the justification here? We feel our answer must take the same form as Luther's, who points out that justification by faith is first indicated in the Scriptures in connection where the Savior is definitely involved, in order that none might venture to dissociate justification from Him." Pink spoke similarly when he said, "In Genesis 15 Abram's faith is directly connected with God's promise respecting his 'seed,' which 'seed' was Christ (see Gal. 3:16)! The faith which was 'counted for righteousness' was the faith which believed what God had said concerning the promised Seed. It was this instance of Abram's faith which the Holy Spirit was pleased to select as the model for believing unto justification."

B. THE COVENANT ABOUT THE INHERITANCE

Now that questions about the heir has been cleared up by God and believed by Abraham, God will now speak to Abraham about the inheritance—specifically the land that God has promised Abraham and his seed. In dealing with this subject, we will note the declaration for Abraham, the desire of Abraham, the duty for Abraham, the disclosures to Abraham, and the demonstration before Abraham.

1. The Declaration for Abraham

As it was with the section in our text on the heir, so it is here in the section on the inheritance—the conversation between Abraham and God begins with a Divine revelation concerning God. "And he [God] said unto him [Abraham], I am the LORD that brought thee out of Ur of the Chaldees to give thee this land to inherit it" (v. 7). Before Abraham will learn more about the inheritance, he will learn more about the God Who will reveal to him more about the inheritance.

Learning about the inheritance is important, but learning about God is more important. This truth about the priority of the knowledge of God needs more emphasis today. Most of our sermons and books and conferences and seminars have little to do with learning more about God. Instead they spend most of their time focusing on other things. Yet, if we do not learn about God, we will not understand other things properly. So Abraham will be given a short lesson on the character of God to help him better understand, appreciate, and accept the information he will be given about the inheritance.

Two things were specifically mentioned about God in this declaration to Abraham: the power of God and the promise of God. Both were vital to the inheritance for Abraham.

The power of God. "I am the LORD that brought thee out of Ur of the Chaldees." Abraham is reminded that it was through God's power that he had made it from Ur to Canaan. Many perils could have destroyed him and his family and possessions on the long and precarious trip from Ur to Canaan, but God's power preserved him from them all. This reminder of the power of God would both humble and encourage Abraham.

First, the reminder of the power of God *humbles*. We all

have a tendency to give ourselves too much credit for our achievements, and it is good to be reminded periodically from whence we obtained the power to gain our achievements. When Abraham met with Melchizedek, king of Salem, after his great victory over Chedorlaomer and his allies, one of the things Melchizedek said to Abraham was, "Blessed be the most high God, which hath delivered thine enemies into thy hand" (Genesis 14:20). Abraham had achieved a great victory in routing the armies of the east, but he was reminded that it was God Who gave the victory. Here Abraham is reminded that it was also God Who made the trip from Ur to Canaan a successful trip.

Second, the reminder of God's power *encourages*. Abraham would see his own forces as wholly inadequate to capture the land or to do anything else to secure the land. But God's power would have no difficulty doing this. Abraham, therefore, can be encouraged by the knowledge of God's power. In like manner, we, too, can be encouraged by the knowledge of God's power when we feel the helplessness of our own strength.

The promise of God. "I am the LORD that . . . [will] give thee this land to inherit it." This is the theme of this section. God is going to give some real estate to Abraham and his seed. The emphasis is on the faithfulness of God in fulfilling His promises. God is the Faithful Promiser. Never has a promise of His failed yet. Therefore, if God predicts, it will come to pass. If God signs on the dotted line, you can count on Him being faithful to the agreement. If God enters into a covenant (which He is going to do with Abraham shortly), He will fulfill His end of the agreement. Do not be concerned about God fulfilling the promises He has given you. Rather be concerned about your fulfilling the precepts He has given you.

2. The Desire of Abraham

"And he said, Lord GOD, whereby shall I know that I shall inherit it?" (v. 8). Again, as in the first section, God's revelation to Abraham prompted him to express one of his chief concerns.

SURETIES FOR PROMISES

Also, as in the first section, it was the last thing God said in this particular revelation that seemed to especially prompt Abraham's concern. In the first section, "reward" was followed by "what wilt thou give me?" In this second section, "give thee this land to inherit it" is followed by "whereby shall I know that I shall inherit it?" Abraham desired to have more assurance about the promised inheritance. We will note the explanation and exemplariness of the desire.

The explanation of the desire. Was this desire for more assurance about his inheriting the land an indication of lack of faith? On the surface it looks that way; for after all, we are to take God at His Word. God has just promised Abraham some land; now Abraham seems to want more than the Word of God to assure him that the promise is valid.

But his inquiry was not filled with unbelief. His inquiry simply said he wanted to know more about God's promise. He wanted to have his faith strengthened. Abraham was not questioning the possibility of the promise but the method by which the inheritance would be made legal and certain. God had told Abraham he would "inherit" the land (v. 7). Inheritances require some legality. Abraham is looking for that, and God gave it to him in the covenant ceremony which follows. While Abraham, in his frailty, may not have had perfect faith; yet unbelief was not the problem here. The proof of this fact is seen in God giving him a covenant concerning the land (God does not respond this way to unbelief) and in his obedience to God's orders about preparing for the covenant ceremony (unbelief does not obey well but faith does).

Inquiries of faith and unbelief often look alike on the surface, but they are far from it in truth. This is illustrated in the first chapter of Luke. Zacharias was given a revelation about John the Baptist. He said, "Whereby shall I know this? for I am an old man and my wife well stricken in years" (Luke 1:18). Later on in the chapter, Mary was given a revelation about the coming of Christ. Her response was, "How shall this be, seeing

I know not a man?" (Luke 1:34). The two responses look almost the same. But Zacharias' response was of unbelief, Mary's of faith. Zacharias questioned the promise about the coming of the child (John the Baptist) because of the circumstances. Mary did not question the promise about the coming of the Child (Jesus Christ); she simply wanted to know the method. One said it cannot be done; the other said it could be done but wanted to know the way it was going to be done. A big difference indeed! And a difference, though not evident on the surface, that exists between the unsaved and saved who both profess to be believers.

The exemplariness of the desire. Abraham wanted to know more about what God had told him. How exemplary was this desire. God had given him a general promise. Abraham wanted to know more; and he learned more, lots more!

So few want to learn more about God's revelation to us. They are satisfied with little information. They study diligently to learn about things that do not matter; but when it comes to the greatest matters of life, their efforts to learn are very small. Such folk will walk in spiritual ignorance, for one of the important prerequisites of learning spiritual truth is the desire to learn it. Hence, those who are ignorant in the area of spiritual truths, only expose their lack of desire to know spiritual truths. These people will seldom read and study the Scriptures and will be most irregular in attendance at church where they could hear the Word taught in service after service. These people will be the first to complain if they think too much Bible is being inserted into the curriculum of a Christian school, and they will be the first to complain if the sermon is too long at church. They insist on limiting their knowledge of God's Word, and so God obliges them. But when an Abraham comes along and wants to know more about God's Word, God will see to it that he learns more.

3. The Duty for Abraham

The answer God gave Abraham to his inquiry was to give him some orders. "And he said unto him, Take me an heifer of three years old, and a she goat of three years old, and a ram of three years old, and a turtledove, and a young pigeon" (v. 9). From this verse about Abraham's duty, we will note the place, the particulars, and the problems of the duty.

The place of the duty. Duty has a very important place in the learning process. We learned above that desire is necessary if we are going to learn more about God. Here we learn that obedience to duty is also involved in spiritual learning. If Abraham wants to know more about God, then let him be attentive to God's assignment. If he wants to know more assuredly about his inheritance, he will have to fulfill his duty. Otherwise he will remain in the dark.

God tests us to reveal if we really want to know spiritual truth or if we are nothing but talk. If it is real, we will do our God-given assignments just as we will do our assignments in the classroom in school if we are in earnest about learning. If we are not earnest, we will not do our assignments well at all. Many folk complain of their spiritual ignorance and blame it on the lack of schooling and opportunity. But the problem is not there; instead the problem is often in their lack of obedience.

The particulars of the duty. "Take me an heifer of three years old, and a she goat of three years old, and a ram of three years old, and a turtledove, and a young pigeon." This seems like a strange thing for Abraham to do. But it really was not. The orders reflected the method used in those days to ratify an agreement. The method was so well known by Abraham that God did not have to tell him what to do with the animals, for Abraham knew immediately what God's orders meant. "And he took unto him all these, and divided them in the midst, and laid each piece one against another: but the birds divided he not" (v. 10). To ratify an agreement, animals were slain then cut in two. The two parts of each animal were laid in two rows opposite each other several feet apart. Then the parties making the agreement would walk between the parts of the animals. This would accomplish the same purpose today as our signing a contract. It confirmed each other's intent to abide by the agreement; and it also implied that if they did not keep their word regarding the agreement, they or their livestock should suffer the experience of the animals. F. C. Cook adds an interesting note: "The very word covenant in Hebrew . . . is supposed by Gesenius to be from a root signifying to cut . . . and the common formula for 'to make a covenant' is . . . 'to cut a covenant.'" The prophet Jeremiah referred to this interesting form of ratification when he spoke of Israel failing to keep their covenant with God. "And I will give [judgment to] the men that have transgressed my covenant, which have not performed the words of the covenant which they had made before me, when they cut the calf in twain, and passed between the parts thereof, The princes of Judah, and the princes of Jerusalem, the eunuchs, and the priests, and all the people of the land, which passed between the parts of the calf" (Jeremiah 34:18,19).

God was about to make a covenant with Abraham regarding the land. He was going to make the inheritance a legally binding promise. Abraham was to prepare the animals for God to walk between (the birds were not divided, therefore, two birds were involved—one bird would be laid on each side), and he faithfully and promptly performed his duty of preparing for the covenant ceremony.

The problems of the duty. Obedience is never easy. After Abraham laid out the carcasses of the animals, three things occurred which made it difficult for Abraham to fulfill his duties and thus learn great truths from God. These difficulties were the devourers, delay, and darkness.

First, the *devourers*. "And when the fowls came down upon the carcases, Abram drove them away" (v. 11). The first problem Abraham encountered in preparing for the ratification of God's covenant about the land was these birds. Carcasses are an open invitation to many birds. As soon as Abraham laid out these divided animals on the ground, the birds would come. It was necessary for him to continually drive the birds away if he was going to preserve the carcasses for the ratification of the covenant. This shows us two lessons: a practical and prophetical lesson.

The *practical* lesson has to do with Abraham's watchfulness in duty. Things (birds) were continually trying to come into his life which would hinder him from performing his duty. These birds could devour the animals which would then make the enacting of the covenant impossible. But Abraham was watchful; and whenever the birds came down upon the carcasses, he "drove them away." Many things, if allowed, will come into our lives and take away our time, energy, concentration, abilities, and other things in order to hinder our service for the Lord. To counter these devourers, we must establish our priorities and drive away all the things which would usurp our priorities. Many pastors need to put more priority on their sermons and drive away the birds of phone calls, civic involvements, attendance at so many meetings, and spending too much time "fellowshipping with the brethren" over coffee and doughnuts. These birds are often very subtle in how they swoop into our lives and devour. Hence, we must be ever watchful for them lest we become unable to fulfill our calling.

The *prophetical* lesson from the birds has to do with the attacks on Israel. These birds represent the nations which over the years have tried to devour Israel before God could fulfill His covenant with them. God could not have ratified the covenant if the animals were eaten up by the birds. Neither could God fulfill the covenant if Israel no longer existed. A great many attempts have been made to exterminate the Jews and thus keep God from fulfilling His covenant. From Egypt trying to destroy Israel prior to the exodus to the present day attempts to destroy the Jews in German concentration camps and by Arab hostilities (symbolized by the remark of Egypt's Prime Minister Gamal Abel Nassar in the 1967 war that they would push Israel into the Mediterranean Sea), the birds have tried to keep God from fulfilling His covenant with Israel.

Second, the *delay*. God did not immediately come and walk between the pieces of the carcasses. Again Abraham faces this problem of inaction. He has done his assignment, but God tarries. This really tests our faith, as we have noted earlier in this chapter. Man does not like waiting and especially so in spiritual matters. But wait he must if he will see the blessing of God. This test, as other tests did, reveals the sincerity of Abraham's request to further his knowledge and strengthen his faith.

Third, the *darkness*. "An horror of great darkness fell upon him" (v. 12). Walking obediently to God's commands does not exempt us from dark places in life. These dark places may be a serious sickness, a grievous sorrow, some severe privation and hardship, or a time of unexplainable doubt. These dark places will often take the joy out of the soul, the energy out of our service, make God seem distant and disinterested, make God's promises seem very remote, and His Word nothing but words. Such dark places can also cause us to wonder if our faith has failed, if we are saved, and if God is real. Like John the Baptist when he was in the dungeon in prison, in such dark times we often ask God, "Art thou he?" (Matthew 11:3).

But though threatening these dark times are, they are not to destroy us. God is simply putting us through dark times in order to produce in us more excellent faith. As a poinsettia plant needs absolute darkness at certain times in order to develop its beautiful blossoms, so the saint needs absolute darkness at times to produce excellence in his faith. Some years ago we read about a greenhouse that was having trouble developing flowers on some of these poinsettias. Then they discovered that on the cash register in the greenhouse was a small light. When the lights of the greenhouse were turned out at night, the cash register light continued to shine. The poinsettias that were close to the cash register got enough light from the cash register light to hinder their development. Absolute darkness was necessary, so the cash register was unplugged at night. In like manner, God may have to unplug some things in our lives in order to bring a darkness that develops excellence in our faith.

4. The Disclosures to Abraham

Here we note some of the valuable faith-strengthening truths which Abraham learned during the time the "horror of great darkness" was upon him. We can learn much in dark times that will improve our faith if we pay attention to what God's Word tells us during these times. If we do not pay attention, then, of course, we will not learn as we ought; and our faith will not be strengthened as it could be. How our dark times will affect us will be determined by how we respond to them.

We note here three truths disclosed to Abraham during the time when "an horror of great darkness fell upon him" (v. 12). These truths are about the residing out of the land, the reposing in the land, and the returning to the land. The residing out of the land involved Abraham's seed sojourning in Egypt, the reposing in the land involved Abraham's peaceful death, and the returning to the land involved Abraham's seed coming back from Egypt to Canaan. Abraham had wanted to learn primarily about the ratification of his inheritance of the land (which we will note a bit later), but he also learned many more truths, too. Faithfulness to God opens the door wide to spiritual knowledge.

Residing out of the land. "And he said unto Abram, Know of a surety that thy seed shall be a stranger [sojourner] in a land that is not theirs, and shall serve them; and they shall afflict them four hundred years; And also that nation, whom they shall serve, will I judge: and afterward shall they come out with great substance" (vv. 13,14). Abraham is told in this revelation what we learn, in more detail, in the latter part of Genesis and in the first half of Exodus. It was quite a revelation for Abraham.

Israel's suffering in Egypt before possessing the land of Canaan as a nation reminds us that affliction precedes inheritance. Before Canaan is Egypt; before the crown is the cross. Paul teaches the same truth when he says, "If so be that we suffer with him, that we may be also glorified together" (Romans 8:17). Many folk want the glory but not the pain that precedes the glory; they want the reward but not the suffering that precedes the reward. It does not work that way, however, especially in spiritual matters.

Reposing in the land. "And thou shalt go to thy fathers in peace; thou shalt be buried in a good old age" (v. 15). There are two parts to this verse: dying in peace and living a long life. The first part can be experienced by anyone who is right with God. The second part, however, may not always be the experience of the godly. The first part can only come to those who know Christ as their Savior. The second part comes as God decrees and is not necessarily based on righteousness, for some godly souls have suffered martyrdom when young in years while some ungodly folk have lived for many years. However, whether we live a long time or do not live a long time is not nearly as important as how we die. Abraham got both long life and a peaceful death. But the peaceful death is the most important. You may live hundreds of years; but if it is not followed by peaceful death, the long years have no value.

Returning to the land. "But in the fourth generation they shall come hither again; for the iniquity of the Amorites is not yet full" (v. 16). Here Abraham is told a great truth which we learn more about in the book of Joshua. Abraham had great spiritual privilege in learning these truths, but do not feel sorry for yourself. We have an even greater privilege; for much more knowledge is available to us than to him. Abraham was a good steward of his knowledge; are we?

The grace of God is most evident in this verse. Much grace on God's part was required to bring the Israelites into the land, for they were a rebelling bunch. But also much grace is involved in sparing the inhabitants of the land (here summarized as the "Amorites") from destruction for centuries. God gave them much time to repent; but they did not repent; and so finally He brought destruction upon them through the armies of Israel.

Oftentimes we become impatient and wonder why God does not judge the wicked sooner. The answer is that God is acting in grace, giving them time to repent. We should not complain, though hard it may be to see the wicked continue; for we also have been a recipient of grace and must not begrudge others having the same experience.

5. The Demonstration Before Abraham

The time has come for God to walk between the pieces and "sign" the covenant concerning the inheritance of the land. It was a demonstration which would be very moving and meaningful. "And it came to pass, that, when the sun went down, and it was dark, behold a smoking furnace, and a burning lamp that passed between those pieces. In the same day the LORD made a covenant with Abram, saying, Unto thy seed have I given this land, from the river of Egypt unto the great river, the river Euphrates" (vv. 17,18). We will note three things involved in this demonstration: the character of God, the confirming of the covenant, and the contents of the covenant.

The character of God. The "smoking furnace" and "burning light" which passed between the pieces of the dead animals represented God Who was making a covenant with Abraham concerning the land. The "smoking furnace" and the "burning lamp" were two parts of the same item. What Abraham saw was "a portable clay oven, a couple of feet high, more or less like an inverted bowl, with a hole on the upper side for draft purposes. This 'firepot' has fire within it kindled and flaming out of the top of the oven like a 'torch.' This firepot plus the flaming torch above pass in between the pieces . . . of the animals" (Leupold). What a moving experience to see this oven passing by itself— unsupported by any human hands—between the pieces of the animals. The drama would be greatly heightened by the fact that "it was dark" at the time. The dark times of life, as we noticed a few pages back, oftentimes give a better background for the display of the glory of God than at other times.

The "furnace of smoke" (the smoke of the furnace would actually be above the fire—the "burning light") speaks of judgment, and thus speaks of the holiness of God which must ever judge sin. After Sodom was judged by God, "the smoke of the country went up as the smoke of a furnace" (Genesis 19:28) which is the picture of judgment.

The "burning torch" speaks of the light, knowledge, revelation, and illumination God gives man. And so Christ, God incarnated, is referred to as "the light of the world" (John 8:12). Maclaren enlarges our thoughts here when he says this "smoking furnace" and "burning light" speak of the "twofold aspect of the divine nature, by which to hearts that love [Him] He is gladsome light, and to unloving ones He is threatening darkness. As to the Israelites the pillar was light, and to the Egyptians darkness and terror; so the same God is joy to some, and dread to others . . . Love and wrath, life and death, a God who pities and who cannot but judge, are solemnly proclaimed by that ancient symbol, and are plainly declared to us in the perfect revelation of Jesus Christ."

The confirming of the covenant. God, represented by this furnace of smoke and fire, passed through the pieces of the animals thus confirming His covenant with Abraham about the land. You will note that Abraham never did walk between the animals. Why? Because this covenant was an unconditional covenant. God would give the land to Abraham and His seed regardless.

In studying the various covenants which God has made with man over the years, you will discover that there are two kinds of covenants: unconditional and conditional. An unconditional covenant means that the fulfilling of it depends entirely upon God's Word. A conditional covenant means that the fulfilling of it is conditioned upon the behavior of man. The covenant which God had with Israel under Moses was conditional, and man failed. Jeremiah 34:18,19, a passage we have referred to earlier, speaks of the failure of the Israelites to keep their end of the bargain. As a result, they experienced Divine judgment. But this covenant about the land is unconditional. This means that Israel has a future in Palestine, in spite of their unbelief and poor behavior at times.

The contents of the covenant. "The LORD made a covenant with Abram, saying, Unto thy seed have I given this land, from the river of Egypt unto the great river, the river Euphrates: The Kenites, and the Kenizzites, and the Kadmonites, And the Hittites, and the Perizzites, and the Rephaims, And the Amorites, and the Canaanites, and the Girgashites, and the Jebusites" (vv. 18–21). The boundaries of the land as well as the the nations then in the land are listed so Abraham would know exactly what land God meant would be his inheritance. Under Solomon, Israel realized more of this covenant than Israel did at any other time. But the time is coming when Israel will realize in a complete way the fulfilling of this covenant. In the future, Israel will possess much more land than Israel has ever before possessed. Pushed into a small bit of land in the Middle East today, Israel someday will possess much land that is now proudly and adamantly held by the Arabs. Jordan, Syria, and Iraq especially have much land that belongs to Israel. While today it does not look like Israel has a ghost of a chance of gaining that land, God will see to it that Israel will someday possess it all. When God makes a covenant, God will fulfill it! Keep your eyes on the Middle East. God has some unfinished business there!

VII.

SCHEME OF SARAH

GENESIS 16

THE DARKEST BLOT in Abraham's life is recorded in the passage of Scripture before us. It is centered around an unholy scheme to obtain the long desired and God-promised son for Abraham. It is hard to believe that the man who performed so well in the three chapters of Genesis prior to this one, and who will perform with such excellence in the chapters following this chapter, could be guilty of such faithless conduct as is recorded of him in our text. But the Bible does not lie. It paints the picture of man with accurate detail. It not only will show us the greatness of a man, but it also will show us the guile of a man. In the Scriptures there will be no whitewashing, no glossing over evil—just the plain, unadulterated truth. And we can be mighty glad the Word of God is that way. If the Scriptures were not true to life, they would lose their value to us. They would be of no help to us where "the rubber meets the road."

To study this defiling scheme of Sarah that gave Abraham the darkest blot on his life, we will consider the proposing of the scheme (vv. 1–4), the problems from the scheme (vv. 4–6), and the policing of the schemers (vv. 7–16).

A. THE PROPOSING OF THE SCHEME

"Now Sarai Abram's wife, bare him no children: and she had an handmaid, an Egyptian, whose name was Hagar. And Sarai said unto Abram, Behold now, the LORD hath restrained me from bearing: I pray thee, go in unto my maid; it may be that I may obtain children by her. And Abram hearkened to the voice of

Scheme of Sarah

Sarai. And Sarai Abram's wife took Hagar her maid the Egyptian, after Abram had dwelt ten years in the land of Canaan, and gave her to her husband Abram to be his wife. And he went in unto Hagar" (vv. 1–4).

This plan which Sarah proposed to gain the promised seed for Abraham constituted the sin of sexual immorality. So in making the proposal, Sarah was urging Abraham to commit an immoral deed. Thus this proposal of Sarah becomes a picture of temptation. We will look at her proposal from that standpoint just as we looked at the proposal the king of Sodom made to Abraham. Both Sarah's proposal and the king of Sodom's proposal give us much valuable instruction on the subject of temptation. Here, in Sarah's proposal, we will note the author of the temptation, the accommodation for the temptation, the appearance of the temptation, the approval for the temptation, the appeal in the temptation, and the agreeing with the temptation.

1. The Author of the Temptation

In coming from Sarah, the solicitation given Abraham to do evil came from a source which made the temptation very strong. No one else could have made such a proposal to Abraham and succeeded in getting Abraham to pay any attention to it. She was the only human who would have to give unqualified approval before Abraham would ever listen, consider, or consent to the plan. Thus when she made the proposal, the temptation to do an immoral deed became very strong.

The source of temptation has much to do with the strength of temptation. It is an old trick of the devil to have temptation come from the places of honor, trust, esteem, position, and popularity. We noted this truth earlier in the temptation Abraham experienced from the offer of the king of Sodom. A solicitation from some tramp on skid row does not have the impact as it does when it comes from some trusted and respected friend or from some highly respected educator or public official or popular person. Therefore, beware that you are not taken in by some evil just because someone with impressive credentials advocates it. We must not do evil no matter who urges us to do so. Paul spoke of this truth when warning about the curse of corrupting the Gospel message. He said, "But though we, or an angel from heaven, preach any other gospel unto you than that which we have preached unto you, let him be accursed" (Galatians 1:8).

2. The Accommodation for the Temptation

"She had an handmaid, an Egyptian, whose name was Hagar . . . go in unto my maid; it may be that I may obtain children by her" (vv. 1,2). There was in Abraham's household that which readily accommodated the temptation. When in disobedience Abraham and Sarah sojourned in Egypt, they picked up an Egyptian maid named Hagar. God worked marvelously to get Abraham and Sarah out of Egypt and back to Canaan. But Hagar, by becoming part of the household of Abraham, provided a ready accommodation for yielding to this temptation. She met all the requirements, physical and otherwise, that encouraged and gave substance to Sarah's proposal. However, had they not gone to Egypt, the temptation would never have occurred.

This situation reminds us that one sin can make it easier to do another sin. Even though God forgives us and delivers us from our sinful ways, we still may have in our lives, as a result of our sin, some Hagars and habits and friends and thoughts that someday can become a ready accommodation and encouragement for future sin. As an example, if you did some indulging in pornography, you brought into your life some memories that will readily accommodate and encourage yielding to the temptation of allowing evil thoughts in your mind in the future. In like manner, if you have developed some unsavory friends by your past sinning, someday they may show up and visit you and provide much opportunity and encouragement for engaging in more sin. All of this is a great warning to never look at any sin lightly. Your sin affects you a lot more than you think it does. If God in grace does not intervene and you do not scorn your sin as earnestly as you ought, you may discover that truth in a most costly and humbling way.

Scheme of Sarah

3. The Appearance of the Temptation

"And Sarai said unto Abram, Behold now, the LORD hath restrained me from bearing . . . go in unto my maid; it may be that I may obtain children by her" (v. 2). This temptation was all dressed up in the noble robes of pious language and self-denial. The negative circumstance (Sarah's barrenness), which is presented as an excuse and justification for the evil, is said to be of God. And Sarah giving Hagar the chance to have the promised child looks like self-denial on Sarah's part; for she is willing to give the privilege, to which she had first claim, to another. But how deceptive is all of Sarah's talk. How cleverly she twists circumstances and situations to sanction evil.

Sarah's actions here instruct us about the deceptiveness of temptation. It is a wolf appearing in sheep's clothing; it is the devil dressed in religious robes; and it is evil cloaked in garments of righteousness. Such deception gives much added strength to temptation, for few evils are so acceptable as those which are done in the name of justice or self-denial or under religious auspices. The devil is a master at dressing up evil in noble apparel. Therefore, keep your vision sharp and keen by studying the Word of God faithfully. Spiritual discernment is a must if we are to see through the deceptive appearances of evil and thus avoid being defiled by it.

4. The Approval for the Temptation

"Sarai said . . . go in unto my maid; it may be that I may obtain children by her" (v. 2). The evil plan that Sarah had for obtaining seed for Abraham had the approval of both society and Sarah. Such approval also strengthened the temptation.

First, *society approved*. This arrangement was common and encouraged among the people of that day. If Abraham is given Hagar as a wife and has a child by her, society will not criticize, frown on the arrangements, or despise the results. Instead they would applaud. What society of that time did condemn and despise was not having any children.

Second, *Sarah approved*. Sarah plainly accepted this plan of society. As we noted above, Sarah's approval of the arrangement would be absolutely essential as far as Abraham was concerned. He must have her unqualified approval, or he would hardly consider such a plan. With Sarah proposing the evil, it made it clear that she did indeed approve of the plan. Abraham could not have gotten a clearer indication of her approval than by having her initiate the idea of him having a child by Hagar.

Hence, Abraham had much approval for accepting Sarah's plan. Society around him approved and his own spouse approved. What more could he ask for? Ah, he could ask for God's approval, for that he did not have! What a warning here on the peril of not making sure we have God's approval before we act. Today we have the Word of God in our hands and can discover quickly what God approves or disapproves. Yet, how little do we seek out the Word to see if our ventures are approved by God. Rather we look around to see what society thinks and what our close friends and relatives think. If they approve, we go ahead and do it. But it is far better that we find out what God thinks and let His Word be final no matter what others say or think. Otherwise we can get ourselves into big trouble as Abraham did, even though he had so much approval for his deed.

5. The Appeal in the Temptation

"Go in unto my maid; it may be that I may obtain children by her" (v. 2). Temptation has to appeal to the tempted one in what it offers, or the temptation ceases to be a temptation. Here in Abraham's case there was indeed some very appealing features in this temptation. The two chief appealing features were sex and a son.

Sex. In Sarah's proposal, Abraham was being urged to have sex with another woman. There is hardly a man in the world who would not understand the strong appeal of this temptation because of what it provided for in regards to the appetite of the flesh. And what made this temptation to have sex with another woman so appealing to Abraham was that the temptation was

Scheme of Sarah

seemingly sanctioned by marriage. Abraham was not being tempted to have a clandestine affair with a woman but to have extracurricular sex in the name of marriage and for the purpose of having a promised son from God. Men have enough trouble with this temptation without it being seemingly sanctioned by such noble causes. So the appeal here to Abraham would be exceptionally strong, in spite of the fact that it was exceptionally evil. But even though "Sarai . . . gave her [Hagar] to her husband Abram to be his wife," God never approved of the marriage. It was, therefore, an unholy adventure which to be labeled correctly can only be labeled sexual immorality, not marriage. A lot of marriages in our day are no different even though some fundamental, Bible-believing preacher performs the ceremony. We will note more of this later.

Son. Abraham and Sarah were frustrated because of the lack of results. They wanted a son, and God had promised them a son. But as yet they had no son. Barren of results, the temptation offered a way to get results in a hurry, to get what seemed like the promises of God in a hurry. No more waiting; no more embarrassment because of the lack of results. God's plan was for them to wait a number of years yet before they got results. But the devil, through this temptation, offers a short cut. How appealing the temptation is because it promises results—and speedily. And these results seemingly were in the area of their faith, too, which would help suppress thoughts about the method being questionable.

It is hard to find a temptation more appealing than one that pampers the appetite of the flesh yet seems also to obtain the goals of faith. And that is exactly the appeal this temptation had to Abraham, and it is exactly what is going on in so many of our churches. Barren of results (and not always because they are not doing God's will, but because the world is not interested in the Gospel message), many churches often resort to flesh-appealing promotional schemes to increase their attendance. Instead of emphasizing the preaching and teaching of the Word, these churches emphasize their fleshly entertainments. These promotional programs are very exciting to the flesh. Karate demonstrations, a marimba player playing "Onward Christian Soldiers" blindfolded, a parachutist jumping from a plane (during Sunday School time) with "Jesus Saves" written on his parachute, a blindfolded sword expert slicing a watermelon completely through while it is laying on the stomach of the Sunday School Superintendent, pie and chocolate chip cookie contests, petting zoos, pony rides, etc., etc. will draw a crowd like garbage draws flies; for the world (and carnal Christians) becomes much more interested in attending a church service if the service majors on entertainment rather than on the preaching and teaching of the Word of God. Though churches spend so much time in the services with their promotional entertainment that Bible lessons and sermons are crowded out or limited to a short few minutes, few complain. And those who do complain are said to be unevangelistic, not interested in souls, and backslidden.

Yes, these flesh-appealing, Hagar-type programs do get results. Many churches have garnered thousands in attendance and built large buildings; and their pastors have become famous as a result of these programs. But the results have been Ishmaels, not Isaacs. Because spiritual discernment in our churches is so poor, few discern that the results are Ishmaels and not Isaacs. Even Abraham had trouble seeing it for many years; for walking in the flesh does not help one's spiritual discernment.

Methods matter in the work of God. The end does not justify the means. Use unholy means, and you will achieve unholy results no matter how holy your objectives are. We do not advance the cause of the Gospel by using unholy methods in our churches. Ishmaels are no substitutes for Isaacs. They will only be a pain in the neck and cause trouble for the church—as we will see in later studies where Ishmael mocked Isaac and had to be removed from the camp. If the work of God is to go forward, our churches will have to remove the Ishmaels out of the church—and for many churches (which includes many of the big churches) that would just about deplete their membership.

6. The Agreeing With the Temptation

"And Abram hearkened to the voice of Sarai . . . And he went in unto Hagar" (vv. 2,4). Abraham quickly went along with Sarah's proposal. He offered no argument or protest, and neither did he seek the counsel of God to see if this was acceptable with Him.

Abraham's agreeing with Sarah's plan is a great warning to all of us to be ever watchful. It makes no difference how long you have been saved or what your spiritual achievements have been, you still can fail miserably in temptation if you take your eyes off the Lord. As we noted in the introduction of this chapter, we find it hard to believe that Abraham, after behaving so nobly in the previous three chapters of Genesis, should act so terribly in this chapter. But Abraham's failure reminds us that no person is immune to failure if he lets his spiritual guard down. King David is another example of this truth. He had led such a great life and was such a great king for Israel. Yet, he let down his guard and, as a result, committed great sins that scarred him terribly. Paul said, "Wherefore let him that thinketh he standeth take heed lest he fall" (I Corinthians 10:12). In view of the great failures of some of the great saints in the Bible, we ought to take earnest heed to Paul's warning.

B. THE PROBLEMS FROM THE SCHEME

The immoral scheme was cleverly made to appear to be that which would solve some problems existing in Abraham's life. But it did not solve any problems. All it did was create problems. Sexual immorality never solves problems but always creates problems. Only a fool thinks otherwise. But the world often plays the fool anyway and laughs at those who warn of the problems of sexual immorality. Such is the wisdom of those who ignore God's Word.

To study the problems of this defiling scheme devised by Sarah, we will note the character of the problems and the catalogue of the problems. This will help us to learn much about the problems of immorality.

Abraham

1. The Character of the Problems

In noting the character of the problems of the scheme and immorality, we will note the swiftness of the coming of the problems, the span of the problems, the sum of the problems, and the seriousness of the problems.

Swiftness. "And he went in unto Hagar, and she conceived: and when she saw that she had conceived, her mistress was despised in her eyes" (v. 4). It did not take very long for the scheme to cause problems. In just a matter of weeks, the troubles of immorality began. No sooner had Hagar perceived that she was pregnant than her attitude towards Sarah became disrespectful and hence very troublesome.

Problems from sexual immorality do not even require pregnancy before they show up, however. The problem of guilt from this sin only requires minutes before it sets in; and venereal diseases often show up in a few days. Listen to and give in to the tempter's subtle justifying of immoral conduct if you will. But before the sweet morsel of sin has hardly been tasted, the poison of the deed will have begun its ruinous work in you. One of the consistent factors about troubles from immoral conduct is that they are extremely swift in coming.

Span. Though the problems of this immoral scheme were swift in coming, they were slow to leave; in fact, they are still with us. Unlike many other problems, the problems of immorality will span ages. They continue on indefinitely. Abraham's immoral venture with Hagar not only caused immediate problems in his household, but it also is still causing many problems for the world today. Much contesting in the Middle East over Israel's land is rooted and grounded in Abraham's sin. Many Arabs lay claim to the land of Palestine because they lay claim to Ishmael as their father. Since Ishmael was Abraham's first born according to the flesh, they believe he should be the one who inherits the land. God, of course, makes it clear in His Word that Isaac, not Ishmael, was the one who obtained that inheritance. But Abraham's disobedience has opened the door for many Arabs to make this claim anyway.

Another problem spanning the years because of Abraham's sin has been Mohammedanism. "The existence of Mohammedanism today is really to be traced to Abram's false step; Mohammedanism which is in some respects the deadliest opponent of Christianity. Isaac and Ishmael still struggle in fierce opposition" (Griffith Thomas).

Yes, the problems of immorality are not short lived. They will plague the immoral person for a lifetime and, after they have died, leave troubles for others for years to come. Let preachers more earnestly proclaim this fact from their pulpits instead of being so lenient towards this evil. Leniency only encourages folks to immorality and thus brings on more and more troubles. It is one of the great disgraces of the modern day pulpit that it does not denounce immorality (including divorce and remarriage) as it ought.

Sum. Many, many problems plague the sin of sexual immorality. It is not just one or two problems or a few here and there, as some would have us believe. But immorality produces many problems. We can see at least a dozen problems from the sin of immorality just by looking at Abraham's case in our text. There were the problems of pregnancy, pride, disrespect, marriage decay, hypocrisy, betrayal, impiety, injustice, cruelty, unemployment, restlessness, and sorrow. We will elaborate on these shortly when we consider the catalogue of the problems from the scheme as listed in our text. But we list the dozen problems here, which are gleaned from our text, to show that the problems of immorality are not few but indeed are many. And these are not all the problems that come from immorality. We can add to these problems such things as guilt, venereal disease, child abuse, and murders (this includes abortion). These problems can be easily observed in everyday life. So to deny that the problems of immorality are many is to deny the facts and to play the fool.

We could stop many problems in our society if we waged war against immorality. But about the only thing our society does regarding immorality is to encourage it. So the problems multiply and ruin society.

Seriousness. Noting all these problems of immorality and their duration, no one can possibly say the problems from sexual immorality are trivial. They are big, big problems which no person in his right mind should want to ever experience. Yet the world continually minimizes the problems, frequently practices sexual immorality, passes out condoms, and gives much more concern to other problems; though these other problems are much less serious and cause much less trouble to society than does immorality. However, let no one ever take a light view of the sin of sexual immorality. Its curse is too great to treat lightly.

2. The Catalogue of the Problems

Here we look more in detail at some of the problems that came into the lives of Abraham, Sarah, and Hagar because of their immoral scheme. As we noted above, we will look at a dozen problems which immorality caused in their case. We note these problems just from a few verses of our text. Many other problems come from immorality, as noted above; but we limit the catalogue of problems here to those seen in the text. They are problems with pregnancy, pride, disrespect, marriage decay, hypocrisy, betrayal, impiety, injustice, cruelty, unemployment, restlessness, and sorrow.

Pregnancy. "She conceived" (v. 4). While pregnancy was first desired in this case, not long after it occurred, it was no longer desired, especially by Sarah. Unwanted pregnancies are always a problem with immorality. People try many things to keep from having this problem and are inventing new methods to permit their sin without this problem. But it still plagues immorality. Today many are even using murder (abortion) to stop the problem, but abortion only aggravates the problem.

Scheme of Sarah

Pride. "When she saw that she had conceived, her mistress was despised in her eyes" (v. 4). Pride manifested itself very quickly after the immoral venture. Hagar's pregnancy, in view of Sarah's failure to become pregnant over the years, caused Hagar to become proud. She had achieved something Sarah had not, and it went to her head.

Immorality does not have to produce pregnancy in order for the evil of pride to show up from this sin, however. Pride simply comes with sexual immorality whether pregnancy occurs or not. This pride will manifest itself in a number of situations. It especially evidences itself in the headstrong attitude of the immoral person when others deal with them about this sin. As an example, if a pastor or church discusses disciplinary measures, the immoral one will generally act arrogant and say such things as "Who do you think you are to discipline me?" or "My private life is none of your business." If parents or others must deal with them about a pregnancy and what to do about it, the immoral are often haughty and very difficult to deal with. All of this reflects pride which is typical of immorality.

Disrespect. "Her mistress was despised in her eyes" (v. 4). Where there is pride there will be disrespect. Sarah was Hagar's boss, and one should respect authority. But immorality eroded that respect in Hagar. Much disrespect in our land today is likewise a result of the immorality of people. Disrespect for man's position is propagated by the women's equal rights movement, and that movement is often led by very immoral women. Disrespect of life is overwhelmingly evident in the abortion advocates, and such advocates are also an immoral bunch to say the least. Much of the disrespect for sacred things (many folk trample on holy things with nary a tremble), of family relationships (these are ridiculed), of decency and honesty (the opposite is advocated), and of law and order (we pamper rioters) can be laid at the feet of sexual immorality.

Marriage decay. "And Sarai said unto Abram, My wrong be

upon thee: I have given my maid into thy bosom; and when she saw that she had conceived, I was despised in her eyes: the LORD judge between me and thee. But Abram said unto Sarai, Behold, thy maid is in thy hand; do to her as it pleaseth thee" (vv. 5,6). No marriage can experience unfaithfulness morally and not have problems! It just does not happen. Immorality will at the minimum always bring decay to the general condition of the marriage. Two problems are most evident in Abraham and Sarah's marriage as a result of immorality. They are the problem of the lack of love and the lack of leadership.

First, there was the problem of *lack of love*. Greater friction than ever before came into the marriage because of immorality. This problem is readily seen in Sarah's denouncing of Abraham about the troubles caused by Hagar's pregnancy. Immorality cooled their love and heated up contention. It always does.

Second, there was the problem of *lack of leadership*. Abraham's leadership in the marriage was eroded. Sarah is upset; so he simply tells her to do what she wants to do with Hagar. That was poor leadership! Abraham did not lead the home well there at all. But immorality causes such problems.

Hypocrisy. "My wrong be upon thee . . . the LORD judge between me and thee" (v. 5). A trademark of the hypocrite is to blame others for the sin the hypocrite is guilty of committing. Man habitually seeks to blame anyone else but himself when he sins. This is certainly evident when immorality is involved. Though Sarah did not commit the sin of immorality, she advocated it earnestly. Now that troubles are coming from following her advice to commit the sin (she called it marriage, but it was still sin), she blames Abraham for the problems while ignoring her own responsibility in the whole case. What gross hypocrisy. But it is a trait of people involved in immorality.

Betrayal. "Behold, thy maid is in thy hand; do to her as it pleaseth thee. And when Sarai dealt hardly with her, she fled from her face" (v. 6). People who instigate sin are unreliable protectorates when the sinner gets in trouble because of the sin. We see this so often in the case of sexual immorality, for this sin is especially filled with betrayal. Hagar found out, as many other girls have discovered over the ages, that those who encouraged her to immoral acts will not stand by her when problems come as a result of her immoral conduct. A boy persuades a girl to act immorally with him; but when she becomes pregnant, he forsakes her. Sarah and Abraham encouraged Hagar to go to bed with Abraham; but when problems arose, Sarah mistreated her; and Abraham went along the mistreatment.

Impiety. "The LORD judge between me and thee" (v. 5). Again we see the dishonoring of God in this immoral situation. Sarah had earlier brought God in on the situation to try to justify her immoral proposal. Now when problems develop because of the immorality, she again brings in God. Sarah represents God as exonerating her and condemning Abraham. But God is a holy God and will condemn both. Sarah makes God something less than holy. She greatly dishonors Him.

Immorality promotes the dishonoring of God. This fact is especially emphasized in David's life. When he committed his immoral act with Bathsheba and then murdered Uriah (immorality and cruelty go hand in hand as we will also see in the case of Abraham and Hagar), the prophet Nathan said, "By this deed thou hast given great occasion to the enemies of the LORD to blaspheme" (II Samuel 12:14).

Injustice. "Do to her as it pleaseth thee" (v. 6). This was Abraham's response to Sarah when she complained of Hagar's conduct after Hagar had gotten pregnant. There is no justice in this remark. Hagar is the only one considered guilty by this remark. Sarah is not condemned. She had encouraged the sin, yet she is given a free hand to do whatever she wants to do to Hagar to counter Hagar's misconduct of despising Sarah. Abraham takes no blame either. He had gotten Hagar pregnant; but he assumes no responsibility. It is the ugly picture of injustice which is one of the products of immorality. This helps explain why the awful deed of abortion, which is primarily a result of immorality, is labeled so unjustly "pro-choice."

Cruelty. "Sarai dealt hardly [cruelly] with her" (v. 6). Wherever immorality is found, cruelty is also found. Immorality does not begat kindness; but it breeds cruelty. Before the act of immorality occurred in Abraham's household, things went along fine. Sarah treated Hagar kindly. But immorality changed all of that. (While Sarah did not commit the immoral act, she advocated it and is, therefore, not immune from the attitude that immorality produces in a person guilty of the act.)

Many cruel crimes we read about and hear about have their roots in some immoral act. The news media, of course, does not discern this; or if they do, they certainly do not tell us (as is the case with them in many problems). As noted above, abortion is bloody, cruel behavior; and it has its roots in immorality. Take away immorality and the abortion businesses will fold up overnight. David committed sexual immorality with Bathsheba; and that was followed by his ordering Uriah, her husband, to his death in battle—a cruel death which God saw as murder. Cruelty and immorality do indeed go hand in hand.

Unemployment. "And when Sarai dealt hardly with her, she fled from her face" (v. 6). Hagar is working for Sarah, but immorality resulted in Hagar being put out in the wilderness without a job. Hence, we have an unemployment problem. This reminds us of a similar labor problem in the Bible. Joseph was working for Potiphar; but because of Potiphar's wife's immoral designs upon Joseph, Joseph lost his job. Joseph, of course, did not lose his job from being immoral himself; for he was impeccably pure. But it was the immoral character of Potiphar's wife that caused him to lose his job. We hear a lot of talk about unemployment today, and politicians have many plans (especially at election time) for solving unemployment. But we notice that none of these plans ever mention improving the morals of

SCHEME OF SARAH

the worker as a means of reducing unemployment. Yet, improving the morals of the worker would stop a surprising amount of unemployment besides a lot of other labor problems. You will not learn this in Economics 101, of course; but you will learn it in the greatest textbook of all—the Word of God—which needs to be taught more in our schools instead of being driven out of our schools.

Restlessness. "She fled from her face" (v. 6). Hagar's fleeing Sarah manifests the problem of restlessness. There was much unrest, uneasiness, and discontent in her life; in short, there was a lack of peace in her life. Isaiah said, "The wicked are like the troubled sea, when it cannot rest . . . There is no peace, saith my God, to the wicked" (Isaiah 57:20,21). Immorality does not help people to settle down. It does not bring tranquility. It does not make people cool, calm, and collected. Rather, it troubles and upsets. It creates turmoil within as well as without. It agitates and vexes the feelings.

Sorrow. Immorality does not make people happy. Our text makes that clear! Sarah is upset. Hagar is upset. Abraham is upset. No happiness there at all, and it all started with immorality. Oh, that we could get people to see this truth. Hollywood, TV, and other things glamorize immoral conduct. They would present it as great fun, wonderful pleasure, and great thrills. But the truth is that immorality fills society with great sorrow. Tears still flow because of the immoral act in Genesis 16, and tears will flow from all immoral acts. Temptation would cover up the sorrow story, but it is still there killing true joy in the hearts and lives of myriads of people.

C. THE POLICING OF THE SCHEMERS

Abraham, Sarah, and Hagar brought upon themselves many problems because of their sin. Then they reacted poorly to the problems which only created more problems. But right after Hagar had run away from Abraham's camp, God, in a great display of grace, stepped in and policed the situation by sending Hagar back to the camp to get all three to deal with their problems in a much better manner. "He interposes in order to bring about the best possible results after the error and sin of His children" (Griffith Thomas).

God's policing of the schemers gives us important lessons in two areas. It instructs us regarding reactions to problems and regarding redemption of sinners.

1. Reactions to Problems

In their poor reactions to their problems, Abraham, Sarah, and Hagar show us three popular, but very bad, ways to deal with problems in our lives. Abraham reacted to his problem by ignoring it. Sarah reacted to her problem by vexing others because of it. Hagar reacted to her problem by trying to run away from it. We will look more in detail at each of these unwise ways of reacting to one's problems and will see how God's plan for dealing with these problems was much better than the way in which Abraham, Sarah, and Hagar were dealing with their problems.

Abraham ignored his problems. When problems began to develop over the immorality of Abraham and Hagar, Abraham's attitude was to tell Sarah to do whatever she wanted with Hagar (v. 6). This meant that Abraham was not going to deal with these problems. He would simply ignore them. Let others deal with them as they will, but Abraham did not want to be bothered with them.

What folly it is to ignore our problems. No problem will get solved that way. They will only get worse. Sometimes folk do not want to admit they have problems, and so they ignore them. Other times they are not willing to deal properly with their problems, and so they ignore them. Whatever the case, they only play the fool and will one day have to deal with bigger problems than their original problems.

Our churches frequently react to problems like Abraham

SCHEME OF SARAH

did. Especially do they react this way in regards to sin problems in the membership. Unwilling to discipline the dissidents, they simply ignore the problems and hope they will go away. But, of course, they do not go away. Rather, they only get bigger and bigger until the problems deal with the church and not the other way around.

When God sent Hagar back to Abraham's camp, He forced Abraham to have to deal with his problem. It was a most needed learning experience for Abraham.

Sarah vexed others because of her problems. When Sarah experienced problems because of the immorality in the home, her reaction was to snap at Abraham with an unjustified sharp and hypocritical tongue and then treat Hagar in an uncalled for cruel manner (v. 6). True, in Hagar's case, there were some disrespect problems; but they did not justify Sarah's harsh treatment of her. Sarah's reaction to her problems only aggravated things. Vexing others because of your problems never helps you with your problems. But Sarah's way of dealing with her problem is a habit many have in dealing with their problems. Sarah's reaction is like those who when they have a problem become a grouch, are short-tempered with those around them, snap unkindly at people, make everyone around them miserable, and in general are very difficult to get along with. If they are in a bad mood because of their problems, they will cause those around them to be in a bad mood. When they experience problems they become a crepe-hanger and a kill-joy. But this kind of reaction only multiplies troubles; it does not mitigate them.

God sent Hagar back to Sarah so Sarah could learn how to be more amiable even though there were many problems in the situation. This would improve character, something Sarah's method of dealing with her problems did not do.

Hagar ran away from her problems. Hagar's response to her problems was to flee from Abraham's camp and head back to Egypt (going "in the way to Shur" [v. 7] is the indication that she was heading back to Egypt). Many try to deal with their problems this way, and it is a great mistake. These kind of people never stick with anything for long. If problems develop on the job, they soon quit the job and move on. If problems develop in the marriage, they are ready to terminate the marriage and move on. If some problems develop at church, they do not take the time to find out what the facts are but speedily move on. They are ever running from their problems. It is the only way they seem to want to deal with them. But one never solves problems running from them any more than one solves his problems by ignoring them or vexing others because of them. Running from one's problems only causes one to run into more problems.

Mercifully, God stopped Hagar from running away from her problem and told her to return and submit to Sarah. While going back to Sarah was not a pleasant assignment, it was God's best for her. When by our sin we forfeit God's first best for us, it may be humbling and trying to the flesh to take second best. But running away from our problem will get us something far worse than second best. Don't be so foolish as to think running away from your problem will eventually put you back in God's first best.

2. Redemption of Sinners

The intervention of God's grace in the problems in Abraham's house gives us in a number of ways a beautiful picture of salvation. This is seen especially in God's dealing with Hagar in our text. Hagar (as well as Abraham and Sarah) had grievously sinned. Judgment was due her. But God in grace stepped in and worked marvelously in her life in many of the same ways He works in the lives of those whom He saves. We want to note some actions of the grace of God in this encounter with Hagar which reflect the work of God in the salvation of a sinner. We will note the pursuing, denouncing, questioning, commanding, instructing, and transforming of the sinner.

Scheme of Sarah

The pursuing of the sinner. Running away from Abraham's camp after being treated cruelly by Sarah, Hagar is seen weary and distraught in the wilderness on her way back to Egypt. Typical of all sinners, she ended up in the wilderness burdened down with troubles she had brought upon herself because of her sin. But then "the angel of the LORD found her" (v. 7) and changed her life. This seeking of Hagar by "the angel of the LORD" is the pursuit of God's grace. This gracious pursuit of the sinner began in the Garden of Eden. After Adam and Eve had sinned and hidden themselves, God in grace came seeking them and "called unto Adam" (Genesis 3:9). This pursuit is the pursuit spoken of in Luke 19:10 where Jesus said, "For the Son of man is come to seek and to save that which was lost."

The pursuer in our text is spoken of as "the angel of the LORD." This is the first time this phrase appears in Scripture. The phrase is very significant, for it refers to a theophany—a visible manifestation of God to man. Only Christ is a visible manifestation of God (Colossians 1:15, Hebrews 1:3). So what is referred to as "the angel of the LORD" here and in other places in the Old Testament is Jesus Christ of the New Testament. "The angel of the LORD" does not refer to just another angelic creature (as some believe) who is a messenger of God. But it is God Himself (attested in our text by "LORD") manifested in Jesus Christ. This is a most important truth; for as Thomas Whitelaw says, "The organic unity of Scripture would be broken if it could be proved that the central point in the Old Testament revelation was a creature angel, while that of the New [Testament] is the incarnation of the God-Man."

"The angel of the LORD" finding Hagar "by a fountain of water" reminds us of a New Testament encounter of God's grace with a sinner. It is recorded in John 4. There Jesus Christ found the woman of Samaria at a well and told her of Himself, the Savior. She, like Hagar, was also an immoral woman (she had gone through five husbands and was at that time living with another man she was not married to, see John 4:18) who needed to experience the grace of God in her life.

ABRAHAM

The denouncing of the sinner. "And he said, Hagar, Sarai's maid" (v. 8). God denounced Hagar here by the way He referred to her. He did not call her Abraham's wife, even though Sarah "gave her to her husband Abram to be his wife" (v. 3). He referred to her as Sarah's maid. That was a stinging and needed rebuke about her relationship with Abraham. Many view God's grace as that which simply winks at sin and lets bygones be bygones. That is an unholy and unscriptural view of God's grace. God's grace is holy and deals sternly with sin, as is seen in God's lack of recognition of Hagar's marriage to Abraham. Divine grace first convicts the sinner of his need before it points to the One Who can solve the need. No one will seek salvation who does not see his need of salvation. Grace would not be grace if it did not deal with sin honestly.

God's refusal to recognize Hagar's marriage to Abraham reminds us that a lot of marriages recognized by man are not recognized by God. We make a mistake of defining marriage only according to the laws of men rather than according to the laws of God. Many marriages may be sanctioned by the laws of man; but in God's sight, they are immoral arrangements though the term "marriage" is assigned to the arrangement. We believe that divorced people who have remarried are in that category. "Whosoever shall put away his wife, and marry another, committeth adultery against her. And if a woman shall put away her husband, and be married to another, she committeth adultery" (Mark 10:11,12); and "Whosoever putteth away his wife, and marrieth another, committeth adultery; and whosoever marrieth her that is put away from her husband, committeth adultery" (Luke 16:18). Churches in our day are more and more embracing lenient views in this area, however, because they reflect more what society thinks than what the Scripture says. Some preachers, instead of trying to lift the standard of morality, busy themselves trying to see how they can twist some texts of Scripture to justify divorce and remarriage.

The questioning of the sinner. "And he [the angel of the

Scheme of Sarah

LORD] said . . . whence camest thou? and whither wilt thou go?" (v. 8). Two questions were asked Hagar by "the angel of the LORD." Both of them were very important. The first question asked about her past; the second addressed the future. These questions which God asked Hagar are inseparably related to the Gospel message and need to be answered by every soul.

First, *consider your past*. The question "Whence camest thou?" involves the whole mess Hagar was in. She came from a sinful situation because of the immorality that was involved. In the matter of salvation, we must consider our past performance; this means we must consider our sinfulness and hence our need of Divine help.

Second, *consider your future*. The question "Whither wilt thou go?" forced Hagar to really ponder thoroughly where she was going, what were the consequences of her heading south, and what eventually would be her situation? Hagar is not the only one who needs to ponder their future. All mankind needs to be brought to the place where they seriously and wisely ponder their future. Where will you spend eternity? Failure to ponder that question will send your soul to eternal damnation.

The commanding of the sinner. "Return to thy mistress, and submit thyself under her hands" (v. 9). God's grace gives Hagar two commands which if obeyed will give Hagar what is best for her. These commands are "return" and "submit." They are the same commands found in the Gospel. "Return" speaks of repentance, for repentance has to do with turning around (or, as we would say in the military, doing an "about face"). And "God . . . commandeth all men everywhere to repent" (Acts 17:30). "Submit" is the acknowledgement that Jesus is Lord of one's life. "That if thou shalt confess with thy mouth the Lord Jesus [that is, Jesus as Lord], and shalt believe in thine heart that God hath raised him from the dead, thou shalt be saved" (Romans 10:9). "Submit" in both Hagar's case and the sinner's case involves a Master and serving. And, as in the case of Hagar, the serving could involve much humility and suffering.

Abraham

The instructing of the sinner. Scripture says the grace of God instructs man. "For the grace of God that bringeth salvation hath appeared to all men, Teaching us . . . " (Titus 2:11,12). Hagar experienced some of this illumination in her encounter with "the angel of the LORD." She was instructed regarding both man and God.

First, she was *instructed about man.* "And the angel of the LORD said unto her, I will multiply thy seed exceedingly, that it shall not be numbered for multitude. And the angel of the LORD said unto her, Behold, thou art with child, and shalt bear a son, and shalt call his name Ishmael; because the LORD hath heard thy affliction. And he will be a wild man; his hand will be against every man, and every man's hand against him; and he shall dwell in the presence of all his brethren" (vv. 10–12). In instructing Hagar about man, "the angel of the LORD" specifically instructed Hagar about Ishmael. He would multiply, be a wild man, his hand would be against every man, and every man's hand would be against him. This description of Ishmael is not unlike the description of mankind in general. Men have multiplied, have behaved poorly, and have been at odds with their fellow man. The world tries to tell us about men, but how often they describe him differently than God describes him here in the Word of God. But when a person gets saved, he thinks differently about man than what the world thinks; for the grace of God teaches him differently.

Second, she was *instructed about God.* In three ways Hagar evidences she was instructed about God: in the name of the son, in the name of God, and in the name of the well. (1) The name of her son told her about God. Hagar was to "call his name Ishmael; because the LORD hath heard thy affliction." The name "Ishmael" means "God hears" or "God shall hear." What an encouragement to know that God hears when we cry out in our troubles. God heard Hagar's affliction. God hears our cryings, too. (2) Hagar "called the name of the LORD that spake unto her, Thou God seest me" (v. 13). Meeting up with the angel of the LORD had convinced her that God sees all. Her life was not hid from God. He is omniscient. (3) The name of "the well was called ['in all likelihood first by Hagar' says Thomas Whitelaw] Beer-lahai-roi" (v. 14). "Beer-lahai-roi" means one who lives and sees. The emphasis is on living. "God is called 'the Living one'" (Leupold). So Hagar has learned that God hears, sees, and is alive. This was quite a contrast to the idols she was accustomed to in her native Egypt. God's grace not only brings salvation to mankind, but it also straightens out one's theology!

The transforming of the sinner. "And Hagar bare Abram a son: and Abram called his son's name, which Hagar bare, Ishmael" (v. 15). What a great transformation in Hagar's attitude and actions occurred when she received the message of God's grace. Both in her walk and in her witness we see the transformation. In the same way we can behold transforming changes in the conduct of the sinner who gets saved. But had Hagar and the sinner not accepted the message of God's grace, the transformation would not have taken place.

First, we see her transformation in her *walk.* Hagar went back to Abraham's camp and served Sarah as her maid again. This took some doings on Hagar's part. When God told her to "Return to thy mistress, and submit thyself under her hands" (v. 9), He did not promise her that Sarah would treat her kindly. In fact, as Whitelaw said, "The verb [submit] here employed is the same as that which the historian uses to describe Sarah's conduct towards her ['dealt hardly' in verse 6]." The verb means "to afflict" (Wilson). Sarah afflicted Hagar; now Hagar was to literally afflict herself; that is, Hagar is to let affliction return upon herself by returning to Sarah and experiencing Sarah's afflicting treatment. As Whitelaw says, she is to "meekly resign herself to the ungracious and oppressive treatment of her mistress." Not an easy command to obey, but she went back as God commanded anyway. How wonderful that God's grace can so change our attitudes and our actions. When a person accepts the message of grace, the Gospel message for our souls, it transforms our behavior. We can do things we could not and would not do before. When a sinner is saved, his conduct is often so transformed that it amazes the world.

Second, we see her transformation in her *witness*. Scripture interestingly reports that when Hagar's son was born, it was Abraham who named the son; and the name given the son was "Ishmael," the name God told Hagar earlier. This says that Hagar told Abraham what the name should be. It was her faithful witness of the message of God's grace to her. She not only went back to serve Sarah, but she also faithfully gave forth the message of God's grace. Those truly redeemed of the Lord have a message they want and should speak to others.

VIII.
SPEAKING WITH GOD

GENESIS 17

AT LEAST FOURTEEN years have elapsed in Abraham's life since God was last recorded as speaking with Abraham (cp. Genesis 16:16 with 17:1). During that time, Ishmael, Abraham's son via Hagar, had been born and grown to a boy of thirteen; Abraham and Sarah had grown to the age of ninety-nine and eighty-nine respectively which made them too old to hope for a child of their own; and the covenant promises had faded considerably in Abraham's mind—especially those about Abraham and Sarah having a son. This period of silence was the longest pause in God speaking to Abraham since Abraham had arrived in the land of Canaan. So it had to be a most welcomed occasion indeed for Abraham when God broke the silence and "talked with him" (v. 3). It was quite a talk, too. God spoke more with Abraham in this session of speaking with him than at any other time He is recorded in Scripture as speaking with Abraham. From verse 1 of this chapter until verse 22 where Scripture says, "And he [God] left off talking with him," there are only two verses (verses 17 and 18) in which God is not speaking directly to Abraham.

God speaking with man is such an awesome thought. But God does condescend to speak with mankind. Today, God speaks to us through the written Word. In Abraham's day, God spoke through visions and, as here, also through the spoken Word. What a choice blessing it is to have God speak to us. Let us, therefore, make sure we are always on good speaking terms with God. Let us be faithful in obedience to His ways so that

His Word will always speak to us and will never become a closed book to our understanding.

In our study of this lengthiest of all times of God speaking with Abraham, we will consider the prelude in the speaking (vv. 1–3), the particulars of the speaking (vv. 4–21), and the postlude to the speaking (vv. 22–27).

A. THE PRELUDE IN THE SPEAKING

"And when Abram was ninety years old and nine, the LORD appeared to Abram, and said unto him, I am the Almighty God; walk before me, and be thou perfect. And I will make my covenant between me and thee, and will multiply thee exceedingly. And Abram fell on his face: and God talked with him" (vv. 1–3). This introduction in God's speaking with Abraham is brief, but it gives us a number of good lessons regarding spiritual illumination. We will note the desire for illumination, the design in illumination, the degrees of illumination, the duty from illumination, and the deference to the illumination.

1. The Desire for Illumination

God desires that we grow in knowledge regarding Him and His will for us; and He provides opportunity to do just that, as He did here. God places no premium on spiritual ignorance. He had spoken to Abraham in the past, and now He speaks again to Abraham to increase Abraham's knowledge about God and His will for Abraham. We want our children to grow and develop, and God also desires that His children grow and develop.

Griffith Thomas rightly said, "The more we know of God, the stronger and richer will be our lives." The problem with man, however, is that God is more interested in our learning of His character and His will than we are. As we have noted in previous chapters, few are interested in growing in spiritual knowledge. They often feverishly strive to gain knowledge of many other things; but when it comes to spiritual knowledge, they put forth small effort at best. The Bible, however, warns us that there is great peril in disinterest and deficiency in spiritual knowledge. This was Israel's situation in Hosea's day; for he said of them, "My people are destroyed for lack of knowledge" (Hosea 4:6). Israel had no excuse for their lack of spiritual knowledge; for as the prophet Jeremiah says repeatedly, God sent His prophets "early" to the Israelites to teach them about Him and His ways. "Since the day that your fathers came forth out of the land of Egypt unto this day I have even sent unto you all my servants the prophets, daily rising up early and sending them" (Jeremiah 7:25, cp. Jeremiah 7:13; 11:7; 25:3,4; 26:5; 29:19; 32:33; 35:14,15; 44:4). Israel, however, was not interested in God's Word. Like most people today, they gave it little if any respect and attention. But it cost them dearly; for it is always to man's great loss that when God would endow him with great spiritual knowledge, he pays no attention, turns up his nose, and goes on his way.

2. The Design in Illumination

Again we see a Divine habit in this speaking of God with Abraham which we have observed in previous occasions when God spoke with Abraham; namely, that the message spoken by God is designed to fit the circumstances of the one to whom it is spoken. God reveals Himself as water to the thirsty, as bread to the hungry, as strength to the weak, and as healing to the sick. God had earlier revealed Himself to Abraham as a protecting shield when Abraham had reason to be concerned about retaliation from the armies he had earlier defeated (Genesis 15:1), and He had revealed Himself as Abraham's reward when Abraham had turned down the reward offer of the king of Sodom (Ibid.). Here God reveals Himself as the "Almighty" God to support the fact that the covenant which God has with Abraham would indeed be fulfilled though at the time it looked nigh unto impossible to natural man. Fourteen times in this chapter we read of God saying "I will" (twice in verse 2, twice in verse 6, once in verse 7, twice in verse 8, twice in verse 16, once in verse 19, three times in verse 20, and once in verse 21). These "I wills" include some pretty big accomplishments; the biggest accomplishment to Abraham would be the giving of a son to him and Sarah. But "Almighty" God can do that without any trouble.

Those who faithfully attend to the Word, be it in personal study or in hearing it taught or preached, will testify, as Abraham could, that often from what they read or hear, a truth is emphasized that especially fits their situation at the time. This is the habit of God in speaking with His own. He speaks just the right word at all times, and "A word fitly spoken is like apples of gold in pictures of silver" (Proverbs 25:11).

3. The Degrees of Illumination

God's speaking with Abraham in our text is an enlargement upon that which God had already spoken about to Abraham in the past. In fact, each time God has spoken with Abraham, it has been an enlargement of previous revelation. Here God tells Abraham more about Himself (in the title "Almighty" which is used here for the first time in the Scripture) and more about the covenant.

All of this teaches us what we are instructed in many other places in Scripture; namely, that Divine truth is learned by degrees. It is "precept upon precept; line upon line . . . here a little, and there a little" (Isaiah 28:10). We do not learn calculus in our first day in first grade, but we must go to class day after day and year after year to learn it. The same is true spiritually.

Learning by degrees requires discipline and dedication to the learning process. It separates the men from the boys, the true disciples from the false disciples, and the sincere from the phony. Learning by degrees promotes humility, not pride; and it helps one to assimilate knowledge better. Like food, we need to digest our knowledge well if it is going to do us any good. Do not be discouraged when you do not learn it all in a few weeks or months. Keep at it faithfully, and you will grow strong in spiritual knowledge. God will see to it that you do.

4. The Duty From Illumination

Divine illumination brings human obligation. Divine revelation is for human regulation, not speculation. Therefore, we should not surprised that right after Abraham was told that God was the "Almighty" God that Abraham was given some practical instructions. They were twofold in this case: "walk before me, and be thou perfect" (v. 1).

Walk before me. This command represents God consciousness. When one walks before someone, he is walking in the sight of that person. That is the picture here. It is true that God can see us no matter where we walk. But to "walk before" God in attitude is to walk with a continual awareness of God seeing all one does; and, therefore, to perform accordingly. Most men act as though there is no God, however. Their actions reflect no awareness of God or of His ways, nor do they reflect any desire for His approval. Hence, it is not surprising that their ways are vile. But when one walks in consciousness of God, he behaves much better than when he walks as though God did not exist. Atheism does not promote holiness!

Be thou perfect. This is the standard and goal that Abraham is to have. It is, however, unacceptably high for much of mankind; and, therefore, many folk want to water it down. As an example, in many books and commentaries, the writers seem very anxious to inform us that the word translated "perfect" does not mean perfect. In fact, they seem so anxious to inform us of this fact that it is generally the first thing that is said regarding the word "perfect" in our text. They tell us that the word means to be complete, whole, sincere, and blameless but not perfect. We should indeed be complete, whole, sincere, and blameless; but perfection can still be our goal. You will seldom, if ever, achieve above your goal; and lowering your behavior goal will not help character achievement. You may never become perfect, but you ought to aim at that goal in character. It should be your model. The Hebrew word translated "perfect" in our text is translated forty-four times "without blemish" in the KJV; and it is translated "perfect" in Psalm 19:7 which says,

"The law of the LORD is perfect." I should think we would want the law of God to be perfect! Not something less as others want us to view the word "perfect" in our text.

Charles Spurgeon said regarding this command of God, "Freely do I admit that the model of sanctification is perfection. It were inconsistent with the character of God for Him to give us any other than a perfect command, and a perfect standard. No law but that of absolute perfection could come from a perfect God, and to give us a model that were not absolutely perfect, were to ensure to us superabundant imperfections, and to give us an excuse for them." So let us not be anxious to water down the meaning of the word. We have enough watering down of God's standards today. Too many seem to want to lower our standards rather than raise them. Preachers are ever looking for loophole texts and toned down word meanings to justify sinful conduct. They need instead to plainly and earnestly condemn sin without all the ifs, ands, and buts of corrupting compromise. But, of course, when you try raising the standard, you will stir up the ire of many church members. And many preachers do not want to do that, for they are more interested in keeping their jobs than in doing their jobs.

5. The Deference to the Illumination

"And Abram fell on his face" (v. 3) is such a great reaction to God speaking to Abraham. It showed his deference to Divine illumination. He greatly respected it. Three things about his posture here shows his great respect for Divine illumination: it was proper, prompt, and productive.

Proper. Regarding this bowing down posture of Abraham, James G. Murphy said in his commentary on Genesis, "This is the lowliest [humblest] form of reverence, in which the worshipper leans on his knees and elbows, and his forehead approaches the ground." Abraham thus expressed great reverence for God and God's Word. Such is certainly a contrast to our day. Disrespect seems to be the "in" thing now. With glee folk trample on flags, morals, duty, and honor; and it is all because folk first trampled on piety. People seem to vie with one another to see who can show the greatest disrespect for the things which we need to give much respect. The way people dress for church today is one illustration of this problem. Folk dress so casually, sloppily, and even immodestly for church which too often reflects a subtle disrespect for the importance of worship. True, the heart is more important than the outward apparel; and some folk cannot afford the clothes that others can. But if the occasion is important, we should endeavor to dress accordingly. Worship is mighty important; and we do not show respect for it by the casual, sloppy, unkempt, and other inappropriate clothes many wear to church. And when we do not show due respect for God, we are headed for Divine judgment.

Prompt. Abraham bowed very quickly when God spoke to him. The quickness with which he bowed indicated that God did indeed have some priority in Abraham's life. When God wanted to speak to Abraham, Abraham did not put God on hold. He put everything else on hold. You put God on hold and He will hang up on you! We will note more about that shortly.

We must bow quickly to God's Word and to God's will for our life. But many exalt their own way above His way. They quickly honor their own wishes and interests but are very slow to give God's wishes and interests any honor. Slowness to bow before God reflects disrespect. And we noted above, there is great peril in disrespect of God's Word and Way.

Productive. Respect for God brings good results. Note that right after verse 3 says, "Abram fell on his face," it next says, "and God talked with him." If you want God to keep speaking with you, you had better show some respect to Him. You will have little revelation without reverence. Where adoration is lacking, illumination will be lacking. Those who honor God will learn from God. Ignorance in spiritual matters is often a result of disrespect. When folk refuse to honor God in obedience, submission, and priorities, God turns the lights out. That is why our world walks in so much spiritual darkness and walks so foolishly in matters that count the most.

B. THE PARTICULARS OF THE SPEAKING

The main subject of God's message to Abraham was the covenant which God had with Abraham. Thirteen times the word "covenant" appears in God's message here; thus leaving no doubt about it being the main subject. This subject was introduced in the prelude (v. 2) of God's message, which would get Abraham's undivided attention right away; for the things of the covenant were of prime importance to him. Sad to say, the great spiritual truths represented in this covenant do not interest many folks, as we will note more about later; but they should be of primary importance to all; for they deal with Jesus Christ and our soul's salvation—nothing is more important.

The particulars of God's message about the covenant are divided into four distinct parts. The four parts are prefaced by the words "As for." First is "*As for* me [God]" (v. 4); second is "*As for* you [Abraham]" (v. 9); third is "*As for* Sarai" (v. 15); and fourth is "*as for* Ishmael" (v. 20). The reader will notice that the "As for you" of verse 9 does not appear in the KVJ. The Hebrew will prefer it, however ["Thou" in verse 9 is better rendered "And thou" which is the same as "As for you"]. However, whether the "As for you" does or does not appear in verse 9, it is easy to see that verse 9 begins a new section in God's message about the covenant.

To study the particulars of God's speaking to Abraham here, we have titled the four parts as follows: the producer of the covenant (vv. 4–8), the precept in the covenant (vv. 9–14), the prodigy of the covenant (vv. 15–19), and the prohibited from the covenant (vv. 20, 21). The producer of the covenant is God, the precept in the covenant is about circumcision which involved Abraham and all the males of his house and seed, the prodigy of the covenant is the son whom Sarah will bare to Abraham, and the prohibited from the covenant is Ishmael.

Speaking With God

1. The Producer of the Covenant

The first "As for" ("As for me" [v. 4]) refers to the producer of the covenant Who is the speaker, Almighty God. The producer of the covenant is, of course, the one who can determine the specifics of the covenant. That God is the producer of this covenant is seen and emphasized repeatedly in this chapter by the covenant being called "my covenant" nine times (verses 2,4,7,9,10,13,14,19,21). We note three things here which the producer of the covenant addresses in speaking to Abraham—things which underscore the fact that God is the producer of the covenant. They are the reassuring of Abraham, the renaming of Abraham, and the reviewing for Abraham.

The reassuring of Abraham. God said to Abraham, "As for me, behold, my covenant is with thee, and thou shalt be a father of many nations" (v. 4). God had visited Abraham on previous occasions in the past and had given Abraham some details of the covenant and some confirmation of the same. But, as we noted at the beginning of this chapter, some thirteen years at least had gone by since the last communication from God; and in that time, one could easily become discouraged and doubtful about the fulfillment and even the existence of the covenant. So here God gives Abraham much reassurance as to the fact that God has indeed made a covenant with Abraham, and it will indeed be fulfilled. In the prelude of the speaking, God began the reassurance; here He amplifies it. As the producer of the covenant, God could give better reassurance than anyone else.

None of us have such great faith that we do not periodically need reassurances to encourage and strengthen our faith. But we have a great advantage over Abraham in obtaining this encouragement. We have always present with us the written Word of God which we can read and study at any time to obtain reassurance. Abraham had to wait on a special visitation from God. While those occasions were special blessings indeed, we need not feel we have been short changed; for we have the Scripture with us all the time. When doubts assail us, we can immediately go to the Scripture. Of course, some do not seek the Scripture when doubts come; and as a result, their doubts get worse and worse. But that is their own fault. We can remove our doubts, if we so desire, by going to the written Word of God.

The renaming of Abraham. "Neither shall thy name any more be called Abram, but thy name shall be Abraham; for a father of many nations have I made thee" (v. 5). Naming someone indicates the authority of the one doing the naming over the one being named. This is seen in other cases in Scripture—God changed Sarah's name (v. 15, we will learn more of this later) and Jacob's name (35:10), Pharaoh changed Joseph's name (41:45), the king of Egypt changed Eliakim's name (II Chronicles 36:4) when he made him the vassal ruler over Judah, and Nebuchadnezzar changed the name of Mattaniah (II Kings 24:17) when he appointed Mattaniah a vassal ruler over Judah. As we pointed out in another book (*Peter*), the wife having her last name changed to her husband's last name reflects the husband's authority over the wife—something not many women accept in our day of women's lib movements. Here in changing Abram to Abraham, God manifested His authority in the covenant making. He was the producer, and, therefore, He could change Abraham's name to fit the promises of the covenant.

The old name "Abram" meant "exalted father." The new name "Abraham" meant "father of multitudes." This new name, which was most fitting for the covenant promises, would, however, be hard to wear at that time; for men could easily mock, laugh, and ridicule Abraham when he informed them of his name change. He had only one child, and that was not by his wife Sarah but by Sarah's maid, Hagar. So to the natural eye, it looked rather ridiculous to name him "father of multitudes" when he had but one child; and at his age, it looked like he could have no other children. But he wore the name anyway; and it eventually fit him, too.

The names, honors, and messages God gives us may not always have the respect and understanding of the world. Much which we prize as a saint, the world mocks. Unbelievers often scorn our convictions and our hopes. But if God says it, it is true; and we can bank on it.

Note that God said, "Father of many nations *have* I made thee." God treats the future like the past ("have") in terms of fulfilling His will. God is so faithful that when He speaks you can count on it as being done already. So even though Abraham is not yet literally the "father of many nations," God is so faithful that He can still say He has already made Abraham the father of many nations.

The reviewing for Abraham. "And I will make thee exceeding fruitful, and I will make nations of thee, and kings shall come out of thee. And I will establish my covenant between me and thee and thy seed after thee in their generations for an everlasting covenant, to be a God unto thee, and to thy seed after thee. And I will give unto thee, and to thy seed after thee, the land wherein thou art a stranger, all the land of Canaan, for an everlasting possession; and I will be their God" (vv. 6–8). God reviews the two main parts of the covenant—seed and soil, people and property, heir and inheritance. In reviewing these two areas (the review includes giving some additional details about the covenant), He emphasizes the fruitfulness, future, and faith of those involved in the covenant.

First, He speaks of *fruitfulness*. God said Abraham would be exceedingly "fruitful." Herein we learn what are some of the things involved in fruitfulness. *Pain* is involved—Abraham had to separate from his homeland, relatives, Lot, and Ishmael. The pain of pruning is a big part of fruitfulness. *Patience* is involved—Abraham had to wait some twenty-five years after the promise was first given before Isaac was born. Patience is so necessary to bearing fruit. As an example, in farming there is the plowing, planting, cultivating and much waiting before the harvest comes. *Power* is also involved—Abraham and Sarah, especially at their age, could not produce Isaac themselves without the power of God. God gives the plant power to bear fruit, and

He must give us power to bear fruit. Power comes after pain and patience in spiritual things, but we often want it first. Power is ability. Pain and patience produce character. Power without character will not honor God. Therefore, it is most important that pain and patience precede power in our lives.

Second, He speaks of the *future*. Twice the term "everlasting" (vv. 7, 8) shows up in this review. God has not used that term before in speaking about the details of the covenant. But now He uses it to show that the covenant involves more than time; it involves eternity (especially is this true in the salvation that comes from Jesus Christ, the ultimate Seed promised in the covenant). The emphasis on "everlasting" reminds us that with God we have a great future; but without Him, we do not! Much of the world leaves out God in their lives; and, therefore, they have no rewarding future at all. How tragic.

Third, He speaks of *faith*. God made plain that the covenant was not for mere material blessing, but it was chiefly for the advancement of faith in Him. Twice this is emphasized in His speaking of the covenant details. "I will establish my covenant between me and thee and thy seed after thee . . . to be a God unto thee, and to thy seed after thee" (v. 7); and "I will be their God" (v. 8). "To be a God unto thee" expresses the primary reason for the covenant. This primary reason for the covenant needs more emphasis, for it is that which makes the covenant so important. The promise of the seed culminates in The Seed, Jesus Christ, Who comes to save men from their sins and give them true and saving faith in God. Nothing is more important to man than this.

We need to look more at our blessings from the spiritual standpoint. God blesses us with many blessings, but we need to remember that the material and physical benefits of our blessings are not the ultimate benefits of our blessings. The ultimate benefits of our blessings are spiritual in nature. Our blessings are primarily to help our faith in God and to help us help others in their faith in God. The greater our spiritual benefits, the greater the blessing we have received.

2. The Precept in the Covenant

The second "As for" tells Abraham about the precept for circumcision which from now on will be inseparably associated with the covenant. "And God said unto Abraham, Thou [As for you] shalt keep my covenant therefore, thou, and thy seed after thee in their generations. This is my covenant, which ye shall keep, between me and you and thy seed after thee: Every man child among you shall be circumcised. And ye shall circumcise the flesh of your foreskin; and it shall be a token of the covenant betwixt me and you" (vv. 9–11).

Circumcision was not something new for mankind here. History tells us that though it was not a common practice, yet it had been practiced at times by other peoples and nations. But now it was to be a special sign of the covenant which God had with Abraham and his seed. And we need to emphasize that it was for a sign, not for salvation. That it did not save is emphasized in the fact that Abraham was declared righteous before he was circumcised (cp. Genesis 15:6 and Romans 4:9–13). However, the Jews frequently tried to attach salvation abilities to circumcision; and in the days of the early church, they tried to incorporate circumcision into the Gospel message. Many have tried to put works of some sort into the Gospel of grace. Some have wanted to make baptism or communion or confirmation or church membership or other things part of salvation. But salvation is totally of grace, not of any works.

We want to note three things about circumcision from this precept text. They are the when in circumcision, the why of circumcision, and the warning about circumcision.

The when in circumcision. "And he that is eight days old shall be circumcised among you" (v. 12). Why did God specify the eighth day? One reason He did it was that the eighth day is the best day medically to circumcise a child. A Christian medical doctor, Dr. S. I. McMillen, in his book *None of These Diseases*, informs us about medical science discovering this truth in our time. Two significant problems are present in circumcision—bleeding and infection. On the eighth day of the new born male child, the blood clotting and infection fighting agents in the blood are at their combined best. Dr. McMillen said, "We should commend the many hundreds of workers who labored at great expense over a number of years to discover that the safest day to perform circumcision is the eighth. Yet, as we congratulate medical science for this recent finding (in the 1940s), we can almost hear the leaves of the Bible rustling. They would like to remind us that four thousand years ago, when God initiated circumcision with Abraham, He said, 'And he that is eight days old shall be circumcised.'" Yes, we can trust the Bible, for it is the Word of God. And God, the Great Creator, knows what He is talking about!

The why of circumcision. "And it shall be a token of the covenant betwixt me and you . . . my covenant shall be in your flesh for an everlasting covenant" (vv. 11,13). Circumcision was done for identification. It was to indicate who were the covenant people. The people of that time living around Abraham and the nations living around the Jewish nation (the seed of Abraham) years later were not circumcised. Circumcision distinguished the Jews apart from other people. In fact, the Jews referred to their heathen nation neighbors as the "uncircumcised." God wants His people to give evidence of their ownership, so He gave a sign which would indicate who were the covenant people.

Circumcision is not the identifying sign of believers today, but we still have significant signs. The Apostle Paul spoke of this identification truth when he said, "Henceforth let no man trouble me; for I bear in my body the marks of the Lord Jesus" (Galatians 6:17). Those marks in Paul's case were scars which he had obtained from persecution. Other prominent marks of belonging to Christ are marks of Christian character, such as, a holy lifestyle, the fruit of the Spirit—love, joy, peace, etc. Some have invented artificial marks like pins, buttons, and bumper stickers (Honk if you love Jesus). But these marks mean little, if anything. Rather it is the marks of Christian character and the scars of persecution for our faith in Christ that evidence our salvation and our relationship to God. Can people tell if you belong to the Lord?

The warning about circumcision. "And the uncircumcised male child whose flesh of his foreskin is not circumcised, that soul [person] shall be cut off from his people; he hath broken my covenant" (v. 14). The warning concerns the failure to be circumcised. Lack of circumcision resulted in Divine judgment. This judgment was not the losing of one's salvation; for, as we have already noted, Scripture says circumcision does not save. This judgment was the exclusion from the temporal blessings of the covenant; it was not a judgment of eternal damnation.

When Moses was about to deliver Israel and lead them back to the land promised the Jews in the covenant, he got a shocking reminder of this judgment. "And it came to pass by the way in the inn, that the LORD met him, and sought to kill him. Then Zipporah took a sharp stone, and cut off the foreskin of her son, and cast it at his feet, and said, Surely a bloody husband art thou to me. So he let him go: then she said, A bloody husband thou art, because of the circumcision" (Exodus 4:24–26). Moses learned that you must not ignore the precept of circumcision in the covenant if you want the promise of the land in the covenant. The same truth is emphasized in Joshua 5. Just after the Israelites had crossed over the Jordan, God commanded Joshua to have the males circumcised. Circumcision had been neglected in the wilderness; but now that they were coming into the land which the covenant had promised, they were going to pay attention to the precept which the covenant had proclaimed. Too often we want blessings from God but not obedience to God. Circumcision reminds us that blessing is tied to obedience.

3. The Prodigy of the Covenant

The third "As for" section speaks about the great prodigy, the great miracle feature of the covenant as far as Abraham and Sarah would be concerned. This "As for" was about the child

Abraham

Isaac which would be born to Abraham and Sarah. God had previously made it very clear that Abraham and Sarah were going to have a son (Genesis 15:4). But He had not given any other details about the son other than the fact that Abraham and Sarah would have one. Here, however, God gives some details about the promised child. And it all comes under "As for Sarai" (v. 15) to emphasize that the promised seed of Abraham is not coming from Hagar or another woman, but from Sarah his wife.

To further examine this section of God speaking to Abraham, we will note the mother of the child, the promise of the child, the laughter about the child, the rival of the child, the name for the child, and the privileges for the child.

The mother of the child. "And God said unto Abraham, As for Sarai thy wife, thou shalt not call her name Sarai, but Sarah shall her name be" (v. 15). Before Sarah has the miracle son, she, like Abraham, is going to have a name change. Her old name, Sarai, will be changed to Sarah. Scholars are not certain what "Sarai" means but are certain of the meaning of the word "Sarah" which is "princess." How fitting that her new name should mean princess; for in the next verse, God says that she is to be a mother of "kings" (v. 16).

Note that God associated Sarah's motherhood with blessing. He said, "I will bless her, and she shall be a mother . . . " (v. 16). Our day certainly needs a lot more emphasis on the blessings of motherhood; for our day views motherhood as a bane and not a blessing, as a hindrance to a career and not a noble career in itself. But God says, "Lo, children are an heritage of the LORD; and the fruit of the womb is his reward" (Psalm 127:3). It is time we got in tune with God's Word and quit honoring such God-forsaken things as women's lib and abortion.

The promise of the child. "And I will . . . give thee a son also of her" (v. 16). This was a fantastic promise at this juncture in the lives of Abraham and Sarah, for they were beyond child producing years as Apostle Paul reminds us so plainly. "He

[Abraham] considered not his own body now dead [no powers to produce a child], when he was about an hundred years old, neither yet the deadness [no ability to conceive] of Sarah's womb" (Romans 4:19). God's promises sometimes are mocked by the circumstances. But God seems to delight to pit His promises against the most mocking of circumstances in order to show His great power. And in the case of Isaac, He certainly did just that. How this should encourage our faith. Too often we let circumstances discourage us and cause us to think that they are too much for God to overcome. But God's promises will eventually mock all circumstances that mock them.

The laughter about the child. "Then Abraham fell upon his face, and laughed, and said in his heart, Shall a child be born unto him that is an hundred years old? and shall Sarah, that is ninety years old, bear?" (v. 17). This laughter must not be construed as laughing in mockery of what God had said. If Abraham had done that, the response of God (which we will see in the next few verses) would have been far different than what it was. You do not laugh at God and get away with it! But Abraham's laugher was not mockery; it was that of wonderment, of astonishment, of laughing for joy at learning that the impossible was going to be accomplished. We have all experienced such emotions and can identify with the feeling.

God is in the business of bringing such laughter to the hearts of those who put their faith in Him. He is the One who is "able to do exceeding abundantly above all that we ask or think, according to the power that worketh in us" (Ephesians 3:20). No laughter is so healthy, so sanctified, and so blessed as the laughter that God gives.

The rival of the child. "And Abraham said unto God, oh, that Ishmael might live before thee!" (v. 18). Abraham's faith is not without weak spots. The flesh dies hard! The next few verses following this one help interpret this plea which Abraham made to God. Abraham wanted Ishmael to also be included with

Isaac in the covenant. But God will not allow that, as we will see more about later. Abraham's desire for Ishmael was not according to God's plan. Ishmael will be given blessings, but they will not include the covenant.

Many times we are like Abraham in pleading for Ishmael. We do not want to give up our Ishmael plans. God's plans may be ever so much better (Isaac is always better than Ishmael), but we try to alter God's plans to include ours. It is the amendment program of the flesh which wants to negotiate with God rather than surrender completely to God. But God tolerates no rivals to His will. You amend God's orders to include some of your desires, and you will amend God's orders to exclude many blessings.

The name for the child. "Thou shalt call his name Isaac" (v. 19). As God did in naming Ishmael so He did with Isaac—God told Abraham what Isaac's name would be before Isaac was born. The name, Isaac, means "laughter" or "he laughs." There certainly was much laughter—some good, some bad—connected with the birth of Isaac. Three times Scripture records laughter regarding Isaac's birth. Abraham laughed for joy when God told him of the promised birth of Isaac (v. 17)—which we just noticed; Sarah laughed in unbelief when she was told about the promise of Isaac's birth (Genesis 18:12–15); and Sarah laughed for joy when Isaac was born (Genesis 21:6).

God has given out three names in this session of speaking to Abraham. The name Abraham speaks of the faithfulness of God—"a father of many nations have I made thee." The name Sarah speaks of the grace of God—being called "princess" after her scheme with Hagar is certainly God's grace. The name Isaac speaks of the power of God—laughter in astonishment at what God will accomplish by His power in enabling Abraham and Sarah to have a child at their age. These three names certainly emphasize what a great God we have, and they should inspire us to much dedication and devotion to Him.

The privileges for the child. "I will establish my covenant with him for an everlasting covenant, and with his seed after him" (v. 19). Isaac will have the same privileges as Abraham. And what great privileges they are! The greatest is that from Isaac's seed will come the Savior, Jesus Christ, the Redeemer of sinful man. But everyone is not enchanted with such spiritual privileges. Esau demonstrated that fact when he sold his birthright, which involved this covenant privilege, to Jacob for nothing more than some pottage. The world is filled with Esaus who have no interest in and put no value on the great spiritual privileges which the covenant speaks about. Their interests and values are so bad that pottage is more important to them than God and their own eternal soul salvation. How sick!

4. The Prohibited From the Covenant

The fourth and final "As for" section concerns Ishmael and his exclusion from the covenant. "As for Ishmael, I have heard thee: Behold, I have blessed him, and will make him fruitful, and will multiply him exceedingly; twelve princes shall he beget, and I will make him a great nation. But my covenant will I establish with Isaac, which Sarah shall bear unto thee at this set time in the next year" (vv. 20, 21). We will note three things from these verses and list them under the heading of words, world, and worth.

Words. We have an interesting play on words by God in our text. The name, "Ishmael" means "God hears." So when God said, "As for Ishmael, I have heard thee," His response to Abraham was a play on words on the meaning of the name Ishmael. The same was true in the giving of the name Isaac. Abraham "laughed" (v. 17) in joy about the promise of the son. In the next verse, God is recorded as telling Abraham that the name of the son would be "Isaac" which name means (as we noted above) "laughter" or "he laughs." So God used a play on words there, too.

For those of us who in our sermons like to use a play on

words or alliterate our outlines (which amounts to practically the same thing), we have a good precedence! These practices are not cheap devices with no purpose, but they are legitimate instructional aids. You will find other instances of a play on words and alliterative practices in the Scripture. Besides being good instructional devices, these instances in Scripture show us the excellence of the literary character of the Scripture. The Scripture is not some hodgepodge of words and phrases jumbled together without rhyme or reason. Rather, the Scripture is a marvelous piece of literature designed by God Himself.

World. God heard Abraham's plea for Ishmael (a plea we noted above) and responded to it. But in saying that He heard Abraham regarding Ishmael does not mean God will do all that Abraham wants, however. Verse 21 makes that plain. Ishmael will be blessed; he will not be left without any blessings in life (that was part of Abraham's concern); but he is definitely not included in the covenant. The covenant belongs to Isaac alone. God will not divide it with Ishmael.

The world needs to pay attention to this dogmatic clarification made by God in verse 21. The "But my covenant will I establish with Isaac" of that verse assures Israel that they will indeed ultimately gain all their land in the Middle East. The "But my covenant will I establish with Isaac" says the Arabs' efforts to push Israel out of Palestine so they can gain the Jews' land is doomed to defeat. And the "But my covenant I will establish with Isaac" should put our nation's support squarely behind Israel in the Middle East land controversy.

The descendants of Ishmael claim that since they are the first born son of Abraham they should have the land (which is part of the covenant blessing), but they ignore Scripture regarding what God said about Isaac having the covenant. Interestingly, they also ignore Scripture about when to circumcise. Instead of doing it on the eighth day, as God prescribed, they do it in the thirteenth year—the time when Ishmael was circumcised at the giving of the circumcision order. In their attitudes, the descendants of Ishmael are like a lot of folk—they want the blessings the Scripture talks about, but they will not give heed to all that God says. They think they can pick and choose what Scripture they are to follow. But it does not work that way. We must take God on all of His terms if we want His favor.

Worth. The great blessing of blessings in this text is the covenant. Ishmael is going to multiply, have twelve princes, and become a great nation; but he will not have the covenant. Today we judge one's success on those things which Ishmael had in abundance, but we do not count what the covenant represents as anything of worth. However, in God's eyes, what the covenant represents are the blessings that supersedes all others. These blessings represent spiritual and eternal blessings in contrast to material and temporal blessings which Ishmael had. We need to take inventory of our possessions to see if we have that which is really of worth. "For what shall it profit a man, if he shall gain the whole world, and lose his own soul?" (Mark 8:36).

C. THE POSTLUDE TO THE SPEAKING

What do you do when God stops speaking with you? What do you do when the sermon is over? And what do you do after reading and studying the Bible? What you do reveals much about your spiritual character. Do you live what you have learned, or do you ignore what you have been instructed? From the looks of things around us, most people ignore their instructions. They are the kind that James condemned in his epistle when he said, "But be ye doers of the word, and not hearers only, deceiving your own selves. For if any be a hearer of the word, and not a doer, he is like unto a man beholding his natural face in a glass [mirror]; For he beholdeth himself, and goeth his way, and straightway forgetteth what manner of man he was" (James 1:22–24). Abraham certainly was not that way, however; for when God "left off talking with him" (v. 22), Abraham went about doing what God in His message had ordered him to do. He circumcised the males in his household. Obedience was his response to God speaking with him. How commendable! But unfortunately, how uncommon.

We will note three things about this obedience of Abraham: it was prompt, complete, and difficult.

1. His Obedience was Prompt

Earlier in this chapter, we noted Abraham's promptness in regards to God—he was prompt to bow before God when God began speaking to him. Here we see this promptness again. This time it is promptness to obey God's precept about circumcision. God had ordered him to circumcise all those in his house, and he did so immediately. Twice we are informed in Scripture of his promptness in circumcision. In verse 23 we are told that all males in his household were circumcised "in the selfsame day" that God had told him about circumcision. In verse 26 the promptness is reported again. "In the selfsame day [which God had told him of circumcision] was Abraham circumcised, and Ishmael his son." The phrase, "in the selfsame day," seen in both verses certainly speaks of promptness. Abraham could say as the Psalmist said, "I made haste, and delayed not to keep thy commandments" (Psalm 119:60).

Punctual obedience brings the blessings on time. If we complain that our blessings are overdue, it just may be that we have not obeyed with promptness. We often get very hypocritical with God regarding the matter of promptness. We expect and want God to be prompt in answering our prayers, but often we do not do well in reciprocating regarding God's commands. There are no dividends in delay. We only lose when we postpone obedience. And the longer we postpone it, the less likely we are to ever obey the command. Multitudes of professing Christians wander about aimlessly in the wilderness of spiritual barrenness because they do not practice promptness in obeying God's orders.

2. His Obedience was Complete

"And Abraham took Ishmael his son, and all that were born

in his house, and all that were bought with his money, every male among the men of Abraham's house, and circumcised the flesh of their foreskin . . . In the selfsame day was Abraham circumcised, and Ishmael, his son. And all the men of his house, born in the house, and brought with money of the stranger [foreigner], were circumcised with him" (vv. 23, 26, 27). Everyone was circumcised that God had ordered to be circumcised—and twice we are told that fact in our text. Twice we were told plainly that Abraham's obedience was prompt; now twice we are told that his obedience was complete. So there is no question about the fact that his obedience was complete as well as prompt.

Completeness is as important as promptness. In fact, if completeness does not accompany promptness, promptness loses its value. Some are prompt in responding to the commands and calls of God; but they never carry through; they never finish their tasks; they never do more than get started before they quit. So their promptness is not impressive. Promptness only counts when completeness accompanies it.

How often we must all confess that we do not obey as completely as we ought. Sometimes we pick and choose what commands we will obey and which ones we will not obey. At other times we become tired or disinterested in continually pursuing a task; so we quit. But completeness in obedience is essential if we expect to reap many blessings of obedience. We will not harvest much blessings if the crop has not been allowed to grow to maturity.

3. His Obedience was Difficult

Few commands of God are easy to obey. The Christian life is not easy to live. It is a lot easier to go in at the wide gate and walk on the broad way than to go in at the narrow gate and walk on the hard path. Abraham found this true regarding circumcision. At least two things made the circumcision a difficult thing to do: it hurt and it humbled.

It hurt. No one is going to argue that circumcision is not painful. A young babe, of course, will not experience this problem as pronouncedly as an adult will. But here many adults and young boys were being circumcised. For them it would take some days for the soreness to wear off. This problem of soreness is seen later in Scripture when we read about the slaughter of the Shechemites. Jacob's daughter Dinah had been morally defiled (Scripture calls sex outside of marriage defiling—something our day does not do, and to their condemnation) by one of the Shechemites who wanted to marry Dinah. Jacob's boys said they would agree to the marriage providing the Shechemites would agree to circumcision—which they did. But it was a trick of Jacob's boys; for "it came to pass on the third day [after the Shechemites had been circumcised], when they [Shechemite males] were sore [from circumcision]" (Genesis 34:25) that Simeon and Levi, two of Jacob's sons, came upon the Shechemite men and killed them. The men of Shechem were too sore from their recent circumcision to defend themselves. Yes, pain was part of the cost in Abraham's obedience here. But he did not let the prospect of pain keep him from obedience.

Obedience is not going to please the flesh very often—if ever. Obedience is not exempt from the pain of troubles, trials, and wear and tear. To obey will involve pain. Abraham is proof of that fact.

It humbled. Circumcision is a humbling act for any except a young babe. So for all those who were circumcised that day in Abraham's camp, it was a humbling experience. For some days the men would be incapacitated. It would be embarrassing to move about. I do not think anyone will argue as to the humbling effect of the situation.

All of this reminds us that to obey God, we are often required to do tasks which do not exalt us in man's eyes. This is too much, however, for many saints; and so they refuse to obey when they fear the loss of honor from men. As an example, this kind likes singing or speaking before the multitudes in a prestigious place; but for them to do the same in some lowly rescue mission is another story. Such folk will not serve the Lord well, for much service requires a willingness to be humble.

We must not judge the importance or value of a deed simply by the esteem and praise given it by mankind. Many very good things would never get done if that were our practice. The world has such poor judgment; therefore, we must not let it determine what is honorable and what is not honorable. Let God's Word tell us that. Abraham listened to God when God spoke to him; therefore he circumcised all the males of his household even though the ordeal was very humbling. But humbling as it may have been before men, it was most honorable before God.

IX.
Strangers From Heaven

Genesis 18

Heavenly guests come to visit Abraham. They were three in number (v. 2) and appeared as traveling strangers when they came to Abraham. While he eventually perceived their heavenly nature, their visit prompted the New Testament exhortation, "Be not forgetful to entertain strangers: for thereby some have entertained angels unawares" (Hebrews 13:2). Of the three "angels," two were ordinary angels; the other "angel" was Jesus Christ.

The identification of Christ is verified in verse 1 where we are told that the "Lord" appeared to Abraham. "Lord" (all caps) refers to Jehovah. As most Bible students know, the Jehovah of the Old Testament is the Jesus of the New Testament. We can learn this by comparing such verses as Isaiah 43:11 with Luke 2:11. The Isaiah text says, "I, even I, am the Lord; and beside me there is no savior." The Luke text says, "For unto you is born this day in the city of David a Savior, which is Christ the Lord." We have only one Savior, and in the New Testament He is called Jesus Christ.

The angelic identification of the other two is found by comparing verse 22 with Genesis 19:1. Verse 22 says, "The men [the two besides the Lord] turned their faces from thence, and went toward Sodom: but Abraham stood yet before the Lord." Genesis 19:1 says of these two when they came to Sodom, "There came two angels to Sodom."

It needs to be pointed out that some interpret the "three" of verse 2 as a reference to the Trinity. These folks believe that it was God in three persons who visited Abraham. Over the years the "Church of England has used this chapter as a Lesson for Trinity Sunday" (Griffith Thomas) because of this belief. But as we have pointed out, the visitors were not the Trinity; rather, they were Jesus Christ and two angels.

In our study of the special visit of heavenly guests with Abraham, we will note the ministering of Abraham to them (vv. 1–8), the messages for Abraham from them (vv. 9–22), and the mediation by Abraham before One of them (vv. 22–33).

A. THE MINISTERING OF ABRAHAM

When guests come into our home, it behooves us to be concerned about ministering to their needs. Abraham did just that when guests from heaven visited him. The manner in which Abraham ministered to his heavenly guests is most exemplary. It gives us an excellent illustration of how all of us should serve the Lord. The excellence of Abraham's service is seen in the swiftness, submission, solicitousness, sacrifice, and steadfastness of his service to the heavenly guests.

1. The Swiftness of His Service

Abraham was swift in his service to these heavenly guests in two ways. He was swift to perceive his duty and swift to perform his duty. Both are very important if our service is to be acceptable to God.

Swift to perceive his duty. "And the LORD appeared unto him in the plains of Mamre: and he sat in the tent door in the heat of the day; And he lift up his eyes and looked, and, lo, three men stood by him: and when he saw them, he ran to meet them" (vv. 1,2). As soon as Abraham saw the three men standing nearby, he quickly recognized his duty of welcoming them and attending to their needs. The phrase "stood by him" means the "three men" were standing at an appropriate distance [enough distance to accommodate the "ran to meet them" by Abraham] as strangers who wanted to visit but who needed an invitation to come farther. Leupold says that this standing nearby was "practically the equivalent of our knocking," and "that there can be no thought of drawing nearer until the one standing has been invited to do so." Hence, the standing of the "three men" indicated duty for Abraham. Just out of courtesy, he needed to recognize and greet those who were standing nearby to see what they wanted.

A mark of a good servant is quickness in recognition of duty. A poor servant can stand beside his duty for hours and never catch on that it is his responsibility. Unfortunately, a good many church members are like that, for they are very slow in recognizing their duty. As an example, when visitors come to church and need to be welcomed by the church members, few members readily perceive their duty to do this. Most of the members gawk at the visitors rather than greet the visitors. Quickness to recognize one's duty in this situation is very important; for visitors need to be given prompt reception so they know where to go, where the nursery is for their little ones, where their Sunday School classes are, etc. But for many church members, it never dawns on them, that this is their duty until some weeks later when the visitors stop coming.

Swift to perform his duty. Abraham was no foot-dragger in doing his duty. The speed at which Abraham did his duty is most evident in our text. Scripture says he "ran" (v. 2) to meet his guests, "hastened" (v. 6) to inform Sarah to get bread ready for the guests, told Sarah to get the bread ready "quickly" (v. 6), and "ran" (v. 7) to the herd to get a calf for the meal. The swiftness of his actions reflected considerable zeal in his service. Especially so when all of this swiftness occurred in the "heat of the day" (v. 1) by a man nearly one hundred years old.

Would that we had more in Christendom today who would serve as zealously as Abraham did in our text. Christians not only ought to serve in this manner in church, but they also need to manifest this kind of service on the job. The sluggishness of performance on the job by many professing Christians does nothing to give forth a good testimony for Jesus Christ.

2. The Submission of His Service

Service requires submission. No one serves well unless they submit to the position and duties of a servant. Abraham evidenced his submission right from the beginning. He "bowed" (v. 2) before the guests and then called himself "thy servant" (v. 3) and "your servant" (v. 5). True, as a servant he was still over others. As an example, we note in verse 6 that he told Sarah to "Make ready quickly three measures of fine meal, knead it, and make cakes upon the hearth" (ERA and other women's lib movements would not like this position of Abraham over Sarah—but they do not seem to like God's arrangements in many other areas of life either). But being over others does not mean he was not under others. "Masters, give unto your servants that which is just and equal; knowing that ye also have a Master in heaven" (Colossians 4:1). Abraham's submission was especially remarkable because of the position Abraham held. He was the head sheik of a large estate. His servants could number over a thousand (as we noted in a previous chapter), and he was a man of great wealth. Yet, in spite of his position in the world, he did not hesitate to take the place of a servant in order to minister to his heavenly guests.

Some folk in our churches could learn a lesson from Abraham here. Because they have high position in the world and are wealthy, some church members think they are above being a servant at church but should be the master. It rankles them if the pastor has more authority than they do to make some decisions in church, and they get mighty upset if they cannot control the actions of the church board (and they really get upset if the church does not vote them on the board). They forget that position and possessions in this world do not remove them from the servant position in the Lord's business. Therefore, Abraham's actions in our text will really rebuke their proud ways. But an even stronger rebuke will come from the actions of Jesus Christ. The Bible says that though He was God, yet He "took upon him the form of a servant" (Philippians 2:7) and "came not to be ministered unto, but to minister" (Matthew 20:28).

3. The Solicitousness of His Service

"My Lord, if now I have found favor in thy sight, pass not away, I pray thee, from thy servant. Let a little water, I pray you, be fetched, and wash your feet, and rest yourselves under the tree. And I will fetch a morsel of bread, and comfort ye your hearts; after that ye shall pass on: for therefore are ye come to your servant. And they said, So do, as thou hast said" (vv. 3–5). Another reason Abraham served well was that he was very solicitous of the needs of his guests. His guests did indeed have needs when they came to Abraham. It was the heat of the day—a time when few people travel—and, therefore, they needed to get in some shade "under the tree" (v. 4) and rest and have their hot and dusty feet washed (which was a very refreshing experience to travelers in those days). Also it was near meal time. Abraham had obviously already eaten, but his guests would not have eaten, for they had been traveling at that time. Abraham evidenced he was much concerned about all of these needs and went about meeting them.

We see so little of this solicitousness in service today. Frequently folk complain about this problem in our hospitals. We can see it often in the clerks where we shop. It is ever present when one needs repairs in the home or for one's automobile. Politicians try to impress us at election time that they have great solicitousness about our needs, but it is all election rhetoric which is quickly forgotten after election day. Many radio and TV religious broadcasters also try to impress you with the idea that they are very solicitous of your needs; but it is only a ploy to get your money, not to help you in your needs. Individually we all often try to make others think that we really care about their needs when in reality we do not. But until there is genuine solicitousness in our service for others, we will not serve well. It will cut short our service and even stop it from starting.

4. The Sacrifice of His Service

No one serves well without being willing to sacrifice. Abraham served well in our text, for he was most willing to sacrifice.

We especially see his sacrifice here in the fact that he "fetched a calf tender and good" (v. 7) to be prepared for the guests' meal. "Tender and good" says Abraham would not serve his guests anything less than the best. He would not serve them leftovers, scraps, something that others did not want to eat, or, as we would say today, something whose shelf-life had expired. He would give them the best he had—which always means sacrifice. The fact that he picked out the calf himself says Abraham was so concerned that his guests have the best that he made the choice himself. The personalness of the choice emphasizes his readiness to sacrifice.

A number of professing believers like to think they are serving the Lord, but their giving often betrays them. They are stingy and miserly (they would balk at having to kill any calf for just three guests). They know little about sacrifice in giving. They not only give little in quantity, but they also give little in quality. They reserve the best for themselves and give God what they do not want. They are like those indicted by the prophet Malachi whose offerings consisted of the "torn, and the lame, and the sick" (Malachi 1:13) instead of the unblemished and healthy and prime animals of the flock. These folk are concerned the church might give too much money to a visiting missionary, while they wine and dine in the most expensive of restaurants. They begrudge the pastor and evangelist a salary anywhere close to their salary, yet they expect these servants of God to work twice as many hours a week as they themselves do. When an unexpected, special offering is solicited for some worthy occasion, they will not, like Abraham, get the best from the herd and give it to the Lord; but they will instead be very slow in opening their pocketbooks. And when they do, it will not be in the category of "tender and good" but more like tight and grudgingly. These folk will know nothing of the joy and excellence in serving the Lord, for such joy and excellence only comes when sacrifice is willingly and unhesitatingly made in order to serve Him.

5. The Steadfastness of His Service

The steadfastness of Abraham's service is especially emphasized in the sentence, "he stood by them under the tree" (v. 8). His standing by the heavenly guests under the tree is the posture of a faithful servant who is ever ready to do the bidding of his master. After getting the meal ready and bringing it to the heavenly guests, Abraham remained at the post of service by standing by them ready to do any further service needed for his heavenly guests. He would serve continuously until his service was no longer needed. Abraham had stamina in his service. He would do a complete job. He would not quit before his work was completed.

Many folk do not serve well because they have little steadfastness. They do not want to stick to their task until it is complete. Difficulties will stop them (in contrast to Abraham, who though nearly a hundred did all this enthusiastic service in "the heat of the day"), distractions will stop them (the average church member is easily distracted—such as by ball games, TV programs, family outings, etc.), and disinterest will stop them (an alarming number of church members have a very short attention span regarding spiritual things). But our accomplishments for the Lord will be small if we will not serve faithfully to the end. This is not a profound truth, but it is a very important truth which is frequently ignored.

B. THE MESSAGES FOR ABRAHAM

After the heavenly guests had partaken of the meal Abraham furnished them, they gave Abraham two messages. The messages spoke about the son (vv. 9–15) and about the Sodomites (vv. 16–22). They spoke about a blessing (the birth of a son) and about a curse (the judgment of the Sodomites).

In our study of the times God has spoken to Abraham, we have noted repeatedly the great blessing it is to have God speak to a person. We note it again here. It may seem almost redundant to note this truth again in our study of Abraham, but mankind simply does not properly value the blessing of having

God's message. Therefore, mankind needs repeated reminders of the great privilege and value of having God's message. Abraham was highly favored of God because God spoke with Abraham a number of times. The Jews were highly blessed of God because they had God's Word. Paul said, "What advantage then hath the Jew? . . . chiefly, because that unto them were committed the oracles of God" (Romans 3:1,2). We are highly favored in our land in having ready access to the Word of God, and churches are greatly favored of God when they have a pastor who can skillfully teach and preach the Word of God.

1. The Message About the Son

Again God gives Abraham a message assuring him that he and Sarah will have a son. While God had just recently told Abraham about the promised son (see our last chapter), He again reassures and encourages Abraham about the coming of Isaac. Would Abraham get tired of hearing messages about his son? Hardly! The more messages about the son the better, as far as Abraham would be concerned. It would be to our great spiritual blessing if we also felt that way regarding messages about The Son, Jesus Christ.

In studying the message about the son, we will note the inquiry before the message, the incredible in the message, the insolence for the message, the indicting in the message, and the iniquity after the message.

The inquiry before the message. "And they said unto him, Where is Sarah thy wife? And he said, Behold, in the tent" (v. 9). Inquiring about Sarah was because this message about the son vitally concerned her, for she was to be the mother of the promised son. The promised son was to be a product of Abraham and Sarah, not of Abraham and anyone else. Abraham and Sarah had evidenced some problem with that fact some years back, and Ishmael was the result. This message on the son will make it crystal clear that Sarah is to be the mother.

The answer to the inquiry about where Sarah was gives us

some instructions about desirable domestic situations. Abraham knew where his wife was, and she was in the home. Unfortunately, not many husbands can say what Abraham said, for they neither know where their wives are, nor are their wives in the home where they ought to be. Not only is Sarah's location an example of being where a wife ought to be; but later in this visit by the heavenly guests, she called Abraham "lord" (v. 12) which the Apostle Peter uses as an example of how wives should respect their husbands (I Peter 3:6). The Bible tells us how a marriage and home should be. The problem today is that we have junked the Bible's way for other ways and, as a result, have made a mess of things indeed!

The incredible in the message. "And he [God] said, I will certainly return unto thee according to the time of life; and, lo, Sarah thy wife shall have a son . . . Now Abraham and Sarah were old and well stricken in age; and it ceased to be with Sarah after the manner of women" (vv. 10,11). The substance of the message is stated here (and will be repeated later). It was a simple message about having a son but an incredible message to the mind of man because Abraham and Sarah were beyond child producing years. As we have noted many times previously, Isaac's birth was going to be a miracle birth.

This message reminds us again of God's great power, and that it is often His habit to let circumstances get their worst before He intervenes so that His power is more wondrously seen. God wants the glory and deserves the glory; and the more impossible the situation, the more glory He obtains in overcoming it. Isaac was not born when Abraham and Sarah were physically able to have children; no, God waited until they no longer had that ability so that His ability would be seen. He did the same for Zacharias and Elisabeth, and He also delights to show His power in the same manner for our blessing.

The insolence for the message. "Sarah thy wife shall have a son. And Sarah heard it in the tent door, which was behind him [eavesdropping is an old habit] . . . Therefore Sarah laughed within herself, saying, After I am waxed old shall I have pleasure, my lord being old also?" (vv. 10,12). Sarah's laughing reaction to the message about the son showed her unbelief in the message and thus greatly insulted God, the Author of the message. We note two significant ways it insulted God. First, it insulted God by *limiting His capability*. It would take the power of God to give Abraham and Sarah a son. But she did not think God could do that. She "laughed" at that possibility. She viewed circumstances stronger than God. How often we do the same to our shame. Second, it insulted God by *libeling His character*. By doubting (laughing at) God's promise, Sarah virtually called God a liar. God said Sarah would have a son. Sarah did not believe what God said—which is the same thing as saying God is a liar. Unbelief is a terrible thing, for calling God a liar is a terrible thing. But all unbelief does just that.

Belittling God's power and calling Him a liar, as Sarah's laughing at God's message did, is what many churches in our land do today. They reject the miracles of God's power which are recorded in the Scripture, and they reject the Bible as true. Yet, they claim to worship God. What a study they are in spiritual hypocrisy.

The indicting in the message. "And the LORD said unto Abraham, Wherefore did Sarah laugh, saying, Shall I of a surety bear a child, which am old? Is anything too hard for the LORD? At the time appointed I will return unto thee, according to the time of life, and Sarah shall have a son" (vv. 13,14). The message continues about the son with an indictment of unbelief about the message. The indicting of Sarah emphasized the omniscience of God, the power of God, and the grace of God.

First, the indictment emphasized the *omniscience of God*. Though Sarah laughed "within herself" (v. 12) and was in the tent unseen, yet God knew she laughed; and He said so. We play the fool if we think we can keep our sins from God's knowledge. God is cognizant of all our actions and knows every thought we think (cp. Psalm 139:1–4). Such knowledge about God ought to clean up our minds and our manners.

Second, the indictment emphasized the *power of God*. The unbelief of Sarah had belittled God's power, as we noted above. God rebuked that belittling by saying, "Is anything too hard for the LORD?" The way most of us act, it seems that a whole lot of things are too hard for God. Sarah thought her age was too much for God's power, and we often wilt before even less imposing circumstances in our lives. But Scripture rebukes that attitude. As an example, Mary was told by the angel Gabriel, "For with God nothing shall be impossible" (Luke 1:37).

Sometimes we confuse the will of God with the power of God. That is, if God does not do what we want Him to do, we think He lacks the power to do it; when, in fact, it is not His lack of power but the lack of His will that stops the action.

Third, the indictment emphasized the *grace of God*. The indictment included a reiteration of the promise of the son ("Sarah shall have a son" [v. 14]). That certainly was grace! After the mocking rejection of the promise, God still promises to bless her with a son. God would have been justified in withholding the blessing. But grace prevailed in a marvelous way. How thankful we can all be that grace prevails in our lives. Not one blessing would be ours if grace were taken away from us.

The iniquity after the message. "Then Sarah denied, saying, I laughed not; for she was afraid. And he said, Nay; but thou didst laugh" (v. 15). Unbelief does not improve one's conduct! We have already seen above that Sarah's unbelief dishonored God by limiting His power and libeling His character. Here unbelief produces falsehood in the mouth and fear in the heart.

First, it produced *falsehood* in the mouth. Sarah denied she laughed. That was nothing but a lie. Unbelief promotes lying. Hence, we should not be surprised that the world is full of lies; for the world is full of unbelief. Sad to say, the church is filled with liars, too; and this indicates a great lack of faith among those in the church. Some of those lies come from evangelists and pastors who cannot report their statistics with much integrity. They frequently embellish them to impress the gullible to gain the applause of men. Rather than showing a great turning to the faith, these statistics, through their lack of integrity, show surprising unbelief.

Second, it produced *fear* in the heart. You cannot reject God's Word and bring peace to your heart. Rejection of God's Word will only foster a deep seated fear in one's heart. Only faith in God can remove fear. The world is filled with fear today because it is filled with unbelief, not faith.

2. The Message About the Sodomites

The second message God gave Abraham was a message about the destruction of Sodom. Gomorrah was also included in the message of judgment, but Sodom was the chief concern for Abraham, for that is where his nephew Lot lived. We will note the courtesy before the message, the clearing for the message, and the contents of the message.

The courtesy before the message. The message about the Sodomites was given to Abraham as the heavenly guests left Abraham's residence and headed for Sodom. "And the men rose up from thence, and looked toward Sodom: and Abraham went with them to bring them on the way" (v. 16). Going with them for a ways to help "bring them on the way" was a noble courtesy. Today, it would be like taking someone to the airport, train, or bus station and then sitting with them until they board their plane, train, or bus.

All through this visit from the heavenly guests, Abraham showed himself a very good host. From the time he graciously welcomed them at their arrival to his accompanying them as they left, Abraham gave them due honor. He, unlike many in our world, gave much honor to the things of heaven. Today, many folk trample on sacred things without hesitation or shame. Legislatures make sure we give little honor to God; while at the same time they make laws which honor the most unholy of things. Courts approve of this, and our schools teach us that this is the way to go. But dishonoring of heavenly things only curses. Honoring God, however, brings much blessing. Here Abraham was given the blessing of a revelation from God about the destruction of Sodom; this revelation would not have come if he had not honored his heavenly guests by accompanying them a ways on their journey. If we want the blessing of hearing valuable truths from God, we must give due honor to God.

The clearing for the message. "And the LORD said, Shall I hide from Abraham that thing which I do" (v. 17). Before important information is given by our government to a person, that person often must be cleared in order to receive the information. A check on the person's character, performance, associations, etc. is done. If everything is okay, then the person is cleared to receive the important information. The same is true regarding Divine revelation. God does not illuminate everyone. He will not cast His pearls before swine. Thus Abraham was examined to see if he was qualified to receive Divine revelation—and he was. He was cleared in both his public life (v. 18) and his private life (v. 19).

First, he was *cleared in his public life.* God said, "Abraham shall surely become a great and mighty nation, and all the nations of the earth shall be blessed in him" (v. 18). Our verse tells us that Abraham's relation to the world scene would be very significant in two ways. He would be the progenitor of a great and mighty nation, and he would be the provider of great blessings to the other nations.

The great and mighty nation of which Abraham was the *progenitor* is Israel. While Israel has had a great past, it is the future which will see Israel's greatest time. Israel in the future will become the absolute greatest and mightiest nation that has ever been on the earth. No nation has a future like Israel.

The chief blessing of which Abraham is the *provider* is Jesus Christ. But also through Abraham would come many other blessings which we noted earlier in this book. Many folk are a curse to the world. The manufacturers of booze and tobacco, the promoters of immorality (Hollywood, filthy magazines, etc.), gambling, and other evils are folk who curse the world, not bless it. Abraham, in contrast, brought much blessing to the world. We need to ask ourselves if we are a blessing or a curse to others.

Being a progenitor of the greatest nation of all time and being a provider of blessing to the world were good reasons to give Abraham important information about the destruction of Sodom. His excellent public life made him a good person to pass on this information to future generations to warn them of the curse of the sins of Sodom. The public needs to know the truth about the destruction of Sodom. But God cannot give everyone the responsibility of carrying such an important message to the public. Those who will not be faithful in their public relationships and whose contribution to society are defiling will not be good messengers. Their character and their reputation will work against them. Their character will make them unfaithful in proclaiming the truth, and their reputation will discredit the message even if they tell the truth. Abraham had to be cleared here from a public standpoint, and he was.

Second, he was *cleared in his private life*. "For I know him, that he will command his children and his household after him, and they shall keep the way of the LORD, to do justice and judgment; that the LORD may bring upon Abraham that which he hath spoken of him" (v. 19). It is popular today to say a person's private life is his own business and should not affect our thinking in regards to his public performance. God does not think that way, however, and neither should we. We are in public what we are in private. If we are corrupt in our private lives, we will sooner or later be corrupt in our public lives. So Abraham needed clearing not only in his public life but also in his private life if he was to receive a special message from God.

Abraham's private life is viewed in prospect here (something only God can do—man can only see the past and present), and his life is outstanding in regards to the home. God said

Abraham would take his proper place of leadership in the home. He would "command" his children and other members of his household, and this commanding would promote holiness in the family. "Command," of course, is not acceptable to much of society today. In regards to our children, the so-called experts tell us that "command" is out and we should only "suggest" or "advise." But God says to "command!" "Advise" or "suggest" is acceptable when children are grown up and on their own; but when they are in your home and care—"command!"

Commanding the rest of the household, too, speaks of the authority of the husband in the entire home. There is no ERA in the Scripture. The order of authority is: "The head of every man is Christ; and the head of woman is the man; and the head of Christ is God" (I Corinthians 11:3). Many men fail to take charge of their homes. This often encourages actions which are opposed to Scripture; for when men leave a void in leadership, woman step in to try and fill it. That is not right; but when man fails, he must take some of the blame for it happening.

With Abraham leading his home well, it is evident that his private life is in order. Therefore, because of his acceptable private life, Abraham is cleared in this area also to be able to receive from God the special message about Sodom. God can trust him with the information about Sodom's destruction.

Before we move on to our next point, we would note a lesson from the last sentence in verse 19 which says, "That the LORD may bring upon Abraham that which he hath spoken of him." Covenant blessings were unconditional. But many other blessings from God were dependent upon Abraham obeying the Lord. Abraham's obedience to God in the matter of leadership in the home was the key to much blessing in the home. It is no different today.

The contents of the message. "And the LORD said [unto Abraham], Because the cry of Sodom and Gomorrah is great, and because their sin is very grievous; I will go down now, and see whether they have done altogether according to the cry of it, which is come unto me; and if not, I will know" (vv. 20,21). God's message to Abraham about the Sodomites was about the sin of the Sodomites. God said three things to Abraham about the sin of the Sodomites. He spoke of the character of their sin, the checking on their sin, and the curse from their sin.

First, the *character of their sin*. The sin of the Sodomites was very bad. We are told this fact in two ways—the "cry [of their sin] . . . is great," and their sin was "very grievous."

"Cry" expresses the cruelty of sin upon others. Thus in the Bible when a sin is said to "cry" out, it means it is a very bad sin in regards to cruelty upon others. As an example, Cain's sin was described in this way: "The voice of thy brother's blood *crieth* unto me from the ground" (Genesis 4:10). Also in James we read, "Behold, the hire of the laborers . . . which is of you kept back by fraud, *crieth* . . . into the ears of the Lord" (James 5:4). In our text here about Sodom's sin, the "cry" is said to be "great" which really emphasizes the great cruelty of Sodom's sin. Sodom was guilty of many sins. As an example, it was said of Sodom, "Behold, this was the iniquity of thy sister Sodom: pride, fullness of bread [indicates a pampering of the appetites of the flesh], and abundance of idleness was in her and in her daughters, neither did she strengthen the hand of the poor and needy" (Ezekiel 16:49). But the chief sin, which made the cities so condemned of God, was their sin of homosexuality. "Even as Sodom and Gomorrah, and the cities about them in like manner, giving themselves over to fornication, and going after strange flesh, are set forth for an example, suffering the vengeance of eternal fire" (Jude 1:7). Homosexuality is a very cruel vice. It makes for the "cry" to be "great" indeed. It does not bring joy and peace. It does not bless others. It leaves terrible suffering and sorrow. It is cruelly aggressive. It does not care if it ruins and destroys morals, character, and lives.

The Hebrew word which is translated "grievous" in our text means "heavy" and "burdensome" (Wilson). Thus in adding the "very" to "grievous," we are told that the sin of the Sodomites, especially the homosexual sin, was, as Whitelaw said, "abundant and heinous." The homosexual sin was abundant in practice and heinous in character. This made it a heavy burden upon society—a burden too heavy for society to carry successfully, for society will always be crushed under the load of this burden. Many think it is a mark of enlightenment and charity to accept homosexuality today. More and more laws are being passed to give the homos not just equality but favoritism over moral people. But all of this only increases the burden of homosexuality upon society; and sooner or later society will break down under the load and be ruined. The problem of AIDS today tells us something about the burden homosexuality brings upon society. No society has survived the toleration of homosexuality.

Second, *the checking on their sin*. God told Abraham that He would "go down now, and see whether they have done altogether according to the cry of it." Thomas Whitelaw said regarding this text, "Judicial investigation ever precedes judicial infliction at the Divine tribunal." God's checking on Sodom does not imply that He is ignorant of what is going on. Rather "God chooses this mode of procedure to make apparent the fact that He, as Just Judge of all the earth, does nothing without first being in full possession of all facts" (Leupold). Whitelaw speaks the same when he says, "The entire verse [v. 21] is anthropomorphic, and designed to express the Divine solicitude that the strictest justice should characterize all his dealings both with men and nations." All too often our courts make corrupt judgment and twist and pervert righteous laws which results in condemning the godly and praising the vile. But God is holy, and so His judgments are always just. Every judgment He renders will be absolutely accurate, true, and fair. His investigation of Sodom emphasizes that fact. Sodom was not destroyed by a cruel, capricious God but by a holy and just God.

Third, *the curse from their sin*. It is not directly said in God's message to Abraham (in verses 20 and 21) that Sodom was going to be destroyed because of its evil. But the implication is so obvious that Abraham said in response, "Wilt thou also destroy the righteous with the wicked?" (v. 23). Abraham knew what God was saying. Sin whose "cry . . . is great" and is described by God as "very grievous" will be judged severely! We especially need to emphasize this truth regarding Sodom; for the sin of homosexuality, which was so prevalent in Sodom (so much so that we often call the sin of homosexuality by the name of sodomy), is becoming more and more accepted today. Sodom was destroyed by fire and brimstone as is seen in Genesis 19. That does not promise a good future for our land if we continue to accept homosexual conduct. Someone said that if God does not do something to the USA soon, He will have to apologize to Sodom and Gomorrah.

C. THE MEDIATION BY ABRAHAM

"And the men turned their faces from thence, and went toward Sodom: but Abraham stood yet before the LORD" (v. 22). The message about judgment upon Sodom caused Abraham to do some mediation on behalf of the righteous in Sodom. This reaction to the message was very noble. Too often when we hear about some terrible thing, we run to the phone and spread the information as quickly (and generally as indiscreetly) as possible with nary an effort to use the information in a constructive way as Abraham did. Abraham took the information straight to the Lord in prayer.

Abraham's mediation for the righteous in our text certainly reminds us of the mediation of Jesus Christ on behalf of those who come to Him for soul salvation. Abraham's mediation was to prevent the righteous from suffering the judgment the wicked were going to suffer—and Abraham was successful in his mediation. Jesus Christ, The Great Mediator (I Timothy 2:5), is also successful in His mediation for the saints; for not one of them will suffer the judgment which comes upon the wicked.

We note three aspects of Abraham's mediation: the closeness for it, the character in it, and the cessation of it.

1. The Closeness for His Mediation

"Abraham stood yet before the LORD. And Abraham drew

near, and said . . . " (vv. 22, 23). Abraham's mediation for the righteous in Sodom did not begin until he drew himself close to the Lord. Drawing near to God will always activate our prayer life. The closer we are to God, the better our prayer life will be. Being close to God may not improve us in sophisticated terminology that impresses people when one prays in public, but it will improve us in the energy and effectiveness of our praying. People who drift away from God instead of drawing near to God are not known for a vibrant prayer life.

We need, of course, to draw near to God for more reasons than just to activate our prayer life. Being near to God is essential for every part of one's life. The Bible exhorts us to draw near to God: "Draw nigh to God, and he will draw nigh to you" (James 4:8). But many folk are doing just the opposite. They are moving farther and farther from God. The outcome of such movement is tragic; for people make many bad decisions and do many bad deeds when they are far from God. And these decisions and deeds can scar one for a lifetime and even for eternity. But when we draw near to God, we protect ourselves from these great problems and make our lives productive in God's sight. No one can perform well for God who does not live close to God.

2. The Character in His Mediation

Abraham's prayer on behalf of the righteous in Sodom (as recorded in verses 24 through 32) is a wonderful prayer. He prayed intelligently, compassionately, humbly, respectfully, resolutely, and successfully.

He prayed intelligently. "Wilt thou also destroy the righteous with the wicked?" (v. 23). Abraham's prayer was guided by Divine revelation; hence he prayed wisely. God had revealed to Abraham that Sodom was headed for destruction and that the destruction was very imminent. Abraham prayed according to this revelation. To have prayed without regard to Divine revelation would have been sheer stupidity. No one prays wisely who does not pray in accordance to what the Word of God says. If you are having trouble with your prayer life, check to see if your prayers are in accordance with the Word.

How different was Abraham's view of Sodom than the world's view of it. When we know the Word of God, as Abraham did, we view things in much different perspective than the world does. Speaking in today's language, worldly guides would be showing off Sodom's rebuilding after Chedorlaomer's invasion (like guides want to show us the rebuilding that has taken place after riots in our cities); they would show big stadiums and boast of the great attendance in them; they would tell that bigotry was being attacked; and, as a result, homosexuals were no longer being discriminated against; and these guides would brag about their stores, their trade, and their tourism. Yes, the world would think Sodom was really doing well. But those who knew the Word knew otherwise. And so Abraham knew that Sodom was headed for destruction; and today, we who study the Scripture, know that this world, our nation, and communities are headed for Divine judgment because of sin. And this knowledge helps us to pray intelligently about our society and world.

He prayed compassionately. "Wilt thou also destroy the righteous with the wicked?" (v. 23). Note that Abraham's compassion was for the righteous. We are not here criticizing a Gospel compassion for sinners. What we note here is that Abraham was concerned about the well-being of the good people. We could use a lot more of this kind of compassion in our land, for it seems today that society is giving more favor to the wicked than to the righteous. Our laws and courts show more interest in protecting the criminal than the innocent. And with our tax money, the government through its welfare program gives more help to the immoral than to the moral. But only when people see to it that it is well with the righteous will a nation do well. "When it goeth well with the righteous, the city rejoiceth" (Proverbs 11:10). The problem in Sodom was that too few cared for the well-being of the righteous. Instead, most of Sodom's citizens were concerned that the wicked prosper.

Abraham

He prayed humbly. The humbleness of Abraham in praying to the Lord is seen throughout his prayer but especially so in verse 27. "And Abraham answered and said, Behold now, I have taken upon me to speak unto the Lord, which am but dust and ashes." The antecedent of "which" in our verse is Abraham, of course, not the Lord as it seems to be in the KJV translation. The more we are in God's presence, the more we are aware and humbled by our smallness compared to God's mightiness and by our sinfulness compared to God's holiness. This is illustrated periodically in Scripture. Abraham, in our text, saw himself as dust and ashes compared to the greatness and holiness of God. The Psalmist, in considering the creation and, therefore, the might of God, was greatly humbled; and said, "When I consider thy heavens, the work of thy fingers, the moon and the stars, which thou hast ordained, What is man, that thou are mindful of him?" (Psalm 8:3,4). When Isaiah drew near to the thrice holy God, he cried out, "Woe is me! For I am undone; because I am a man of unclean lips, and I dwell in the midst of a people of unclean lips" (Isaiah 6:5). And after God spoke with Job, Job said, "Wherefore I abhor myself, and repent in dust and ashes" (Job 42:6). The arrogant soul who hesitates not to boast of his greatness and his own righteousness has not walked with God!

He prayed respectfully. Abraham spoke most respectfully of God in his prayer. As an example, he called God by the highly respected title of "Judge of all the earth" (v. 25). When we pray, we need to be careful how we address the One to Whom we are praying. Beware of subtle disrespect of God in the cheap terms used for God in some people's praying. God is not "the man upstairs" or "big Daddy" as some like to refer to Him. As a former military man, I recall how we were duly instructed in how to address our superior officers. It was not "Hi Joe, nice morning"; but it was "Good morning, Sir!" If it is appropriate in the military to speak respectfully to one's superiors (and it certainly is), how much more appropriate is it to speak respectfully when we are speaking with God.

He prayed resolutely. This aspect of Abraham's prayer is probably the most noticed one. Abraham was very determined that the righteous in Sodom would be spared. His determination was so great that he worked down the number needed to spare Sodom—and hence the righteous—from fifty to ten. And he evidenced concern that his great resoluteness was perhaps making God angry (vv. 30,32). Most of us are not that resolute in pursuit of our spiritual goals. We would never upset God because of too much resoluteness in our spiritual life—we only make Him angry by our lack of resoluteness. We would have stopped at fifty, for we do not have the spiritual determination to strive for more from God. God is anxious to grant us answers to our sanctified requests, but we are too often not interested enough to pray for as many answers as God would like to give us. We cut short our own blessings, for we do not persist in our tasks and are not determined enough in our efforts to accomplish much.

He prayed successfully. Though Sodom was destroyed (see Genesis 19), Abraham still got his prayer answered. He made six requests in his prayer. He asked God to spare the city for fifty righteous (v. 24), forty-five (v. 28), forty (v. 29), thirty (v. 30), twenty (v. 31), and ten (v. 32). In each request, God promised to do as Abraham had requested—which certainly is the answering of his prayer. Furthermore, God also answered the principle of Abraham's prayer—that the righteous would not be destroyed with the wicked (v. 25)—for He delivered Lot from the destruction of Sodom. "God remembered Abraham, and sent Lot out of the midst of the overthrow, when he overthrew the cities in which Lot dwelt" (19:29).

But though his prayer was answered, Abraham did not know it at the time; for when Abraham "gat up early in the [next] morning to the place where he stood before the LORD [in prayer for Sodom the preceding day]" (19:27) and "looked toward Sodom and Gomorrah" (19:28) to check on the situation, all he saw was "smoke" (Ibid). That had to be very discouraging. But sometimes that is about all we see after we have prayed, and in our discouragement we question the value of prayer. Faith, however, must see through the smoke and remember that we do not pray in vain to God—which the next verse (19:29) emphasizes. Prayer does accomplish great things. Lot was delivered, though Abraham did not know it at the time. So keep praying, you may be accomplishing much more through prayer than you realize.

With Abraham's praying resulting in the deliverance of Lot from destruction, this becomes the second time that Abraham has rescued Lot. He rescued Lot "The first time by the sword [Genesis 14] . . . the second time by supplication [Genesis 18]" (Griffith Thomas).

That Abraham should have his prayer answered here is not difficult to understand; for as we have noted, he was praying according to the Word of God, with compassion for the righteous, with humility, with respect for God, and with resoluteness. Such praying by Abraham not only helps us to understand why Abraham's prayer was answered, but it also helps us to understand why many of our prayers are not answered.

3. The Cessation of His Mediation

"And he said, Oh let not the LORD be angry, and I will speak yet but this once: Peradventure [suppose] ten shall be found there. And he said, I will not destroy it for ten's sake" (v. 32). We will note two things about the cessation of Abraham's prayer: the expectation of righteousness and the evaluation of the righteous.

The expectation of righteousness. Sometimes, if not oftentimes, folk criticize Abraham and wonder why he did not continue to go farther instead of quitting with ten. But it is not Abraham that we should criticize in this number; it is Lot that needs to be criticized! Abraham can be justified in quitting at ten, for he was simply expecting that Lot would have at least seen to it that his family was righteous. That would number at least ten. We can discover this fact in Genesis 19. There we are told that Lot had "two daughters who have not known man"

(19:8), at least two "sons-in-law" (19:14) which would add at least two more daughters, and at least two sons as indicated by "thy sons" (19:12). These unmarried daughters, married daughters, sons-in-law, and sons plus Lot and his wife would make a minimum of ten. There may have been more; but at a minimum, Lot's family would number ten. Hence, if Lot saw to it, as a good father should, that at least his family was in the fold, it would have been enough to spare Sodom. But as we learn in Genesis 19, the whole family was not in the fold. In fact, only Lot, his wife, and two daughters were taken out of the city. And his wife did not get far before she turned into a pillar of salt which does not encourage one to think she was righteous, for she did not escape Divine judgment.

Some tell us today that we underestimate the number of people that are saved. We are told that there are a lot more saved people here and there than we realize. We do not agree with this assessment. To the contrary, we believe there are a lot less saved folk than we think. The count at Sodom encourages us to think this way. We live in a day like Sodom—and with our society's conduct being like Sodom, we have no reason to believe the number of conversions would be any different. We have learned that a great portion of the people who made "decisions" for Christ at large evangelistic meetings, such as the Billy Graham meetings, were not saved. We also need to recognize, more than we do, that many folk who sign cards and help many churches achieve record breaking Sunday School attendance (through the gimmick program) are not saved either. Their lives definitely do not show it; and their lack of desire for the true teaching and preaching of the Word says so, too. When a person is truly saved, his appetite will show it—his appetite for the Word. Yes, you can be sick and not want food. But when multitudes of our "decisions" never manifest much interest in the Word, chalk them off as phony "decisions." We have a lot less saved folk in our land and world than most realize. Of course, some will be in glory we did not expect to see. But the great surprise will be the number of those not there that we thought would be there.

The evaluation of the righteous. From the cessation of Abraham's prayer, we learn a very important lesson about the value of righteous people to society. Only ten righteous people would have spared the city of Sodom from terrible fire and brimstone judgment! During the early stages of World War II when the pilots of Great Britain's planes had staved off the bombers of Germany, Winston Churchill, then Prime Minister of England, paid great tribute to these RAF pilots in a speech before the House of Commons by saying, "Never in the field of human conflict was so much owed by so many to so few." The pilots, though few in number in comparison to the number of people they saved, had kept Great Britain from being defeated by the German war planes. The owing of much by many to so few is even more true concerning the righteous in society. Few though they are, the righteous have year after year spared many cities and many nations from Divine judgment. You may not have political power, be famous, be a genius, or have a great fortune; yet you may be of tremendous value to society simply because you are living a holy life. Little do your neighbors or community or city or state or nation know how valuable you are to their well-being simply because you live a holy life. Holy living is mighty important to society. The world honors those they think are the MVPs of society, but they never honor the right people. The MVPs of society are the godly people. They are the ones who keep a society from the anathema of God. Where would the United States be today if it were not for the remnant of the righteous?

X.
SHAME IN GERAR

GENESIS 20

ONCE MORE SCRIPTURE records a great failure on the part of Abraham. It is the third major failure of Abraham recorded in Scripture after he came into the land of Canaan. The first of these failures was his lie in Egypt that Sarah was his sister. The second failure, the worst of the three, was having a child via Hagar. His third major failure, the subject of this study, was a repeat of the first failure—he lied about Sarah being his sister. This third failure by Abraham, especially in view of the recent promise that he and Sarah were shortly to have a son, was great enough that Joseph Parker said, "To us the Almighty seems to have a just cause for contracting Abraham to Abram, and sending him back to his own country a sadder but a wiser man."

Any admirer of Abraham could wish that this great failure of his was not recorded in Scripture for all to see. But as Arthur Pink says about this recording of Abraham's failure in Scripture (which is something that could be said about the recording of any of the failures of the great saints in the Bible), "The contents of Genesis 20 furnish a striking proof of the Divine inspiration of the Scriptures. No fictitious historian would have recorded this dark blot on the life of such an illustrious personage as Abraham. The tendency of the human heart is ever toward hero worship, and the common custom of biographers is to conceal the defects and blemishes in the careers of the characters which they delineate, and this, had it been followed, would have naturally forbid the mention of such a sad fall in the life of one of the most venerated names on the scroll of history.

Ah! but herein the Bible differs from all other books. The Holy Spirit has painted the portraits of Scripture characters in the colors of nature and truth. He has given a faithful picture of the human heart such as is common to all mankind." Charles Simeon in like thinking says, "We admire the fidelity of Scripture history. There is not a saint, however, eminent, but his faults are reported as faithfully as his virtues."

To examine this failure of Abraham, we will consider the resorting to deceit by Abraham (vv. 1,2), the reprimanding of evil by God (vv. 3–13), and the reconciling of men by Abimelech and Abraham (vv. 14–18).

A. THE RESORTING TO DECEIT

"And Abraham journeyed from thence toward the south country, and dwelled between Kadesh and Shur, and sojourned in Gerar. And Abraham said of Sarah his wife, She is my sister: and Abimelech king of Gerar sent, and took Sarah" (vv. 1,2). Abraham thought his move to Gerar put him in a life-threatening situation. He thought someone in Gerar would kill him in order to obtain Sarah for a wife (v. 11). To protect himself, he resorted to deceit about his relationship with Sarah. Instead of telling them the truth about her being his wife, he said she was his sister.

From the first two verses of our text for this chapter, we want to note three things about this deceitful conduct on the part of Abraham (and also Sarah, for she was likewise deceitful, cp. v. 5): the practice, place, and peril of this deceit.

1. The Practice of This Deceit

As we noted in our introduction, this failure of Abraham had been practiced before. It was a repetition of his failure of twenty to twenty-five years earlier. After coming into the land of Canaan, Abraham experienced a famine in the land. He then moved to Egypt, and while there he deceived the Egyptians about his relationship with Sarah. He said she was his sister and did not tell them she was his wife (see 12:11–13). Now he does it again in Gerar, a major city of the Philistines.

Shame in Gerar

The practice of deceit was a weakness in Abraham's character. Thomas Whitelaw said, "The character of the patriarch, otherwise so noble, appears to have had a natural bias towards deception." Deceit was Abraham's besetting sin. Again we quote Whitelaw who in commenting on this passage, said, "A sin once committed is not difficult to repeat . . . How hard it is to lay aside one's besetting sin." Yes, even great saints can fail again in the same area in which they failed years before. No one is exempt from repeating a serious failure. It matters not how many years you have been in the faith, how experienced you are, or how many great battles you have won; you can still fail again in the same sin in which you failed long before if you are not continually cautious about that sin in your Christian walk.

We all have character weaknesses. We do not all have the same weaknesses; but whatever our weaknesses, it behooves us to be especially watchful in that particular area. Others, who do not have that particular weakness, may not have to be as watchful as we need to be in that area; but that does not lessen our need of watchfulness. In the physical, as an example, diabetics must watch their diets much more carefully than non-diabetics. Now if we recognize that truth in the physical area, how much more do we need to recognize that truth in the area of character. We must realize that we have to be much more careful in a weak area of our life than others who do not have a weakness there. We also need to realize that those who do not have our weaknesses will often not be very sympathetic about the extra caution we must take in certain areas of our lives. Even though the critics are professing Christians, they still may try to tell us that we are fanatical, too straight-laced, and legalistic because we do not do some things and go some places in which they see no harm. But we must not let this unsympathetic attitude of others cause us to cease our extra caution in the weak areas of our lives, or we will fail—and when we do fail, the critics will be of little help but will even chide us for not being more cautious. So be careful to recognize your weaknesses and take due caution. Also, do not be like your critics, but be charitable and recognize that others have their weaknesses, too; and when they take extra caution in those areas, do not be critical even though you do not need to take extra caution in those areas.

2. The Place of This Deceit

Abraham's deceit occurred in Gerar, a major city of the Philistines. He had been living for some time in Hebron. But suddenly he "journeyed from thence toward the south country [south of Hebron and on the way to Egypt], and dwelled between Kadesh and Shur, and sojourned in Gerar" (v. 1). This move certainly did not reflect wisdom on Abraham's part, for Abraham thought the city was so impious that someone might kill him to gain Sarah for a wife (v. 11). If the city is that bad, why move there? The only reason for moving to such a place would be if God plainly ordered the move. But Scripture does not give the slightest hint that God ordered the move. Therefore, Abraham's moving there only causes trouble. It jeopardized the well-being of he and Sarah and the Philistines, and it greatly encouraged the sinful actions of he and Sarah.

Temptation will come no matter where we are, but in the wrong place temptation has more power to overcome us than when we are in the right place. There are places we must not go to if we are to have victory over temptation and over our besetting sins. Abraham is walking right into the kind of situation he faced in Egypt, which caused him to lie about Sarah's relationship to him.

We note in passing another reason which made Abraham's move to Gerar very unwise. God had just promised that Sarah would have a son within the year. To then bring about the disturbance of moving his household does not make sense—unless, of course, God had ordered the move. But, as we just noted, there is not the slightest evidence that He did so. Instead of moving, it was a time when Abraham should have stayed put, taken extra care for Sarah's well-being, and made arrangements for Isaac's coming. How true it is that when we do not follow the will of God, we do some very foolish things.

3. The Peril of This Deceit

"Abimelech king of Gerar sent, and took Sarah" (v. 2). The lying of Abraham and Sarah resulted in imperiling the princess (the meaning of Sarah's name), imperiling the promises of the covenant, and imperiling the Philistines. When God called Abraham, God said Abraham was to be a blessing to mankind. But living disobediently in Gerar, he was a curse instead of a blessing. He brought peril instead of prosperity to man. Disobedience to God always does that.

It imperiled the princess. Fortunately, the taking of Sarah by Abimelech was not for immediate marriage. "When Abimelech takes Sarah, that implies, not as the phrase sometimes means to take in marriage, but only to take into his harem" (Leupold). But that was bad enough, for the fact that Sarah was in Abimelech's harem meant that in due time she would be corrupted morally. So the lying of Abraham and Sarah greatly imperiled the virtue of Sarah. Truth does not imperil virtue, but lying certainly does.

Today, there are many lies circulating in society which result in the corrupting of people's character. We are told that sex outside of marriage is not all that bad, that gambling is good for the economy of a community, that alcohol is the life of the party, that abortion solves problems, and that homosexuality is a valid sex practice. All these lies, like Abraham's lie, lead men to corruption. Beware of the philosophies of the world that do not give due honor to virtue.

Some folk wonder what Abimelech saw in Sarah, who was then eighty-nine years old. What Abimelech saw in Sarah was her beauty. In our times, we do not think that eighty-nine year old women have the outward beauty to attract male attention. But Sarah had some things going for her that women do not have today. First, women lived much longer than they do now; so eighty-nine years would not affect a woman's appearance then like it does now. "Sarah, though now eighty-nine years of age, was as youthful in looks as a person of forty would now be" (James Murphy). Second, God had just rejuvenated Sarah physically so she could bear a child. That this would improve her outward beauty is not unreasonable thinking. Third, it was only twenty years or so earlier that Abraham had said in Egypt, "Behold now, I know that thou art a fair [beautiful] woman to look upon" (12:11); and the Egyptians beheld that "she was very fair [beautiful]" (12:14). These observations in Egypt about Sarah's beauty were made when Sarah was in her late sixties. So to conclude she still was attractive and desirable to men in that day is very justified. And we might add, Sarah had not hurt her looks through tobacco, strong drink, and wild living—habits which wreck many women's looks quickly.

It imperiled the promises. God had just promised that within a year Sarah would bear Abraham the promised son Isaac. But when Abimelech took Sarah into his harem, the fulfillment of that promise was greatly imperiled. Abraham would no longer be able to father a child via Sarah, for with Sarah being in Abimelech's harem, she was no longer available to Abraham.

This imperiling of the promise regarding the chosen seed reflects the ever on going enmity of Satan against the seed of the woman (Genesis 3:15), particularly The Seed, Jesus Christ. The attack on the promised seed began with the slaying of Abel by Cain. Abel, at first, appeared to be the seed through whom the Redeemer would come; so Satan went after him through Cain. The attack continued by so polluting the human race in Noah's time that it looked like Satan would be successful in blocking the coming of The Seed. The decree to kill all the male Jewish babies in Egypt was another attack by Satan to eliminate The Seed. The attempt to kill the Jews in Esther's time and the decree by Herod to kill the babies in Bethlehem were likewise Satan's attempt to eliminate The Seed. Here in our text, we see the hand of Satan in the deceit of Abraham. Putting Sarah in Abimelech's harem looked like a master stroke to stop the coming of The Seed. But Satan was not successful in his attempt to stop the coming of The Seed through Abraham's lie or through any of his other attempts. God is still on the throne; and no matter how man acted or Satan schemed, The Seed came as God planned and predicted.

It imperiled the Philistines. As we will note more about towards the end of this chapter, the taking of Sarah by Abimelech resulted in God bringing an affliction upon the Philistines which affected many. Abimelech and his wife and maid servants became sick (v. 17) which made it impossible for any in Abimelech's household to bear children (v. 18). Abraham's sin of deceit was imperiling many people. This is true of any sin. "For none of us liveth to himself, and no man dieth to himself" (Romans 14:7). If our sin only imperiled ourselves, it would be bad enough; but the fact that it adversely affects many others makes it much worse. Our conduct affects so many more folk than we realize that it is very difficult to compute all the many people that have been harmed by our sin. If we have any kindness in our hearts at all, that fact should do something about improving our conduct.

B. THE REPRIMANDING OF EVIL

Sooner or later, man will be reprimanded for his sin. Thankfully, it came "sooner" for Abimelech and Abraham, which stopped their sins from causing disastrous, irreparable damage. God reprimanded Abimelech, and Abimelech reprimanded Abraham.

1. The Reprimanding of Abimelech

The first reprimanding in the case before us is God's reprimanding of Abimelech. We will note the elucidation, explanation, exoneration, education, exhortation, elaboration, and extrication involved in this reprimand.

Elucidation. "But God came to Abimelech in a dream by night, and said to him, Behold, thou art but a dead man, for the woman which thou has taken; for she is a man's wife" (v. 3). How very important this information was which Abimelech received from God. It was life and death information. If there was anything Abimelech needed to pay attention to at this time, it was what God spoke to him about his situation with Sarah.

Abimelech learned from the Word of God (spoken Word here) what is right and wrong. We can all do the same. It is the Word that is our rule, our guide, and our authority for what is right and wrong morally and spiritually. When men ditch the Word and try to make their own rules, they really botch things up in a hurry. Their rules will always bring lower morals and character and, therefore, will bring much trouble to society. Legalizing sin, which our land and many nations are habitually and earnestly doing, does not take away the sinfulness of sin; it only makes sin a greater plague to society, for it encourages it.

God's message here, like the Gospel message, told Abimelech the way of life. Abimelech because of his sin of taking Sarah was under the sentence of death, but the Word of God showed him the way of life. So it is in the matter of salvation. We all are under the curse of death, but the Word of God shows us in Christ the way of life. Do not despise the Word of God as so many do, for it is what shows us the way of life.

Explanation. "But Abimelech had not come near her: and he said, Lord, wilt thou slay also a righteous nation? Said he not unto me, She is my sister? and she, even she herself said, He is my brother. In the integrity of my heart and innocency of my hands have I done this" (vv. 4, 5). While guilty of having Sarah, and thus under a curse, Abimelech did not have bad motives in taking Sarah. To the shame of Abraham, it was Abimelech, not Abraham, who came off the better man in this incident of Genesis 20. In a demonstration of commendable conduct, Abimelech had obviously investigated to make sure Sarah was fair game; for he states that both Abraham and Sarah said she was his sister. Abimelech evidences good character in this whole business about taking Sarah. The inner motivation ("integrity of my heart") was proper, and the outward deed ("innocency of my hands") was likewise proper. Leupold adds an illuminating note about the expression "innocency of my hands." He states that the word "hand" means "the palm of the hand," which means his hands were open and not concealing anything—a good expression for innocence.

We should see to it that every action we take can be as defended as Abimelech's action was. It will keep us out of a lot of trouble. Abimelech would have been in a lot more trouble than he was had he not had the "integrity of my heart" and "innocency of my hands" involved in his conduct about Sarah. God saw that integrity and, as a result (which we will note more about later), gave him opportunity to extricate himself from the situation and remove the curse from his household.

Note that Scripture makes it a point to tell us that Abimelech "had not come near her [Sarah]." This is important; for it makes certain that Isaac was the seed of Abraham and Sarah as God had promised, not the son of Abimelech and Sarah.

Exoneration. "And God said unto him in a dream, Yea, I know that thou didst this in the integrity of thy heart; for I also withheld thee from sinning against me: therefore suffered I thee not to touch her" (v. 6). Motivation is very important. In this story of Abraham in Gerar, we have a man (Abraham) speaking words of truth but being condemned severely for lying because his motivation was to deceive. And then we have another man (Abimelech) who did a very terrible deed of taking another man's wife, yet escaping the condemnation (death) for the deed because his motivation did not correspond to the actual deed. God looks on the heart when He judges man (I Samuel 16:7). Therefore, while you may fool man or be misjudged by man, you will never fool God or be misjudged by God.

God's exoneration of Abimelech did not mean that his taking Sarah was right to do. That was a very wrong act, and Abimelech was under the sentence of death for doing it. But God's exoneration of Abimelech meant that He recognized that Abimelech did not have evil intent in his heart in taking Sarah. Because the action was wrong, however, God ordered Abimelech to restore Sarah to Abraham.

In restraining Abimelech from immoral conduct with Sarah, God informs us that He gives special protection to those whose heart is proper in regards to conduct. Those who do evil and know they are doing evil do not have that assurance of protection from God. If we want God to protect us from trouble, we need to make sure our hearts are right in all that we do.

Education. "I also withheld thee from sinning against me" (v. 6). In speaking with Abimelech, God did some educating of Abimelech about the primary harm of sin. God said that if Abimelech had corrupted Sarah morally, it would be "sinning against me." Yes, it was sin against a lot of others, too. But the emphasis is that sin is primarily against God! David acknowledged this truth after his awful sin with Bathsheba and subsequent ordering of Uriah's death when he said in the Psalms, "Against thee, thee only [chiefly], have I sinned, and done this evil in thy sight" (Psalm 51:4). Nathan also acknowledged this truth when he said to David, "Because by this deed thou hast given great occasion to the enemies of the LORD to blaspheme" (II Samuel 12:14). We need this truth taught more today. It is education we are sorely lacking. To be cognizant of the fact that all our sin is against God will do much to stop our sinning.

Exhortation. "Now therefore restore the man his wife; for he is a prophet, and he shall pray for thee, and thou shalt live: and if thou restore her not, know thou that thou shalt surely die, thou, and all that are thine" (v. 7). Divine revelation is for our regulation. Illumination is to be followed by application. God does not give us information simply to fill our minds with facts and figures to satisfy our curiosity. The information given Abimelech was for the purpose of directing Abimelech's action.

Our sermons ought to reflect this truth. But, of course, when we preachers begin to apply Divine truths to everyday living we can step on a lot of toes. It can cross the will of many people. So the compromising preachers and teachers simply give out interesting facts without application (and in giving out the facts, they often try to impress their audience with their intelligence—compromising people are always anxious to gain the accolades of man more than the accolades of God). Giving out facts without application to our faith and conduct is a far cry from what is involved in God's commission to proclaim His truth. Yet many do it anyway. Preachers, teachers, books, and commentaries too often reflect this problem. They give out a lot of information but they seldom make any application to everyday living.

Elaboration. "For he is a prophet" (v. 7). God gave some additional information to Abimelech about Abraham's identification. He told Abimelech that Abraham was "a prophet." That God had to tell Abimelech that Abraham was a prophet is an indictment upon Abraham's conduct. Abraham's conduct should have evidenced the fact that he was a prophet of God. But it did not, and so God had to inform Abimelech of Abraham's office of a prophet.

It is a pretty sad commentary on our life if others cannot figure out by our conduct that we are a Christian. But some folk who claim to be Christian give so little evidence of the fact of their salvation that others have to be told of the fact. Sometime later, Abimelech did see evidence in Abraham's life of his relationship with the Lord. "Abimelech . . . spoke unto Abraham, saying, God is with thee in all that thou doest" (Genesis 21:22). Abraham's conduct had become much improved, and it gave obvious evidence of a good relationship with God. Towards the end of the book of Genesis, we have a similar commentary about Joseph's life; for it is said that others could tell that God was with Joseph (cp. Genesis 39:3; 41:38). Our Christian profession should be so evident in day-to-day living that everyone will know that we are Christians. If they have to ask to find out, we are either in a serious backslidden state or a counterfeit.

Extrication. "Therefore Abimelech rose early in the morning, and called all his servants, and told all these things in their ears: and the men were sore [very much] afraid" (v. 8). Abimelech believed God, and early in the morning he began the process of extricating himself from his forbidden situation with Sarah. The "arose early in the morning" spoke very well for Abimelech. It said he was very prompt in obeying God's orders to extricate himself from a very bad situation. He was not like some who, in a church service, promise God they will serve Him; but then as soon as the service is over, they go on their way ignoring all their impressive statements of dedication. We all need to be a man of our word about our commitment to truth and righteousness as Abimelech was. Talk is cheap; it is walk that proves our profession.

The first thing Abimelech did when he got up early in the morning after God had spoken to him in a dream was to tell his servants about the dream. This was important; for they, too (vv. 17,18), were suffering from the malady which came from Abimelech having Sarah and, therefore, needed to know why they had the problem. Otherwise they would not have opportunity to learn from this situation the value of virtue. That the servants were "sore afraid" spoke well of them. They did not despise and mock God's message but evidenced some godly fear. Oh, that more men would tremble at God's message of judgment upon sin. It would have a purifying affect upon society like few other things do.

2. The Reprimanding of Abraham

After informing his servants of the situation, Abimelech calls Abraham and reprimands him for the evil Abraham had done. In studying this reprimand, we will note the confronting of Abraham about his sin and the contending by Abraham in trying to excuse his sin.

The confronting of Abraham. "Then Abimelech called Abraham, and said unto him, What hast thou done unto us? and what have I offended thee, that thou hast brought on me and on my kingdom a great sin? thou hast done deeds unto me that ought not to be done. And Abimelech said unto Abraham, What sawest thou, that thou hast done this thing?" (vv. 9,10). In confronting Abraham with his sin, Abimelech makes four statements—three are questions, one a simple declaration. These four statements deal with the injury of Abraham's conduct to others, the innocence of Abimelech in provoking Abraham's conduct of lying about Sarah, the iniquity of Abraham's conduct, and the instigation of Abraham's conduct.

First, the *injury* to others. "What hast thou done unto us?" (v. 9). As we noted above, this lying of Abraham imperiled many Philistines. The result of the lying was that "the LORD had fast [completely] closed up all the wombs of the house of Abimelech, because of Sarah Abraham's wife" (v. 18). Some sort of affliction came upon many Philistines from which they needed to be "healed" (v. 17). Abimelech, by this question, caused Abraham to address the problems caused by his conduct.

Abimelech was wise in his approach to Abraham; for before you can get one concerned about their evil, you must first show them the evil they have done. The idea that we can preach salvation without first showing mankind they are sinners is an idea that did not come from Scripture. It is the so-called "positive" Gospel that some, who have neither the courage nor integrity to show people their sins, want to preach.

Second, the *innocence* of Abimelech. "[In] what have I offended thee, that thou hast brought on me and on my kingdom a great sin?" (v. 9). This question is the kind in which the answer is implied. By the question, Abimelech reminds Abraham that he had done no harm to Abraham to give occasion for Abraham to do evil back to him. That Abimelech was not a provoker of Abraham's action only intensifies the guilt and seriousness of Abraham's conduct of lying. As we noted above, Abraham's concern that the fear of God was not present was only a suspicion of his. It was not fact. We need to be charitable enough in judging people that we do not convict them by mere suspicion. It can cause a lot of trouble as it did in Abraham's case.

Third, the *iniquity* of Abraham's conduct. Abimelech plainly denounced Abraham by stating that Abraham's conduct was wrong. He told Abraham, "Thou hast done deeds unto me that ought not to be done" (v. 9). We need preachers like Abimelech who will with plainness expose evil as evil. The world may have all sorts of arguments to insist that their evil deeds are not evil (Abraham had his arguments as we will note shortly). But sin is sin, and the true preacher will declare this fact even if the whole world disagrees.

One of the big problems we have in our churches today is the unwillingness of the church to take a good stand against sin. Churches are smiling benevolently on much conduct today which they denounced with a fervor several generations back. Both pastor and people have gone soft on sin. This helps explain why our churches are so corrupt today.

Fourth, the *instigation* of Abraham's conduct. "What sawest thou, that thou hast done this thing?" (v. 10). This question is similar to the second one but is broader in scope. The second question addressed Abimelech's conduct and said it was not a reason for Abraham's evil. This question searches the whole heart of Abraham and seeks for the reason whatever it was. The question implied an answer, just as the second question did. And the answer was that Abraham did not have any good reason for his deceitful conduct. It is the same conclusion that we must make about all sin—we have no excuse (Romans 1:20).

The contending by Abraham. When Abimelech finished reprimanding Abraham, "Abraham said, Because I thought, Surely the fear of God is not in this place; and they will slay me for my wife's sake. And yet indeed she is my sister; she is the daughter of my father, but not the daughter of my mother; and she became my wife. And it came to pass, when God caused me to wander from my father's house, that I said unto her, This is thy kindness which thou shalt show unto me; at every place whither we shall come, say of me, He is my brother" (vv. 11–13). Abimelech's four-pronged reprimand of Abraham was a good one, and it ought to have brought Abraham to his knees in humble confession and apology. But shamefully for Abraham, it did

Shame in Gerar

nothing of the sort. Rather than apologize for his sin and ask Abimelech's forgiveness, Abraham contended that his deceitful conduct was excusable. To Abraham's shame, his reaction to being reprimanded for sin was certainly different than Abimelech's reaction to being reprimanded for sin.

Abraham gave at least five excuses for his conduct. He tried to excuse his sinful conduct on the character of Gerar, on the preservation of life, on the relationship of Sarah to him, on the orders of God for his life, and on the kindness of the deed. Pitiful, pitiful are his excuses. What twisted thinking they reflect. They do not exonerate him but only condemn him more. A good number of folk are no better today, however. In fact, they give even more pitiful excuses to justify their evil and demonstrate even more twisted thinking in their excuses.

First, the *character of Gerar*. Abraham first tried to excuse his deceit by his suspicion that the fear of God was not in the place; and, therefore, his life would be in jeopardy. "Because I thought, Surely the fear of God is not in this place; and [therefore] they will slay me for my wife's sake" (v. 11). This excuse condemned him instead of exonerating him. We cite two reasons why it condemned him, both of which we have already noted. One, the conclusion was based merely on suspicion, not fact. Two, if the area had that kind of character, he should not have moved there.

Though unacceptable this excuse was, what Abraham said about an impious society is true. When a society lacks piety, its members will lack protection. The less men respect God, the less men will respect their fellow men. The more godless our land becomes, the more perilous it will be for our lives. Drive out God and you drive out good. You can make zillions of laws to protect the citizen; but if the fear of God is lacking, the citizen will always be in great peril regardless of the laws.

Second, the *preservation of life*. Abraham next tried to excuse his lying by saying that lying was necessary to save his life. He felt that if he did not lie by saying that Sarah was his sister instead of his wife, "they will slay me for my wife's sake"

(v. 11) In making this excuse, he plainly says to Abimelech that self-preservation was more important to him than virtue. He was more interested in saving his life than in speaking the truth and in protecting Sarah from immorality. Security was more important to him than character. Anytime we think like that, we are headed for trouble. But a lot of folk ignore that fact, and so virtue has a very low priority in their lives. Generally society in our land gives popularity, money, position, and other things preference over virtue.

Third, the *relationship of Sarah*. Another way in which Abraham tried to excuse his deceit was by the fact that Sarah was actually his half-sister. "Yet indeed she is my sister; she is the daughter of my father, but not the daughter of my mother" (v. 12). It was a clever lie but still corrupt. One may actually be speaking the truth but in such a way as to mislead. The fact that what was said is the truth will not nullify the lie. God judges our speech by what our intentions are. Abraham intended to deceive and did, even though he spoke the truth. Many folk do the same. They continually deceive, even though what they say is actually the truth. A host of ministers are no better. They manipulate actual facts and figures to make it appear they are doing more than they are. They lie just as Abraham did.

Fourth, the *orders of God*. Abraham's worst excuse was to blame his conduct on the way God ordered his situation. The statement "It came to pass, when God caused me to wander" (v. 13) shows this abominable excuse. Abraham makes it sound like God put him in circumstances that required the use of deceitful methods to protect himself. Barnhouse says, "There is a terrible meaning in this verb 'wander' which Abraham uses. The Hebrew word occurs exactly fifty times in Scripture and never in a good sense. It is used of animals going astray, of a drunken man reeling or staggering, of sinful seduction, of a prophet's lies causing the people to err, of the path of a lying heart. Six other words are translated 'wander,' any one of which Abraham might have used, but he used the worst word available [using the worst word made God look bad and to blame]. One of the terrible fruits of sin is that it casts the blame back upon God. Adam said, 'The woman thou gavest me . . . ' And Abraham here shows the traits inherited from Adam." No excuse is so unjustified as blaming God for our failure. Such excuses greatly dishonor the character of God.

Fifth, the *kindness of the deed*. Abraham also tried to excuse his deceit by claiming it was a kind act. "This is thy kindness which thou shalt show unto me" (v. 13) was the way Abraham described the agreement with Sarah to be deceitful. My, how gifted is humanity at labeling evil deeds with lovely names in order to justify the deeds. Pro-abortion has become pro-choice. Habitual drunkenness has been labeled with a respectable title of disease. No longer do we say folk are living in adultery when they live together without marriage. We call it a common law marriage. Homosexuality is not called an abomination (as God calls it) but simply another sexual orientation. Nice names for naughty deeds do not change a naughty deed to a nice deed. It only encourages more naughty deeds.

Note that this "kindness" was very one-sided. It was only for Abraham. How extremely selfish! What sort of kindness was Abraham showing Sarah? "True love would have made Abraham willing to sacrifice his life for Sarah" (Barnhouse). True love is not selfish. The application of "kindness" here is limited just like "pro-choice" in abortion. It is a one-way street. It is unkind to Sarah and no-choice for the unborn child.

When we try to excuse our evil, we make a fool of ourselves and expose defects in our character. Abraham certainly looked terrible in his contending about his conduct.

C. THE RECONCILING OF MEN

With Abraham's deceitfulness about Sarah causing strained relations between he and Abimelech, reconciliation is needed if these two men are going to get along together in the future. Fortunately, reconciliation did occur. To note the details of the reconciliation, we will look at the propitiating by Abimelech and the praying by Abraham.

Abraham

1. The Propitiating by Abimelech

Abimelech, to his credit, initiated the reconciliation of the two men. He did three things to propitiate Abraham and thus help to reconcile the two men. The three acts of propitiation were the presentation of gifts, the restoration of Sarah, and the invitation to dwell anywhere in Philistia.

The presentation. "And Abimelech took sheep, and oxen, and menservants, and womenservants, and gave them unto Abraham . . . [with] a thousand pieces of silver" (vv. 14,16). This was a most liberal gift. And Barnhouse says, "The Philistine king is now heaping coals of fire upon the head of Abraham." That Abimelech made the gift to Abraham and not the other way around really shames Abraham. But it is Abimelech, not Abraham, whose behavior is exemplary in Genesis 20.

The gifts to Abraham were Abimelech's way of acknowledging the wrongness of his taking Sarah. Yes, he was innocent in that Abraham and Sarah lied. But it was still wrong for a man to have another man's wife, and Abimelech was acknowledging that fact and bending over backwards to make things right. Abraham, on the other hand, tried to excuse his sin even though he was by far the greater sinner of the two in this episode and even though of the two he was the one who belonged to God. But when a saint is disobedient, the behavior of people of the world is often much better—to the shame of the saint and to the dishonoring of God. We who profess to know the Lord ought to show it with conduct that is far superior in character to that of the world. In this day and age that should not take much; but shamefully, professing Christendom too often has difficulty looking better than the world in the matter of conduct.

The gift of "a thousand pieces of silver" for "a covering" figures prominently in giving us some illustrations of the Gospel message in the episode of Genesis 20. So we will note here some Gospel lessons from this chapter in Genesis.

First, one man's sin (Abraham's sin) caused others (Abimelech) to sin. Romans 5:19 says, "For as by one man's disobedience many were made sinners."

Second, man sinned willfully. Abraham and Sarah sinned willfully just as did Adam and Eve and everyone after them.

Third, sin brought the condemnation of death upon the sinner. God told Abimelech that he was but a dead man for taking Sarah. Romans 6:23 says we are all under the condemnation of death because of sin.

Fourth, the way of salvation is revealed to man by the Word of God. It was the spoken Word of God that told Abimelech how he could be saved from his condemnation. It is the written Word of God that tells us how our soul can be saved.

Fifth, salvation was of grace. This is especially seen in Sarah's deliverance. Ephesians 2:8,9 emphasize this truth in soul salvation.

Sixth, one man's obedience (Abimelech's) caused others (Abraham and Sarah) to be made righteous in their living. Romans 5:19 says, "By the obedience of one shall many be made righteous."

Seventh, salvation provided a covering. The silver Abimelech gave to Abraham was to provide "a covering" (v. 16) to counter the evil that had been done. Isaiah 61:10 describes soul salvation covering thusly: "He [God] hath clothed me with the garments of salvation." God clothing Adam and Eve after their sin also pictures the same truth.

Eighth, salvation is by the redeeming blood. As most Bible students know, silver is used for redemption money in the Old Testament and, therefore, speaks of the blood of Christ.

Ninth, the redemption price was paid by the one who was sinned against. Here it is paid by Abimelech. In soul salvation it is paid by God.

The restoration. "And restored him Sarah his wife" (v. 14). From this restoration of Sarah to Abraham by Abimelech, we note three things: the proving of sincerity, the condemning of sin, and the rebuking of Sarah.

First, the *proving of sincerity.* God had ordered this restoration (v. 7) when speaking to Abimelech in a dream. When God told Abimelech his situation, Abimelech pleaded innocence. He said his heart was innocent and his hands were clean in the matter. The restoration of Sarah proves it! As we noted above, many people talk piously when all that is required at the time is talk. But when the time comes to translate the talk into walk, they do very poorly; for their piety is nothing but talk. Their talk is not sincere. Abimelech is a contrast to all of that poor behavior.

Second, the *condemning of sin*. The restoration of Sarah again shows us that Genesis 20, unlike our society, really condemns the evil of a man taking another's man wife. Previously in this chapter, Abimelech called such action "a great sin" (v. 9); and God so condemned the deed that He told Abimelech he was "but a dead man" for having Sarah (v. 3). But the Bible's condemnation of taking another man's wife is not the attitude of many about this conduct today. Society generally condones what Scripture condemns. Adultery is approved; wife swapping is acceptable; and divorce and remarrying someone else (generally another person's former mate) is so respected that even when one opposes it in the church, such opposition is often considered unforgiving and unloving.

Third, the *rebuking of Sarah*. When speaking to Sarah in restoring her to Abraham, Abimelech spoke of Abraham as "thy brother" (v. 16). That was a well deserved rebuke! Sarah had been in on the deceit and had said Abraham was her brother (v. 5). Abimelech reminds her of this deceptiveness in order to give her a needed rebuke. He had rebuked Abraham earlier, but now he gives Sarah a rebuke also.

Sin needs to be rebuked, not excused or watered down. Failure to rebuke sin encourages the guilty to think their conduct is acceptable, and it encourages them to sin some more. Our churches, by their failure to rebuke sin, have encouraged much sinful conduct when they—of all organizations—ought to be discouraging sinful conduct.

The invitation. "And Abimelech said, Behold, my land is

before thee: dwell where it pleaseth thee" (v. 15). The first time Abraham lied about Sarah being his sister, he was sent away (12:20) by the king he deceived. This time the king he deceived invited Abraham to stay in the land and dwell wherever he thought best.

One of the wise attitudes Abimelech evidences in inviting Abraham to stay in the land is his value of having a prophet of God in the midst. God had informed Abimelech that Abraham was a prophet and could pray for him (v. 7). Unlike some, Abimelech valued the presence of godly people in his country (Abraham being a prophet, not his deception, is in view here in his designation as godly). He was a wise man in this attitude. So many nations have been just the opposite. Instead of being kind to God's people, they have persecuted them. But such a wicked attitude by governments will result in loss of much blessing and the eventual destruction of a nation.

Our land certainly needs to take note here. It seems to be more interested in having the ungodly around than the godly. The laws being made today seem mostly to favor the wicked, not the righteous. Government leaders are making it increasingly clear that the righteous are not wanted.

2. The Praying by Abraham

"So Abraham prayed unto God: and God healed Abimelech, and his wife, and his maidservants; and they bare children. For the LORD had fast closed up all the wombs of the house of Abimelech, because of Sarah Abraham's wife" (vv. 17,18). Finally Abraham begins to act better. Until these last two verses in Genesis 20, Abraham has not performed well at all in this chapter. But somewhere between his excuses and his praying, Abraham had a change of heart and saw his wrong and got it straightened out with God. Otherwise his praying would not have been as successful (cp. Psalm 66:18).

God had told Abimelech earlier to restore Sarah to Abraham and then Abraham would pray for him (v. 7). There was a real need of prayer for Abimelech and his household. As we have noted earlier, God had brought a curse upon Abimelech's house because of Sarah being taken into his harem. Some sort of sickness had come upon the household of Abimelech which affected both the men and women and made having children impossible. They needed to be healed, and they were healed when Abraham prayed.

All of this drives home the important truth that immorality is plagued with various illnesses. But tell the world it is God's judgment upon immoral conduct, and they will laugh. But Abimelech did not laugh. He paid attention to God and got the sickness cleared up! Today we face the devastating disease of AIDS. Rooted in homosexuality, it is also spreading to the innocent via incidental contacts. Unless God intervenes, as He did in the case of Abimelech, the results will snowball into a horrible plague that could wipe out nations. Our text makes it very plain that God does indeed send physical illnesses when men depart from the moral laws of God. AIDS is without question the Divine judgment of God upon an immoral generation. Let people get on their knees in confession of their sins and then forsake their evil ways, and you will see a marvelous decrease in the AIDS problem.

Had Abraham prayed before he commenced his move from Hebron, all his praying now would be unnecessary. Many of the problems we spend a lot of time praying about and soliciting others to pray about would not have come if we had prayed earlier about our conduct. Prayer is a wonderful thing. But it is not to be used just to get us out of our troubles; it is to be used to keep us from getting into trouble.

XI.

SON OF PROMISE

GENESIS 21:1–19

THE PROMISED SON of Abraham and Sarah finally comes on the scene. After Abraham and Sarah had moved to Canaan, God had repeatedly promised them a son. He had even told them what to name the son. But they had to wait twenty-five years after moving to Canaan before the promised son was born.

Two main promises formed the covenant God gave to Abraham. They were the promise of the seed and of the soil. With the birth of Isaac, the promise of the seed began to be fulfilled long before—in fact, four hundred years before—the promise of the soil. Without question, this would be the preference of both Abraham and Sarah. The seed was more important to them than the soil. When Isaac was born, Abraham and Sarah were still only sojourners in the land, not owners. God had not yet given Abraham and Sarah "even a foot-breadth of the soil" (James Murphy). But it was not lack of soil that bothered them, it was lack of seed (cp. 15:2; 16:2).

The priority of interests which Abraham and Sarah had regarding the seed and the soil needs more emphasis in our materialistic age. Parents become so obsessed with making money, buying houses, cars, boats, stocks, and bonds that they ignore some of the most precious possessions God ever gave them, namely, their children. What blessings we miss by not spending much time with our children. Today, mothers give birth to them then hand them to the baby sitters and go off to work—so they can have more money to buy more things. Fathers are too busy with work and these "things" to hardly speak with the children, let alone spend quality time with them. But the seed is more important than the soil. Our children are more important than "things."

The seed is more important than the soil regarding another son, too; for the promise of a son for Abraham and Sarah—as important as that was—also involved the promise of The Son, Jesus Christ the Savior of mankind. Through the descendants of Isaac would come Christ, and how much more important it is to have The Seed, Jesus Christ, than any soil. Christ can save our souls, and soul salvation is more important than all the soil in the world. Jesus Himself told us that truth when He said, "For what shall it profit a man, if he shall gain the whole world, and lose his own soul?" (Mark 8:36).

In this study of Abraham's promised son, we will consider the birth of Isaac (vv. 1–8) and the belittling of Isaac (vv. 9–19).

A. THE BIRTH OF ISAAC

The birth of Isaac was one of the most significant and celebrated births ever recorded in the Scripture. Robert Candlish, a famed Scottish pastor of the 1800s, said, "If there be an occasion on earth fitted to call forth the songs of heaven, next to the birth of Jesus, and not second to the birth of his forerunner John, it is the birth of Isaac. Upon no event, between the fall and the incarnation, did the salvation of men more conspicuously depend."

In examining the birth of Isaac, we will note the character of God, the compliance of Abraham, the carol of Sarah, the celebration for Isaac, the coming of the Christ-child, and the conversion of sinners.

1. The Character of God

The announcement in Scripture of Isaac's birth emphasizes at least three important aspects of the character of God. It emphasized the faithfulness of God's Word, the greatness of God's power, and the deliberateness of God's actions.

The faithfulness of God's Word. "And the LORD visited

Sarah as he had said, and the LORD did unto Sarah as he had spoken. For Sarah conceived, and bare Abraham a son in his old age, at the set time of which God had spoken to him" (vv. 1,2). Three times in these two verses we are told that God acted just as He said He would ("as he had said . . . as he had spoken . . . which God had spoken"). In commenting on these verses, Barnhouse rightly said, "God is a God of His word. If He were not, the universe would fall apart."

A man's character is greatly honored when it can be said of him that he is a person of his word. Of no one can this be said more than of God! Joshua emphasized this truth when he said, "Not one thing hath failed of all the good things which the LORD your God spake concerning you; all are come to pass unto you, and not one thing hath failed thereof" (Joshua 23:14, cp. Joshua 21:45). God's Word had not failed even though difficulties sometimes seemed to predict failure. When God's promises are made, circumstances often mock. But the mocking will eventually stop, for all of God's promises will be fulfilled, for God's Word is true. God had promised Abraham and Sarah a son, but their circumstances were so bad that Sarah laughed at the promise. However, her laughter of unbelief turned to the laughter of great joy when the promise was fulfilled in the manner in which God said it would be.

We can trust God's Word if we can trust anything. Do not hesitate to build your creed, your convictions, your hopes, your consolations, your inspiration, your joys, and your all upon God's Word. It will not fail. We trust men's word today in many important matters of life. But men often fail. God never fails! His Word will ever abide faithful. Sarah finally and wisely came to the place where "she judged him faithful who had promised" (Hebrews 11:11), and we need to do likewise.

The greatness of God's power. "For Sarah conceived, and bare Abraham a son in his old age . . . And Abraham was an hundred years old, when his son Isaac was born unto him . . . I have born him a son in his old age" (vv. 2,5,7). Many times already we have had the truth of God's power emphasized in regards to the coming of Isaac. Now at his birth, we again have this truth emphasized. Isaac's birth was a miracle. Three times our text emphasizes the problem of age which required a miracle of God's great power to bring the birth to pass. Just as our text emphasized the faithfulness of God's Word in a threefold way, so our text emphasizes the greatness of God's power in a threefold way.

Our text only emphasizes the need of a miracle on Abraham's part regarding the coming of Isaac. But Scripture elsewhere tells us that Sarah also needed a miracle of Divine power to conceive and bear Isaac. Apostle Paul told us of the miracle needed in Sarah when he spoke of "the deadness of Sarah's womb" (Romans 4:19). Hebrews 11 likewise speaks of Sarah's inability. "Sarah herself received strength to conceive seed, and was delivered of a child when she was past age" (Hebrews 11:11). All of this emphasizes God's great power.

Frequently Scripture likes to emphasize the difficulty of the circumstances which confront the promises of God in order to show us the greatness of God's power. God's power is not just for easy circumstances—the extent of the faith of most of us—but it is also for the most difficult of circumstances. Yet, how little of this truth do we apply to our daily lives. Our prayers and our hopes are frequently an insult to God's power. Were others to judge the power of God by most of our prayers and expectations, they would conclude God was much weaker than man.

The deliberateness of God's actions. "Sarah conceived, and bare Abraham a son . . . at the set time of which God had spoken to him" (v. 2). God always moves at a deliberate pace. He never rushes around in a panic as we often do, nor does He act delinquently as we also often do. His pace is according to His "set" times. This means He is always on time, in time, at the right time, at the best time, and at the promised time. Abraham and Sarah, however, did not readily submit to God's set time. Impatient in waiting for God's set time, they resorted to the scheme of having a child via Hagar. But that was the wrong time as well as the wrong way, and all it did was bring trouble and show the folly of not submitting to God's set times.

If we want to keep our lives from many troubles, we must submit to God's set times and adjust our walk to God's cadence. Satan, however, is ever attacking God's set times. The temptation scene with Jesus Christ evidences this fact. There Satan urged Christ to receive the kingdom from him right then rather than receiving it from God later at God's set time. Satan continues to attack God's set times today. One area in which he especially attacks today is God's set time in the matter of sex. God's set time for that is after marriage. Satan, however, urges mankind not to wait till marriage. But the consequences of listening to Satan have made our nation a moral cesspool and have ruined and wrecked countless lives; all of which reminds us forcefully of the folly of not submitting to God's set times.

2. The Compliance of Abraham

"And Abraham called the name of his son that was born unto him, whom Sarah bare to him, Isaac. And Abraham circumcised his son Isaac being eight days old, as God had commanded him" (vv. 3,4). Two duties came to Abraham when Isaac was born: naming his son and circumcising his son. God had specified the name for the child, and He had specified the act and the time of circumcising the child. Abraham complied wonderfully to God's orders, for he did exactly what God told him to do.

To some, Abraham's obedience may seem to be nothing special and to even look easy. But no obedience is without difficulties, and difficulties would be present in doing these two tasks.

First, there were *difficulties in regards to the name*. The name Isaac was not nearly as impressive in meaning as the names Abraham, Sarah, and Ishmael. Abraham meant father of multitudes, Sarah meant princess, and Ishmael meant God hears. But Isaac only meant laughter. However, Abraham did not change the name to some name with a more impressive meaning. He did not give "him some other name of a more pompous signification" (Matthew Henry) as many would do today who are more interested in impressing the world than God. No, he named him what God wanted him named.

Second, there were *difficulties in regards to circumcision.* The cries of Isaac and the protests of those opposing circumcising such a small child could cause difficulty for Abraham in circumcising Isaac, but he did it anyway. And he did this duty at the exact time God specified. Matthew Henry said, "God had kept time in performing the promise, and therefore Abraham must keep time in obeying the precept [of circumcision]."

The only acceptable obedience is to do exactly what God wants us to do. Yet, we so often try to alter, amend, and revise His orders. Such action spells rebellion. The submissive heart will do exactly what God says without complaint, knowing that God knows what is best.

3. The Carol of Sarah

"And Sarah said, God hath made me laugh, so that all that hear will laugh with me. And she said, Who would have said unto Abraham, that Sarah should have given children suck? for I have born him a son in his old age" (vv. 6,7).

Sarah's comments about the birth of Isaac, though not lengthy, are considered a song (especially are they a carol here; for carol means a "song of joy, rapture, or gladness" which is what Sarah's song certainly was). Her song is considered a forerunner of the song which Hannah sung after the birth of Samuel (I Samuel 2:1–10) and of the song which Mary sung shortly after she had conceived Christ (Luke 1:46–55). That Sarah's comments are a song is seen in "the use of a [Hebrew] poetical word (*millel*) for 'said,' instead of the more common [Hebrew] words (*dibber* or *amar*); and also in the appearance of regular parallelism of the members of the sentence" (F. C. Cook).

In this song we again see a play on words in Scripture. In speaking words of great rejoicing, Sarah uses the meaning of

SON OF PROMISE

Isaac's name to express her great delight over having a son. She tells of her laughing (Isaac means laughter) at the wonderfulness of having a son. When God blesses, the laughter of joy is real and virtuous; but the laughter of the world is far different.

Sarah's rejoicing over having a child is not difficult to understand. When we first met Sarah in Scripture, her barrenness was emphasized. "But Sarai was barren; she had no child" (Genesis 11:30). This was a great stigma to a woman in Bible times. They could accept about anything better than barrenness. So with the coming of Isaac, she had a heavy reproach of many, many years removed. That would bring much rejoicing indeed.

Sarah's song is a good song. God's blessings inspire good songs. We note three good things of which Sarah's song spoke. It spoke of the power of God, the witness for God, and the responsibility from God. What a different message is found in this song than in the songs of the world and even in the many new songs being sung in church today.

The power of God. "Who would have said unto Abraham, that Sarah should have given children suck? For I have born him a son in his old age" (v. 7). We earlier noted this statement by Sarah as one of the three times the power of God was emphasized in the reporting of Isaac's birth in Scripture. This part of Sarah's song tells us that Sarah has learned that nothing is too hard for God. Sarah did not always believe this. When God gave the promise about a year earlier, Sarah had laughed at the promise (18:12). God rebuked her laughter by saying, "Is anything too hard for the LORD?" (18:14). Sarah's song says she has now learned her lesson about God's power.

Sarah's song reminds us that God is able to do "exceeding abundantly above all that we ask or think" (Ephesians 3:20). Her song also reminds us that not many folk encourage one to believe God has such great power. "Who would have said?" tells us that fact. The world around us does little to encourage our faith but God does much. Therefore, let us pay more heed to what God says than to what unbelieving man says.

The witness for God. "All that hear will laugh with me" (v. 6). Note it is not laugh *at* me but *with* me. Sarah is not being mocked, but her life is now a witness of God's power. When Sarah's unbelief was replaced by belief, great things happened in her life; and, as a result, "all that hear" will rejoice in God's blessing. Her faith caused others to honor God by rejoicing ("laugh with me") in what great things He had done. This is a challenge to our witness for God. Do what people hear of us cause them to rejoice in the Lord or to reject the Lord? Does it cause them to honor faith in God or belittle it? Let us so live that what people hear of us will give much honor to God.

The responsibility from God. The responsibility truth taught in the song comes from the words "given children suck [nursed children]." Sarah would have available through her servants many who could have done this task for her. But in spite of the fact she was the wife of the head sheik of a large estate, she assumed the mother duties herself. That is a rebuke for our day. Mother duties are so despised today that if a woman wants to be a mother—that is, stay home and take care of the kids instead of being a so-called career woman—she is looked down upon as some sort of second rate individual who lacks ambition and "self-esteem" (a favorite expression of our sick age). But God thinks differently! The women who scorn mother responsibilities will be in for a shock when they stand before God. What choice blessing to have children, and what important responsibility to be a mother to them. Never play down the duties of motherhood. Exalt them. God does!

4. The Celebration for Isaac

"And the child grew, and was weaned: and Abraham made a great feast the same day that Isaac was weaned" (v. 8). The birth of Isaac was followed by the healthy development of the child. This is fittingly recorded right along with the report of his birth. Isaac grew up. He did not stay in babyhood all his life like many saints do. The average saint does not evidence he or she has ever been weaned spiritually. They have never grown up, but they are still in the baby crib and on the bottle. Hebrews helps us understand this situation, "For every one that useth milk is unskillful in the word of righteousness; for he is a babe. But strong meat [solid food] belongeth to them that are of full age, even those who by reason of use have their senses exercised to discern both good and evil" (Hebrews 5:13,14). Those in the spiritual babe/milk stage have considerable trouble discerning right and wrong. In observing the difficulty which most professing Christians have in discerning right and wrong, it is obvious that most professing Christians are in the babe category. If they were to grow up, it would indeed be a cause to celebrate.

5. The Coming of the Christ-child

The birth of Isaac was a type of the birth of Jesus Christ. We should not be surprised at this fact; for, as we noted earlier, the most important seed promised to Abraham and Sarah in the covenant was not Isaac but Jesus Christ. The covenant would lose its worth if Jesus Christ was not in it.

We will note five areas in which Isaac's birth was a type of Christ's birth. These areas are the mother of the child, the name of the child, the time of the birth of the child, the circumcising of the child, and the joy in the child.

The mother of the child. Four parallels exist between Sarah, the mother of Isaac, and Mary, the mother of our Lord.

First, each was given a Divine revelation of the child's birth before they conceived (Genesis 18:10–14; Luke 1:26–33).

Second, each had a Divine miracle worked in them physically in order to give birth to the promised child (Genesis 18:10–14; Luke 1:35).

Third, each recognized the great difficulties of their having a child as God promised (Genesis 18:11,12; Luke 1:34).

Fourth, each was given a heavenly message about the power of God being able to overcome their situation so they could have the child as promised (Genesis 18:14; Luke 1:37).

The name of the child. Three parallels exist here in regards to the name of Isaac and Jesus.

First, both Isaac and Jesus were given their names before they were born (Genesis 17:19; Matthew 1:21).

Second, both Isaac and Jesus had their names revealed to the husband of their mother before they were born (Genesis 17:19; Matthew 1:20,21).

Third, the names of both Isaac and Jesus had a twofold meaning. They spoke of the failure of man and also promised a blessing to man.

In regards to failure, Isaac's name meant "laughter"; and the laughter of unbelief (a failure to believe God's Word) was associated at times with his coming (Genesis 18:11,12). When telling Joseph to name the child Jesus, the angel said, "For he shall save his people from their sins [a failure to live righteously]" (Matthew 1:21).

In regards to blessing, Isaac's name, meaning laughter, promised rejoicing which came because of blessing. The angel telling Joseph that Jesus would be the Savior promised the greatest blessing man could ever have.

The time of the birth of the child. The punctualness of God is emphasized conspicuously in the birth of both Isaac and our Savior. As we noted at the beginning of this chapter, this fact about Isaac was emphasized in the report of his birth—"at the set time of which God had spoken" (v. 2). This same truth concerning the time of Christ's birth is emphasized in Galatians where Paul writes, "But when the fullness of the time was come, God sent forth his Son, made of a woman, made under the law" (Galatians 4:4). God is always punctual in fulfilling His promises. If we are anxious about an unfulfilled promise, it is because we are looking at the wrong clock.

The circumcising of the child. Scripture reports the circumcising of both Isaac and Christ, and it reports that both were done on the eighth day as Divine precept prescribed (Genesis

21:4; Luke 2:21). Hence, parental obedience was conspicuous in the birth of both Isaac and Jesus in regards to this Divine precept. A lot of today's problems would be prevented if we had more parental obedience in raising children.

The joy in the child. Great joy conspicuously accompanied the birth of both Isaac and Jesus.

In regards to Isaac, our text tells us how Sarah rejoiced (v. 6). With the stigma of her barrenness and with the long wait for her son, her joy over the birth was obviously extremely great.

In regards to Jesus Christ, the message of the angels expressed great joy at His birth. They said we "bring you good tidings of great joy" (Luke 2:10). While Christmas has been terribly commercialized, yet the spirit of joy that permeates the season can not be accounted for apart from the fact that the birth of Christ is a source of great joy.

6. The Conversion of Sinners

Not only does the birth of Isaac foreshadow and picture the birth of Christ, but it also is a picture of the new birth which is the spiritual birth that takes place when a sinner puts his faith in Jesus Christ for his soul's salvation. It is the same birth which Jesus Christ referred to when He told Nicodemus, "Ye must be born again" (John 3:7).

We note four ways in which the conversion of sinners is seen in Isaac's birth: a miracle was performed, a deadness was present, a new creature was produced, a heritage was procured.

A miracle was performed. As we noted earlier, Scripture repeatedly reminds us of the Divine miracle factor in Isaac's birth. In the promises of the birth of Isaac and in the account of Isaac's birth, the miracle factor is made plain. Abraham and Sarah could not produce Isaac in their own strength. Hence, God had to work a Divine miracle to bring Isaac on the scene.

In like manner, Scripture repeatedly shows us the inability of man to bring about his own new birth. We cannot save ourselves; for we are "without strength" (Romans 5:6) and "we are all as an unclean thing, and all our righteousnesses are as filthy rags" (Isaiah 64:6). Therefore, only a miracle can save us. And that miracle occurs when the sinner comes to Jesus Christ for his soul's salvation.

A deadness was present. Abraham was considered dead in his ability to father children (Romans 4:19), and Sarah was considered dead in her ability to conceive and bear children (Ibid.). In like manner, the unsaved are "dead in trespasses and sins" (Ephesians 2:1); and it was "when we were dead in sins, [that God] hath quickened us [made us alive] together with Christ" (Ephesians 2:5).

A new creature was produced. Isaac was not Ishmael reformed and made over. Isaac was an entirely new creature. So Paul tells us that "if any man be in Christ, he is a new creature; old things are passed away; behold, all things are become new" (II Corinthians 5:17). Jesus told Nicodemus, "Ye must be born again" (John 3:7), not reformed, made over, redecorated, etc.

Because some pervert the "old things are passed away; behold, all things are become new" to encourage such things as remarriage after divorce if one has been saved since being divorced, we want to note here what does not change and what does change when a person is saved.

First, *what does not change*. When a man gets saved, his age does not change, his marital status past or present does not change, his physical disabilities do not change—if he is missing a leg, he will continue to miss a leg; if he has false teeth, he will continue to have false teeth; if he is blind, he will continue to be blind, etc., etc.

Second, *what does change*. When a man gets saved, there is at least a threefold change. First, his *destiny* changes. Before coming to Christ, one is headed for eternity in hell fire. After coming to Christ all of that is changed, for the saved one is headed for heaven, not hell. What a glorious change! Second, his *deportment* changes. One of the most notable evidences of salvation is the change from bad to good behavior. Third, his *devotion* changes. One's interests, affections, desires, objectives, and values will change. Jesus Christ will be revered, honored, and loved.

A heritage was procured. By virtue of his birth, Isaac automatically gained an inheritance. And what a great inheritance it was! His father Abraham was not poor. He owned a vast estate of livestock and servants. In like manner, by virtue of the new birth, the redeemed gain a great inheritance. Their heavenly Father is not poor either. He possesses an even greater estate than Abraham, to say the least. We can even compare it in terms of livestock, if you please. Abraham owned cattle on a few hills. But the Psalmist says God owns the "cattle upon a thousand hills" (Psalm 50:10). Isaac was an heir of a man, but believers are "heirs of God, and joint heirs with Christ" (Romans 8:17). The heritage salvation brings to the redeemed is so great that the human mind cannot fully comprehend it. We once heard a preacher say, "There ain't nothing the Lord ain't got that I ain't gonna get when I get to heaven. Now that ain't good English, but it sure am good theology." We agree on both accounts.

With such a tremendous heritage, let the redeemed not become so taken up with the material of this world that they lose sight of the tremendous inheritance that is coming their way in eternity. In eternity, God will have no poor children! And taxes will not be a problem either.

B. THE BELITTLING OF ISAAC
Ishmael did not like Isaac coming into Abraham's home. For fourteen years Ishmael had been the darling of the home (with the exception of Sarah). But when Isaac came into the home, things changed—Ishmael was no longer the sole object of affections. Furthermore, and even more importantly, Isaac's presence challenged Ishmael's claim of heirship to Abraham. Ishmael's inheritance rights were unchallenged when he was the only son

of Abraham. But now it was evident that the son who was the heir was the son of Sarah, not Hagar. All of this change in Ishmael's situation resulted in his mocking Isaac. This belittling of Isaac became such a problem that it eventually necessitated Abraham taking serious action to stop the problem.

To examine this mocking of Isaac, we will note the severity of the mocking, the scope of the mocking, the separation from the mocker, and the saving of the mocker.

1. The Severity of the Mocking

"And Sarah saw the son of Hagar the Egyptian, which she had born unto Abraham, mocking. Wherefore she said unto Abraham, Cast out this bondwoman and her son; for the son of this bondwoman shall not be heir with my son, even with Isaac" (vv. 9,10). We note the severity of this mocking in three ways: in the record of it in the New Testament, in the repetition of it from the word renderings, and in the reaction to it by Sarah.

Severity in the record of it. The Hebrew word translated "mocking" does not necessarily have to be interpreted in a negative sense. It comes from the same root word as the word Isaac. It means to laugh. As a result, some translators over the years have interpreted it far differently than hostile action. As an example, the Septuagint went so far as to translate it "playing with Isaac," which was a poor translation indeed. But the interpretation of the meaning of the word in this text is not one we have to be uncertain about. The meaning is forever finalized by the Apostle Paul when he says "persecuted" (Galatians 4:29) when referring to Ishmael's mocking. "Persecuted" says that the mocking was severe, that Ishmael was being very hostile towards Isaac.

Severity in the repetition of it. The mocking of Ishmael was not just a once only act occurring at the weaning of Isaac (v. 8) as some think. It was a repeated action. Leupold emphasizes this character of the mocking by translating "mocking" as "always mocking." Wuest does likewise by translating "persecuted" in Galatians 4:29 as "constantly persecuting," which is proper because the word is in the imperfect tense. The continuous habit of the mocking makes the mocking something more than a harmless bit of ridicule at a celebration. It shows more than a passing emotion, but rather it shows a deep-seated heart attitude which says Ishmael's belittling of Isaac had a lot of venom in it.

Severity in the reaction to it. "Wherefore [because of the mocking] she said unto Abraham, Cast out this bondwoman and her son" (v. 10). Sarah's reaction to the mocking was very pronounced. While she did not have warm feelings for Ishmael, hardly would such a strong demand be made if the mocking was just playful and harmless. But Sarah saw danger in the mocking. She was concerned about the harm it might cause Isaac and about Isaac remaining the heir of the covenant. So when telling Abraham to cast Ishmael and his mother out, she mentioned this concern. "For the son of this bondwoman shall not be heir with my son, even with Isaac" (Ibid.).

Mockers do not stop with verbal attacks especially when verbal attacks are continuous as here. Sooner or later physical force will follow when opportunity permits—this is the nature of persecution. Therefore, Ishmael's mocking warned of peril for the young child Isaac. His constant belittling of Isaac implied thinking which said, "Get rid of Isaac, and the inheritance is mine." Sarah's awareness of this serious peril is seen in her reaction. Ishmael's descendants still verbally and physically mock and thus imperil Isaac's descendants in the Middle East. And the intent is still the same—it is to gain some of that inheritance. They want Israel's land.

2. The Scope of the Mocking

Mocking Isaac involved a good deal more than just Isaac. It represented a wicked heart attitude which made the mocking of Isaac also an attack upon the people, the power, the promises, and the provision of God.

It attacked the people of God. Isaac is an important representative of the people of God. Hence, Ishmael's mocking of Isaac was an attack upon God's people. The people of God are hated by evil. "But as then he that was born after the flesh persecuted him that was born after the Spirit, even so it is now" (Galatians 4:29). This explains a lot of the hostility the world exhibits towards believers and the church. The world may try to disguise it as something else, but the fact is the world hates God's people. Therefore, we must not be surprised when the world attacks God's people. Just because we serve God well does not mean we will be praised by the world. To the contrary, we may be especially attacked by the world. Matthew Henry said, "God's favorites are often the world's laughing-stock."

It attacked the power of God. Isaac was a result of a miracle of Divine power. Therefore, in mocking Isaac, Ishmael evidenced he had no respect for the great work God had accomplished through Abraham and Sarah. This is always the habit of this evil world. It ever belittles the work of God. This belittling of God's work was pronouncedly present when the Jews were rebuilding the wall of Jerusalem under Nehemiah's leadership. The enemy "mocked" (Nehemiah 4:1) the rebuilding and went so far in their belittling of this work as to say that "if a fox go up, he shall even break down their stone wall" (Nehemiah 4:3). We see the same belittling of God's work today from the world. Let the church have special meetings that result in souls being saved and character changed, and the world will ridicule it as a bit of religiosity that accomplishes little. But let the world organize a project for reforming some segment of society; and you will hear all sorts of accolades praising it as a great and mighty work; even though all it does is cost taxpayers more money. With this in mind, let us not be discouraged by the mocking evaluations of the world. Evaluate things as God does, not as a mocking world does.

It attacked the promises of God. Isaac was to be the progenitor of a great nation and a provider of great blessings to the world. In mocking Isaac, Ishmael evidenced no respect for the promises. Every generation has their Ishmael characters who mock the promises of God's Word. From the promise of judgment upon sin to the promise of the return of Christ, the world mocks. But "Whoso despiseth the word shall be destroyed" (Proverbs 13:13).

It attacked the provision of God. The great provision in Isaac was the Savior, Jesus Christ. Thus, Ishmael's mocking manifested "a spirit entirely out of sympathy with the best treasures known to the household of Abraham, the hope of the coming Savior" (Leupold). People are still mocking Christ. They mocked Him at the crucifixion (Mark 15:31), and He is mocked in our day. But no mocking will get you in more trouble than the mocking of Jesus Christ.

3. The Separation From the Mocker

Ishmael's mocking of Isaac resulted in the separation of Ishmael and his mother Hagar from Abraham's household. Abraham had once before experienced separation from close family members when Lot was separated from him (13:9). Now he experiences it again in the separation of Ishmael from his home.

In examining this separation, we will consider the demand for it, the distress about it, the decree for it, the doing of it, and the declaration in it.

The demand for it. "Wherefore she [Sarah] said unto Abraham, Cast out this bondwoman and her son; for the son of this bondwoman shall not be heir with my son, even with Isaac" (v. 10). We note three things in this demand: the righteousness in it, the reaping in it, and the recognition in it.

First, the *righteousness* in the demand. This demand for separation was justified. But because we have noted this fact above and will note more about it a bit later, we will only briefly review here that the separation was needed because of the seriousness of the mocking. The mocking threatened the life of Isaac and his obtaining the inheritance. The mocking attacked the people the power, the promises, and the provision of God. Such attacks cannot be tolerated by society without greatly hurting society.

Second, the *reaping* in the demand. The demand for separation reflects the fact that Sarah again is reaping what she sowed. She was the one who sowed the wild oats of immorality when she initiated the scheme of Abraham having a son via Hagar. But when Hagar became pregnant, she despised Sarah which really upset Sarah. That was the first conspicuous reaping she did. Now she is doing some more reaping.

Unholy plans, like Sarah's plan of having Abraham have a child via Hagar, seem so promising. Even though they give troublesome indications that they do not fit God's plan, we resort to twisted rationalizing to justify following the unholy pathway anyway. But we cannot obtain God's best without living God's way. The future will be filled with great trouble if we go the way of the flesh, and those troubles will cause us to loathe the day we chose to go that way. Be it a marriage, job, money-making scheme, choice of a school, or other decision, when we go contrary to God's will, we will soon discover what Sarah discovered; namely, that which we thought so great will be absolutely intolerable to us.

Third, the *recognition* in the demand. Note that in this demand, Sarah calls Hagar "bondwoman." She gave Hagar to Abraham for a "wife" (Genesis 16:3). But God never recognized the "wife" designation; and when the scheme turned sour, Sarah also stopped recognizing the "wife" designation. Sooner or later we will recognize God's designations are the right ones. But the worst way to finally recognize them is through the bitter results of our rebellion.

The distress about it. "And the thing was very grievous in Abraham's sight because of his son" (v. 11). Abraham is also experiencing chickens coming home to roost. He followed a wrong pathway to obtain a son, and now it is causing him much grief. Ishmael has been around for at least seventeen years (if Isaac was weaned at three, then Ishmael was at least seventeen here; for he was fourteen years older than Isaac); and in that amount of time, Abraham had his heart very wrapped up in Ishmael in spite of the coming of Isaac. To send Ishmael out of the household is going to tear a big chunk out of Abraham's heart.

Oh, how we need to be careful about where we put our affections. And how careful we need to be about doing things which cause us to put our affections in the wrong place (such as Abraham's having a child via Hagar). We cannot put our affections on the wrong objects without some day having a terrible heart-wrenching experience. What grief Abraham could have avoided had he not gotten involved in the unholy union with Hagar. Folk, in every age, who have married outside the will of God know much about this grief.

The decree for it. "And God said unto Abraham, Let it not be grievous in thy sight because of the lad, and because of thy bondwoman; in all that Sarah hath said unto thee, hearken unto her voice; for in Isaac shall thy seed be called. And also of the son of the bondwoman will I make a nation, because he is thy seed" (vv. 12,13). Some may be surprised that God approved of Sarah's demand. When we first read of Sarah's demand and then read of God's approval, we are tempted to conclude that great injustice was done. It seems so cruel to throw out a teenage boy and his mother just because he had been mocking his baby brother. But God never acts unjustly; and, as we noted earlier, Ishmael's mocking was something far more than just harmless teasing. It represented a great dishonoring of important spiritual truths, and it also represented a serious threat upon Isaac's life and upon Abraham's willingness to give the full inheritance to Isaac. "Ishmael . . . did afford something for nature's affections to entwine themselves around, thus furnishing a more difficult task for Abraham to perform afterwards" (C. H. MackIntosh).

Those things which hinder our performance of the will of

God and which hinder the work of God need to be dealt with firmly. We cannot be gentle with these things, or they will defeat us and greatly dishonor God. Compromise, however, always wants to tolerate these things. It does not want to make a clean break with evil. In our personal lives, it causes us to refuse to give up friendships and habits that hurt our spiritual growth and service. In the church, it causes us to refuse to deal with the Ishmael dissidents who continually cause a bad spirit in church which keeps the Holy Spirit from working in the church. If we are going to have the victory over evil, do a work for God, and be steadfast in obeying God, we will have to separate from our Ishmaels even though it is a "very grievous" thing to do.

It is important to note that our text shows us that though difficult our tasks may be, God will always give us some encouragement for the doing of them. In this case, God promised Abraham that Ishmael would become a nation (v. 13). This said that though he was cast out, he would survive and not die. That would help Abraham immensely in dealing with Ishmael. Look for those encouragements from God when He gives you difficult assignments. Rather than complain about the duty, busy yourself in discovering the encouragements God has given to do your duty and then meditate on them. It will make a big difference in the character of your performance.

The doing of it. "Abraham rose up early in the morning, and took bread, and a bottle of water, and gave it unto Hagar, putting it on her shoulder, and [gave her] the child [a Hebrew word used for person from youth all the way to young manhood], and sent her away: and she departed" (v. 14). We note the promptness and the provisions in Abraham's doing as God commanded.

First, the *promptness*. As distasteful as his duty was, Abraham did it promptly. Promptness is seen in the "rose up early in the morning." God told him what to do and Abraham did not delay. Any delay would have made obedience that much more difficult and could have broken down his will to do the task. Delay assaults the will of men. We cannot allow our desire to do

God's will to be assaulted continually by delay, for our desire cannot survive delay well. Promptness is always the best way to dispose of distasteful duties. Postponing them, whining about them, or trying to get out of them is a very poor way to take care of these duties.

Second, the *provisions*. Abraham gave Hagar and Ishmael bread and a skin of water as their provisions for leaving the household. The provisions Abraham gives Hagar and Ishmael certainly seems stingy and mean. But Charles Simeon has a good answer for this. He says, "The provision which he gave them for their journey, was not such as might have been expected from a person of his opulence; but we can have no doubt but that he acted in this by the divine direction, and that the mode of their dismission as well as their dismission itself, was intended for their humiliation and punishment."

The declaration in it. In contrasting Ishmael and Isaac in Galatians 4:22–31, the Apostle Paul declares that these "things are an allegory" (Galatians 4:24) about the separation of law and grace in the matter of salvation. Ishmael, being a child of a bondmaid, represents the law. Isaac, being a child of a freewoman, represents grace—and it is one born apart from the law that is the heir. So the lesson of this allegory is that we are saved by grace not by the law. How mighty thankful we can be that salvation is by grace and not by keeping the law. The law cannot not save a soul, but grace (which comes via faith) can save anyone (Galatians 2:16). However, there are many religions which do not want to separate from Ishmael. They want works included in salvation. But salvation is "by grace . . . not of works" (Ephesians 2:8,9).

4. The Saving of the Mocker

God is faithful, and He demonstrated it in saving Ishmael from death shortly after He ordered his expulsion from Abraham's house. God had promised Abraham that Ishmael would become a nation (v. 13). The fulfillment of that promise looked in jeopardy shortly after it was made. But no matter how bleak the prospects may be for the fulfilling of a Divine promise, it will be fulfilled!

The things our text mentions which are involved in the saving of Ishmael from death give us such a good picture of the salvation of sinners that we are going to look at Ishmael's deliverance from that standpoint. We will note the destitution of the sinner, the compassion for the sinner, the proclamation for the sinner, the illumination of the sinner, and appropriation by the sinner, and the evangelization of the sinner.

The destitution of the sinner. "She departed, and wandered in the wilderness of Beer-sheba. And the water was spent in the bottle, and she cast the child under one of the shrubs. And she went, and sat her down over against him [apart from him] a good way off, as it were a bowshot; for she said, Let me not see the death of the child. And she over against him sat [apart from him], and lifted up her voice, and wept" (vv. 14–16). We will note three ways the destitution of the sinner is seen in these verses. They are the lost, lifelessness, and lamentation conditions of the sinner as reflected in Hagar and Ishmael.

First, *lost.* "Wandered" indicates this. Here it means Hagar "lost her way" (Whitelaw). Likewise, the sinner is "lost" not knowing where he came from (the sinners' theory of evolution tells us that fact) or where he is going. Hagar was, of course, Ishmael's guide. Her being lost is a good picture of the guides the world is following today. It is the blind leading the blind.

Second, *lifelessness.* They were without water. Water was life. Ishmael is left to die because they lack water. "The wages of sin is death" (Romans 6:23) for the sinner.

Third, *lamentation.* Hagar "lifted up her voice, and wept." That Ishmael also cried out is discovered when God later says He "heard the voice of the lad" (v. 17). Sin produces great sorrow. And when the sinner comes to the end of his way, there will be much lamentation as "weeping and gnashing of teeth" (Matthew 8:12; 22:13; 24:51; and 25:30) attests.

The compassion for the sinner. "And God heard the voice of the lad . . . God hath heard the voice of the lad where he is" (v. 17). We have another play on words. "God heard" is the meaning of Ishmael's name. Here it speaks of the compassion of God. The compassion of God is great. God "so loved the world" (John 3:16) that He provided a way of salvation. "God commendeth [proved] his love toward us, in that, while we were yet sinners, Christ died for us" (Romans 5:8). God's compassion is all of grace. Ishmael certainly did not deserve to have God hear his cries, for Ishmael had despised the things of God. Yet, God in compassion still heard and took action to save. Truly, "by grace are ye saved" (Ephesians 2:8); and "not by works of righteousness which we have done, but according to his mercy he saved us" (Titus 3:5).

The proclamation for the sinner. "And the angel of God called to Hagar out of heaven, and said unto her, What aileth thee, Hagar? fear not; for God hath heard the voice of the lad where he is. Arise, lift up the lad, and hold him in thine hand; for I will make him a great nation" (vv. 17,18). This message from heaven was filled with great truths which all sinners need. We note four of these truths.

First, it *rebuked sin.* "What aileth thee, Hagar?" is a question that rebukes failure (cp. Isaiah 22:1). In salvation, the first message we must always preach is the failure of man to live righteously. The sinner must be brought face to face with his sin if he is ever going to listen to God about how to be saved.

Second, it *removed fear.* "Fear not" is part of the message of salvation. When Christ was born, the angels' message was "fear not" (Luke 2:10). When salvation comes on the scene, fear is removed. The fear of the second death will be taken away.

Third, it *raised the sinner.* Hagar was instructed to "lift up the lad." The Gospel message if heeded (as Hagar heeded the message) will always "lift" the sinner. The world, however, has no message that will "lift" the sinner. The only message the world has lowers the sinner.

Fourth, it *reported a great future*. "I will make of him a great nation." Only the Gospel message can promise man a great future. And it is a great future indeed—all eternity in heaven with God.

The illumination of the sinner. "And God opened her eyes, and she saw a well of water" (v. 19). A well of water that was necessary to save Ishmael was right near them, but God must illuminate, or Ishmael will perish. The same is true regarding the sinner and salvation. Though the message of salvation may be near, though the sinner may sit in church and hear it week after week, the Holy Spirit must open the understanding of the sinner in order for him to comprehend the Gospel message. Today we seem to have forgotten or are ignoring this fact in our preaching. Instead we think that the more clever our argument the more likely people will get saved. But that is not a Scriptural idea. We can give the best of messages, the most logical of salvation arguments; but until the Spirit of God opens the eyes of the sinner to understand, our message will not sink in. We are to give the best message and argument possible, but we must also look to God to open the sinner's eyes to understand the message. When folk are saved, we cannot take the credit. It is a Divine work.

The appropriation by the sinner. "And she went, and filled the bottle with water" (v. 19). Showing Hagar the well was one thing; getting water from the well was another thing. In like manner, bringing the water to Ishmael was one thing; Ishmael drinking was another. Hagar must appropriate the truth and get water from the well; Ishmael must appropriate truth and drink the water. We must have our eyes open to the truth, but we must then apply the truth if it is going to do us any good.

The evangelization of the sinner. "And gave the lad drink" (v. 19). When Hagar obtained the water, she gave it to Ishmael, the one who was perishing. Hagar did with the water what we must do with the message of salvation—we must give it to those who are perishing. It is the water of life for their souls.

Many think other things besides the water of life need to be given to the perishing. Some would fix up the area in which Ishmael was lying down and make a nice comfortable bed for him with more shade. But that would not save him—neither will a Gospel of improved environment save souls. Some would tell Ishmael all about the desert—but like education, that would not save him, either. It only makes the sinner an educated sinner. The sinner needs the water of life if he is to be saved. Stick with the Gospel message if you would give sinners true help. The apostate churches have many programs to meet the temporal needs of mankind, but these churches never give out the water of life, the Gospel of Jesus Christ, to meet the spiritual needs of mankind. The world loves these programs that emphasize the temporal and makes much over them, but they are like trying to help Ishmael without giving him the water of life.

Hagar could not have helped Ishmael if she had not filled her vessel with water. This is a good and needed truth for preachers and teachers to ponder. On too many occasions, we have heard preachers and Sunday School teachers try to preach a sermon or teach a class when it was evident they had not first filled their vessels with water. Before you teach or preach—get a message! Go to the water of the Word and fill your vessel full so you can give the listener a soul satisfying draught of Divine truth. Empty-bottle ministries abound; and it is time a lot of preachers and teachers got out of the seminars, symposiums, workshops, etc., and got into the Word of God instead. Then they would have something worthwhile to say on Sunday!

XII.

SUMMIT WITH ABIMELECH

GENESIS 21:22-34

ABRAHAM HAS A second encounter with Abimelech, the king of the Philistine city of Gerar (his first meeting with Abimelech was recorded in Genesis 20, a meeting we dealt with two chapters previous). As a matter of introduction to this second meeting, it is helpful to note three features about it.

First, the *importance* of this meeting. The importance of this second encounter is emphasized by the fact that "Phicol the chief captain of his [Abimelech's] host [army]" (v. 22) accompanied Abimelech as he came to meet with Abraham. Thus the meeting took on the character of a summit; for it was a meeting of two men who were the heads of their respective domains—Abimelech was king of Gerar, and Abraham was the head sheik of a large estate.

Second, the *time* of this meeting. This second encounter with Abimelech took place approximately four to six years after the first meeting; for the summit "came to pass at that time" (v. 22) which was the time following the weaning of Isaac and the casting out of Ishmael, events we have just finished studying. The first meeting occurred about a year before Isaac was born; so with Isaac being weaned from three to five years after his birth, it would make the time between the two meetings about four to six years. Therefore, Abraham would then be 104 to 106 years old at the time of the second meeting, for he was 100 at the birth of Isaac. Much had happened in the life of Abraham during those four to six years. And, as we will note shortly, it was all very impressive to Abimelech.

Summit With Abimelech

Third, the *contrasts* of this meeting. This second meeting has some significant contrasts to the first meeting. In the first meeting, Abraham was rebuked; in the second meeting, Abimelech was rebuked. In the first meeting, Abimelech gave gifts to Abraham; in the second meeting, Abraham gave gifts to Abimelech. In the first meeting, Abimelech came to Abraham to upbraid him; in the second meeting, he came to Abraham to praise him. But as contrasting as these meetings were, they both ended in peace for the two men.

To further study this summit which Abraham had with Abimelech, we will consider the request in the summit (vv. 22–24), the reproving in the summit (vv. 25–31), and the results of the summit (vv. 32–34).

A. THE REQUEST IN THE SUMMIT

Abimelech wanted a covenant (a formal swearing—"Now therefore swear unto me here by God" [v. 23]) with Abraham to deal peacefully with one another. Today, this would be like a peace treaty between nations. Though Abraham did not represent a nation then (God promised to make of him a great nation in the future, however) as did Abimelech, who at that time was a king and so represented a nation, this was not an unusual request; for in those days, even individuals of large estates sometimes had these covenants, too. As an example, Abraham already had a covenant with others; for he had a confederacy (14:13) with Mamre, Eshcol, and Aner. Now a king wants to have a covenant with him.

To examine Abimelech's request, we will look at the inspiration for the request, the specifications in the request, and the accommodation to the request.

1. The Inspiration for the Request

"Abimelech and Phicol the chief captain of his host spake unto Abraham, saying, God is with thee in all that thou doest" (v. 22). That which inspired Abimelech to request a peace treaty with Abraham was the evidence that Abraham and God were on very amiable terms. In those intervening years between meetings with Abraham, Abimelech had been observing Abraham; and it was very obvious from his observations that Abraham enjoyed in a blessed way the presence of God in his life. Hence, his comment: "God is with thee in all that thou doest."

Abimelech's comment, which showed the inspiration for his desire for a covenant with Abraham, spoke of the promises of God, the performance of Abraham, and the policy of rulers.

Promises of God. Abimelech's comment showed that God was beginning to fulfill several promises given years earlier to Abraham; namely, that He would bless Abraham, and that He would make Abraham's name great (12:2). Abimelech had observed some of the blessings. He could see Abraham's continual prosperity, the increase of his large estate, and he would hear of the miracle birth of Isaac. The blessings were most obvious, and they contributed to his greatness, for his estate had now become so impressive that even a king wants a covenant with him. Leupold said this "incident shows forth clearly how influential and prominent a personage Abraham had become . . . neighboring kings were concerned about retaining his goodwill; he ranked on a par with the mighty men of his day."

Yes, God had promised to bless Abraham and to make his name great. At the time of the giving of the promises, Abraham's circumstances did not promise much blessing; and his being a stranger in the land did not promise much greatness. But God's promises are sure and will be fulfilled. Abimelech's request for a peace covenant verifies that fact.

Performance of Abraham. Abimelech's comment not only showed that God was fulfilling some of the promises He had made to Abraham, but it also showed that Abraham's lifestyle was evidencing considerable godliness, for to say "God is with thee" is a great compliment about the godliness of your conduct. "God is with thee" is not said of wicked people, but it is said of righteous people. This is seen in the case of Joseph (Genesis

SUMMIT WITH ABIMELECH

39:2, 3, 21, 23) as well as Abraham. Abraham was performing a lot better in his conduct than he had done earlier. When Abraham was living a lie about Sarah, God had to tell Abimelech that Abraham was a prophet. But when Abraham was living obediently, Abimelech did not need anyone to tell him that Abraham was living for God—he could see it plainly.

The same thing is true about every Christian. If a Christian is living disobediently, others will have difficulty seeing that he is a Christian and may not even believe it when someone tells them the disobedient one is a Christian. But if a Christian is living obediently, others will have no trouble knowing that he is a Christian, for it will show in every area of their life. Does your life tell others that you are a godly person? Do you live so worldly, in such an unglued, confused, helter-skelter way, unashamedly embracing low standards that the world looks upon you with disgust and abhorrence, never realizing that you are a Christian? Our faith or lack of it will show up in every facet of our lives. If others have to inquire if we are a Christian, we are either very backslidden or we do not have the faith.

Policy of rulers. That Abimelech, a king, wanted to be at peace with a godly man speaks very well of Abimelech. It is to the great advantage of rulers to seek to be in the good graces of the godly. All rulers should seek to be at peace with the godly. In fact, rulers should seek to be in favor with the godly more than any other group. Failure to be at peace with the godly will spell destruction for any nation. Tragically, the majority of the leaders of our land are today more interested in being in favor with the ungodly. Through legislation and money handouts, they court the favor of such evil people as the homosexuals, the abortionists, the gamblers, the evolutionists (the favored ones in education), the women's rights groups (who disdain the Biblical place of women), and the makers and sellers of alcohol. The righteous, on the other hand, are scorned and legislated against. They are often not allowed to display Christian symbols at Christmas time, pray, or read the Bible in some public places even though the most vulgar and filthy of artists are funded by the government to display their filth in public places in the name of the freedom of expression. But "righteousness exalteth a nation" (Proverbs 14:34), not wickedness. Rulers who cater to the wicked only harm the nation.

2. The Specifications in the Request

"Now therefore swear unto me here by God that thou wilt not deal falsely with me, nor with my son, nor with my son's son: but according to the kindness that I have done unto thee, thou shalt do unto me, and to the land wherein thou hast sojourned" (v. 23). Abimelech's request specified four things about the covenant. They are the integrity, duration, kindness, and coverage of the covenant.

The integrity of the covenant. "Thou wilt not deal falsely with me" shows Abimelech's desire to have a covenant with Abraham that emphasized integrity in their dealings with one another. The request was a reminder of Abraham's deceptive past. While Abraham had proven himself a better man than his deceitful conduct of a few years back indicated, the fact is— once a liar always a suspect. All of this tells us it often takes a long time to prove to others that we are a changed person. Therefore, a change in behavior after conversion will not be readily accepted by the world until the convert has proven over a number of weeks, months, or even years that the change is real and lasting. The same is true for those in the church who have grievously sinned. These folk often expect immediate restoration when they say they have confessed their sin to God. But they need to realize that they must give proof of their change before they experience much restoration, and that proof requires much time before the genuineness of the change can be verified.

The duration of the covenant. Abimelech did not want the covenant just for his lifetime; but he also wanted it continued through the days of his "son" and "my son's son." Abimelech

Summit With Abimelech

wanted Abraham to commit himself to something more than just a short term arrangement. Abimelech wanted Abraham to make a covenant that would require a lifetime commitment.

This sort of commitment does not appeal much to most folk in our churches today. It is hard to get folk to be anything but temporary in their service for the Lord. They will serve if nothing else interferes. They do not want to be "tied down" (as they say) indefinitely to some job at church. Oh yes, they want the Lord to be faithful all the time; but they have a double standard when it comes to their own commitment, for they do not seem to want to be faithful any of the time. Such folk can learn from Abimelech's appeal. He wants lifetime commitment—so does the Lord. If there is not lifetime commitment here in the covenant, it greatly decreases the value of the covenant. In like manner, if there is not lifetime commitment in serving God, it decreases greatly the value of our service. Lack of lifetime commitment insults God and is grossly ungrateful to God.

With the numbers of divorces skyrocketing, we need to also emphasize here lifetime commitment in marriage. Preachers need to stop trying to find devious ways to sanction divorce and instead spend more time emphasizing lifetime commitment in marriage. We expect to see divorce in the world; but the church is being smitten by it now, too. Preachers who justify divorce are not helping the matter at all.

The kindness of the covenant. Abimelech wants a covenant with Abraham which specifies that "kindness" will characterize their relationship with each other. This request goes along with the earlier request for truthfulness in their relationship. Being truthful is being kind. When Abraham was dishonest with Abimelech about Sarah, he was mean to Abimelech, not kind.

Abimelech refers to the kindness which he had showed Abraham in the past (restoring Sarah, giving Abraham gifts though Abraham had wronged him, and inviting Abraham to dwell in the land) as the sort of kindness that is to guide their covenant relationship. As "I have done unto thee, thou shalt do unto me" is the guide Abimelech wants Abraham to follow. We call this the golden rule. Jesus stated it thus: "And as ye would that men should do to you, do ye also to them" (Luke 6:31). If we took seriously this rule to guide our conduct, it would indeed make us kind to people. Of course, we have some who want and insist that others be kind to them even though they are not kind to others. That is not the golden rule; that is the hypocrites' rule!

The coverage of the covenant. Abimelech specified that the covenant should not only cover him and his descendants, but he told Abraham it should also include those of "the land wherein thou hast sojourned." Abimelech wanted the covenant to cover all the people of Abimelech's nation. Hence, it was a covenant with a nation as well as with an individual family. Abimelech was not selfish. He wanted peaceful relations with Abraham not just for himself and his descendants, but for all his land. He was not a self-serving politician like so many politicians in our land today. He did not seek benefits for himself, but not for the people. So if he was a politician in our land, he would not vote to raise his pay while voting to reduce the people's pay (via a raise in taxes). He would not be controlled by special interest groups who would buy him off to pass legislation favoring them but not the whole land. Would that we had more politicians in our land with the unselfish attitude of Abimelech!

3. The Accommodation to the Request

"And Abraham said, I will swear" (v. 24). Abraham was very accommodating to Abimelech's request. He quickly agreed to make the requested covenant with Abimelech. A man of character will not hesitate to accept such a proposal. There was nothing in the proposal that was wrong or shady or tricky. It simply called for honest and kind behavior.

There is no problem here, as some may think, in having a covenant with an unbeliever. Abraham is simply agreeing to live peaceably in a righteous way with his neighbors. We ought to live that way with our neighbors—covenant or no covenant. The

Apostle Paul exhorts us along this line when he told the believers in Rome, "As much as lieth in you, live peaceably with all men" (Romans 12:18). Too many professing Christians, however, are quarrelsome, cannot get along with anyone, are always agitating, bickering, and irritating. It does not speak well of their faith and, in fact, makes us wonder if they are truly in the faith. Such folk need to start agreeing to live peaceably.

Some, such as the Quakers, have difficulty with the swearing part in this agreement between Abraham and Abimelech. It is a result of their misunderstanding of the Matthew 5:33–37 text. But in that part of the Sermon on the Mount, Christ is not condemning the taking of a solemn and formal oath to speak truthfully or to give formal assurance of your upright intentions. What He does condemn in that text is perjury and profanity. The word "swear" has several meanings. It not only means to curse, to take the name of the Lord in vain; but it also means to make a solemn pledge or vow often with an appeal to God or some sacred thing for confirmation. Good men are most willing to give proper assurances of their intentions to be honest and upright. If they testify in the court, they are glad to let people know in a formal way that they intend to speak the truth. If they borrow money, they are glad to sign papers to agree to monthly payments to pay back the loan. Failure to give formal assurances in these and similar situations does not speak well of one's intentions. There are many texts in Scripture which sanction the taking of formal oaths with an appeal to God for confirmation. As an example, "Thou shalt fear the LORD thy God . . . and shalt swear by his name" (Deuteronomy 6:13; cp. Genesis 24:2,3; 47:29–31; Isaiah 45:23; Jeremiah 4:2; 12:16; II Corinthians 1:23; Galatians 1:20; and Revelation 10:6).

B. THE REPROVING IN THE SUMMIT

While Abraham quickly agreed to have a covenant of peace with Abimelech, the covenant was not ratified before Abraham reproved Abimelech about some iniquitous conduct by Abimelech's servants. We will note the reason for the reproving, the response to the reproving, and the repeating of the reproving.

1. The Reason for the Reproving

"And Abraham reproved Abimelech because of a well of water, which Abimelech's servants had violently taken away" (v. 25). Water is extremely vital for any people, and in those days wells were especially important for people in such lands as Palestine, for Palestine did not have frequent rains and a resulting number of creeks and rivers which run continually throughout the year. Their rains only come in early spring and late fall. Hence, wells were absolutely vital to having an adequate water supply. So to steal a well was a most serious crime. And not only had Abimelech's servants taken the well, but they had "violently" taken it. This means they took it by force, which implies physical injury to at least some of those who were defending the well. Thus, before Abraham ratifies a peace treaty that involves "kindness," this evil must be duly reproved; for you cannot have peace if transgression is not reckoned with and put in its place.

This principle, which says we must duly reprove evil before we can have peace, needs more attention today; for we are trying to establish peace in many situations—in individuals in the matter of salvation, in communities, and with nations—without first dealing properly with wickedness.

An *individual* will never be saved and thus gain peace with God—the greatest peace of all—until his sin problem is dealt with properly. His sin must be washed away by the blood of Christ, and the righteousness of Christ be imputed to him if he wants peace with God; for "there is no peace, saith my God, to the wicked" (Isaiah 57:21).

A *community* will not have peace until the lawless element is dealt with properly. All the talk about peace in our land is sheer folly when our government sanctions lawless living and is so lenient with criminals. Righteousness is what brings peace, not wickedness. Virtue, not vice, brings tranquility.

And *nations* will not have peace with other nations until the belligerency of offending nations is dealt with properly. Signing a peace treaty (like Korea and Vietnam) without putting evil in its place is a study in stupidity. Belligerent attitudes and people must be put down firmly, or the treaty will be worth less than the piece of paper upon which it is written.

2. The Response to the Reproving

"And Abimelech said, I wot not [know not] who hath done this thing; neither didst thou tell me, neither yet heard I of it, but today" (v. 26). Abimelech's response to the reproving by Abraham was to insist he was innocent of any guilt in the stealing of this well. He claimed innocence by saying he did not know about the crime and by the fact that Abraham had not told him about it until now. Abimelech's answer indicated that he did not approve of the stealing of the well, and he would correct the situation. Hence, the covenant of peace could be ratified; for evil had been duly dealt with by Abraham.

While Abraham is to be commended for reproving this evil before he made a covenant of peace with Abimelech, the complaint that he had not heretofore informed Abimelech of the grievance is a valid one. Abraham should have told Abimelech about the problem before he did. "It is as much the duty of him who has a grievance to reveal it, as it is the duty of him who has caused the grievance to remove it" (Whitelaw). If a grievance needs to be made known, it should in most cases be made known promptly. Why? In order to promptly stop whatever evil may be involved, to eliminate any inaccurate charges, to avoid misunderstanding, and to maintain peace. Belated revealing of grievances often times (though not in our text) causes one to wonder about the motives of folk who delay the reporting of a grievance. As an example, there are some church members who practice this sort of thing frequently in order to make their pastor look uncaring and unkind. If they make a trip to the hospital, they will not tell the pastor so they can later berate the pastor for not caring because he did not call on them when they were in the hospital. You do not have to pastor long before you experience this charge.

3. The Repeating of the Reproving

During the ratification of the covenant, which was done by Abraham giving Abimelech some gifts ("And Abraham took sheep and oxen, and gave them unto Abimelech; and both of them made a covenant" [v. 27]), Abraham discreetly repeated his reproving about the stealing of the well. He did it by giving an additional gift of seven ewe lambs to Abimelech. "And Abraham set seven ewe lambs of the flock by themselves. And Abimelech said unto Abraham, what mean these seven ewe lambs which thou hast set by themselves? And he said, For these seven ewe lambs shalt thou take of my hand, that they may be a witness unto me, that I have digged this well" (vv. 28–30).

There was much wisdom in Abraham's actions. While "seemingly betraying a secret suspicion of the prince's veracity, the act aimed at preventing any recurrence of the grievance . . . Good men should not only rectify the wrongs they do to one another, but adopt all wise precautions against their repetition" (Whitelaw). This action of Abraham promoted genuine peace. There were no cover-ups or winkings at evils—a practice that only encourages evil to continue. Peace treaties which our nation has made with other nations have often lacked these necessary reproving reminders of grievances in order to insure a better peace. Politicians seem so anxious to gain the praise of man in signing a peace treaty that it is peace at any price. They will sign treaties which do not properly deal with evil. Thus they do not really stop the belligerency that destroyed peace.

Interestingly, the wronged (Abraham, who had a well stolen from him) in this meeting gives the gifts just as the wronged (Abimelech, who was lied to about Sarah) gave the gifts in the last encounter between these two men. This also happens in soul salvation. God is the One that is wronged by our sins; yet it is God, not we the sinner, who gives the gift, namely, Jesus Christ (John 3:16), Who is the means of the salvation of our soul and our reconciliation with God. This wonderfully shows the work of grace in salvation. Peace with God does not come by merit, but by mercy.

C. THE RESULTS OF THE SUMMIT

The covenant brought good results. Thomas Whitelaw, in *Pulpit Commentary*, points out two important results which came to Abraham. They were the establishment of peace and the enjoyment of peace.

1. The Establishment of Peace

"Thus they made a covenant at Beer-sheba: then Abimelech rose up, and Phicol the chief captain of his host, and they returned into the land of the Philistines" (v. 32). After the making of this covenant, Abraham had peace with the Philistines for the rest of his life. Thus the covenant brought peace for approximately seventy years; for, as we noted earlier, Abraham was between 104 and 106 years years of age when the covenant was made; and he died at 175 (25:7).

But shortly after Abraham died, peace began to be disturbed by failure of succeeding generations to abide by the terms of the covenant. Isaac disturbed the peace when like his father, he lied about his wife and said she was his sister (26:6–11). That violated the terms of the covenant to be truthful. The Philistines also disturbed the peace when they went back to hostilities regarding the wells. After Abraham died, they filled up some of the wells he had dug (26:18). That violated the terms of the covenant to be kind.

Later on, when we get into the book of Judges and into the history of Saul and David, the first two kings of Israel, peace was so disturbed between the Philistines and Israel that we forget all about the fact that Israel and the Philistines were at one time at peace with each other. In Judges and in the reigns of Saul and David, one of the main enemies of the descendants of Abraham was these pesky Philistines. But we should not be surprised. Their attitude towards God was not the same as that of Abimelech. Abimelech, on the occasions we see him in the Scripture, was not anti-God. He paid great respect to Divine revelation (about Sarah being Abraham's wife); and he evidenced, in this desire to have a peace treaty with Abraham, that he wanted to be in favor with God's people. Such attitudes which Abimelech embraced will promote peace. But when the idol Dagon takes over the affections of the people (I Samuel 5) and God is defied as Goliath defied Him (I Samuel 17:45), peace will not survive. The covenant Abimelech had with Abraham will not be respected. True peace will never come unless there is a proper attitude towards God Almighty. That explains why the godless world of ours has very little genuine peace.

2. The Enjoyment of Peace

"And Abraham planted a grove in Beer-sheba, and called there on the name of the LORD, the everlasting God. And Abraham sojourned in the Philistines' land many days" (vv. 33,34). Scripture shows us three ways in which Abraham evidenced the enjoyment of peace from the covenant: the planting of a tree, the practicing of worship, and the place of residence.

Planting of a tree. "And Abraham planted a grove in Beer-sheba." There is confusion and concern about this action which needs to be cleared up in order to show that the action was part of the blessing of peace. Because the "planted a grove in Beer-sheba" is immediately followed by "and called there on the name of the LORD," many readers may be alarmed that Abraham is going into idolatry; for the mention of groves in Scripture is usually associated with idolatry. But this is definitely not the case here. We cite two reasons that should cancel out that alarm. First, the grove planting was a separate action in itself. If you read verses 33 and 34 carefully, you will see that the Scriptures report three separate actions of Abraham—not two. The planting of the grove and worship are not one action. They are separate actions. As listed in our text, the three actions are planting a grove, "and" calling on the name of the LORD, "and" sojourning in the Philistines' land. Second, the meaning of the word "grove" eliminates idolatry. The word translated "grove" here is a different word than the words translated grove or groves elsewhere in the Old Testament, which are so closely associated with idols. The word here simply means a tree (and here it is singular), specifically a "tamarisk tree" (an evergreen tree similar to a cypress). The word translated grove or groves which is associated with idolatry does not refer primarily to trees but to idol poles.

Abraham's planting of a tree reflected peaceful circumstances. Some believe he planted the tree as a memorial of the peace covenant. Whether this is so or not, the fact is that we seldom do much landscaping in a situation in which peace does not abound. Peace means you can enjoy where you live. Planting a tree or trees or doing other landscaping reflects that fact.

Practicing of worship. "Abraham. . . . called there [Beersheba] on the name of the LORD, the everlasting God." One of man's greatest blessings is to be able to worship without the harassment of hostile surroundings. Peace in the land provides good conditions for having public worship services. In regards to Abraham's public worship here, we note first, the concern for worship and second, the correctness of worship.

First, the *concern for worship*. Abraham worshipped because he was concerned about worship. His heart desired to worship God. You will not do much worshipping if the heart concern is not present. Folk with Abraham's concern for worship will be in church every Sunday; and when they move to a new neighborhood or community, they will put high priority on finding a good church in which to worship. If one claims to be a believer and yet does not show much concern for worship, he is nothing but a hypocrite.

Abraham took advantage of his peaceful situation to promote his public worship. This is a rebuke to those who when given good situations do not use them to promote their spiritual lives, but instead they use them to promote their own selfish pursuits. Though we are privileged today to have nice homes, nice cars, nice roads, and nice church buildings, many still have trouble getting to church regularly. How shameful to so misuse our blessings.

Second, the *correctness of worship*. In worshipping God, Abraham called Him the "LORD, the everlasting God." Abraham already knew God as the "most high God" (14:18) and the "Almighty God" (17:1). Now here he uses a new name (as far as Abraham is concerned) for God, a name which expresses the eternal nature of God. Abraham has grown in the knowledge of God over the years since he has moved to Canaan, and this growth in the knowledge of God has been very beneficial to him. It has helped him worship better, and it has also helped his faith to be stronger.

No knowledge is so beneficial to us as the knowledge of God. Therefore, it is important that we all grow continually in the knowledge of God as we make our way through life. The better we know God, the better we will worship God; and the better we know God, the better we will trust God. Lack of knowledge of God will make our worship and our faith defective. But we cannot afford to be defective in these areas for no areas in our lives are more important than these areas.

To know that God is eternal is a great solace for the soul. So many things around us will not last—even "heaven [not the eternal abode of the believer, but the sidereal heavens] and earth shall pass away" (Mark 13:31). But God and His Word will not pass away. They will remain forever. This means His promises for our eternal salvation shall never fail. Therefore, when Christ says, "I give unto them eternal life" (John 10:28), it means "they shall never perish" (Ibid.). Yes, it is wonderful to know that God is eternal. It is wonderful to know that "The eternal God is thy refuge, and underneath are the everlasting arms" (Deuteronomy 33:27). God will always be our help; He will never fail. This truth is great comfort indeed.

Place of residence. A good place to reside was another result of the peace from the covenant. "And Abraham sojourned in the Philistines' land many days" (v. 34). Matthew Henry says, "Abraham, having got into a good neighborhood, knew when he was well off, and continued a great while there." We, at first, cringe at that statement; for the mention of the Philistines does not give us ideas of a good neighborhood. But we must remember that Abimelech was not typical of the Philistines of later generations. As we noted above, he respected Divine revelation and wanted to be in good favor with God's people. This was not the characteristics of the Philistines in the book of Judges and during the reigns of Saul and David. To settle down and live with that bunch would be a mark against you. But the Philistines of Abraham's day were much different.

It is good to live in a neighborhood which respects the Word of God and wants peace with God's people. Many people do not always have a choice as to where they live. But when we do have a choice, certain guidelines should dictate where we choose to live. Foremost among these guidelines are the piety of the place. Lot chose to live in godless, immoral Sodom and it ruined him. Abraham chose differently and the results show it.

XIII.

Sacrificing of Isaac

Genesis 22:1–19

THE GREATEST TEST Abraham ever experienced was the sacrificing of Isaac. Verse 1 says God did "tempt" (v. 1) Abraham regarding the sacrificing of Isaac. But "test" is a better translation than "tempt," for it conveys more accurately the action by God. We normally think of "tempt" as a solicitation to evil, but God does not do such a thing to men. "Let no man say when he is tempted, I am tempted of God; for God cannot be tempted with evil, neither tempteth he any man" (James 1:13). The difference between temptation and testing is very great. Temptation is to pollute and weaken us; testing is to purify and strengthen us. Temptation offers immediate pleasure and gain; testing offers immediate pain and loss. Temptation seems reasonable to the flesh and appeals to the flesh; testing does neither.

Warren Wiersbe said, "In the 'School of Faith' we must have occasional tests, or we will never know where we are spiritually." Abraham was in the School of Faith; and, therefore, we should not be surprised to read of his experiencing many tests—the one in our text being the greatest. You could almost write his entire life under the headings of his various tests. To emphasize this fact, we list twenty-five tests which can be detected in his life (the names of six tests—2,4,7,8,12,18—are suggested by Wiersbe in his book on Abraham from the "Be" series).

1. The *forsaking test*: leaving his land and relatives to come to the land of Canaan.

2. The *famine test*: experiencing a famine in Canaan shortly after arriving there.

3. The *falsehood test*: lying in Egypt about Sarah being his sister instead of his wife.

4. The *fellowship test*: separating from Lot.

5. The *first-choice test*: letting Lot have first choice in the selecting of the land.

6. The *forgiveness test*: rescuing greedy and disrespectful Lot when Lot was captured by Chedorlaomer's armies.

7. The *fight test*: attacking Chedorlaomer's armies to free Lot and Sodom, even though he had much fewer soldiers than Chedorlaomer's coalition.

8. The *fortune test*: turning down the king of Sodom's offer to take all the goods of Sodom.

9. The *fear test*: fearing retaliation after defeating Chedorlaomer's armies—his fear is revealed in the fact that God told him to "Fear not" (Genesis 15:1).

10. The *faith test*: believing God about the promised son and, as a result, being declared righteous.

11. The *faithfulness test*: abiding patiently by the animals he had slain at God's command to confirm the covenant.

12. The *fatherhood test*: having a son via Hagar.

13. The *forbearance test*: having to put up with Sarah, Hagar, and Ishmael after Hagar and Ishmael had returned from fleeing Sarah's harsh treatment.

14. The *flesh test*: circumcising all the males in his household after God commanded him to do so.

15. The *friendship test*: showing God and the two angels great hospitality when they visited him.

16. The *fervency test*: asking God repeatedly to spare the city of Sodom.

17. The second *falsehood test*: lying in Gerar, as he had done in Egypt, about Sarah being his sister.

18. The *farewell test*: casting Ishmael and Hagar out of his household after Ishmael had mocked Isaac.

19. The *flattery test*: reproving evil before making a covenant with Abimelech who had greatly complimented Abraham when requesting the covenant with him.

20. The *foremost test* (the one we are concerned about in this study—we could also call it the fiery test): submitting to God's command to offer Isaac for a burnt offering.

21. The *funeral test*: experiencing the death of Sarah.

22. The *financial test*: dealing honestly and wisely in buying a burying place for Sarah.

23. The *father-in-law test*: seeing to it that his son Isaac obtained the proper wife.

24. The *family test*: enlarging his family through Keturah which was a questionable situation.

25. The *fidelity test*: administrating the distribution of his estate so that Isaac received the covenant inheritance just as God had decreed.

Doubtless there were other tests in Abraham's life; but we list these twenty-five tests to emphasize the fact that his life, like the life of anyone desiring to walk by faith, was filled with tests. Abraham did not pass all of these tests but failed some of them miserably. However, he did not quit the School of Faith when he failed a test. He continued on, just as we should after we have failed. The greatest failure occurs when we quit after we have failed.

The severity of this test of sacrificing Isaac (James Murphy calls it "The grand crisis" in Abraham's life) was a compliment for Abraham, for God does not test one so severely unless that person has grown strong in the faith. The toughest tests are for the strongest saints. Few saints, however, ever advance far enough in the School of Faith to experience very severe tests. Oh, we often think our tests are severe; but compared to Abraham's test, they certainly are not. But if we are experiencing a severe test, we do not have to always feel we have miserably failed. To the contrary, the test may indicate that we have greatly succeeded in our spiritual growth. Of course, the disobedient will frequently confuse severe chastisement for their sin as a test. Instead of seeing a reprimand for their sin, they think the chastisement indicates they are growing spiritually.

One of the most significant features of this great test of

SACRIFICING OF ISAAC

Abraham is that the story provides us a really great type of the sacrifice of Jesus Christ at Calvary. This chapter and Exodus 12 are the greatest and most detailed Gospel pictures in the Old Testament. Long before Christ came to earth and died for our sins, God gave excellent foreshadowings of it in the Old Testament. With our text being such a great picture of Calvary, we will, in this study, be frequently pointing out the comparisons of the sacrificing of Isaac with the crucifixion of Christ.

To study in detail this sacrificing of Isaac, we will consider the command given to Abraham for the sacrificing (vv. 1,2), the conduct of Abraham in the sacrificing (vv. 3–14), and the consequences for Abraham and others from the sacrificing (vv. 12,14,15–19).

A. THE COMMAND FOR THE SACRIFICING

"And it came to pass after these things, that God did tempt [test] Abraham, and said unto him, Abraham: and he said, Behold, here I am. And he said, Take now thy son, thine only son Isaac, whom thou lovest, and get thee into the land of Moriah; and offer him there for a burnt offering upon one of the mountains which I will tell thee of" (vv. 1,2). There are three parts to this command: whom to sacrifice, when to sacrifice, and where to sacrifice.

1. Whom to Sacrifice

There is no question as to whom Abraham is to sacrifice for a burnt offering. In a very plain and repetitive way (in verse 2), God made it very, very clear that Abraham is to offer Isaac for a burnt offering. It is "thy son," "thine only son," "Isaac," "whom thou lovest," and "him."

The extreme clarity of God's command about whom to sacrifice instructs us that when God tells us to do some unusual deed, He will make it very clear to us what that deed is. God never asks us to take extremely unusual action without giving us much assurance as to what the action is. This truth not only encourages us, but it also warns us that before we make any unusual decision or take any drastic action, we need to be certain that we have clear and strong commands from God for it. Some have run clear off the reservation with hardly a hint that God has so ordered them to take such extreme action. Then when failure results (and it will when we lack God's orders), they blame God. They are all wrong, of course; for if we act as God says, though extreme the action may be, there will be no failure.

From verse 2 and several later verses in Genesis 22, we note here three important descriptions of Isaac, the one to be sacrificed. These three descriptions of Isaac are the lone son, the loved son, and the law-abiding son. These descriptions will help us to better see the nature of the sacrifice Abraham had to make and will show us how wonderfully Isaac foreshadows Christ.

The lone son. The first description of Isaac by God in speaking to Abraham was "thine only son" (v. 2). This phrase, "thine only son," is repeated in verses 12 and 16. Each time this phrase appears in these verses, the word "son" is in italics in our translation which means it is not in the original; but it was added by the translators to, as they thought, clarify the reading. Such additions by the translators often did clarify the reading; but in this case it probably would have been better to have left out the added "son"; for without the word "son," we can see more clearly the strong emphasis on the "only" aspect of the description of Isaac. Three truths are seen in the "only" description.

First, "only" underscores the *magnitude of the sacrifice*. When Isaac is sacrificed, there will be no son left. Hence, Abraham is being asked to give his all. We may give a lot, but if we have a lot left, the sacrifice is not nearly as great as it is when we have nothing left. It is what is left that determines the real size and cost of our sacrificing. This is the lesson Jesus taught when He commended the giving of the poor widow. Though she only gave two mites, she gave all she had (Luke 21:4). Others gave more in terms of money but not in terms of sacrifice.

How very few are willing to go so far as to give their all in obeying God. Many cannot even tithe, though they have good incomes. Others cannot sacrifice weekends at their cabins by the lake to attend a worship service. A good number find the price too high to give up a few weekday nights to attend a week-long series of special meetings at church. Sad to say, many professing believers are not willing to pay much of a price to obey God. Yet, they still claim to be a follower of the One Who gave His all for their salvation on Calvary. There is a word for this kind of professed believer—the word is "hypocrite!"

Second, the "only" addresses the *matter of statistics*. It tells us how God counts. While Abraham had another son in Ishmael, Ishmael does not count in God's eyes. Isaac was the only son of Sarah and the only son who was heir to the covenant. God only counts the one that counts.

Many times we make the mistake of counting things which God does not count. Someone has said, "Only one life 'twill soon be past, only what's done for Christ will last." We could change the last line to read, "Only what's done for Christ will count"; and it will give us the message here. We count Ishmaels but God does not. Preachers often count a lot of decisions, which God does not count, in order to pad their statistics. God only counts Isaacs, not Ishmaels. Others count up their works for salvation, but God does not; for they are only Ishmaels. The works of the flesh will never save a soul. Learn to count as God counts, if you wish to count correctly.

Third, the "only" is a *mark of our Savior*. As Isaac was Abraham's only son, so Jesus Christ was God's only Son. Both Isaac and Christ are, in fact, particularly called "only begotten son" (Hebrews 11:17, John 3:16). Yes, God, like Abraham, also had other sons (Job 1:6 and 2:1, Romans 8:14, and John 1:12); but Christ was still the "only" One. There are angelic "sons," and the redeemed are brothers of Christ. But He is still "only." Speaking of this picture of Christ from Isaac, Barnhouse said, "Here is an only son who had a brother! God is showing us a pageant, a type, a parable of the heavenly Father offering up His only begotten Son."

What a great price God paid for our salvation. Do we reciprocate in our sacrificing to serve Him? Or do we play the hypocrite as we noted above.

The loved son. Isaac is also described by God as the son "whom thou lovest" (v. 2). Here God is emphasizing the heart in Abraham's duty. Abraham had previously demonstrated that his love for God was greater than his love for Ishmael. Though he loved Ishmael very much, he obeyed God's orders to send him away. Now Abraham is tested to see if he loves God more than Isaac. Abraham is asked to give up Isaac, the son he loved the most. Abraham is asked to do more than just send him away (which would not kill Isaac); he is asked to slay him. What a great test of the heart's affection this test is for Abraham!

The heart must be examined to determine the character of our sacrifice. "My son, give me thine heart" (Proverbs 23:26) is God's plea to man. That is the main thing God wants from us. If He has our heart, He has everything about us. We may sacrifice much; but if the heart is not in it, the sacrifice loses much of its value. Abraham demonstrated, in his willingness to sacrifice Isaac, that God was his first love. That is the way it ought to be for all of us. Christ exhorted that God is to be our first and foremost love when He said the first and great commandment was "Thou shalt love the Lord thy God with all thy heart, and with all thy soul, and with all thy mind" (Matthew 22:37), and "If any man come to me, and hate not his father, and mother, and wife, and children, and brethren, and sisters, yea, and his own life also, he cannot be my disciple" (Luke 14:26). The "hate," of course, is a comparative term. It does not mean to have malice in one's heart for those mentioned; but it means that our love for God should be much, much greater than our love for man.

We see precious little of this priority in love today. As an example, young people will not give up their unholy boy friends or girl friends for God, and men everywhere are "lovers of pleasures more than lovers of God" (II Timothy 3:4). This lack of priority is why so many church members miss a lot of church services. There is a lot of talk about love today, but it certainly is not about loving God.

The typology of Christ is not difficult to see here. Just as Isaac was greatly loved by his father, so Jesus Christ was greatly loved by His Father. "This is my beloved Son" was God's comment of His great affection for Christ, a comment He made at both the baptism (Matthew 3:17) and transfiguration (Matthew 17:5) of Christ. To further the typology, we note that not only did both Abraham and God greatly love their sons, they also both willingly sacrificed their beloved sons.

The law-abiding son. Isaac submitted completely to his father's will in this whole ordeal. While this truth does not come from the description of Isaac in verse 2 but from later verses, we still wanted to consider it here; for it is also a very significant part of the description of the son who was to be sacrificed. Isaac's submission can be seen in his going with Abraham (v. 3), in his carrying the wood for Abraham (v. 6), and especially in his not being recorded as uttering a word of complaint or protest when bound and laid on the altar (v. 9).

This submission of Isaac is a striking foreshadowing of the law-abiding character of Jesus Christ, Who submitted totally to the wishes of His Father. Christ's submission was a hallmark of His character. "My meat [food] is to do the will of him that sent me" (John 4:34); "Lo, I come . . . to do thy will, O God" (Hebrews 10:7); "I delight to do thy will, O my God" (Psalm 40:8). And like Isaac, the greatest evidence of Christ's submission had to do with His being sacrificed. He was "obedient unto death, even the death of the cross" (Philippians 2:8); "when he suffered, he threatened not; but committed himself to him that judgeth righteously" (I Peter 2:23); "he is brought as a lamb to the slaughter, and as a sheep before her shearers is dumb, so he openeth not his mouth" (Isaiah 53:7).

Some may argue that Isaac does not foreshadow Christ's obedience as strongly as we insist; for he was only a "lad" (v. 5) and, therefore, could not resist or understand the situation he was in. But Isaac was a good deal older than a young child. We can ascertain this fact in several ways. First, a "lad" of a young age would have difficulty carrying the wood (v. 6). Second, the Hebrew word translated "lad" is not limited to a small child. It is used of anyone from youth to manhood. In fact, "lad" is even used of Benjamin (Genesis 43:8) when he was a father of ten boys (Genesis 46:21). Therefore, Isaac certainly does not have to be a small child in this experience. In view of the typology and the context, we believe Isaac was close to or, more likely, at the age of Christ when He was crucified. The next chapter says Sarah died at 127 years of age, which would make Isaac 37 then. Thus, for Isaac to be the age of 33 (the age of Christ at His crucifixion) when he was laid on the altar in Moriah, Sarah's death would have to be four years later—a most acceptable time span between the events. For Isaac to be offered on the altar at age 33 would seem most fitting, for so many things said of Isaac in Genesis 22 foreshadow Christ in such close detail.

The willingness of Isaac to be bound and placed on the altar when he was old enough to easily have resisted Abraham makes Isaac's submission so great in this episode that if it had not been for the greater performance of Abraham in the story, Isaac would have been the star of the story. Leupold states this conviction when he says, "Usually too little consideration is given to Isaac's heroism, which, if it were not for the marvelous faith heroism of his father, could justly be classed as among the mightiest acts of faith."

The Christ-like submission which Isaac so wonderfully demonstrated is that which ought to characterize the saints, too. But instead of submitting, we argue, complain, interpret the Scriptures pervertedly to try to void our duties, or simply ignore God's orders altogether. Then we stupidly wonder why our life does not experience the blessings of the saints of old, who submitted so completely to God's will. But if we want God's blessings, we must submit to the Word of our Heavenly Father as Isaac submitted to the words of his earthly father. The Word of God must be our supreme authority at all times.

Sacrificing of Isaac

Before we pass on to our next thought, we want to note here that Isaac's submission in carrying the wood foreshadows Christ in at least two significant ways. First, it foreshadows Christ carrying the cross to Calvary. "And he bearing his cross went forth into a place called the place of a skull, which is called in the Hebrew Golgotha, Where they crucified him" (John 19:17,18). Second, it foreshadows Christ bearing our sins. As Abraham, the father of Isaac, "took the wood . . . and laid it upon Isaac his son" (v. 6); so God, the Father of Jesus Christ, "laid on him [Jesus Christ] the iniquity of us all" (Isaiah 53:6).

2. When to Sacrifice

"Take now thy son . . . and offer him" (v. 2). Abraham was to sacrifice Isaac "now." The "now" of the command emphasizes the suddenness of the test. One night, without any warning whatever, God came to Abraham and told him to sacrifice Isaac and to do it "now." For a number of years Abraham had been living a quiet, peaceful life and enjoying the company and the development of his son Isaac as Isaac grew from childhood up to manhood. Then suddenly into his life came the greatest test Abraham ever experienced.

The suddenness of the test is a forceful warning to us. It tells us we need to always have our spiritual dues paid up. We need to always be at our spiritual best so we are always ready for the battle. We can never afford to be caught off-guard for either a testing from God or a temptation from Satan. Paul warns us about this need of being prepared when he says, "Watch ye, stand fast in the faith, quit you like men, be strong" (I Corinthians 16:13) and "watching thereunto with all perseverance" (Ephesians 6:18). When we fail in testing or temptation, it is not without reason. It is because we have neglected our spiritual health. Firemen are constantly busy keeping their trucks and equipment in the best of condition so that whenever a fire call comes, they are well prepared to answer the call. Emergency rooms in hospitals are staffed with the proper personnel and stocked with the proper supplies so that no matter what sort of case is brought into the emergency room, they are prepared to handle it efficiently. Oh, let us be the same way spiritually. Let us use our opportunities to maintain our spiritual strength so that at any time we can respond successfully to testings and temptations. "Now" comes without warning, but it does not need to come without our readiness. Abraham was obviously ready for the testing. During those calm and blessed years between the casting out of Ishmael and the offering of Isaac, he had not drifted away from the Lord and weakened himself spiritually. Significantly, one of the last things we read about Abraham before chapter 22 is that he was worshipping God. No wonder he passed this test with flying colors, as we will see later.

With the sacrificing of Isaac so clearly and forcefully foreshadowing Calvary, the "now" also reminds us how one needs to respond to the call to be saved. Salvation is an urgent matter. Putting off salvation is to risk eternal damnation. Therefore, heed God's Word when it says, "Behold, now is the accepted time; behold, now is the day of salvation" (II Corinthians 6:2).

3. Where to Sacrifice

"Get thee into the land of Moriah; and offer him there . . . upon one of the mountains which I will tell thee of" (v. 2). This place where Abraham was to sacrifice Isaac was in the area later known as Jerusalem. It was a three days' journey (v. 4) north of Beer-sheba. The name "Moriah" is found only one other time in Scripture besides our text. But this other reference is very significant, for it confirms the location of Moriah as being in the Jerusalem area. This second reference to Moriah speaks of a Mount Moriah, which is a mount in Moriah named after the region. It is connected with David's sacrificing after the three days' pestilence and with Solomon's Temple. "Solomon began to build the house of the LORD at Jerusalem in Mount Moriah, where the LORD appeared unto David his father, in the place that David had prepared in the threshing floor of Ornan the Jebusite" (II Chronicles 3:1).

Being in the Jerusalem area, the significant feature of the

location for the sacrificing of Isaac is its obvious relationship with Calvary and Christ; for this location is where Christ was crucified. The Bible tells us that Christ was crucified just outside of Jerusalem (Hebrews 13:12). We have no difficulty believing that the crucifixion of Christ occurred not only in the general area but also right at the very place Abraham offered Isaac. Charles Simeon said, "Mount Calvary was one of the mountains in the small tract of country called the land of Moriah: and from verse 2 it can scarcely be doubted, but that it was the very spot pointed out by God. It could not possibly be far from the spot; and, therefore, when the place for the sacrifice of Isaac was so accurately marked, it can scarcely be thought to be any other, than the very place where Jesus was offered two thousand years afterward." So again we see plainly Christ and the Gospel in the sacrificing of Isaac.

There is an important lesson here in the manner in which God disclosed the exact place where Abraham was to offer Isaac. Our text says that God told Abraham to go into the land of Moriah and offer Isaac upon one of the mountains "which I will tell thee of." Abraham had to travel several days before the rest of the will of God was made known. The lesson in this is that we will *learn* the will of God as we *do* the will of God. God seldom discloses to us all the directions and orders at once. We normally receive just enough instruction to guide us a step at a time. So Abraham had to go to Moriah before God would tell him the exact location. The flesh would like to know the location before it even begins the journey. But it is not necessary to know the location to begin the journey. However, it is necessary to begin the journey if we are to know the exact location. Obedience is a mighty important key to knowing the will of God. Disobedience will keep you in the dark about God's will. If you are always having trouble ascertaining the will of God, your problem is likely your lack of obedience.

B. THE CONDUCT IN THE SACRIFICING

Abraham's response to God's command to offer up Isaac was so noble that it is esteemed as one of the greatest acts of obedience ever. Barnhouse says it was "obedience unparalleled." With the exception of the obedience of Jesus Christ, it would be hard to find any act of obedience that surpasses the excellence of Abraham's conduct in this experience.

To study the excellent way in which Abraham conducted himself in obeying God to sacrifice Isaac, we will look at eleven things concerning his conduct. They are the problems for his conduct, the promptness in his conduct, the preparations for his conduct, the particularity in his conduct, the perseverance in his conduct, the privacy in his conduct, the promise about his conduct, the perplexity about his conduct, the persuasiveness of his conduct, the provision for his conduct, and the proof from his conduct.

1. The Problems for His Conduct

God's command to "Take now thy son, thine only son Isaac, whom thou lovest, and . . . offer him . . . for a burnt offering" (v. 2) presented some real problems for Abraham's faith and obedience. We note five major problems which confronted him in his obeying God's orders. They are an endearment, explanation, ending, evil, and esteem problem.

First, the *endearment problem*. Abraham had great affection for Isaac. This affection could easily argue for disobedience. As we noted before in Abraham's life, one's affections can hinder our obedience to God. It was doubtless the biggest problem of all in sacrificing Isaac.

Second, the *explanation problem*. God did not give any explanation for sacrificing Isaac. All He gave Abraham was a command. It takes strong faith to obey God when His commands are without good explanations and seem senseless. But faith knows a command is all we need to justify doing God's will, for God's wisdom controls His every command. It is nice to have explanations in hand at the time, and God sometimes gives them with the command. But when He does not give them, be sure that He will give them later on—to the delight of

Sacrificing of Isaac

obedience, but to the shame of disobedience.

Third, the *ending problem*. Sacrificing Isaac seemed to cancel out the promises God made to Abraham in the covenant. Was this not the promised son? Was not the seed of Isaac to be a blessing to mankind? Slaying Isaac seemed to end all prospects of the promises concerning Isaac ever being fulfilled. To experience loss from obeying God's commands makes it very hard to obey. The greater the apparent loss, the more difficult to obey. The world does not help matters here, for it will quickly tell us (and with much exaggeration) what great losses we will experience from obedience. It takes the keen eye of faith, which Abraham certainly had, to see that obedience only adds to the promises, not subtracts from them.

Fourth, the *evil problem*. Slaying Isaac seemed so evil, so cruel. It seemed to be that which would bring great suffering. How cruel to Isaac to kill him. How cruel to Sarah to kill her only son. And it also seemed to be very cruel to Abraham, too. What heartache to kill his son. Suffering is another formidable problem that is very difficult to overcome in order to obey God's will. It takes very strong faith to obey when suffering is involved. But faith knows that suffering in the will of God ultimately brings the greatest pleasures. No pleasures are greater than the pleasures salvation brings. But salvation required the greatest of all suffering—Jesus Christ on Calvary.

Fifth, the *esteem problem*. How could Abraham, in obeying the command to slay Isaac, demonstrate that the God he worshipped was a better God than the gods of the heathen, who were capriciously cruel and often demanded people to sacrifice their own offspring? When disobedience appears to promote the glory of God, how very difficult it is to obey. But true faith knows that if we want to honor God and enhance His esteem before others, we will do it best by obeying His commands.

Abraham faced some very great problems in his obedience. But he obeyed anyway. His faith was exceptionally strong, so he gave priority to God's precepts and not to the problems. Alexander Maclaren said that the "best way of knowing ourselves is to observe our own conduct, especially when it is hard to do nobly." The problems Abraham faced in sacrificing Isaac certainly would evidence, in a very clear and unmistakable way, the excellent character of Abraham's faith. No wonder Abraham's obedience brought the great comment from heaven "Now I know that thou fearest God" (v. 12), a comment we will look at more fully later on. Some folk look very good in nice weather; but when the storms of trials come, it really separates the real from the phony. Into what category do trials put your faith?

2. The Promptness in His Conduct

"And Abraham rose up early in the morning" (v. 3). God had spoken to Abraham in the night. Though the duty which God gave him was extremely unpleasant, Abraham got up early in the morning to pursue the duty anyway. Abraham had also responded in the same excellent way when told to cast Ishmael and Hagar out of his household (21:14). Abraham could say with the Psalmist, "I made haste, and delayed not to keep thy commandments" (Psalm 119:60). Promptness provides great assurance that the duty will be done.

As we pointed out in Abraham's casting out of Ishmael and Hagar, the best way to deal with difficult and distasteful duties is to do them promptly. Postponing the doing of such duty (or any duty) only makes it more difficult to do it. Matthew Henry said, "While we delay, time is lost and the heart is hardened." When difficult and distasteful duties encumber us, the temptation is often to oversleep, to sit, to complain, to brood, and to try and rationalize away our responsibilities. But that only makes matters worse. Great men of God in the Scriptures were characterized by early rising to pursue their duties. Moses (Exodus 24:4; 34:4), Joshua (Joshua 3:1; 6:12; 7:16; 8:10), David (I Samuel 17:20), Hezekiah (II Chronicles 29:20), Job (Job 1:5), and Christ (Mark 1:35) all illustrate this excellent characteristic.

3. The Preparations for His Conduct

Abraham "saddled his ass, and took two of his young men

SACRIFICING OF ISAAC

with him, and Isaac his son, and clave [cut] the wood for the burnt offering . . . and he took the fire in his hand, and a knife" (vv. 3,6). Abraham made sure that everything necessary to fulfill his duty was taken along on the trip to the land of Moriah. The ass was needed to carry the wood (Leupold informs us that the Hebrew word translated "saddled," means to prepare the ass to carry a load, not to ride it). The two servants were taken along for needed assistance on the journey and to take care of the ass when Abraham and Isaac went on alone to do the actual sacrificing. The wood was necessary for the burnt offering, the fire was necessary to start the burning of wood on the altar, and the knife was necessary for killing Isaac. The wood speaks of the cross (as we have already noted and will note more about later). It, like the cross, was laid on Isaac; and he was later put on the wood as Christ was put on the cross. The fire and knife speak of God's holy judgment upon sin. The fire and knife are combined in the "flaming sword" of Genesis 3:24; and at Calvary we see the two in "I thirst" (John 19:28, cp. Luke 16:24 for the spiritual significance of "I thirst"), and the spear thrust into the side of Christ (John 19:34).

The ability to fulfill our duty has much to do with how well we prepare to do our duty. Had Abraham failed to include any of these items, he would not have been able to obey the precept. We need to give more attention to this needed preparation in our churches today, for failure to adequately prepare for service is very evident in the church. Preachers and Sunday School teachers are notorious for lack of adequate preparation for their preaching and teaching work. In fact, it is one of the most conspicuous problems we observe in churches on Sunday. The Sunday School lessons are so weak and sick. The poorly prepared teacher has little of substance to say and tries to kill time through class discussions. The pastor is often no better. His sermons reflect the fact that he has spent most of his time running around during the week instead of earnestly studying the Word of God. Our pulpits are most barren of worthwhile messages. Lack of preparation is one of the main reasons for the problem.

If we want an excellent performance like Abraham's, however, we must prepare with the same excellence as Abraham did.

4. The Particularity in His Conduct

Abraham went "to the place which God had told him of; and Abraham built an altar there, and laid the wood in order" (v. 9). Abraham was very particular in his conduct in obeying God's command to sacrifice Isaac. We especially see this in our text in the location of the sacrificing and in the laying of the wood in order upon the altar. These actions, which may seem unimportant to some, reflect attitudes one must possess in order to have a good performance in doing our duty.

The location of the sacrificing. God made it very clear where Abraham was to sacrifice Isaac, and the location was more important than Abraham could ever have realized at the time of the giving of the instructions. It was there where he would find the ram to offer in place of Isaac; and we believe it was also there where, some two thousand years later, the Great Seed of Abraham would be sacrificed for the sin of man. So it was very important for Abraham to go to exactly the right place. Failure would have missed the ram and would have obscured typology (and obscuring typology does not go over well with God as is seen in what He did to Moses for obscuring typology when he hit the rock for water, see Numbers 20:7–12).

Often we fail to be particular in our obedience simply because at the time we do not see any need to be so particular. Yet, we need to realize that there is very good reason for the specifics of God's precepts—whether we know it or not. Therefore, we need to obey to the letter Some will call this legalism, but it is not legalism. It is simply full obedience, for to not fulfill the specifics of God's orders is disobedience.

The laying of the wood. Laying the wood in order reflected the noble attitude of taking the time to do things right even in small matters. Abraham did not throw the wood on the altar in a haphazard way. In spite of the distastefulness of his duty, he still insisted on taking care to lay the wood in order. Laying the wood in order was important, for it would make the fire burn more efficiently. Laying the wood in order and also the pieces of the sacrifice in order are commanded later in Leviticus in such texts as 1:7,8,12; 6:12.

Much work done in the church today is not wood laid in order; rather it is wood hurriedly thrown in a heap. But those who throw the wood in a heap at church often get pretty fussy about how things are done in their personal lives. Let someone work on their auto or house and they will scrutinize it with a fine tooth comb. They will carefully pick up the grass at their house when they mow their weedless lawn, but at church they will blow it over everything and let the weeds multiply. Abraham was not that way, however. He cared enough to take the time to do God's work right. So should we.

5. The Perseverance in His Conduct

"Then on the third day Abraham lifted up his eyes, and saw the place afar off" (v. 4). One factor which made Abraham's obedience so noble is that it was something more than just a passing notion. The command from God specified that Abraham go to the land of Moriah to make the sacrifice. As verse 4 notes, the distance to Moriah required three days to complete. This meant that Abraham had to keep up his resolve over a longer period of time than just a few minutes or hours. Hence, the perseverance in his conduct was outstanding. His commitment to God's orders was very strong. Maclaren said, "How much the long protracted tension of the march increased the sharpness of the test! It is easier to reach the height of obedient self-sacrifice in some moment of enthusiasm, than to keep up there through the commonplace details of slowly passing days. Many a faith, which could even have slain its dearest, would have broken down long before the last step of that sad journey was taken."

A major problem in Christian service today is lack of resolve and commitment. Folk will sign up for work at church if it does not involve much commitment. But God wants your complete commitment. He wants you to commit your money, time, and effort to His work week after week. Folk are committed to pleasure-seeking and to increasing their possession of personal toys and gadgets. But commitment to God is lacking because their heart is not right with God. Abraham is a welcomed difference to what is in our churches today.

The mention of the "third day" in our text speaks very strongly of the resurrection of Christ. For three days Isaac was dead in the mind of Abraham. But after three days of viewing Isaac as a dead man, God gave Isaac back to him. Seeing the resurrection here is not some fanciful imagination but is supported by Scripture. Scripture says that by faith Abraham "Accounting that God was able to raise him [Isaac] up, even from the dead, from whence also he received him in a figure" (Hebrews 11:19). So here is another detail in this episode which speaks of the work of Christ.

6. The Privacy in His Conduct

"And Abraham said unto his young men, Abide ye here with the ass; and I and the lad will go yonder and worship, and come again to you" (v. 5). The actual sacrificing of Isaac on the altar will be done in private. Only Abraham and Isaac will be present. The servants will not be allowed to witness the scene. From Abraham's command to secure privacy for the sacrifice, we note the prudence of Abraham and the picture of the crucifixion.

The prudence of Abraham. Commanding his servants to stay behind while he and Isaac went on alone was very wise action by Abraham. Had the servants gone along with him and Isaac, they could very well have hindered Abraham's obedience in sacrificing Isaac. Not understanding or appreciating Abraham's faith, they would doubtless attempt to stop Abraham (and two could overcome one, especially when the two would be young men and the one an aged man).

Those who would walk by faith must expect to walk alone

at times out of necessity. We must separate from anyone and anything which would hinder our worship of God and our walk according to His ways. Take note of the people and activities which cool your ardor for the Lord and then take proper action to keep them from hindering your walk and worship. Separate from friends, events, activities, pleasures, and places which hinder you from fulfilling your obligations to the Lord. Otherwise you will not do well in obeying God.

The picture of the crucifixion. Two aspects of the crucifixion are seen in Abraham securing privacy for sacrificing Isaac. They are the darkness which accompanied the crucifixion and the thieves which were associated with the crucifixion.

First, the *darkness accompanying the crucifixion.* The privacy of the sacrifice of Isaac foreshadows the privacy of the sacrifice at Calvary. For three hours a great darkness came over the earth when Christ was on the cross. "Now from the sixth hour there was darkness over all the land unto the ninth hour" (Matthew 27:45). This darkness shut the world out so God the Father and God the Son could deal with the sacrificing at Calvary alone. As the sacrificing of Isaac was a private father and son scene, so the transaction that took place on Calvary between God the Father and God the Son was a private scene.

Second, the *thieves associated with the crucifixion.* How significant that just two others besides his father went along with Isaac on this trip to Moriah. The two servants, therefore, foreshadow the two thieves who were associated with Christ in His crucifixion. Some may argue that the two servants did not go to the place of sacrifice as did the two thieves. True, the two servants did not go to the place of the altar; but types do not necessarily foreshadow in every detail. However, being separated from Isaac as a result of Abraham's command helps the two servants to foreshadow the two thieves in their seclusion from the scene on the cross by the darkness during the crucifixion. For three hours they (as were all other people) were shut out by darkness from viewing Christ on the cross.

7. The Promise About His Conduct

"And Abraham said . . . I and the lad will . . . come again to you" (v. 5). Abraham promised the two servants that both he and Isaac would return to them. Here is one of the great statements of Abraham's faith that is found in this episode. He believed that Isaac would come back with him! Why? Because he believed Isaac would be raised from the dead. "By faith Abraham . . . offered up Isaac . . . Accounting that God was able to raise him up, even from the dead, from whence also he received him in a figure" (Hebrews 11:17,19). This is a tremendous act of faith. Abraham had no precedent for the resurrection. All he had was God's Word which said He would "establish my covenant with him [Isaac] for an everlasting covenant, and with his seed after him" (Genesis 17:19). God could not fulfill these predictions about the covenant if Isaac was dead. But Abraham had heard the Word of God and believed! "Faith cometh by hearing, and hearing by the word of God" (Romans 10:17). And like the Psalmist, Abraham could say, "I believed, therefore have I spoken" (Psalm 116:10). He spoke of the promise that he and Isaac would return to the servants.

It is the Word of God which we need if we want true faith. Apart from the Word, Abraham would have nothing in which to hope. His entire hope of returning with Isaac to the servants relied upon the Word of God. Oh, how important is the Word to our faith. Yet, today in our churches there is much de-emphasis on the Word. Churches are ever expanding their programs and services. But they do not expand their teaching and preaching of the Word, for these increased services are mostly in the social and recreational area. Busy, busy, busy is the church schedule. But all the busyness has little to do with teaching and preaching the Word. In fact, even the services which used to major on teaching and preaching the Word are no longer majoring on this great work. Entertainment, films, musicals, and what all are increasingly cutting into the preaching and teaching time of the services. No wonder we have so little faith today.

8. The Perplexity About His Conduct

"And Isaac spake unto Abraham his father, and said, My father: and he said, Here am I, my son. And he said, Behold the fire and the wood: but where is the lamb for a burnt offering? And Abraham said, My son, God will provide himself a lamb for a burnt offering" (vv. 7,8). Isaac was justifiably puzzled that Abraham was planning to offer a burnt offering but had no lamb. Both the asking by Isaac and the answering by Abraham about the missing lamb will instruct us in important truths.

The asking. Isaac's question, "Where is the lamb?" indicated Isaac had been duly instructed regarding sacrifices. Abraham had obviously seen to it that Isaac knew vital truths regarding worship. God had earlier predicted Abraham would do this. "For I know him, that he will command his children and his household after him, and they shall keep the way of the LORD" (18:19). Abraham did what all parents should do—he diligently instructed his children in the things of God.

Isaac's knowledge that the lamb was missing exceeds the knowledge of many folk today. A good number of folk in our churches would not know the Lamb was missing. They are so spiritually dull they cannot tell the difference between a sermon that honors Christ and a sermon that leaves Christ out entirely. Even some theologians do not know the Lamb is necessary, let alone missing. They embrace a theology that brings salvation without Jesus Christ, the Lamb of God. Give Isaac great credit, for he knew what was missing! He knew the lamb was essential for a sacrifice for sins. He knew you could not worship without the lamb. Fire and wood are not enough. You must have the lamb. Churches are seldom without either the fire of emotionalism or the wood of formality; but most of them lack the Lamb, the most important ingredient of all in worship.

The answering. Abraham's answer, "like many other prophetical expressions, conveyed more than he himself probably was aware of at the moment" (Simeon). "God will provide himself a lamb" (v. 8) not only says God will provide a lamb to take Isaac's place; but it also says at least three things about the provision of Jesus Christ, the Lamb of God. First, it says that God will provide a Lamb. God provided Jesus Christ for man to be man's Savior from sins. Man did not provide himself with a Savior. Second, it says God is providing Himself a Lamb; for He needs a Lamb, too, if He is going to save people. And, third, the English rendering can also be read to say that God will Himself be the provided Lamb—which is true, in that Jesus Christ is God Incarnated. Yes Abraham certainly said a good deal more in his answer to Isaac than he realized.

The answer to Isaac's question was not only given by Abraham, but it was also given even more plainly by John the Baptist. "John seeth Jesus coming unto him, and saith, Behold the Lamb of God, which taketh away the sin of the world" (John 1:29). John the Baptist left no doubt as to Who The Lamb was.

9. The Persuasiveness of His Conduct

"Abraham took the wood of the burnt offering, and laid it upon Isaac his son . . . and they went both of them together . . . and Abraham said, My son, God will provide himself a lamb for a burnt offering: so they went both of them together . . . and Abraham. . . . bound Isaac his son, and laid him on the altar upon the wood" (vv. 6,8,9). We have earlier viewed Isaac's cooperation with Abraham as a type of Christ's submission to the Heavenly Father. Here we look at Isaac's cooperation as evidence of the persuasiveness of Abraham's faith upon Isaac. Isaac continued with Abraham when Abraham put the heavy load of wood on him. He continued with Abraham after Abraham told him God would supply a lamb. And he did not protest when Abraham bound him and put him on the altar. Such cooperation by Isaac with Abraham indicated that Abraham's faith was strong enough and genuine enough to convince Isaac to go along with his father. The persuasiveness of Abraham's faith is very evident in the "they went both of them together" which we read twice in our text.

SACRIFICING OF ISAAC

Abraham's influence over Isaac is a great challenge to all parents. Is our faith persuasive in our children's eyes? Do we live our faith well enough so they are encouraged to embrace it? Many children do not follow their parents' professed faith. Why is this? The answer is that too often their parents are more talk than walk. They may talk nice at church, but in their personal lives they do not reflect their faith well at all. They do not evidence their faith well enough to do much persuading of their children to embrace this faith.

10. The Provision for His Conduct

"Abraham built an altar there, and laid the wood in order, and bound Isaac his son, and laid him on the altar upon the wood. And Abraham stretched forth his hand, and took the knife to slay his son. And the angel of the LORD called unto him out of heaven, and said, Abraham, Abraham: and he said, Here am I. And he said, Lay not thine hand upon the lad, neither do thou anything unto him; for now I know that thou fearest God, seeing thou hast not withheld thy son, thine only son from me. And Abraham lifted up his eyes, and looked, and, behold behind him a ram caught in a thicket by his horns: and Abraham went and took the ram, and offered him up for a burnt offering in the stead of his son. And Abraham called the name of that place Jehovah-jireh" (vv. 9–14). How wonderfully God provided for Abraham here at Moriah. No wonder Abraham named the place "Jehovah-jireh" (v. 14) which means Jehovah will provide. Abraham would never forget this providing ability of God.

That which we want to especially note here from this provision of a ram for Abraham is the fact that Christ is very conspicuous in it all. He is seen in our text as the substitute for sinners, as the supplier of needs, and as the speaker from heaven.

Substitution for sinners. The ram caught in the thicket became a substitute for Isaac in that Abraham "offered him up for a burnt offering in the stead of his son." Instead of Isaac having to die, the ram died. "In the stead of" is the substitution truth of the Gospel. "Christ died for the ungodly" (Romans 5:6), "Christ died for us" (Romans 5:8), "For Christ also hath once suffered for sins, the just for the unjust" (I Peter 3:18). The ram—the substitute for Isaac just as Christ is a substitute for sinners—was near, free, and appropriated.

First, the ram was *near*. The ram was caught in the thicket just "behind" Abraham. Abraham could easily see and quickly obtain the ram. In like manner, Christ is near; for He came to the world where the sinner was. He is as near as the prayer of the heart. A sinner may call upon Him to be saved at anytime and at anyplace. You cannot get any closer than that.

Second, the ram was *free*. It cost Abraham nothing. He had no one to pay. All he had to do was take the ram. Christ is also free. Salvation cannot be bought but is freely offered to man. "Being justified freely by his grace through the redemption that is in Christ Jesus" (Romans 3:24). "And whosoever will, let him take the water of life freely" (Revelation 22:17).

Third, the ram was *appropriated*. The ram was in the thicket ready for Abraham, but Abraham had to take the ram if the ram was going to be a substitute. Abraham could look at the lamb all day; but until he appropriates it for his offering, it will not take Isaac's place. It is the same with Christ. Christ is offered to sinners; but sinners must receive Him if they want salvation. "As many as received him, to them gave he power to become the sons of God" (John 1:12). Folk may learn of Christ and know that He can save them from their sin; but until they call upon Him for salvation, they will not be saved. Christ must be appropriated if the sinner wants to escape eternal judgment.

Supplier of needs. The ram supplied a great need for Abraham, for the ram provided the sacrifice for the burnt offering. The ram was the fulfillment of the promise stated earlier that "God will provide himself a lamb" (v. 8). Christ, The Lamb, is likewise the great supplier of our needs. He supplies our need of salvation, which is our greatest need. When we have Christ, we have all we need to be saved. Christ also is the means by which

Sacrificing of Isaac

God supplies our other needs; for as Paul said, "My God shall supply all your need according to his riches in glory by Christ Jesus" (Philippians 4:19).

From this providing of the ram for Abraham, we learn some instructive truths about the where, when, and how of the supplying of our needs by God.

First, *where* our needs are supplied. Our needs will be supplied in the place of obedience. Abraham was told where to go, and he went to that exact place, and the need of a lamb was provided. Had he gone elsewhere, he would not have found the ram in the thicket. We also learn the same lesson several times from the life of Elijah. God told him to go to Cherith and then said, "I have commanded the ravens to feed thee *there*" (I Kings 17:4). Later God told Elijah to go to Zarephath and then added, "Behold, I have commanded a widow woman *there* to sustain thee" (I Kings 17:9). *There* was the place of obedience. *There* was where his needs would be supplied. If we are lacking in our needs (be careful not to mistake wants for needs), it may be that we are not where God wants us to be.

Second, *when* our needs are supplied. The ram was supplied when Abraham needed it. God will supply our needs in time. Sometimes He supplies our needs at the last minute; other times He provides them in advance. But whatever the case, He always provides in time.

Third, *how* our needs are supplied. The means God uses to supply our needs will vary greatly. He supplied Abraham's need by a ram caught in the thicket. He used ravens and a destitute widow to supply food for Elijah. He used the Wise Men to supply the needs for Joseph and Mary so they could take Jesus to Egypt when peril threatened. He provided a coin in a fish's mouth to pay the Temple tax for Peter and Christ. Using various means to supply our needs is a good thing, for it keeps our eyes focused on the Provider of our needs rather than on the means. It is "God will provide" (v. 8) that we need to emphasize, not some particular method.

Speaker from heaven. Christ is also seen in this experience of Abraham at Moriah in the one who called unto Abraham "out of heaven" (v. 11), for that one was none other than Jesus Christ Himself. It was the "angel of the LORD" (Ibid.) Who, as we have pointed out in previous studies, is the Old Testament manifestation of the Second Person of the Trinity. How fitting that Christ should be the One here to show Abraham the lamb that was to be sacrificed. For the lamb typified Christ Who would, some two thousand years later, sacrifice His life as the Lamb of God in that very location.

11. The Proof From His Conduct

"And he said . . . now I know that thou fearest God" (v. 12). H. C. Leupold rightly says, "The acme of true fear, i.e., reverence of God, consists in complete subjection to His sovereign will." Abraham's conduct in his sacrificing of Isaac demonstrated "complete subjection to His sovereign will" more than anything else did in his life heretofore or afterward.

This verse raises a question: did God not know before now that Abraham feared Him? Of course He did, or else He is not omniscient. So how then do we explain this statement in our text? Charles Simeon explains it well when he says, "There are in the Holy Scriptures many expressions, which, if taken in the strictest and most literal sense, would convey to us very erroneous conceptions of the Deity. God is often pleased to speak of himself in terms accommodated to our feeble apprehensions, and properly applicable to man only . . . in the passage before us, he speaks as if from Abraham's conduct he had acquired a knowledge of something which he did not know before . . . [but] Strictly speaking, he needed not Abraham's obedience to discover to him the state of Abraham's mind: he knew that Abraham feared him before he gave the trial to Abraham: yea, he knew, from all eternity, that Abraham would fear him. But it was for our sakes that he made the discovery of Abraham's obedience . . . for it is in this way that we are to ascertain our own character, and the characters of our fellow-men."

Does our life offer much proof that we fear God? What does our meager giving to the Lord's work prove? What does our skipping church to pursue worldly pleasures prove? What does our disinterest in the Word of God prove? What does our worldly lifestyle prove? What do all the hours we spend before TV soaking up the vileness of its programs and advertisements prove about our fear of God? These traits certainly do not show the kind of proof Abraham's performance did regarding offering up Isaac. If we are going to show proof in our life of our professed fear of God, of our professed faith in God, it will have to be better than what most folk are doing. "It is no ordinary proof that will satisfy God, as to the love of our hearts. He Himself did not rest satisfied with giving an ordinary proof. He gave His Son, and we should aim at giving very striking proofs of our love to Him who so loved us, even when we were dead in trespasses and sins" (MackIntosh). Yes, "God commendeth [proved] his love toward us, in that, while we were yet sinners, Christ died for us" (Romans 5:8). Do we offer any proof at all of our affection, of our holy reverence for God?

C. THE CONSEQUENCES FROM THE SACRIFICING

Many wonderful blessings came to Abraham because of his obedience to God's command to sacrifice Isaac. We should not be surprised, for God is the Great Rewarder. No one rewards better. So when you perform like Abraham did, you can expect to receive tremendous blessings like Abraham did.

Abraham was not the only one blessed as a result of his obedience. Blessings came and continue to come upon countless others as a result of his obedience. That is always the way it is; for Scripture says, "None of us liveth to himself" (Romans 14:7). We often use this verse in Romans to show the problems one person's sin causes other people. But people not only cause problems to come upon others by the way they live, they also can cause blessings to come upon others by the way they live. Our problem is that we have too many folk in the former category and not enough in the latter category.

We will consider seven valuable blessings which came as a result of Abraham's excellent compliance to God's command to sacrifice Isaac. They are commendation, illumination, confirmation, multiplication, domination, salvation, and jubilation.

1. Commendation

Abraham received repeated praise from God for his obedience to the command to sacrifice Isaac. The first commendation came when the "angel of the LORD" said, "Now I know that thou fearest God" (v. 12). We have just looked at that comment above. There we noted that the comment spoke of the proof in Abraham's conduct. Here we note that the comment also praises Abraham. Two other commendations of Abraham's conduct in sacrificing Isaac are in "thou hast done [obeyed] this thing" (v. 16) and "thou hast obeyed my voice" (v. 18).

The world is not interested in the commendation of God and certainly does not view it as a blessing. They only value and are interested in the praise of man. But how mixed up they are. It is the praise from God, not the praise from man that is the real blessing in life. You may have everything this world can offer; but if you do not have praise from God, you are a total loser. On the other hand, you may have very little of what this world offers; but if you have praise from God, you are a big, big winner. Covet God's praise more than you covet any other praise. Do not be like some Pharisees in Christ's time who in public "did not confess him . . . For they loved the praise of men more than the praise of God" (John 12:42, 43).

2. Illumination

Obedience really helps to increase our knowledge about God. We have emphasized this again and again in our studies, for it is taught again and again in Scripture, and it is taught in this experience of Abraham. He obeyed God about sacrificing Isaac; and, as a result, he grew in the knowledge of God. This is seen in the name which Abraham gave to the place where God had directed him to sacrifice Isaac. "And Abraham called the name of that place Jehovah-jireh" (v. 14). The name means God will provide. Through his obedience, Abraham had learned that God was indeed The Great Provider. God had wonderfully provided a lamb to offer instead of Isaac. This great provision Abraham would never forget, and it taught him very forcibly a great truth about God. But had he not obeyed the command of God to sacrifice Isaac, he would not have learned so well this knowledge about God. He would have missed out on this blessed learning about God.

Growing in the knowledge of God is a choice blessing. The more we know about God the better. Deficiency in the knowledge of God curses. The prophet Hosea said of Israel in his day that there was no "knowledge of God" in the land (Hosea 4:1) and that this would result in terrible consequences on the land: "My people are destroyed for lack of knowledge [of God]" (Hosea 4:6). While the knowledge of God is one of the greatest blessings that can come to mankind, you would never realize this fact by how the knowledge of God is valued today. Few give it much value at all. Man seeks to increase in knowledge in a host of many areas—which is not necessarily wrong—but few seek to grow in the knowledge of God. The Apostle Paul, however, so valued the knowledge of God that he said, "I count all things but loss for the excellency of the knowledge of Christ Jesus my Lord" (Philippians 3:8) and prayed for the Colossian saints to "be filled with the knowledge of his will" (Colossians 1:9) and to be "increasing in the knowledge of God" (Colossians 1:10). But however great a blessing the knowledge of God is, we must remember that our increase in the knowledge of God is tied inseparably to our obedience.

3. Confirmation

"And the angel of the LORD called unto Abraham out of heaven the second time, And said, By myself have I sworn, saith the LORD . . . That in blessing I will bless thee . . . " (vv. 15–17). Another great blessing which came to Abraham as a result of his obedience in sacrificing Isaac was to be given more confirmation concerning the covenant blessings. God had given these promises to Abraham before (cp. 12:2,3; 13:14–16; 15:5; and 17:1–8), but once again He gives assurance to Abraham of the great covenant blessings. And He gives this assurance in the strongest possible way by saying, "By myself have I sworn." Never before had God confirmed the covenant promises in this manner. To confirm the promises in this manner, God "in a most solemn manner pledges the perfection of his Divine personality for the fulfillment of his promises" (Whitelaw). Scripture says that to swear by Himself is the strongest, most solemn oath and confirmation God could possibly make. "For when God made promise to Abraham, because he could swear by no greater, he swore by himself" (Hebrews 6:13). The importance of and respect for this oath is seen in its being referred to periodically in Scripture (Genesis 24:7; 26:3; 50:24; Exodus 13:5,11; 32:13; 33:1; Isaiah 45:23; Luke 1:73; and, as just noted, Hebrews 6:13).

Such a strong and solemn confirmation of the covenant blessings was in itself a great blessing. We will look at the covenant blessings under separate headings shortly, but here we want to particularly note the blessing of assurance. What great assurance God gave Abraham by this oath. Anyone who has had doubts about their salvation—and has at times gone into the "slough of despond" because of these doubts—will not have any trouble appreciating this blessing of assurance. One cannot have too much assurance. While God only has to say it once to make it so, we still like to have it repeated and confirmed again and again to assure our hearts. As no husband gets tired of having his wife tell him she loves him and no wife gets tired of being assured by her husband that he loves her, so likewise we prize as a great blessing our spiritual assurances. Assurance is a mighty big blessing, and Abraham obtained this wonderful blessing through obedience. While not all doubts come to us through disobedience, a great portion of them do. Disobedience does not produce assurance but lack of assurance. Assurance is a product of obedience.

4. Multiplication

"That in blessing I will bless thee, and in multiplying I will multiply thy seed as the stars of the heaven, and as the sand which is upon the sea shore" (v. 17). The blessings under the heading of multiplication are twofold: an abundance of prosperity and an abundance of posterity.

Prosperity. "Blessing I will bless thee" is translated by the respected Hebrew scholar, H. C. Leupold, "I will most abundantly bless thee." Already Abraham has known something of this abundant blessing in the covenant. But his obedience in sacrificing Isaac ("because thou hast done this thing . . . I will bless thee") simply enhanced the blessing the rest of his life. Prosperity was a constant companion of Abraham, and this prosperity continued on to his descendants when they, too, obeyed God.

Of course, earthly prosperity does not always come with obedience to heavenly commands. But it is not necessary for us to have earthly prosperity to experience an abundance of blessings for our obedience. God may save many of our blessings for heaven. And because any blessing we get in heaven will far exceed any blessing we get on earth, we should not complain if some of our blessings are saved for heaven. Obey God and you will never be disappointed in the blessings you receive as a result of your obedience.

Note that these great blessings are often associated with suffering. Abraham experienced great suffering—the great suffering of sacrificing Isaac—to obtain these abundant blessings. And those who expect to enjoy great blessings from God will find their pathway is not without suffering either. "And if children, then heirs; heirs of God, and joint-heirs with Christ; if so be *that we suffer with him*, that we may be also glorified together" (Romans 8:17). The greatest blessing of all—our soul salvation—came as a result of the greatest suffering of all, namely, the suffering that Jesus Christ went through in order to obtain our redemption.

Posterity. "In multiplying, I will multiply thy seed as the stars of the heaven, and as the sand which is upon the seashore." God uses two illustrations—the stars of the sky and the sand upon the seashore—to drive home the truth of the great multiplying of Abraham's seed.

God never short changes anyone. If you must give up something for God, He will pay you back so very much more. Abraham was willing to give up his "only" son. But God paid him back with so great a number of sons that Abraham could never begin to count them. Matthew Henry said, "Those that are willing to part with any thing for God shall have it made up to them with unspeakable advantage." Jesus Christ spoke the same message when He said, "For whosoever will save his life shall lose it; but whosoever shall lose his life for my sake and the gospel's, the same shall save it" (Mark 8:35). How fearful we often are of giving up things for God. We cling to our money, our time, our possessions, our friends, our popularity, and our positions with a great tenacity; for we are fearful that if we give these things up for God, we will lose everything and become destitute. That is not, however, the message of our text! Nor do we find that message anywhere in the Scripture! It is the message of Satan, and it is a lie. Give up your Isaacs, and they will come back with a multiplied number of Isaacs that will stagger your imagination.

5. Domination

"Thy seed shall possess the gate of his enemies" (v. 17). To possess the gate of a city meant to control the city, to dominate the city, to rule the city. The promise here is a promise of power. True power comes via obedience. "Because thou hast done this thing" (v. 16) you will possess the gates of the enemy.

This principle that power comes via obedience is demonstrated repeatedly in the history of Israel. When Israel obeyed God, they could walk around the walls of Jericho, and the walls would fall down, and Israel could easily conquer Jericho (Joshua 6). When Israel obeyed God, they could go forth singing to meet the enemy; and the enemy would destroy themselves (II Chronicles 20:20–25). When Israel obeyed God, they were strong and mighty; but when they disobeyed God, they became weak and were easily overcome. So it is individually. The person who obeys God has power over temptation that the disobedient person knows nothing about. Some people lead such wonderful victorious lives over evil. What is the secret? The secret is they are careful to obey God in their daily walk. Abraham's obedience brought the blessing of power. It is a great blessing. You may not be able to do a lot of things because you lack skills and opportunity. You can, however, obey; and that obedience will give you more power than many folk who are more famous and more skilled than you will ever be.

6. Salvation

"And in thy seed shall all the nations of the earth be blessed, because thou has obeyed my voice" (v. 18). This promised blessing given to Abraham for his obedience speaks of the salvation of a multitude of souls. This consequence of Abraham's obedience touches men in every age with the greatest blessing that can ever come to mankind.

In this promised blessing from God to Abraham, we will note the Provider of salvation and the proclaimer of salvation.

The Provider of salvation. Christ, the Provider of man's salvation, is in our verse. Paul confirms this fact when he comments upon this promise, "Now to Abraham and his seed were the promises made. He saith not, And to seeds, as of many; but as of one, And to thy seed, which is Christ" (Galatians 3:16). Earlier in that chapter of Galatians, Paul gave us another Gospel interpretation of a promise given to Abraham. When Abraham had just entered Canaan, God promised, "In thee shall all families of the earth [nations] be blessed" (12:3). Paul said of that promise, "God . . . preached before the gospel unto Abraham, saying, In thee shall all nations be blessed" (Galatians 3:8).

Christ said that "Abraham rejoiced to see my day; and he

saw it, and was glad" (John 8:56). Abraham may have had a glimpse of it in the previous repeatings by God of the covenant promises about the seed, but there is no question that he saw it on the mount in Moriah. The lamb substitute, the "Jehovahjireh" illumination, the promise of blessing all the earth through his seed (singular as Paul pointed out) opened Abraham's eyes to see Christ. And seeing Christ brought the blessing of joy ("rejoiced . . . was glad"). Not everyone will be glad to see Christ, however. Only those who welcome Him into their lives will delight to see Christ. For unbelievers, seeing Christ in the last days will be terrorizing. "And [unbelievers] said to the mountains and rocks, Fall on us, and hide us from the face of him that sitteth on the throne, and from the wrath of the Lamb; For the great day of his wrath is come, and who shall be able to stand?" (Revelation 6:16,17).

The proclaimer of salvation. Abraham's obedience resulted in a great testimony of the Gospel. In fact, as we stated at the beginning of this chapter, it is one of the best pictures of the Gospel given in the Old Testament. Disobedience would have ruined the portrayal of the Gospel. But obedience proclaimed the message of salvation well.

Obedience promotes the proclamation of the Gospel. In the last several generations, we have seen many clever and innovative programs and schemes introduced into the church to proclaim the Gospel message. Not all of these programs are bad, but a good many of them smack of carnality and reflect the world's way of doing things instead of God's way of doing things. In it all, the church has neglected to emphasize the most effective way of proclaiming the Gospel of Jesus Christ—obedience to God. If church members would simply live obedient lives, the witness of Jesus Christ would go forth far better than it does with all these new programs.

7. Jubilation

"So Abraham returned unto his young men, and they rose

up and went together to Beer-sheba; and Abraham dwelt at Beer-sheba" (v. 19). This verse does not specifically say that Abraham was jubilant, but it does not have to tell us that. It is the most obvious feeling he could have. For three days Isaac—his only son, his beloved son—was dead in his eyes. But now he is alive! He is alive because God provided a lamb to die in Isaac's stead. Added to this great blessing was the confirmation of great and wonderful covenant blessings and his seeing Christ's day which, as we have already noticed, caused him to rejoice and be glad (John 8:56), and which affirms he was indeed full of joy here though our Genesis text does not specifically say so. Yes, Abraham could not be anything but jubilant as he journeyed back home. One wonders if his feet even touched the ground as he went down the hill to rejoin his two servants and travel back to Beer-sheba. The greatest trial of his life was over, and he had come out victoriously.

If you want joy, be obedient. If you want to be happy, be holy. True pleasure is not apart from purity. This, of course, is not the message we hear from the world. The world's wine, women, and song message is to seek pleasure apart from purity, and joy apart from obedience. One only has to look around even casually to see that this program of the world is a total failure! The world's program for happiness will never bring the jubilation Abraham experienced. Their program leads to guilt, sorrow, tragedy, and worse—eternal torment in hell fire which is hardly a picture of jubilation.

XIV.
Sepulcher for Sarah

Genesis 23

THE SUREST THING about life is death, for "it is appointed unto men once to die" (Hebrews 9:27). We are reminded of this truth in our text; for in this twenty-third chapter of Genesis, we have the record of the death and burial of Sarah, Abraham's wife of many years. One may be puzzled as to why so much is recorded about the death and burial of Sarah. Few in Scripture have as much said about their death and burial as Sarah does. So what makes her death and burial so important to have so much said about it? The answer to that perplexity is that Abraham's response to Sarah's death, both in his mourning and especially in his purchase of a grave, gives excellent testimony of the great faith Abraham had in God and His Word. Leupold says, "The seemingly unimportant event of this chapter, an event that could have been reported far more briefly, is recorded at greater length because it is an act of faith, in fact, a rather outstanding act." The death of Sarah provided a good opportunity for Abraham to demonstrate in a substantial and public way how sincere and great his faith was in God and His Word.

Death always affords the believer a great opportunity to show his faith, for faith responds so distinctly differently to death than the way the world responds to it. Of course, there are times when professing believers do not respond much differently to death or other trials than the world does. Such a response dishonors God and His Word, and it also discredits the claim of these professing believers about their having faith. Their talk about having faith is just that—talk. It is not walk.

SEPULCHER FOR SARAH

To study this event in Abraham's life, which is primarily centered around his purchase of a sepulcher for Sarah, we will consider the occasion for a sepulcher (vv. 1–4) and the obtaining of a sepulcher (vv. 3–20).

A. THE OCCASION FOR A SEPULCHER

"Sarah was an hundred and seven and twenty years old: these were the years of the life of Sarah. And Sarah died in Kirjatharba; the same is Hebron in the land of Canaan: and Abraham came to mourn for Sarah, and to weep for her" (vv. 1,2). The reason Abraham needed a sepulcher was that Sarah had died and needed to be buried. In considering the occasion for the sepulcher, we note from these two verses the time of Sarah's death, the town of Sarah's death, and the tears over Sarah's death.

1. The Time of Sarah's Death

Sarah died when she "was an hundred and seven and twenty years old" (v. 1). In noting the time of Sarah's death, we will examine the measuring, mention, and manner of Sarah's years.

The measuring of Sarah's years. With Sarah dying at 127 years of age, Abraham would be 137 and Isaac 37 at the time of her death. Therefore, Sarah had lived long enough to enjoy seeing Isaac grow up into adulthood. Since she was 65 when she and Abraham moved to Canaan (cp.12:4 with Abraham's age, who was ten years older than Sarah), she had lived 72 years after the great move of faith. Scripture had called Sarah and Abraham "old and well stricken in age" (18:11) 38 years earlier when God promised that in a year they would have a son. Sarah agreed that they were both "old" (18:12), and we would not argue, for at the time she was 89 and Abraham was 99. But by faith, she and Abraham were rejuvenated by God's power to have Isaac. As a result of the rejuvenation, not only was Isaac born, but also the "old" woman lived 38 more years; and the "old" man doubled that by living 38 years longer than Sarah. All of this was a testimony of their great faith in God and of God's great power—a wonderful combination for accomplishing great things for God.

The mention of Sarah's years. Sarah is the only woman outside of Jairus' daughter who has her age revealed in Scripture. Anna, an aged saint of the New Testament, is thought by some to have her age reported; for Scripture said she was "a widow of about fourscore and four years" (Luke 2:37). However, the 84 years is generally thought to speak of the years she was a widow, not the years of her life. But whether or not it was her actual age, it is true that Scripture only mentions the age of women a few times. So we could say (in humor, of course) that women have a good precedence for not revealing their ages. However, age needs to be mentioned when it is a testimony of faith in God and of the power of God, as it was in Sarah's case.

The manner of Sarah's years. Much of what Scripture records about Sarah's years on this earth are about her failures. Scripture records her going along with the lie in Egypt about her relationship with Abraham, her urging Abraham to have a son via Hagar, her treating Hagar cruelly when Hagar became arrogant after getting pregnant by Abraham, her laughing at God when she was promised a son, her lying to God by denying she had laughed, and her dishonesty in Gerar when she lied again about her relationship to Abraham.

But Scripture also says some good things about Sarah. Scripture reports her song of faith after Isaac was born and her desire that Ishmael be cast out so Isaac would obtain the inheritance (a desire which on the surface did not look good, but which was sanctioned by God). Scripture, in the great faith chapter of Hebrews 11, reports her faith in the birth of Isaac (she and Rahab are the only women found in that chapter on the list of worthies who exemplified faith in extraordinary ways). Giving birth to Isaac meant she was an ancestress of Jesus Christ. Little did she realize when she married Abraham what eternal honor would come to her by being married to him. Also, in spite of her failures, Sarah is pointed out by Scripture as an example for Christian women to follow in the area of submission to their husbands. "Wives, be in subjection to your own husbands . . . Even as Sarah obeyed Abraham, calling him lord" (I Peter 3:1,6). God notes our failures, but He also notes our faith. Sarah's life reminds us that our faith can overcome our failures. This is a great and most encouraging truth. It is, in fact, the message of salvation; for though we have failed miserably to live righteously, yet faith in Jesus Christ will result in our salvation and will indeed overcome our failures.

2. The Town of Sarah's Death

"And Sarah died in Kirjath-arba; the same is Hebron in the land of Canaan" (v. 2). Hebron is much associated with Abraham and with fellowship with God. Abraham and Sarah first moved to Hebron after their split with Lot (13:18). Their move to Hebron is what first brings Hebron into Scripture prominence. Besides their abode in Hebron giving it attention, further attention is given to Hebron because of the memorable visit of God and two angels to Abraham there. This visit brought with it the wonderful promise that the birth of Isaac would take place within the year. It was also in that same visit that Abraham made his famous prayer to God to spare Sodom. Then Hebron is given prominence as the place where Sarah died (Isaac also died there). Later in Scripture Hebron comes into prominence again when Caleb is given the area for his inheritance in the days of Joshua and when David reigned from there as king for seven years before he moved to Jerusalem.

Abraham and Sarah moved away from Hebron shortly after the visit from God which promised them a son within the year. They dwelt in Gerar and then in Beer-sheba for the next thirty or so years. Since Abraham returned to Beer-sheba after he and Isaac made the famous trip to Moriah, the return to Hebron would not be long afterward; for we believe Sarah died only a few years after Isaac was put on the altar.

While Sarah died in a city which was much associated with

God, it matters not where we are when we die. What matters is where we go when we die. Most of us have our preference in where we want to be when we die. But we cannot control those circumstances. We can control, however, where we will go when we die—and that is what is really important. We cannot determine the exact length of this life, but we can determine our eternal destiny. Some complain about what they are not allowed to control, but we should not complain, for we can control the most important things in life. We can control our eternal destiny. Is there anything more important than that?

3. The Tears Over Sarah's Death

The death of Sarah brought considerable sorrow to Abraham, as would be expected. Of course, he was not the only one that sorrowed. Doubtless the many servants who knew Sarah mourned; and in Genesis 24:67 we are informed that Isaac also, and not surprisingly, sorrowed over his mother's death. But here we will look only at Abraham's sorrow, for that is all the Scripture reports in this chapter of Genesis. We will note that Abraham's tears were legitimate and limited.

Legitimate. "Abraham came to mourn for Sarah, and to weep for her" (v. 2). The tears of Abraham were legitimate in that they were both sanctified and sincere.

First, the tears were *sanctified*. Weeping is not necessarily wrong or a sign of weakness. Abraham showed respect and affection in his weeping over the death of Sarah. Peter justifiably wept in remorse over his sin of denying Christ (Mark 14:72). The Ephesian converts understandably wept on Paul's neck when he was leaving for Jerusalem and they knew they would not see him again (Acts 20:37,38). And Jesus gave weeping a very noble status when He "wept" (Luke 11:35) over the death of Lazarus. But the weeping of our sinful world is seldom sanctified. The world weeps over what it should not weep over (such as TV soaps), it weeps for lack of hope because it rejects Christ, and it weeps because of the destruction caused by its sin.

Sepulcher for Sarah

All this weeping is unsanctified, for it is weeping that could be and should be avoided. There is nothing noble in such weeping.

Second, the tears were *sincere*. Our text says Abraham came to both "mourn" and "weep." The word "mourn" is translated from a Hebrew word "referring to the beating of the breast as a sign of grief" (Whitelaw), and the word "weep" is translated from a Hebrew word which means to "flow by drops" (Ibid.). Hence, "mourn" speaks of the outward show of sorrow (Orientals show their grief with much less restraint than we Occidentals do); but "weep" speaks more of the inward sorrow. Beating of the breast can easily be artificial; but a flow of tears speaks more of grief of heart—and, hence, sincere sorrow.

While Abraham's sorrow was sincere, we see no evidence that it was filled with regret. He had lived a long life with Sarah; and though he and Sarah certainly did not behave perfectly at all times, yet Abraham would not have to weep out of regret for all the things he should have done for her but did not. Unfortunately, much sorrowing over the loss of loved ones is filled as much with regret for failures in the relationship as for the missing of the loved one. It is hard sometimes to detect in these people's weeping what causes them to lament the most. Joseph Parker said that to avoid the sorrow of regret, "Make your homes happy, banish from the sacred enclosure of the family all meanness, hardness, suspicion, and unkindness; that when the dark day comes as come it will too soon, your deep and tender sorrow may not be mixed with bitterness of self-reproach." Don't wait until the funeral to buy flowers and say nice things about the deceased. Don't wait till the funeral to spend generously on the loved one. Some spend little during lifetime for the one who has passed away; but then after they die, they spend lavishly for casket, service, and tombstone. This sort of expenditure does not demonstrate their love, as they think it will; but instead it demonstrates their guilt for lack of love and/or their desire to gain the plaudits of the world for being so devoted to the one passed away—something they were not.

Limited. "Abraham stood up from before his dead" (v. 3) and ended his tears by promptly and properly assuming the duty of obtaining a burying plot. Tears do have their place, as F. B. Meyer so eloquently said: "Tears relieve the burning brain, as a shower [does] the electric clouds. Tears discharge the insupportable agony of the heart, as an overflow lessens the pressure of the flood against the dam. Tears are the material out of which heaven weaves its brightest rainbows. Tears are transmuted into the jewels of better life, as the wounds in the oyster turn to pearls." However, tears are not to go on forever. Tears are like rain—some rain is a good thing, but too much rain will bring destructive floods. Scripture does not condemn sorrowing over the loss of loved ones; but it does exhort us "that ye sorrow not, even as others which have no hope" (I Thessalonians 4:13). Some, however, who claim to be believers do not evidence much faith by the way they sorrow over lost loved ones; for they sorrow overmuch. Abraham did not, for his faith was strong.

How to end the tears is always a problem with man, however. The world often struggles with this problem, for they have not God. Some seek grief therapy which is the "in" thing today. But it is a sick invention of modern psychology which leaves out the wonderful grace of God, prolongs the problem of grief by continually opening old wounds, and produces more problems that it solves. Some try to end their tears with booze or a wild pursuit of sinful pleasure. But that only multiplies and complicates their problems. Scripture shows us, in the illustration of some great lives, that the best way to end our tears is to address ourselves to our duty. Sorrow, discouragement, and distress can best be handled by getting busy with our responsibilities. If we lay around lamenting all the time, we will increase our grief. Getting busy with our duties demonstrates our faith in God to strengthen us and to give us the grace we need to carry on. Always despairing and putting off doing things insults God and indicates that God is not strong enough in a time of sorrow to help us do what needs to be done. Abraham did not overly mourn; he got busy in the matter of obtaining a burial plot.

B. THE OBTAINING OF A SEPULCHER

Abraham did not have a cemetery plot bought and paid for years in advance of the death of a member of his family. So when Sarah died, this became an urgent need. There are considerable benefits in having some funeral and cemetery arrangements taken care of before one dies, but it is not necessary to do this to evidence faith. Some cannot afford such arrangements, and others move frequently and have no settled place where they could make such arrangements. The lesson here in Abraham's conduct is not whether or not you have advanced arrangements; it is how you act when you make the arrangements. Abraham's action in obtaining a sepulcher was a great demonstration of his faith. It is why, as we noted earlier, it is reported in such detail.

In examining his purchase of a sepulcher, we will note the confession of Abraham, the concern of Abraham, the compliments for Abraham, the courtesy of Abraham, the compensation from Abraham, the consistency of Abraham, the currency of Abraham, the certification for Abraham, and the commitment of Abraham.

1. The Confession of Abraham

"I am a stranger and a sojourner with you" (v. 4). To begin his request to his neighbors, the Hethites (the Hittites were descendants of Heth), for a sepulcher for Sarah, Abraham describes himself simply as a "stranger and a sojourner with you." On the surface this description seems to be nothing more than a humble approach of a person who is requesting a favor of another person. But the statement says much more. From the great faith chapter in Hebrews, we learn that this statement is a strong confession of faith. The writer of Hebrews says that those who "confessed that they were strangers and pilgrims on the earth . . . declare plainly that they seek a country" (Hebrews 11:13,14). What kind of a country do they seek? "They desire a better country, that is, an heavenly" (Hebrews 11:16). This confession of Abraham said that all his hopes and ambitions were not here on earth, but his chief interests were in heaven and his main affections were above, not below.

True believers will evidence to those around them that their main interests are in the eternal, not temporal; in the spiritual, not physical; in heaven, not earth. But many in this world see nothing but this world. Their interests, investments, and involvements are for this life and this life alone. Speak to those like that about the Gospel, and they are completely turned off, for the blessings of the Gospel come chiefly in those areas of which they have no concern. But how eternally tragic to be so shortsighted in one's view of life. How foolish to give the chief emphasis in life to that which only lasts for a very short time while ignoring that which lasts forever.

In view of this truth, one wonders about the genuineness of the faith of many professed believers who show little priority or interests in spiritual matters—such as skipping church in order to pursue some worldly pleasure. Such emphasis betrays the phoniness of their profession of faith.

2. The Concern of Abraham

"Give me a possession of a buryingplace with you, that I may bury my dead out of my sight" (v. 4). Abraham's concern was to obtain a grave for Sarah so he could bury her "out of my sight." There are at least two lessons from this concern of Abraham which was voiced in his request to the children of Heth. One pertained to sorrow, the other to the soul.

Sorrow. While the decay of the human body made it necessary to quickly put the human body out of sight, there is another good reason to do this; and that is sorrow. Matthew Henry said, "While she was in his sight, it renewed his grief, which he would prevent." Henry knew what he was talking about, for his first marriage ended in the death of his wife, and three of his nine children died in infancy. Putting the dead loved one out of sight does not instruct us that when a person dies we should put everything out of sight that would in any way remind us of them and, thereby, cause us grief. But it does instruct us to avoid the habit of some who must keep every memento of the deceased in plain sight and will not change a thing in their living quarters in order that the dead one will be constantly brought before their minds. Such action prolongs grief and promotes emotional stress which makes a person morbid in attitude and action, and depressing to be around. One of the problems with the modern day "grief therapy" program is that its practices are akin to this unwise practice of keeping in sight what should be put out of sight. They want the sorrowing person to go through all the steps of grief (steps which they have invented); and to do that, they keep grief before the sorrowing one unnecessarily and harmfully long.

Soul. Abraham did not give undue emphasis to the grave. In seeking for a sepulcher for Sarah, Abraham evidenced he was more concerned about the reposing of one's soul than one's body. He simply asked for a suitable cave for a burying place. He was not concerned about obtaining a huge pyramid or impressive looking mausoleum. He took action to obtain a fitting grave when the time was necessary, but he was not so wrapped up in the grave that he lost sight of eternal things. This does not condemn prepaid and prearranged funerals and the buying of cemetery lots years in advance. What it does condemn is giving more attention, as many do, to the reposing of one's dead body than to the eternal rest of one's soul. Some folk have gone to elaborate extremes to obtain the most prestigious grave possible. They buy a big and expensive tombstone (to the delight of tombstone makers) to mark their own grave or that of their loved ones. But when it comes to the eternal resting place of their soul, they give very little thought and time to that subject. Let us make the planning for the resting of our soul of far greater importance than the planning for the resting of our body.

3. The Compliments for Abraham
"And the children of Heth answered Abraham, saying unto him, Hear us, my lord: thou art a mighty prince among us; in the

choice of our sepulchers bury thy dead; none of us shall withhold from thee his sepulcher, but that thou mayest bury thy dead" (vv. 5,6). The response of the children of Heth to Abraham's request for a sepulcher was a double compliment for Abraham. They complimented him in the title they gave him and in the offer they made him.

The title they gave him. The children of Heth called Abraham, "a mighty prince among us" (v. 6). The term "mighty prince" is indeed a compliment, but the compliment is even greater than what the English translation makes it. It means "a prince of Elohim" (Whitelaw), that is, "a prince of God." So Leupold translates it, "Thou art a prince of God among us." This title was a great compliment of the way Abraham was living his faith. In his day-to-day conduct, Abraham lived such a godly life before the children of Heth that they esteemed him a prince of God. The world may not accept our faith, but they will watch how well we practice it. Too often in observing the conduct of a professing Christian, the world asks in great surprise, "Is he a Christian?" But with Abraham it was a far different story. He lived his faith with such excellency that his neighbors knew he had a good relationship and standing with God.

That was not always the case in Abraham's life, however. When he first moved to Gerar and lied about Sarah's relationship to him, God had to tell Abimelech the king that Abraham was a prophet (Genesis 20:7). Abimelech would never have guessed it by the way Abraham was acting then. But that is not the case here. His conduct is obviously godly. Everyone could tell he belonged to the Lord.

The offer they made him. The response of the children of Heth to Abraham's request for a burying place was very generous. They said they would let him bury his dead in the "choice" of their sepulchers, not just any sepulcher, but in a "choice" sepulcher. That was quite a compliment. It gave much honor to Abraham. It, like the title they gave him, emphasized the fact that Abraham had lived his life before others in a very noble manner which was worthy of high honor. It said that they, because of his good life, were not disgraced by his presence or hesitant to deal with him.

Believers ought to perform so well in their daily lives that they will not be unwanted by decent company or be someone no person wants to do business with because of their poor behavior. True, believers are hated by the world and often cast out and rejected by the world because of their faith. But what we are speaking of here is that we believers should make sure that the rejections of us are not because we have behaved in an ill-mannerly way; rather, the rejections are because our faith offends those who reject us. When we apply for a loan, our credit should not be so bad that the banks would be afraid to loan money to us. When we apply for a job, our work record should not be so bad that employers would be afraid to hire us. Our character should be so noble that we will be trusted above our peers. We should excel in integrity, good work ethics, and reliability.

4. The Courtesy of Abraham

"And Abraham stood up, and bowed himself to the people of the land, even to the children of Heth. And he communed with them, saying, If it be your mind that I should bury my dead out of my sight; hear me, and entreat for me to Ephron the son of Zohar, That he may give me the cave of Machpelah, which he hath, which is in the end of his field; for as much money as it is worth" (vv. 7–9). The decorum of Abraham here is outstanding. In spite of the fact that he had just lost his wife of many years, he still conducted himself in a very gracious manner in purchasing a burying place. He did not let his personal problems cause him to be inconsiderate of others.

It is in the time of trial that we really see the quality of a person's faith. One may be kind and courteous in good times; but if when trial comes, they cannot speak kindly, are always complaining, and are so wrapped up in their own problems they are inconsiderate of others, their faith is small.

Abraham was not that way. In dealing with the children of Heth, he manifested the finest of courtesies. We see this in our text in his gracious standing when he spoke, in his bowing before them in humility when making his request (as one should do in those days in that situation), and in asking those at the gate to mediate for him with Ephron. The latter act may not be understood well in our culture as a courtesy. But in those days it was very important that you ask the council of the city (whom Abraham was addressing—more on this later) to mediate for you; rather than mediate with the person yourself. This gave due honor and respect to the council, and it promoted good feelings with all concerned. Ephron happened to be present at the time and appears to be on the council also. But Abraham courteously maintained the proper formal approach throughout the meeting.

Charles Simeon, in noting the courtesies of Abraham, remarked, "It were well if, in all our intercourse with mankind, we were careful to maintain a similar deportment. But there are many Christians who seem almost to forget that God has said unto them, 'Be courteous' [I Peter 3:8]. They are arrogant and assuming towards their superiors; they are haughty and imperious towards their inferiors; they are ready to claim as their right what they ought to ask as a favor; and, if they grant a favor, they confer it in so ungracious a way, as to destroy all sense of obligation in him who receives it."

5. The Compensation From Abraham

When the children of Heth indicated they were most willing for Abraham to bury his dead in their land, Abraham then made an offer for the particular piece of real estate he wanted, namely, the cave of Machpelah. The offer he made spoke of good character on his part. He said he would give "as much money as it is worth" (v. 9) to the owner. The words "as much money as it is worth" are translated "for the full price" in I Chronicles 21:22. In the First Chronicles text, David insisted on paying the full price for Ornan's threshing floor so he could offer a sacrifice to God on it. In like manner, Abraham said he would compensate the owner of the cave at the full price. Abraham was not trying to sponge off his neighbors or trying to use his sorrow to gain economic sympathy from the seller—a disgusting tactic not infrequently used by greedy souls.

It is not wrong to shop for the best price and to take advantage of advertised sales. What is wrong, however, is the attitude that is always groveling and chiseling for a cut-rate price but expecting, on the other hand, that the product give a full-price performance. It is the attitude which wants and expects others to fulfill their obligations to the fullest, but it does not want to reciprocate. It is bad enough to see this attitude permeate the world; but disgustingly, we see this attitude oftentimes very pronounced in Christian circles. As an example, we see this attitude oftentimes in Christian day schools. Everybody wants a discount at Christian schools. Nobody wants to pay full tuition, full fees, or full anything. However, if the school has to close because of financial problems, these discount happy people will be the first to criticize and complain and blame everybody but themselves for the demise of the school. Christianity could do a great deal for the improvement of its witness if it followed Abraham's example of being willing to pay the full price for a full performance.

6. The Consistency of Abraham

Abraham had indicated he would pay the full price for the burial place; but when the owner of the property became involved in the business negotiations, it presented a situation in which Abraham could have backed down on his word. However, he did not back down. He remained consistent throughout the entire bargaining session. Just because the seller was being crafty did not mean Abraham had to be crafty. He maintained his high character all through the negotiations. His word was something upon which you could depend at all times. That is a trait that is rare even among those who claim to be God's people. But it ought to be the rule of conduct, not the exception, for all believers.

Abraham

In order to better appreciate the noble consistency of Abraham's conduct in his business dealings with Ephron, the owner of the property which Abraham wanted for a burial place, we need to first consider how Orientals did business. "Those who have witnessed bargain-making in the East say that Genesis 23 depicts it to a nicety. The seller opens the transaction by assuring you, with an expressive 'shalom' [peace], that everything he has is yours, and bidding you take just what you want. You return the salutation, and protest against such kindness; he continues to urge you to oblige him by taking whatever you desire. This . . . meaning no more than, 'I am at your service, command me.' When you at length get nearer business, and he condescends to name a price, which he does in an offhand way as a matter of no importance, it is sure to be six times the real value; 'but what,' he asks 'is that between thee and me?' With much maneuvering and leisurely disregard of time, the negotiation then proceeds, till the seller is brought to the reasonable terms and a bargain is struck" (James Strahan).

The description in our text of the dealing of Ephron with Abraham compared to the above quote certainly manifests how noble Abraham's conduct was but how lacking in nobility was Ephron's conduct. Ephron first offered to give the property, as was the custom. "Hear me: the field give I thee, and the cave that is therein, I give it thee" (v. 11). But, of course, he did not mean at all to give it. All he meant by this statement was that he was willing to sell the property. And do read carefully what he offered to give. It was a crafty bit of greedy dealing. He included the field around the cave as well as the cave. Abraham only wanted the cave. But Ephron knew he had Abraham at a great disadvantage. Abraham needed a grave immediately; and so Ephron indicated, by his "give thee," that Abraham had to also buy the field if he wanted the cave. Ephron is like many in every age who hesitate not to take advantage of another person's disadvantage. He is like the service stations on expressways which charge high prices on service and products because they know that you are stuck if they do not supply your needs.

When Abraham continued to insist on paying for the property (which now included the field), Ephron put a price on the property at four hundred shekels of silver; but he tried to play down the inflated price (some scholars say it was even exorbitant) by saying, "What is that betwixt me and thee?" (v. 15). Ephron would make a typical car salesman! His actions are the same that are condemned in Proverbs 20:14. "It is nought, it is nought, saith the buyer; but when he is gone his way, then he boasteth." Ephron was the seller here, but the principle is the same. He tried to say his price was nothing; but when he gets the money, he will go on his way delighting in what a good deal he got out of Abraham.

Abraham was not dissuaded by all this customary wheeling and dealing from keeping his word to pay the full price. He was absolutely sincere throughout the negotiations for the property. He consistently conducted himself in the highest manner in the negotiations. The council at the gate would be able to easily see the contrast in the character of his dealings with the character of Ephron's dealings. Some, like many of the world, would snicker up their sleeves thinking Abraham was dumb not to indulge in craft and intrigue with Ephron. But the world does not appreciate the wisdom of character. God's people ought to, however. Let God's people make their word as trustworthy as God's Word. That may cost them sales and money, but it is better to be known as a man of your word than to be known as a man of wealth whose word is not reliable.

7. The Currency of Abraham

"And Abraham weighed to Ephron the silver . . . four hundred shekels of silver, current money with the merchant" (v. 16). Explaining "current money with the merchant," Leupold says, "Abraham used the higher standard [of currency] . . . i.e., accepted on every hand as full value." C. F. Keil speaks similarly when he says, "Current with the merchant" is "the shekel which passed in trade as of standard weight." The currency Abraham used said in today's language that Abraham's check would not bounce. It said that when his credit card was run through the computers, it would come back approved. Abraham paid his bill with the best of money, and that included paying promptly. His money was valid the very moment the deal was consummated. As soon as the deal was agreed upon, Abraham got out his billfold.

We should be able to say that in Christian circles this practice of Abraham is universal. But unfortunately, Christians do not seem to have a much better record regarding money responsibilities than the world. They write checks that are no good. They borrow money from friends and make all sorts of glowing promises about paying it back, but their promises are worthless. They run up charge accounts; then they make little attempt to pay them on time or even at all. And when these folk go to church, they cause the church to do the same. Some churches are so poor at paying bills that their testimony among the merchants in their community will never be anything but disgusting. God's people should use the best currency; their checks should be valid; their credit excellent; and their bills paid promptly.

8. The Certification for Abraham

At least nine times in our text, we have reference to the fact that Abraham took care to have his business dealing for a burial plot certified by the most legally accepted witnesses. Today we would say he was careful to do everything legally correct. To do things legally proper in those days, you did your business "at the gate" (v. 10) of a city. This is where the elders or councilmen of the city sat with whom legal business must be transacted. It was also a gathering place for the citizens of the city which would thus provide ample witnesses. Doing business at the gate meant you would make certain that the business transacted would be strongly attested, legally sound, and very secure (cp. "made sure" of verses 17 and 20).

The first of the nine references to the fact that this buying of a burial place was being done with utmost propriety is found in verse 3: "the sons of Heth." That phrase must not be construed as just a mere reference to a man and a few sons. It refers rather to the leaders of the people in that city. The reference changes in words periodically in the other eight references which helps us see the largeness and legality of the witnesses. It is "children of Heth" (vv. 5,7), "the children of Heth, even of all that went in at the gate of his city" (v. 10); "in the presence of the sons of my people" (v. 11); "before the people of the land" (v. 12); "in the audience of the people of the land" (v. 13); "in the audience of the sons of Heth" (v. 16); and "in the presence of the children of Heth, before all that went in at the gate of his city" (v. 18).

Abraham gives us a good example of how to do business matters right. It is an example we need to be more careful about following both individually and in our churches. Failure to handle business matters properly seems especially to be a problem in our churches. Financial books need to be kept accurately and properly, and tax laws need to be known. The selling of bonds needs to have a sinking fund for paying them off instead of assuming the church people who bought the bonds will say "forget it" when it is time to pay them back—something some churches have assumed. Buying and selling property needs more than a handshake; it also needs surveys, examination of abstracts by title companies, legal papers to signify ownership, and filing of ownership with proper authorities. Constructing buildings also needs to be done right. Building codes must be known, and construction must follow professional guide lines. The do-it-yourself church building program looks very economical, and those who give a lot of time and effort to help such a project certainly demonstrate dedication. But if this work lacks the supervision of competent men, it will bring many problems to the church in later years. We have personally seen many serious problems in these areas over the years, as have many other pastors; and the problems can be very upsetting to the work of the Lord. Abraham saw to it that he conducted his business affairs with wisdom. It is a mark of faith and is a good example for us individually and also for our churches.

9. The Commitment of Abraham

"And the field of Ephron, which was in Machpelah, which was before Mamre, the field, and the cave which was therein, and all the trees that were in the field, that were in all the borders round about, were made sure unto Abraham for a possession in the presence of the children of Heth . . . And after this, Abraham buried Sarah his wife in the cave of the field of Machpelah" (vv. 17–19). Abraham had confessed that he believed God about the covenant promise concerning the land of Canaan. Buying the cemetery plot put his money where his mouth was. He invested in God's promises. Buying this burial place was a testimony to all his seed after him that he believed God would give them the land of Canaan for a possession.

Joseph had a similar testimony. He believed God's promise about the children of Israel returning to Canaan and, therefore, instructed that his body should be kept in a coffin until the day of their return so he could be buried there (Genesis 50:24–26). His coffin in Egypt was a continual testimony of his faith in God's promise. Scripture also records another testimony like Abraham's in the book of Jeremiah. The prophet Jeremiah purchased the rights to a field from his nephew during the time when the field was actually under the control of Babylon's armies (Jeremiah 32:6–15). Jeremiah had prophesied, under the inspiration of God, that the day would come when the land would be returned to the Israelites. At the time, it certainly did not look like that would happen. But Jeremiah believed the promise God gave him to the extent that he bought the property from his nephew. Like Abraham, he put his money where his mouth was. He was committed to his faith.

We would like to see more saints doing the same. Some sound very supportive and enthusiastic about the work of God; but if you look at their contributions in the offering plate, it betrays their lack of sincere commitment. Their support and enthusiasm is not real. They are unwilling to back up their talk with money. Others tell you how much they love the Lord and His Word, but you will have a hard time finding them in church on a regular basis. They are unwilling to back up their talk with their time. God wants commitment in our faith. When we say we believe, we are to evidence that fact in our walk.

Sarah was not the only one put in this grave. Abraham, Isaac, Rebekah, Jacob, and Leah were all buried there (Genesis 49:31; 50:13). Every burial gave strong testimony to faith in the promises of God. And it all began with Abraham. He led the way. His example caused others to follow. What kind of example of faith are you giving others? Are you making lifetime commitments that would make worthy examples to follow?

XV.
SPOUSE FOR ISAAC

GENESIS 24

THREE YEARS AFTER Sarah died, Abraham decided it was time to find a wife for his son Isaac, who was then forty years old (25:20). This gives us the beautiful and instructive account in Scripture of how Rebekah became Isaac's wife. In our day of scorn for family values—which is evidenced in such things as the despising of morality, wifely submission, lifetime commitment in marriage, and respect and authority for parents—it is most refreshing to read and study this Biblical record of Abraham obtaining a wife for his son Isaac; for it champions many important values which society in our day despises with shocking shamelessness. This text of Scripture is a great and welcomed contrast to the godless, crude, vulgar, and morally rotten lifestyles so popular in our day.

In this study of Abraham obtaining a wife for Isaac, we will consider the choosing of the girl (vv. 1–28), the communication for the girl (vv. 34–52), and the choice by the girl (vv. 54–67).

A. THE CHOOSING OF THE GIRL

The choosing of a wife for Isaac was certainly done differently than the way we choose our marriage partners today. In seeking a wife for Isaac, Abraham ordered the "eldest servant of his house, that ruled over all that he [Abraham] had" (v. 2) to do the choosing of the girl to be Isaac's wife. Isaac was not consulted about it at all! That amazes us and is definitely not the way we want our marriage partners chosen. We pick our own marriage partners today and would not possibly give that choice to our parents or to a servant or employee of our parents. Especially would we never consent to their making the choice without our being consulted. But before we get too critical and scornful of how some had their marriage partners chosen for them in Abraham's day, we need to check on how well our marriages are doing today. When we do that, we will be forced to conclude that our method of selecting mates certainly has not improved the general quality of marriages compared to those in Abraham's day. Why? Because good marriages are not so much the result of who makes the selection, but what the guidelines are in making the selection.

Our day habitually uses very poor and unintelligent guidelines for selecting a marriage partner. Computers, money, fame, position, and witchcraft are some of the various unsanctified guides used by folk in choosing a marriage partner. Some students in our Christian colleges have resorted to their version of a "Gideon's fleece" test. As an example, they will tell the Lord in their devotions that if their current girlfriend or boyfriend wears a certain colored sweater the next day, they will take that as a "sign" that he or she is the one. But all of these kinds of means for selecting the right mate are totally unnecessary, woefully untrustworthy, and just plain ludicrous.

Genesis 24 gives us far better guidelines for choosing one's marriage partner. It is, in fact, one of the best texts in Scripture regarding the choosing of a marriage partner. Because of this fact, it would highly benefit every man and woman who is contemplating marriage to read and study this chapter thoroughly in order to become acquainted with the excellent guidelines found in this chapter for choosing a marriage partner. And even if folk are already married, it will still do them good to become acquainted with these guidelines for selecting a mate so they will be able to give good advice to others who are contemplating marriage. If people would follow these guidelines laid down in this chapter of Genesis about selecting a marriage partner, marriages would be a lot better than most of them are today.

We will examine here some of the guidelines given in this

chapter of Genesis concerning choosing a marriage partner. We will look at them under two headings: what to look for in a mate, and how to look for a mate. These guidelines will be seen in the instructions Abraham gave his servant, in the servant's actions and prayer, and in information our text gives about Rebekah.

1. What to Look for in a Mate

If one does not know the important things to look for in a mate, a poor marriage is in the making. Our text, however, will give us great help in knowing what to look for in a mate and thus help us choose a good mate. From the passage of Scripture before us, we will note nine important character requirements which need to be present in a person before you marry that person. They are the spiritual, the role, the dependability, the appearance, the moral, the unselfishness, the manners, the industriousness, and the family relationship requirements. In examining these requirements, we will discover what a good girl Rebekah was and, hence, what an excellent choice the servant made in selecting a wife for Isaac.

The spiritual requirement. This first requirement is seen in Abraham's orders to his servant about whom to choose for Isaac's wife. Abraham started with this requirement, and we all need to start here. He told his servant, "Thou shalt not take a wife unto my son of the daughters of the Canaanites" (v. 3). The Canaanites were pagans. In New Testament terminology, they were the unsaved. The principle expressed in New Testament language is "Be ye not unequally yoked together with unbelievers" (II Corinthians 6:14). Mixed marriages are a nightmare for both partners. Neither is going to be happy. How can they be happy when they disagree on the most important issues of life?

Many believers have tried mixed marriages even though the Scripture forbids them. They have often twisted Scripture to try to justify the marriage. But when problems come from the forbidden yoke, no twisting of Scripture will solve the problems or remove the misery of that marriage.

Those who want to marry the unsaved not only twist Scripture to try to justify their unholy desires, but they frequently also try to justify the unequal yoke by pointing to a mixed marriage they know about in which the unbeliever in the marriage eventually became saved. They think that because the unsaved got saved in a mixed marriage they know about, it will also happen in their case. But it is a bit of unholy and unwarranted thinking. That an unbeliever got saved in a mixed marriage simply shows the grace of God. It does not nullify God's command forbidding the saved from marrying the unsaved, nor does it eliminate the chastisement which comes as a result of disobeying God in marrying an unsaved person. Yes, there will indeed be chastisement for the believer when he or she marries an unsaved person, and that chastisement will come whether or not the unsaved mate gets saved. Also the chastisement will be severe enough that no pleasure from the mixed marriage will adequately compensate for the pain of the chastisement.

In view of the fact that Scripture forbids the saved from marrying the unsaved, it is therefore most unwise for the saved to even date the unsaved. Many do, however. But they insist they will not marry the unsaved—they will only date them. But experience shows that such resolves seldom hold up long. Some like to tell us that they are trying to win the unsaved to the Lord by dating them, but that is definitely not a Scriptural method of evangelism! Furthermore, experience shows that the unsaved generally drag down the saved instead of the saved lifting (saving) the unsaved date. Those who would defend dating of the unsaved only reveal how duped by the devil they are. Dating the unsaved is the devil's bait to get them to go farther and marry them, and it is effective bait once it is taken by the disobedient. The more they date the unsaved, the more they become infatuated with them. The more they become infatuated with them, the weaker their resolve becomes to not marry the unsaved. And the weaker the resolve becomes, the more likely a tragic marriage will result. When you date the unsaved, you are dating with danger, courting with corruption, romancing with ruin, and flirting with failure.

The role requirement. This requirement, unfortunately, is seldom considered in selecting a mate. But if a mate does not know their proper role in marriage or will not practice it, marriage problems will be big and bad. The role requirement is seen in our text in another of Abraham's orders to his servant. Abraham told his servant, "Beware thou that thou bring not my son thither again . . . if the woman will not be willing to follow thee, then thou shalt be clear from this my oath: only bring not my son thither again" (vv. 6,8). Abraham did not want Isaac leaving Canaan and going back to Haran—the place Abraham had left at God's command some sixty-five years earlier to come to the land of Canaan. Hence, the woman to be Isaac's wife must make her life subservient to Isaac's life. It is his career, not hers, that has priority in marriage. That thinking, of course, does not go over well in our society today. Women's movements champion the woman doing her thing regardless of what her husband does. But Scripture says to wives, "Submit yourselves unto your own husbands" (Ephesians 5:22). One of the significant indications of the crumbling of society is the general disrespect and ignoring of that command in Scripture.

The role requirement is not limited to wives. Husbands also have a role to play in marriage, and those looking for a husband need to be sure he knows his role and will practice it. He is to be the leader in the home. He is to take responsibility, guide the home, and supply for the home. Many men do not do well here. They are not against having the respect of the head of the home; their problem is they do not want to fulfill the responsibilities of the head of the home.

The importance of fulfilling one's role and the great problems that come when that role is not fulfilled can be easily observed by considering a football team. When the quarterback calls a play, each player has his own personal assignment. The team will do well if each player does his own assignment well.

Spouse for Isaac

But if the players decide they want to do one of the other player's assignments instead of their own, you will see chaos on the playing field. It is no different in marriage. Therefore, a girl should not marry a boy she can boss around, and a boy should not marry a girl that is headstrong and domineering.

The dependability requirement. This requirement (and also some of the other requirements we are looking in "what to look for in a mate") is gleaned from the prayer of Abraham's servant. When Abraham's servant arrived in Haran, he prayed a most interesting prayer to God (vv. 12–14). Some think he was putting out the fleece as Gideon did. But this was a good deal different than putting out the fleece. The servant's wise prayer—wiser than most people realize—was only asking for a girl with some good character traits. The conditions he sagaciously laid out in his prayer were simply conditions that would reveal, in a very clear manner, whether or not the girl had these good character traits which the servant required for Isaac's wife and which should always be required in selecting a marriage partner.

The first character requirement which we glean from his prayer addressed the dependability requirement. This is seen in the fact that his prayer specified that the selection be made from among those coming to the well (vv. 13,14). This meant that the girl would be dependable, for it was "evening . . . the time that women go out to draw water" (v. 11). Those who would come to the well at evening would be dependable girls. You could count on such girls to do their duty when it was to be done. In selecting a wife for Isaac, the servant wanted a dependable girl. So he wisely went to the well where such girls could be found and then prayed to God that the choice for Isaac's wife would come from these dependable girls. He did not pray that the choice would be from among all the girls in Haran be they dependable or not. No, he prayed that the choice of a wife for Isaac would be a girl from only the dependable kind.

The axiom "the best ability is dependability" has a great deal of truth to it. If a marriage is going to be successful, it must have a lot of dependability in it. If a husband or wife cannot depend on their partner, they can depend on having problems. If they are not faithful before marriage, they will not be faithful after marriage. If a prospective mate is not reliable, that person will be a liability in marriage.

It is not difficult to detect unfaithfulness in a person. It shows up in little matters as well as in big matters. If it shows up in a prospective mate, that prospect needs to become a former prospect.

The appearance requirement. Abraham's servant did not ignore appearance as one of the requirements for Isaac's wife. In praying to God, he said, "And let it come to pass, that the damsel *to whom I shall say* . . . " (v. 14). He was not going to approach any damsel that came along. Looks were clearly an important part of the choice. Therefore, when Rebekah, a girl who was "very fair to look upon" (v. 16), came along, he was obviously impressed; and so he approached her after she had made a trip down into the well (vv. 16,17) and thus evidenced her dependability.

Many well-meaning folk are going to argue and say appearance should not be classed as a character requirement. After all, these folk argue, we cannot control our appearance; and everybody does not have the good fortune of being good looking like Rebekah was. But we beg to differ. It is true that not everyone is blessed with extra ordinary good looks, but a good appearance does not require extra ordinary natural beauty. In fact, natural beauty can easily be hidden by one who does not take care of themselves as they ought; and on the other hand, one not greatly endowed with natural beauty can still look very attractive simply by taking good care of themselves. That the servant could see that Rebekah was good looking even when she was doing her chores of getting water spoke well of Rebekah; for it indicated that she took good care of herself. This was not a banquet or some other dress-up occasion which would aid in one's appearance, but it was a working place. To look nice at the well, a girl had to take especially good care of herself, whether she possessed a lot of natural beauty or not.

Therefore, a good appearance speaks of more than just natural beauty. It speaks of good habits—habits which are essential to the well-being of a marriage. Lack of good habits regarding one's appearance can cause serious problems in marriage. Marriage counselling will attest to that fact. If the wife always looks like a hag and the husband always looks like a bum, that marriage will have problems. If the only women the husband ever sees that look nice are women other than his wife, that wife may have trouble holding on to her man. If the only men the wife ever sees looking nice are men other than her husband, that husband may have trouble keeping his wife. Therefore, appearance needs to be duly considered in selecting a mate. If a girlfriend seldom looks like anything but a sloppy Jane, the boy needs to look elsewhere. And if a boyfriend generally looks likes a sloppy Joe, the girl needs to find someone else.

The moral requirement. Rebekah was "a virgin, neither had any man known her" (v. 16). The moral purity of Rebekah is emphasized in our text by the double statement of her purity. Not only does the text say that she was a "virgin," but it also repeats the fact by saying "neither had any man known her."

This emphasis in our text on Rebekah's purity emphasizes the importance of moral purity in marriage. This was a qualification which the servant would certainly insist upon for a wife for Isaac. It was understood in those days that he was to look for a virgin. That does not have to be written out in bold letters in our text for us to know that. It was simply something that decent people practiced. Hence, the servant was not looking for some divorced girl or unwed mother or prostitute! He would not have pursued Rebekah for Isaac had she not indicated virtue. Virtuous women then, as in our day, were not difficult to detect. They generally dressed differently and definitely behaved differently.

Moral purity cannot be stressed too much in selecting a mate. A good marriage is not obtained easily. It takes much strength of character to produce a good marriage. But lack of good morals is indicative of a very great weakness in character, and such a weakness is prohibitive to a strong marriage bond. Not only is immorality a tremendous character liability for marriage (which is its most significant problem), but it is also a great health risk. Medical authorities tell us that whomever you have sex with, you are having sex with whomever your partner has had sex with in the last ten years. With the presence of deadly and contagious venereal disease and also the great potential that venereal disease of any kind has in bringing serious birth defects to children, just the health problem alone ought to scare off anyone from marrying the immoral.

So if you want a good marriage, you must marry one who has impeccable morals. This means you should not marry a divorced person or a person who has been guilty of sex outside of marriage. Furthermore, if a boyfriend can't keep his hands off a girl, wants to spend dates in dark and secluded places such as in parked cars, is ever talking about sex, and wants to frequent x-rated movies, the girl does not need a computer, a psychologist, or a heavenly sign to discern that he is not the one and that she ought to drop him with dispatch. If the girlfriend is immodest in dress, encourages cuddly conduct, does not hesitate to use back alley language, and cannot walk without unnecessary body motion, the boy has a very plain mandate to drop the girl and quickly. Remember that those not morally careful before marriage will not be morally careful after marriage. Marriage is for life. Pick the best. Why settle for a morally defiled mate?

The unselfishness requirement. The conditions the servant laid out in his prayer to God for discerning which girl should be Isaac's wife indicated that unselfishness was also a character attribute he was looking for in the girl. The servant prayed, "Let it come to pass, that the damsel to whom I shall say, Let down thy pitcher, I pray thee, that I may drink; and she shall say, Drink, and I will give thy camels drink also; let the same be she that thou hast appointed for thy servant Isaac" (v. 14). If the girl

Spouse for Isaac

is going to stop her work and give a stranger a drink and then volunteer to water his camels—she is definitely not selfish! In fact, she is extraordinarily unselfish. Giving the servant a drink was one thing; offering to water the camels was another thing. Both acts were unselfish, but the watering of the camels really verified her unselfishness. The servant demanded strong evidence on the unselfish issue, and Rebekah gave it to him.

Unselfishness is extremely important if a marriage is to last and be pleasant, for marriage is a life of sharing and helping. The husband is to provide for the home, and the wife is to be a "help meet" for her husband. Selfishness will do poorly in both accounts. A selfish husband is the kind who will seldom take his wife out for a nice outing but will not hesitate to leave her at home struggling with the care of the children while he goes out and has a good time with the boys going to ball games, playing golf, fishing, hunting, or pursuing some other pleasure. A selfish wife is the kind who insists on having her own way in everything, demands that they see her relatives frequently but will not give equal time to his relatives, and spends nearly all her husband's hard-earned money on herself, caring not that she leaves very little for him. Selfishness thrives under pressure, and marriage generates much pressure. With selfishness being such a menace to a good and pleasant marriage, it behooves those looking for a marriage partner to be alert to selfishness. Therefore, if one's date is self-centered, monopolizes the conversation and talks only about themselves, and always insists on doing only what they want to do—beware. This is not the one to marry. Faults in small letters before marriage come out in capital letters after marriage. If selfishness is easily seen before marriage, it will be an impossible trial after marriage.

The manners requirement. The conditions stipulated by the servant in his prayer for the right girl for Isaac would also give opportunity to observe the girl's manners. How would she respond to the servant's request for water? Would it be a kind, courteous, and respectful response or a rude, crude, and ill-mannerly response? We've already seen that her response was unselfish. Here we note that it was very mannerly, too. This is all seen in just three words. The three words are "Drink, my lord" (v. 18). This was her answer to the servant when he requested a drink. The answer was kind—she would give him a drink, it was courteous—she responded in an obvious pleasant manner, and it was respectful—she said, "My lord." Some may say that "my lord" was just a small thing and that you cannot tell much from that. But not so! It spoke well of Rebekah's manners. Persons who say, "Yes, sir" and "No, sir" to their superiors and elders indicate they are a much better mannered person than the ones who say, "Yah" or "Okay" or "Yep" or "Nope." Speaking to others respectfully reflects good manners.

Good manners are vital if a marriage is to last and have quality to it. Lack of good manners can cut deep wounds in a marriage relationship. A girl looking over a boy should steer clear of the boy who knows little of opening car doors and other doors for her, who speaks disrespectfully to teachers and elders, who is in such a rush to get in line he cannot wait for her, and who walks into a building ahead of her. The same principle goes for a girl's conduct. If she cannot say "thank you" for favors done, lacks politeness and respect in addressing teachers, parents, and others, and hesitates not to kick, pinch, or hit her date—she needs to be dumped. She is no one to marry. She will make marriage difficult, not delightful.

The industriousness requirement. To discover if the girl had the industriousness required to be a good wife, the servant stipulated in his prayer that she should volunteer to water his camels. This seems on the surface to be asking too much of the girl. But it was a wise stipulation by the servant, for it would really reveal the quality of her industriousness. To water the camels meant the girl would have to go down the steps into the well time and time again. And the servant stipulated in his prayer that she should volunteer to do this (v. 14). To volunteer meant she could see when work needed to be done and would do it. That is a better person than those who only work when told to do something. Those who only work when told to work have a problem with industriousness. They have to be constantly pushed. But a volunteer is a different story. Part of industriousness is being able to recognize when work needs to be done as well as doing the work. Lazy people have trouble not only in doing the work but also in recognizing when work needs to be done. Rebekah really demonstrated that she was a very industrious woman. Not only did she volunteer to water the camels, but she also volunteered to water them "until they have done drinking" (v. 19). The servant had ten camels (v. 10), and camels can drink a lot of water! They can drink up to ten gallons of water at a time! Rebekah was volunteering for a long, backbreaking task, a task only a girl who was not afraid of hard work would do. But Rebekah did it; and she did it enthusiastically; for "she hasted, [hastened] and emptied her pitcher into the trough, and ran again unto the well to draw water" (v. 20). The "hasted" and "ran again" say plenty about her work ethics. She was a super good worker! She was industrious with a capital "I."

Industriousness is another important requirement one needs to duly consider in a marriage prospect before hitching up with that person for life. Sloth creates much stress in marriage. To have a good marriage takes a lot of hard work by both partners. So if a boyfriend is lazy, is not interested in working, cannot hold a job because he does not work well, the girl better not hold hands with him and should look for another. If a girlfriend is the type that camps out much of the day before the TV, does not help around the home in house cleaning and washing clothes and dishes, is not diligent about doing her school studies, and when on the job is not a good worker, the boy contemplating her for a possible mate should cease the contemplation immediately. She is unfit for marriage and will make marriage intolerable.

We read and copied from some source we cannot remember a humorous but wise statement by Dr. Bob Jones, Sr. about a girl who was not very industrious. We quote it here. He said, "Young man, have you been going with one of those painted dolls who lets her mother do all the work? Have you been keeping company with a girl who does not get up in time for breakfast, who leaves it to mother to wash the dishes while she spends all her time on looking pretty and pleasing herself? If she one day tells you that she likes you very much and admires you but somehow she simply cannot love you and that she will always be just your good friend; and if you hear soon thereafter that she is engaged to marry another man, don't you play the fool and go and kill yourself! No, go buy them a wedding present! And don't be stingy; make it a thank offering! Then get down on your knees and thank God that He saved you from marrying a parasite who never learned to work, and who could not make a good wife because she was not a good woman."

The family relationship requirement. After Rebekah had finished watering the camels, the servant gave her some gifts and then asked two questions: "Whose daughter art thou?" (v. 23); and "Tell me, I pray thee: is there room in thy father's house for us to lodge in?" (Ibid.). The first question spoke of the first requirement, the spiritual requirement. Abraham had specified that Isaac's wife should come from "my kindred" (v. 4). Rebekah's answer to this first question (v. 24) gave Rebekah passing marks on this requirement. Since we have already dealt we that requirement, we will not deal further with it here.

The second question dealt with the family relationship requirement which we will deal with here. The servant asked for lodging. Rebekah's answer provided lodging in her home and an opportunity for the servant to observe her relationship with her family. Her answer said, "We have both straw and provender enough, and room to lodge in" (v. 25); then opportunity came quickly for the servant to observe her family relationship, for as soon as Rebekah invited him to lodge at her home, she "ran, and told them of her mother's house these things" (v. 28). Good girl. She got along well with her mother—and father, too; but in those days the men lived separately from the ladies; and so Rebekah would first tell her mother who would then in turn

Spouse for Isaac

relate the news to the others in the family.

One needs to pay much attention to their prospective mate's attitude about their home and their conduct in their home before saying, "I do," for it tells volumes about what kind of home that prospect will produce in their marriage. What a prospective mate's attitude is about their parents says much about the prospects of a good marriage. If the father is the "old man" and the mother is the "old lady," and curfew hours, rules, and regulations given by parents for the date are scorned and disregarded, this person is not a good prospect for a marriage partner. If in the home a prospective mate's conduct is disrespect, cold, and indifferent towards parents and other family members, one needs to find another prospect. How one's relationship is with the members of that one's family will tell what sort of relationship they will have with their mate after they are married.

Of course, we have an abundance of broken homes today in which it is difficult to observe family relationships. But even then, the one with the broken home will reveal much by what their attitude is about the home's problems and about proper family relationships. How they have adjusted to the troubles and trials of their home will also tell much about how they can adjust to troubles and trials that come into marriage. Marriage is not without problems, and ability to react properly to these problems has much to do with maintaining a good marriage.

2. How to Look for a Mate

Not only is it important to know what to look for in a mate, but it is also important to know how to look for a mate. You may know all the right qualifications needed to make a person an acceptable mate; but if you do not know how to look for a mate, you will not be very successful in finding a person with those right qualifications. From the servant's actions, we learn some important ways about how to look for a mate. He looked prayerfully, obediently, deliberately, logically, and responsibly.

Prayerfully. When the servant arrived at the town where he was sent by Abraham, he prayed (vv. 12–14). We have already examined the contents of his prayer; here we note the fact of his praying. He was a wise man to pray about the choice of the spouse. This was an extremely important decision he had to make, and such decisions ought to be accompanied by prayer. We are exhorted to pray for all things ("every thing" [Philippians 4:6]) which means we are to pray for small matters as well as big matters. If we are to pray for small matters, how much more ought we to pray about the very big matter of marriage. Outside of salvation, no decision in your life will be more important than that which has to do with the selection of your marriage partner. How foolish, then, to not pray about the decision. This should be one of the most important items on your prayer list. If folk prayed as earnestly about their choice of a partner before marriage as they pray about their troubles with their partner after marriage, they would not have had to pray so earnestly about their troubles with their partner after marriage.

Prayer not only needs to be an important part in the selection process, as it was with the servant, but it also needs to be an important part of keeping the marriage going once it has occurred. Interestingly, both Isaac and Rebekah demonstrate the wisdom of prayer after marriage. Twice the Scripture records significant times when they prayed concerning their problems about having children. The first time was when Rebekah was barren, and so "Isaac entreated the LORD for his wife" (25:21). The second time was when Rebekah was pregnant and "the children struggled together within her . . . [so] she went to inquire of the LORD" (25:22). "Pray together and you will stay together" is a saying with a good deal of validity to it. But if you want that saying to be true, you need to start praying before you get married.

Obediently. Abraham told the servant, "The LORD . . . will send his angel with thee, and prosper thy way" (v. 40). But to prosper in choosing a wife for Isaac required the servant to walk obediently in the right way. And the servant did. Therefore, he could say later, "I being in the way [of obedience], the LORD led me" (v. 27) to the right person.

Walk where God wants you to walk; and you will meet that person who is just the right one for you to marry, if God wills that you are to be married (some do not get married because it is not God's will for them to marry). Walk disobediently and providence will not be on your side to meet the right person. Rather, walking disobediently can cause you to meet the wrong one and make a mistake that will plague you the rest of your life. Unfortunately, a number of folk can testify that they got into a bad marriage situation because they were backslidden at the time they chose their marriage partner. Get out of the will of God in life, and you will imperil the right choice in marriage.

Deliberately. While Rebekah was chosen in a matter of hours and was on her way to Isaac within a day, this choice still reflected deliberateness. If we do not consider the custom of the day in Abraham's time, we will be aghast at the speed in which Rebekah was chosen. However, considering the day in which Abraham lived, this choice was made acceptably and did indeed reflect wise deliberation. The deliberateness of the action is especially seen in the servant's patience at the well. Rebekah volunteered to water the camels "until they have done drinking" (v. 19). That was a very impressive promise; but the servant waited to see if she could keep this big promise, which required long and hard labor, before he proposed for Isaac. So "it came to pass, as the camels had done drinking" (v. 22) that he gave her the gifts and inquired about her home. He proved the prospect before proposing to the prospect. He waited to see if she would fulfill her promise before he further pursued her for Isaac.

Many, many marriages have failed because one or both of the married couple were not deliberate enough in making their choice. Some girls, impatient to get married, go with boys they should not go with and make their decision for marriage based only on the promise of their unsavory boyfriend to quit drinking or smoking or gambling or keeping company with bad people.

They do not wait until he has proven reform in his life. Some who want to get married in a hurry will promise the world in an effort to convince the other person to marry them. But promises need to be proven before you can believe the great promise to be faithful "until death do us part."

Hasty marriages, made before either person has a chance to duly learn if the other person is a good prospect for marriage, are a predictor of big trouble in marriage. Hasty marriages lead to hasty separations. Those in a hurry to get married will probably be in a hurry to get divorced.

Logically. You must look in the right places if you want to find the right partner. Where you look for a mate will have a lot to do regarding finding a good mate. Abraham's servant wanted a bride for Isaac who had character, and so logically he looked in a place where character could be found and where character could be examined.

First, he looked *where character could be found.* Abraham instructed the servant where to look for a mate. He told him not to look for one among the Canaanites. He would not find character there, for they were pagans, and their conduct was most unholy. They would not, therefore, make good marriage partners. The servant instead was told to look for a girl from among Abraham's kinfolk—a much more logical place to look for character. The Canaanite character problem is verified several chapters later in Genesis when Esau's marriages to some Canaanite girls are mentioned. "Esau was forty years old when he took to wife Judith the daughter of Beeri the Hittite, and Bashemath the daughter of Elon the Hittite. Which were a grief of mind unto Isaac and to Rebekah" (26:34,35). Esau got married at the same age his father Isaac did. But his wives were certainly not like Rebekah. They were both Canaanites (and they were two in number which was also wrong). Abraham bought a grave from these folks, but he did not want a girl from them. They would be a grief of mind to any godly parents.

Therefore, do not look in Canaan for a marriage partner.

Spouse for Isaac

You will not find character in dance halls, playhouses, or other dens of iniquity. Nor will you find character on the beach or in some park late at night. You will have better success in finding character if you go to Christian gatherings. Church, Christian schools and colleges, and camps, as an example, are logical and good places to find good people.

Second, he looked *where character could be examined*. The servant went to the well where he would be able to witness a girl doing daily tasks. There he could easily observe the character of a person. The servant also asked and was invited into Rebekah's home. The home is another very good place to observe the true character of a person, as we have noted earlier.

One will be limited in examining the character of a prospective mate if the only time one ever sees their date is when their date is all dressed up and they are going to some special event where they will be putting their best foot forward. Where you can observe character well, however, is in such places and situations as the home (as we noted earlier), in school (when the prospective mate is under the stress of school work), on the job or any place where the prospective mate is working with others, and you can even observe the prospective mate's character when their favorite team loses (yes, that reveals more about one's character than you might expect). All places show character, but some places show it a lot more than others. Look where character can be readily examined if you want to be sure of getting a mate with character. It is only logical to do so.

Responsibly. When the camels had finished drinking, and the servant was therefore convinced Rebekah was the girl for Isaac, the servant "took a golden earring of half a shekel weight, and two bracelets for her hands [wrists] of ten shekels weight of gold" (v. 22, cp. v. 47) and gave them to her. Later, after Rebekah's family consented to the servant's proposal that Rebekah be Isaac's wife, the servant "brought forth jewels of silver, and jewels of gold, and raiment, and gave them to Rebekah: he gave also to her brother and to her mother precious things" (v. 53). In giving all these gifts, the servant demonstrated that he was acting very responsibly in seeking Rebekah's hand in marriage for Isaac. These were not cheap gifts. As Leupold said, "Their weight indicates that they were gifts worthy of the master and of the occasion." The gifts he gave Rebekah were worthy "engagement" symbols, and the gifts he gave the family were worthy dowry—dowry was especially to give proof of the financial competence of the prospective bridegroom. The gifts, therefore, demonstrated that Isaac could indeed take excellent care of Rebekah.

Looking for a marriage partner is a two way street. Not only was Rebekah to meet some very high requirements to be Isaac's wife, but the servant demonstrated by the gifts that Isaac was also able to meet high requirements to be her husband. Part of looking for a mate is demonstrating that you are worthy of the one you desire for a marriage partner. A girl may be a wonderful girl; but if the boy seeking her in marriage does not demonstrate he can fulfill his marriage obligations well, he cannot complain if she will not marry him. It is not necessary to go bankrupt buying an engagement ring, but a cheap ring may be an ominous indication of the boy's inability (or even desire) to take proper care of the wife. A boy insisting a wonderful girl marry him even though he cannot adequately support her is selfish, and it is not the way to look for a good wife. On the other hand, if she insists on the most qualified of men for a husband and yet has not busied herself to be able to cook and fulfill other wifely responsibilities, she is not looking for a husband the right way either; for she is not looking for a mate responsibly. To obtain a good marriage partner, one needs to look responsibly.

B. THE COMMUNICATION FOR THE GIRL

After being welcomed and lodged by Rebekah's family, the servant of Abraham gave them a message. It was a message for the girl—it was for the securing of the girl from her family to be the bribe of Isaac, and it was for the hearing of the girl to inspire her to want to be the bribe of Isaac. This communicating of the message was extremely important to the servant's mission to Haran. In fact, it was so important that if you leave out the message, the servant has no reason for journeying to Haran. So it is with the Gospel. Without the message, we have no reason for the mission. The reason for going "into all the world" (Mark 16:15) is to "preach the gospel" (Ibid). The same principle applies to church. Leave out the message and we have no reason for having church. But we notice that churches have a lot of meetings without the message. Such meetings have little value. We need to get back to the place where the message is a vital part of our church services and where pastors are primarily preachers of God's Word instead of directors of religious country clubs.

In examining the message of the servant, we will note the person of the message, the priority of the message, the proof of the message, and the proposal in the message. In each of these four parts of the message, we will not only note how they relate to the obtaining of a wife for Isaac; but we will also note how they speak clearly of the Gospel message, which is the obtaining of a bride for Christ.

1. The Person of the Message

"The LORD hath blessed my master greatly; and he is become great: and he hath given him flocks, and herds, and silver, and gold, and menservants, and maidservants, and camels, and asses. And Sarah my master's wife bare a son to my master when she was old: and unto him hath he given all that he hath . . . thou shalt go unto my father's house, and to my kindred, and take a wife unto my son" (vv. 35, 36, 38). The message which Abraham's servant gave to Rebekah's family had to do primarily with Isaac. Everything else that he said was in one way or another to enhance the person of Isaac in their eyes. So telling of the greatness of his father Abraham meant Isaac was heir to greatness; and telling of his miracle birth enhanced his being a special person. It was Isaac that was to be the bridegroom, and he needed to be emphasized and glorified in the message, and the servant faithfully did just that.

In considering the person of the message, we note the essentialness of the emphasis on Isaac and the essentials in the message about Isaac.

The essentialness of the emphasis on Isaac. For Rebekah, the message about Isaac would be very exciting news. In fact, it was glorious news. Here was a maiden, employed in humble duties in the home, being told of a marriage opportunity that would immediately lift her greatly in position, possessions, and pleasures. But had the servant not told her of Isaac, the message would have contained no excitement, no promise, no prospects for Rebekah. What a loss it would have been for Rebekah if all she had been given was a few pieces of jewelry and had never been told about Isaac! We would never have heard of Rebekah again. She would have never been the ancestress of Christ. The loss she would have experienced if she had not been told about Isaac is so great that it is impossible to compute the loss.

So it is with the Gospel message. Christ is the main theme. Leave Him out and you do not have a message of hope for the world. But many leave Christ out of the message anyway. If these folk were the servant, they would only emphasize the gifts; they would not tell about Isaac. This is what the cursed social gospel is all about. It only emphasizes the material provisions of man in this life. It does not proclaim the Redeemer Who can cleanse the soul from sin and give eternal life in heaven. What a tremendous loss the social gospel message brings to man. It may fix him up well in this life with plenty of food and clothes and other material things, but what good are all these things if one goes to hell when he dies? Christ must be the central theme of our message just as Isaac was the central theme of the servant's message for Rebekah if we are to give man the best blessings. Leaving Christ out and going the social gospel route is cruelty in the extreme.

The essentials in the message about Isaac. The important

truths the servant told about Isaac really parallels some of the truths we should preach about Jesus Christ. The servant told about how great the father was, that Isaac was of unusual birth, and that Isaac was heir to all that the father possessed and could, therefore, deliver Rebekah from her lowly situation which was caused by her birth. So we are to proclaim the greatness of God the Father, the miracle birth of Jesus Christ, and that Christ is able to deliver man from his lowly sin-cursed situation caused by his birth.

That, however, is not the message we hear from many pulpits today. Instead of proclaiming the greatness of God, these pulpits criticize Him and make Him out to be a weakling or a figment of one's imagination. We are not told from these pulpits that He created the universe or that He controls everything. Furthermore, these pulpits do not tell about the virgin birth of His Son Jesus Christ or that His Son is the only One Who can deliver us from our sin-cursed condemnation. Instead, they tell us that Christ is only human and that He is nothing more than an example and at best just a martyr. These pulpits give us no bridegroom/Redeemer facts. And a message which leaves out and denies the important and glorious truths about Jesus Christ will do nothing for the sinner but leave him in his sins; just as a message about Isaac which left out and denied the important and glorious truths about him would leave Rebekah in Haran with no prospects whatever for leaving there.

2. The Priority of the Message

The message about Isaac, which Abraham's servant was to give to Rebekah and her family, was so important that the servant said to them, "I will not eat, until I have told mine errand" (v. 33). The family in inviting and welcoming him into their home for lodging had just prepared him a meal, but he would not eat of it until he could give them this all-important message. Food could wait as far as Abraham's servant was concerned. The message was more important. He was sent to obtain a bride for Isaac, and he was concerned that this fact be made known even before they began eating.

The message of salvation through Jesus Christ is certainly more important than eating, even more so than the servant's message. Eating has its place, but soul salvation is more important. The world, however, puts the emphasis on the physical over the spiritual, and so it is more concerned about the stomach than the soul, about meal time than the message. This is why at rescue missions we must preach before we set the table of food before the listeners. It is why medical missionaries must preach to the crowd before they treat their physical ailments. If the food and the medicine were first, hardly anyone would stay around for the spiritual help.

All of this exposes the fallacy of the social Gospel which places the emphasis on providing man with physical needs before spiritual needs. Critics argue that a person with an empty stomach will not listen well to the Gospel. But experience says that those with full stomachs are even poorer listeners. Mark 8:36 puts it in perspective. In that verse Jesus said, "For what shall it profit a man, if he shall gain the whole world, and lose his own soul?" We do not wish an empty stomach or ill-health on anyone. But a saved soul is infinitely more important than both a full stomach and good health.

3. The Proof of the Message

The servant's message about Isaac was an exciting and wonderful message. But was it true? How would Rebekah and her family know the servant was speaking the truth? Can the servant's message be substantiated? The answer is a very strong "Yes!" The servant's message was verified in two significant and forceful ways. Both providence and provisions gave ample proof as to the authenticity of the servant's communication.

Providence. When speaking to Rebekah's family, the servant emphasized that providence was working on his behalf. He told them that Abraham had predicted that God would "prosper thy way" (v. 40) in seeking a wife for Isaac; and that in his seeking of a wife for Isaac, the circumstances had really worked out beautifully in fulfillment of that prediction of Abraham. He especially mentioned two circumstances which reflected Divine providence in guiding him in selecting a wife—circumstances Rebekah and her family were acquainted with. First, he mentioned his prayer that the girl he would ask for a drink at the well would also volunteer to water his camels (vv. 43,44)—which Rebekah did. Second, he mentioned that, upon inquiry, Rebekah turned out to be from the very family from whom Abraham had instructed the servant to obtain a wife for Isaac. The world would call that "lucky" or "coincidental." But the servant saw it far differently. He told Rebekah's family that with the circumstances working out so wonderfully, he "blessed the LORD God of my master Abraham which had led me in the right way" (v. 48).

This pointing out of providence by Abraham's servant was most convincing to Rebekah's father Bethuel and to her brother Laban. Therefore, they said in response to the servant's message, "The thing proceedeth from the LORD" (v. 50). They saw that the circumstances were indeed evidencing Divine direction; and this fact helped them to believe that the servant's message about Isaac was true.

Provisions. Another great proof of the veracity of the servant's message was in the provisions which the servant brought along with him. Rebekah and her family could see by the gifts he had given Rebekah and others in the family that he represented a good deal of wealth. The servant had indicated that he was Abraham's servant (v. 34) and that "the LORD hath blessed my master greatly" (v. 35). The gifts substantiated the claim. Greedy-eyed Laban, whose greed is described later on in Genesis, had no trouble understanding this fact. He saw just from what the servant had given Rebekah at the well that the servant represented great wealth. "And it came to pass, when he [Laban] saw the earring, and bracelets upon his sister's hands, and when he heard the words of Rebekah his sister saying, Thus spake the man unto me; that he came unto the man . . . And he said, Come in, thou blessed of the LORD" (vv. 30,31). Note it was the jewelry given Rebekah that is first mentioned as catching Laban's attention. Apart from the jewelry, Rebekah's words concerning what the servant told her would have meant little to Laban. It was obviously the jewelry that really convinced Laban. One can just hear Laban's rather ostentatious welcome, "Come in, thou blessed of the LORD," as he greedily drooled at the sight of all that wealth. Yes, the provisions of the servant strongly substantiated his message as well as providence did.

As the servant's message could be well substantiated, so also can the Gospel message be well substantiated—and even more so. "He showed himself alive after his passion by *many infallible proofs*" (Acts 1:3) is a good summation of the support we have for the veracity of the Gospel message. The "many infallible" proofs emphasize the greatness of the verification of the Gospel message. Such things as the fulfillment of prophecy, the archeologist's spade, the testimony of history and of personal experience by those who have received Christ, all substantiate the Gospel message in a great way. The Gospel message is not built on sand but on the Rock of Gibraltar of facts.

4. The Proposal in the Message

The servant did not tell Rebekah and her family this information about Isaac simply to let them know how their relatives were doing down in Canaan. He told them all this information in order to make a proposal for Rebekah to be Isaac's wife. "And now if ye will deal kindly and truly with my master, tell me [that they will give Rebekah to be Isaac's wife]; and if not [that they will not give Rebekah to be Isaac's wife], tell me; that I may turn to the right hand, or to the left" (v. 49). The servant had informed them of the choice of Rebekah to be Isaac's wife. Then he formally proposed. This made it decision time. Would the proposal be accepted, or would it be rejected? To the servant's delight, the proposal was quickly accepted. "Behold, Rebekah is before thee, take her and go, and let her be thy master's son's wife, as the LORD hath spoken" (v. 51).

The Gospel message also has a proposal; and it, like the servant's proposal, also involves becoming a bride—the bride of Christ. In the New Testament the redeemed are referred to as and put in the place of the bride of Christ. John the Baptist initiated this bride relationship when he referred to Christ as the bridegroom. "He that hath the bride is the bridegroom; but the friend of the bridegroom, which standeth and heareth him, rejoiceth greatly because of the bridegroom's voice: this my joy therefore is fulfilled" (John 3:29). The book of Revelation plainly speaks of the redeemed as the bride of Christ when it says, "Come hither, I will show thee the bride, the Lamb's wife" (Revelation 21:9). But you cannot become a member of the bride of Christ unless you accept the proposal of the Gospel which is to receive Jesus Christ as your Savior. The servant's proposal must be accepted, or Rebekah does not become Isaac's bride. The Gospel's invitation must be accepted, or a person does not become saved and become a part of the bride of Christ.

C. THE CHOICE BY THE GIRL

While the custom of Abraham's day generally had the parents making the entire choice as to what man would be their daughter's wife, the choice in Rebekah's case also involved her own decision. In fact, the making known of her choice is what really decided the case.

To further study her choice, we will note the resistance to her choice, the revealing of her choice, and the results of her choice.

1. The Resistance to Her Choice

After staying overnight at the home of Rebekah's family, the servant wanted to leave immediately to return to Canaan. He said, "Send me away unto my master" (v. 54). They had promised the day before to do this. "Behold, Rebekah is before thee, take her and go" (v. 51). But now the family resisted. They were not ready to send Rebekah away. "And her brother and her mother said, Let the damsel abide with us a few days, at the least ten; after that she shall go" (v. 55). The servant would have none of the delay; and so "he said unto them, Hinder me not, seeing the LORD hath prospered my way; send me away that I may go to my master" (v. 56). We note the subtleness of the resistance and the source of the resistance.

The subtleness of the resistance. Resistance to Rebekah becoming Isaac's wife came in the form of procrastination. While the opposition to her going to Isaac did not come right out and say, "No," this was the message of the procrastination—an all too frequent message of procrastination. Procrastination is subtle. Under the guise of putting off something for awhile, it really is trying to put it off forever. Though the family had earlier consented to letting Rebekah become Isaac's wife, they were now recanting through procrastination. The servant, however, saw through this procrastination and immediately and wisely protested.

Procrastination is also used to oppose sinners coming to Christ. It is a very subtle tool of the devil; for it does not appear to man as an overt, vehement rejection of the Gospel. It does not openly and obviously scorn the Gospel message. It simply says to put it off for awhile, don't be in a hurry, take your time, don't get excited, think it over. But putting it off awhile only encourages more delay which finally leads to denial. Procrastination gives time for the enemy of our souls to move in and begin his clever, but corrupt, arguments to try and persuade otherwise. It gives time for the enemy to build up his forces; so he can attack with greater power and, hence, greater effectiveness.

The source of the resistance. The resistance to Rebekah being Isaac's wife came from those closest to her. It was Rebekah's family, of all people, who were keeping her from the great blessings of going to Isaac. It was not some jealous girl or others who did not like Rebekah who were hindering her going to Isaac. Rather, it was those who would profess to have her best interests at heart. And so the source of the resistance would make the request for the delay look like charity—give Rebekah some time to say farewell to her family, etc. But it was not charity; it was cruelty; for it was keeping her from great blessings.

This same problem occurs in the work of the Gospel. Oftentimes the greatest hindrance to a person becoming saved comes from those who profess to be the best friends of the unsaved. This makes the opposition very effective, for the devil works most effectively when his workers are disguised as friends. But these friends are not true friends. No one is a true friend who hinders you from the blessings of salvation. Such folk are your enemies, not friends.

2. The Revealing of Her Choice

In a beautiful but short exchange, Rebekah reveals her choice to be Isaac's wife. On a stand-off with the servant, Rebekah's family said, "We will call the damsel, and inquire at her mouth. And they called Rebekah, and said unto her, Wilt thou go with this man? And she said, I will go" (vv. 57,58). We note the faith, firmness, and fidelity in Rebekah's choice to be Isaac's wife.

The faith in her choice. Rebekah's acceptance of the invitation to become Isaac's bride is a great illustration of faith. She committed herself to become the wife of a man she had never seen and to live the rest of her life in a place where she had never been, and she did this all on the word of the servant. Receiving Christ as Savior is done in a very similar way. We accept a Bridegroom (Christ) Whom we have never seen and agree to go to a place we have never been (heaven) and from which we will never leave. And we do this all on the basis of the word of servants of God (the word which under the guidance of the Holy Spirit is the Word of God). How strongly this exhorts us to preach the Word. It is the Word of God that is the basis of our faith. Leave it out and you eliminate saving faith.

The firmness in her choice. Rebekah's "I will go" was a very firm commitment. It left no doubts as to her desire and willingness. She did not say "perhaps" or "maybe" or "possibly" or "I'm not sure." No, her answer was a simple and strong "I will go." Her answer reminds us of what Ruth told Naomi: "Entreat me not to leave thee, or to return from following after thee; for whither thou goest, I will go; and where thou lodgest, I will lodge: thy people shall be my people, and thy God my God. Where thou diest, will I die, and there will I be buried; the LORD do so to me, and more also, if aught but death part thee and me" (Ruth 1:16,17). Rebekah's answer was just three words in our translation, but it embodied everything Ruth said. It reflected a firmness of choice that was committed to going all the way in the matter of being Isaac's wife. Nothing was held back; everything was given. Oh, to see more of this sort of commitment for God in our churches today.

The fidelity in her choice. Rebekah's "I will go" sounded so great. But did she mean it? Indeed she meant it, for Scripture says a bit later that "Rebekah arose . . . and followed the man" (v. 61). Following the servant to go to Isaac was the great proof of the fidelity in her professed choice. She put feet to her faith, walk to her talk, and conduct to her confession. Had she not done that, her stated choice would have been proven false.

The same is true with the Gospel. We have many decisions today but few disciples, for few follow-up their decision with "follow." Some eighteen times in the Gospels, we read of Christ saying, "Follow me." That is what the Gospel is all about. Signing a decision card does not a disciple make; it is following Christ that makes a disciple. If our churches and evangelistic campaigns were to count only those that followed Christ rather than those who signed decision cards, they would not be so anxious to let everybody know how many folk made decisions in their meetings. Many decisions lack fidelity because they lack the all important "follow" part. Not so with Rebekah. Her professed "I will go" was also her practice as "follow" evidenced.

3. The Results of Her Choice

"And Isaac brought her into his mother Sarah's tent, and took Rebekah, and she became his wife; and he loved her: and Isaac was comforted after his mother's death" (v. 67). The results which Rebekah experienced because of her choice were very, very great. They were life-changing. The same is true regarding the Gospel. If man accepts the invitation to take Jesus Christ as his Savior, tremendous and blessed life-changing results will happen.

We will consider eight results which Rebekah experienced by becoming the wife of Isaac; and in each of the results, we will see a parallel Gospel application. These eight results involve acceptance, abode, advancement, affluence, affection, associations, acclaim, and achievement.

First, the *acceptance* of Rebekah. "Isaac . . . took Rebekah." The servant brought Rebekah to Isaac and he accepted her. He did not reject her. In fact, as we can see from reading the entire verse, the acceptance was very warm. This, of course, would be a great blessing to Rebekah. We all like to be accepted. In fact, people crave acceptance so much that many times they even do bad things they should not do just to be accepted by some. Rejection is a bitter pill to swallow. But Rebekah did not have to swallow that pill. She was accepted by Isaac.

We have a beautiful type of the Gospel in this acceptance. Jesus said, "Him [or her] that cometh to me I will in no wise cast out" (John 6:37). Rebekah came at the bidding of the servant to be Isaac's wife and was accepted. So is everyone who comes to Christ at the bidding of the Holy Spirit. No one will be rejected no matter how sinful they have been. What a blessed promise Christ gave of acceptance. You may be rejected by all mankind, but if you are accepted of Christ that is what really matters. You can survive human rejection, but you cannot survive Divine rejection.

Second, the *abode* for Rebekah. "Isaac brought her into his mother Sarah's tent." The choice to become Isaac's wife resulted in a great change of abodes for Rebekah. She moved from Haran to Canaan and from her mother's tent to Sarah's tent. This change in abodes was a most blessed change, a most honorable change, and it was a lasting change—for it was for the rest of her life. Being a lasting change really enhanced her blessings, for it meant her blessings were also lasting blessings. Receiving the Gospel message will also result in a honorable change, a blessed change, and a lasting change of abodes for the believer. Instead being in hell for eternity, the believer will abide in heaven for eternity. Rebekah's choice resulted in a very great change of abodes, but nothing is greater and more blessed and wonderful than the change of abodes which results when one receives Christ as Savior.

Third, the *advancement* of Rebekah. "Isaac brought her into his mother Sarah's tent." Rebekah replaces Sarah as the head woman of a large estate. Heretofore, she had been a lowly maiden going daily to the well to get water for the family. Now, as a result of her choice to become Isaac's wife, she is advanced beyond any position she could have obtained in her home.

Advancement is also a result of choosing to receive the Gospel message. When we choose to accept Jesus Christ as our Savior, we are advanced in position beyond anything this old world could advance us. For one thing, "We shall reign on the earth" with Christ during the millennium (Revelation 5:10; 20:6; cp. II Timothy 2:12). What a great promotion that will be.

Fourth, the *affluence* for Rebekah. "She became his wife." As a result of making the choice to become Isaac's wife, Rebekah came into great wealth. The servant had said that Isaac's father was "great . . . [in] flocks, and herds, and silver, and gold, and menservants, and maidservants, and camels, and asses" (v. 35) and that he had given Isaac "all that he hath." (v. 36). So now by virtue of her relationship to Isaac, she came into that wealth. She will possess and enjoy great riches. In like manner, one of the results of accepting the Gospel message is also to possess and enjoy great riches. Believers, because of their relationship to Jesus Christ, become joint heirs with Jesus Christ (Romans 8:17); and there is no greater wealth than that.

Spouse for Isaac

Fifth, the *affection* for Rebekah. "He loved her." What a beautiful statement, and what a cherished blessing for Rebekah. All the riches and position she gained as a result of making her choice for Isaac would not equal this blessed result. She could have been accepted as Isaac's wife and given high position but still not be loved. But that was not the case, for Isaac loved her. But Rebekah would never have experienced the love of Isaac had she not made the choice to be his wife. The same is true regarding the Gospel. "God so loved the world" (John 3:16); but until a person receives His Son as their Savior, they will not experience His great love in the wonderful way He wants to manifest it to them.

Sixth, the *associations* of Rebekah. "Isaac brought her into his mother Sarah's tent." Another result of her choice to be Isaac's wife was that she would gain an entirely new set of associations. There would be a new family, new friends, and new companions. With the exception of her nurse (v. 59) and a maid or two from home (v. 61), which were given her by her family when she left home, all other acquaintances of Rebekah would be new as a result of her choice.

A similar experience comes to those who choose to accept the Gospel message. Such folk become members of God's family, they are children of God, and they gain new friends (and much better friends, too) among the redeemed.

Seventh, the *acclaim* for Rebekah. "She became his wife." Rebekah's choice, to accept the invitation to be Isaac's wife, resulted in her going from a lowly, humble maiden, stuck away in obscurity in Haran to becoming the wife of one of the most famous men in history. By choosing to be Isaac's wife, she became a world famous woman whose fame has reached around the world and abides through some four millenniums. Girls in every age are still named after her. No woman in our age has ever had her great abiding acclaim. Furthermore, by becoming Isaac's wife, she became the ancestress of Jesus Christ. Indeed, what great acclaim came to her through receiving the message about Isaac.

The believer in the Gospel message will also experience much acclaim as a result of his receiving Christ as Savior; for "Whom he justified, them he also glorified" (Romans 8:30). No living man can fully comprehend the great glory for the saint that is predicted in that statement. We may still be in the Haran of the world, obscure and a nobody. But eternity is ahead, and there we will discover glory as no man has ever achieved it on this earth.

Eighth, the *achievement* by Rebekah. "She became his wife . . . and Isaac was comforted after his mother's death." Choosing to have Isaac as her husband resulted in Rebekah being able to help Isaac. She was a true "help meet." Here in our text it specifically states that she was a great comforter for him. Doubtless she also helped him in many other areas over the years of their married life. But had she not chosen to come to Isaac, she would never have been able to serve him at all.

In Gospel application, we have a lesson here on serving Christ. We are of no service to Him until we come to Him for our salvation and are made part of the bride of Christ. Then we can serve Him. But many, unlike Rebekah's help to Isaac, are poor servants of Jesus Christ. Instead of helping Him, they actually hinder Him. Let us not be that way. Let us pray daily that we will be a true servant of Jesus Christ and give Him much delight because of our excellent service.

XVI.
Servant of Abraham

Genesis 24

THE PERSON WE read about the most in Genesis 24 is the eldest servant of Abraham. Though the main focus of this chapter in Genesis is on the obtaining of a spouse for Isaac—which we examined in our last study—yet the servant plays a very significant part in the whole proceedings; for he was the one who did the actual obtaining of the wife for Isaac. He traveled all the way to Haran, selected the girl (an excellent selection indeed), gave her some gifts, requested from her family her hand in marriage for Isaac, paid the dowry, and then brought her safely back to Canaan to Isaac. His performance in selecting a wife for Isaac, as instructed by Abraham, showed what a valuable servant he was to Abraham. It was a great day when Abraham obtained this servant. He proved to be Abraham's best and most trustworthy servant. Griffith Thomas said of this servant of Abraham, "We may . . . fitly regard him as a model for all who are called upon to work for God."

In considering some helpful lessons from Abraham's best servant, we note the calling, consecration, and comparison of the servant—this last point being a comparison of the servant with the Holy Spirit.

A. THE CALLING OF THE SERVANT

We will look at six important things involved in the servant's calling which are also involved in the calling of any of God's servants. These six things are the authority for his calling, the assignment in his calling, the assurance of his calling, the assistance for his calling, the accounting in his calling, and the anonymity in his calling.

1. The Authority for His Calling

"And Abraham said unto his eldest servant . . . go unto my country, and to my kindred, and take a wife unto my son Isaac" (vv. 2,4). Service begins with authority. First there is a master, then there is a mandate. Without these two aspects of authority, service is presumptuous and counter productive. Abraham's servant had both the master and the mandate in our text.

The master. To serve well, you must give due recognition and honor to your master. This is basic and fundamental. Abraham's servant certainly did this. Some nineteen times in Genesis 24, he refers to Abraham as "my master." Those who would serve God well must keep the "master" rank of God before them at all times. Bringing God down to our level will kill our service for Him. Many popular songs today have so cheapened God and Christ that they are not given much "master" respect. This takes away from the authority of His commandments and promotes our own will instead, and that diminishes our service for Him.

The mandate. Service is doing the orders of the master. The servant did not venture out on his own to get a bride for Isaac. He went according to Abraham's orders. It would have been extremely foolish and produced many great problems had the servant presumptuously gone out looking for a wife for Isaac on his own. Likewise anyone who desires to be a good servant of God must serve only as the He bids. No calling is valid unless it has the authority of God behind it. To presumptuously assume a calling is as foolish as it would have been for Abraham's servant to take off on his own to find a wife for Isaac. Yet some do presume and get into the ministry who are not called of God. The glamour of the call or emotions or friends or family have influence some folk more than God has to enter a calling. This produces many problems in God's work and in the presumers' lives.

2. The Assignment in His Calling

The assignment which Abraham gave his servant was extremely important. In fact, it would doubtless be the most important assignment ever given to the servant. Being given this important assignment was a great compliment to the servant. Abraham, like any wise master, would not assign just any servant to such an important task of selecting a bride for Isaac; but the extreme importance of the task would mandate that his very best servant would be assigned the job. So Abraham assigned the task of selecting a wife for Isaac to the servant who "ruled over all that he [Abraham] had" (v. 2). This fact of ruling over all that Abraham had tells us much about the good performance of the servant. It tells us he had performed so well over the years that he had advanced to the job of ruling over all that Abraham had, and that he was doing this job so well that Abraham could trust him to select a bride for Isaac.

Assignments from God are not given out at random. The more important the assignment, the more character will be required to be given the assignment. If you want to be given important assignments from God, you will have to first prove yourself faithful in the lesser assignments He gives you. Some complain they are never given important tasks. Generally the problem is they have never done a good enough job in the tasks already given them to merit being given a higher assignment. If you cannot be faithful in the least, you will not be given a promotion to more. Our present callings reflect the quality of our past faithfulness.

3. The Assurance of His Calling

The servant was very wise in that he made certain of the details of his calling. After Abraham had told him to "go unto my country, and to my kindred, and take a wife unto my son Isaac" (v. 4), the servant asked, "Peradventure the woman will not be willing to follow me unto this land: must I needs bring thy son again unto the land from whence thou camest?" (v. 5). It was a good question, and the servant got a quick and plain response from Abraham which really clarified the details of his calling. Abraham's response to the question was "Beware thou that thou bring not my son thither again" (v. 6).

We need to be certain of our calling. Certainty greatly helps us to fulfill our calling. To gain certainty about our calling, we need, like Abraham's servant, to speak to our Master in prayer and become acquainted with the Word of our Master. When you pray and study the Word with a sincere heart, you will be certain of your calling; God will see to that. Just as Abraham made the details of the servant's calling very plain to the servant, so God will do likewise to His servants who, like Abraham's servant, are earnest in knowing their calling. Those who seem to never quite know what the will of God is for themselves indicate a lack of earnestness in doing their calling. Continued uncertainty is not God's fault. We may only know enough to take a step at a time, but we will know where to take each step if we are earnest in wanting to step where God tells us to step.

4. The Assistance for His Calling

Abraham's servant received Divine help to perform his task of selecting a wife for Isaac. We note the necessity of Divine help, the promise of Divine help, and the qualification for Divine help.

The necessity of Divine help. The servant had an important but very difficult task to perform. He must travel some five hundred miles (the least difficult part of the task) and pick out a girl that was just right for Isaac and then convince her to leave her home and come to a strange land to be a bride of a man she had never met. He needed help, Divine help, to accomplish his task successfully. That he recognized this fact is seen in his praying at the well concerning the choice.

Anyone who would serve Christ successfully needs Divine help. God's work cannot be done in our own strength and wisdom. Christ affirmed this fact when He said, "Without me ye can do nothing" (John 15:5). But with Him it is a far different story; for "I can do all things through Christ which strengtheneth me" (Philippians 4:13). With God's help the waters of the Red Sea will part, the Jordan River will part, the walls of Jericho will fall down, Goliaths will be slain, and prison doors will be opened. But without God's help, we will trip over our own shadow.

The promise of Divine help. Abraham told his servant that he would be given Divine assistance for the task. Abraham said, "The LORD . . . will send his angel with thee, and prosper thy way" (v. 40, cp. v. 7). This information had to be a great encouragement to the servant. He needed help for his task, and now he was told he would be given Divine help.

Divine callings come with Divine enablings. In fact, the presence of Divine enablement is an obvious evidence of one's calling. When the servant of God is tempted to faint before the difficulty of his assignment, he can find great inspiration in the promise of God's help to do the assignment.

The qualification for Divine help. Divine assistance is related to obedience. Our text emphasizes this truth in a statement by the servant. After the servant had seen the wondrous hand of Divine providence in leading him to Rebekah, he said, "I being in the way, the LORD led me" (v. 27). The servant had walked on the path of obedience and, as a result, experienced the leading of the Lord which he so greatly needed. Walk in obedience to God's calling, and you will know plenty about God's assistance. But walk in disobedience, and you will become unplugged from God's power and "be like any other man" (Judges 16:17).

5. The Accounting in His Calling

It is an universal and logical principle that we must give an accounting to those we serve. Christ spoke of this principle a number of times; such as, when He spoke of a "king, which would take account of his servants" (Matthew 18:23). Abraham's servant was concerned about this accounting (which helps to explain why he was such a good servant) and, therefore, inquired about what he was expected to do. As we noted above, he wanted to know what to do if the girl he chose for Isaac would not come to Canaan. Abraham told him that if she would not come, the servant would not be faulted. "If the woman will not be willing to follow thee, then thou shalt be clear from this my oath: only bring not my son thither again" (v. 8).

Abraham's statement embraced a great truth. It says we are judged not by results but by our faithfulness. The servant may not be successful in bringing back a wife for Isaac; but if he is faithful in following the guidelines laid out by Abraham in going to Haran, the servant will not be condemned. In our day there is a much greater emphasis on results than on faithfulness. The emphasis on results is so great and the emphasis on faithfulness is so small that many folk ignore the proper methods for getting results. Instead they embrace and practice the corrupt philosophy which says the end justifies the means. But that is not God's philosophy. God rewards according to obedience.

Men may criticize a minister if he does not baptize a certain number of converts every year; but if he has faithfully proclaimed God's Word, God will not criticize. Many faithful servants of God who have labored hard and long and honestly with few outward results feel like saying, "I have labored in vain, I have spent my strength for nought, and in vain" (Isaiah 49:4). But they need to read on to the next verse in Isaiah; for it says, "Though Israel be not gathered, yet shall I be glorious in the eyes of the LORD" (Isaiah 49:5). One may not be glorious in the eyes of man, but that is not what matters. Unfortunately, a lot of preachers are primarily concerned about being glorious in the eyes of men; and so they adjust their ministry to obtain that glory. However, "Every man's work shall be made manifest . . . [to see] what sort it is" (I Corinthians 3:13). Every man will give an accounting! And in the accounting, it will not be the size that matters but the sort that matters. Large churches and many decisions may impress men; but though the size is great, it is obvious that often the sort is not! This does not condemn all large churches and all the reports of many decisions. But it is evident in our day that many of these ministries which are long on size are very short on sort.

6. The Anonymity in His Calling

Though we read more of the servant than anyone else in Genesis 24, yet not once is he named. All except a few references to him are in humble terms. Fourteen times in Genesis 24 he is called "servant," and nine times he is simply called "man." One time Rebekah called him, "My lord" (v. 18) in a demonstration of good manners; and one time Laban, being impressed with the wealth the servant had brought with him, ostentatiously called him, "Thou blessed of the LORD" (v. 31). But the rest of the time it was humble terminology. Others were named in this chapter—Abraham, Sarah, Isaac, Rebekah, Bethuel, Milcah, Nahor, and even greedy Laban—but not the servant. His identity is shrouded in obscurity. Some believe he was "Eliezer of Damascus" (15:2), and he well could have been. But in Genesis 24, he is never named. He is anonymous.

The anonymity of the servant instructs us in a much needed lesson. It is the lesson of humility in service. The servant made no attempt to exalt himself. If he could have read the account in Genesis, he would not have been upset that his name was not mentioned. He was concerned about exalting Abraham and Isaac and selecting a bride, not about gaining personal honor and recognition. He was not like some who get all bent out of shape if their name is omitted in the Sunday church bulletin.

Anonymity is not easy for the flesh to take. The flesh wants to be up front and duly noticed. It wants its name at the top of the list and in bold print. Abraham, Isaac, and others can be named; but he prefers that their names follow his on the list and not be in as big a type or as bold a type as his name. The flesh forgets whom it is serving. Whatever it does in service is arranged to exalt itself.

This does not mean it is wrong for a pastor to have his name listed in the bulletin or on the church sign out front of the church. Also, it is not wrong having his name mentioned as the speaker on some radio program or having his picture beside an article he has written. What is wrong is his desire and efforts to be the main focus instead of giving God the main focus. What is wrong is spotlighting the servant rather than the Savior. We see so much of this today. Some men's magazines have so many pictures of themselves in the magazine you wonder it if isn't their personal photo book. Some talk so much about themselves (and always as the hero) in their sermons that you wonder if the sermon isn't an autobiography of the speaker. Others use their sermon time to tell about their family or their troubles. It makes no difference what the text is, they find some way to use it as a springboard to talk about their family or their current problems. The true servant is not like this, however. He does not exalt himself but rather he exalts God and His Word.

B. THE CONSECRATION OF THE SERVANT

A calling will never be fulfilled unless there is considerable consecration by the one called. The performance of Abraham's servant makes it most evident that he was a very consecrated servant. We note his consecration in his pledge for service, his preparation for service, his praying in service, his passion in service, and his priority for service.

1. His Pledge for Service

"And Abraham said unto his eldest servant of his house, that ruled over all that he had, Put, I pray thee, thy hand under my thigh; And I will make thee swear by the LORD, the God of heaven, and the God of the earth, that thou shalt not take a wife unto my son of the daughters of the Canaanites, among whom I dwell . . . And the servant put his hand under the thigh of Abraham his master, and sware to him concerning that matter" (vv. 2,3,9). Here is the earnest commitment to serve. Here is the signing of one's name on the dotted line.

Many talk big about desiring to serve the Lord; but they

never come to the place where they make a no-turning-back, strong commitment to serve. They want an arrangement in service that allows them to back out whenever anything else comes along which they would rather do. You can never get this kind to be definite about doing anything at church. Their language is, "I will serve *if*" rather than "I will serve *regardless*." This bunch wants the respect of being committed but not the responsibility. Such attitudes God does not tolerate. He does not want that kind in His service. Neither did Abraham. He wanted his servant to commit himself wholly to his task. And the servant did. Would that we had more like him.

Before going on to the next point, we want to note a lesson gleaned from part of what Abraham said in the oath. Though it is not on the subject of service on which we are presently focused, we did not want to pass by this good and needed lesson. In the oath, Abraham said God was the "God of heaven and the God of the earth" (v. 3). Some folk leave God in heaven and forget He can also help us here on earth. Some leave God at church and forget to bring Him into everyday life. God is both the God of the sanctuary and the God of the shop. He is both the God of the celestial and the God of the common. God not only can save us for eternity but can also help us in everyday life.

2. His Preparation for Service

"And the servant took ten camels of the camels of his master, and departed" (v. 10). Why did the servant take so many camels? The answer is that he needed them in order to successfully perform his calling. The trip to Haran to look for a bride for Isaac was going to be a long, long trip. It was some five hundred miles to Haran. So the entire trip would cover approximately a thousand miles and would last in the neighborhood of a couple months. He needed, therefore, to carry a goodly amount of supplies to support himself and the servants who went with him and also to provide for the bride's well being on the trip from Haran to Isaac's home in Canaan. And, of course, the servant needed to carry with him a goodly amount of samples of

Abraham's wealth in order to substantiate his claim about Abraham's wealth plus give the chosen bride a proper "engagement" gift and pay a fitting dowry for the bride. Therefore, the servant needed all those camels if he was going to have a successful journey. Taking the ten camels says the servant prepared most adequately for the trip.

Preparation is so vital in service. The servant had to do much preparation or the trip would have been a disaster. The same is true in Christian service. This does not mean one needs to go to school until he has a number of degrees behind his name—an obsession of some which speaks more of pride than of preparation, for much preparation is not going to some college but is preparation in personal Bible study and prayer. But when a person today does not evidence much concern about schooling or drops out after a year or two, he is evidencing that he is not very interested in getting adequately prepared for service. Seldom does this kind amount to much in God's service. Unwillingness to prepare reveals poor consecration to service.

We would urge preachers to take this preparation exhortation to heart in regards to their sermons. Today's pulpit is so anemic. The sermons are a farce. Preachers often bluff their way through the sermon Sunday after Sunday. Yes, we know from many years of pastoring that there are so many calls on the pastor's time that he hardly has time to study. But he needs to put some priority on the pulpit! He needs to do a lot more preparation to preach and not just for special Sundays when a big crowd is present. Let him put a sign on his desk which says "Ten camels" and let it prod him to prepare his sermons so earnestly each week that when he walks into his pulpit in Haran, he will have something of great value and substance to give his people.

3. His Praying in Service

We noted in our previous chapter that the servant prayed (vv. 12–14) regarding the selection of a spouse for Isaac; and we emphasized that we, too, should pray in the matter of choosing a marriage partner. Here the lesson from the servant's prayer at the well is applied to prayer in Christian service, for it was not only a prayer for selecting a mate, but it was also a prayer for help in service. We note three truths here about the servant praying in his service: the indispensableness of his praying, the ingredients in his praying, and the influence for his praying.

The indispensableness of his praying. The consecrated servant will be a praying servant, for he knows that without prayer he will not do well in his service. We must pray or we will fail. This is seen so clearly in the praying of Abraham's servant at the well. Had the servant not prayed at the well, there would have been great failure. The prayer provided the way by which God could show the servant the wonderful character of Rebekah and thus show him that she was the one to be Isaac's bride. Prayer was absolutely vital for the servant to be successful in his service, and it is absolutely vital for any of us to be successful in our service. E.M. Bounds was right when he said, "What the church needs today is not more machinery or better, not new organizations or more and novel methods, but men whom the Holy Spirit can use—men of prayer, men mighty in prayer."

The ingredients in his praying. The servant's praying not only involved requests, which we mostly think of when thinking of prayer; but it also involved thanksgiving, which we seldom think of when thinking of prayer. Twice we see him evidencing gratefulness to God for directing his ways so prosperously. We first see his thankfulness to God in his reaction at the well when he found out from what family Rebekah came and that he could find lodging at her family's home. "And the man [the servant] bowed down his head, and worshipped the LORD. And he said, Blessed be the LORD God of my master Abraham, who hath not left destitute my master of his mercy and his truth: I being in the way, the LORD led me to the house of my master's brethren" (vv. 26,27). The second time we see his gratitude to God is in his reaction to Rebekah's family's good response to his desire to take Rebekah for Isaac's wife. "And it came to pass, that, when Abraham's servant heard their words, he worshipped the LORD, bowing himself to the earth" (v. 52).

Thankfulness is a big part of a successful prayer life. But it seldom is more than a small part of our praying. We make many requests but seldom give much thanks. If we are disappointed at not having more requests answered, the reason may be in our lack of thankfulness for the prayers already answered. Also, note that the servant teaches us by his example that not only should part of our prayer life be thanksgiving; but our thanksgiving ought to also be prompt. The servant's thanksgiving came quickly after the blessing came. Giving thanks needs to be done promptly if it is to be done honorably. Delay in giving thanks is evidence of ungratefulness.

The influence for his praying. The fact of the servant's praying and giving thanks so commendably tells us something about Abraham's good influence upon the servant in the matter of spiritual things. Abraham had lived his faith so well that his servant had obviously been converted. The servant would be well able to observe the way Abraham lived from day to day; and so he would see that Abraham's faith was real, not some cosmetic he put on at certain times. We read earlier that Abraham would be this way. God said, "I know him, that he will command his children and his household after him, and they shall keep the way of the LORD, to do justice and judgment" (Genesis 18:19). When we ponder that verse we usually think of Abraham's influence over his own family—which is indeed part of the verse. But what we do not ponder so much is that "his household" was also included. That would include his chief servant as well as other servants. Would to God that we all lived in a way that would commend our faith to all those around us. Unfortunately, professing Christians often do just the opposite.

4. His Passion in Service

The consecrated servant will serve with zeal. The whole

record of the servant's actions in Genesis 24 reflect a man who was very earnest in what he was doing. As an example, he had to put forth considerable energy and effort to travel the thousand mile round trip. This was not an easy task, but a laborious one. But he had the dedication not only to do the task but also to do it with enthusiasm. We want to note one verse especially which shows the enthusiasm of his service. When the servant first saw Rebekah coming up from the well with water, he "ran" (v. 17) to meet her. His running says much about his consecration. He was not dragging his feet, doing only what he had to, showing up late for the church service, and sliding into the back pew; nor did he have to be called on the phone repeatedly to be reminded and urged to get busy with his task. Rather he "ran" to accomplish the work. About the best we see today in our churches is a saunter. Folk can get excited and enthused about ball games, making money, politics, and other things. But when it comes to God's business, most people yawn and take a leisurely stroll to meet Rebekah. Is is any wonder our service is so unsatisfactory and unproductive?

5. His Priority for Service

We have already spoken in our last chapter of this evidence of the servant's consecration when we noted the priority he placed on the message he gave to Rebekah's family. He would not eat until he had told them the purpose of his trip (v. 33). Here we again see the emphasis on priority in service but in a different area, and it underscores the priority he gave to his entire task of obtaining a bride for Isaac. "And he said unto them, Hinder me not, seeing the LORD hath prospered my way; send me away that I may go to my master" (v. 56). Rebekah's family wanted to delay Rebekah's trip to Canaan. The servant would not allow that at all. He had a job to do, and that was to bring back a wife for Isaac, and it had priority over a few weeks' fellowship with Rebekah's family.

We would like to see more of this priority in Christian service in the churches today; and it could come in the same matter, too. Family reunions and "family time" are often used as excuses for not serving. Family reunions and "family time" are certainly not wrong. The wrong is giving them priority over service. A person will do little serving of the Lord if he does not place a high priority on serving.

So many interruptions subtly try to take away time and attention to what should be done. The interruptions look so innocent and harmless. But if they hinder or delay service, they are evil indeed. Therefore, we must deal firmly and forcefully with these interrupters whoever and whatever they are if we are going to be successful in serving our Lord.

C. THE COMPARISON OF THE SERVANT

In previous studies, we have noted that Isaac in his birth and in his being offered up on the altar at Moriah, is a wonderful type of Christ; and that Rebekah in becoming his bride typifies the church, the bride of Christ. This brings us to the typology of the servant who had such a large and influential part in obtaining a bride for Isaac. In comparing the servant's ministry with that of the Holy Spirit, we can see some significant ways in which the servant typifies the Holy Spirit. We note four of these ways: the sending of the Spirit, the seeking of the Spirit, the speaking by the Spirit, and the supplying by the Spirit.

1. The Sending of the Spirit

The sending of the servant to take a bride for Isaac foreshadows the sending of the Spirit in a twofold way. First, the servant was sent by the father. Abraham, the father of Isaac, was the one who gave the orders which sent the servant to Haran to find a bride for Isaac. Jesus spoke likewise of the Holy Spirit when He said, "The Comforter, which is the Holy Ghost, *whom the Father will send* in my name" (John 14:26). Second, the servant was sent in the name of (on behalf of) the son. Abraham sent the servant to take a bride for Isaac; hence he was sent in the name of Isaac. Again we look at John 14:26 which records Christ as saying the Holy Spirit was sent "in my name."

2. The Seeking of the Spirit

The servant sought out Rebekah to be Isaac's bride. In doing this, we see the work of the Spirit in apprehending the sinner, awakening the sinner, and abiding with the sinner.

Apprehending of the sinner. The servant "ran to meet her" (v. 17) was how Rebekah's attention was arrested. She did not know this meeting was going to come about. John 3:8 describes this action of the Spirit when it says, "The wind bloweth where it listeth [willeth], and thou hearest the sound thereof, but canst not tell whence it cometh, and whither it goeth; so is every one that is born of the Spirit."

Awakening of the sinner. The servant soon made Rebekah aware of the situation of Isaac and of her need of him as her husband if she would enter a new and glorious life. Informing her of these things would make her weary of her present life and cause her to desire the much better situation of being Isaac's bride. This work types the work of the Holy Spirit Who awakens us to the curse of our sin and to our need of a better life in Jesus Christ. "When he is come, he will reprove the world of sin, and of righteousness, and of judgment" (John 16:8); and He "shall testify of me" (John 15:26).

Abiding with the sinner. The servant sought Rebekah to abide with her till he could present her to Isaac. Once Rebekah accepted the invitation to be Isaac's wife, the servant never left Rebekah until he brought her to Isaac (vv. 58–67). The Holy Spirit does not leave the redeemed either until they come into the presence of Christ. "I will pray the Father, and he shall give you another Comforter, that he may abide with you forever" (John 14:16).

3. The Speaking by the Spirit

Another area in which the servant of Abraham foreshadows the Holy Spirit is in his speaking to Rebekah and to her family.

In his speaking he exalted the son, emphasized the son, and enlightened about the son.

He exalted the son. If the servant is going to influence Rebekah to want Isaac for a husband, he is going to have to speak well of him—and he most certainly did. He described how great and wealthy Isaac's father was and then said all of this was Isaac's. This portrayed Isaac as a most worthy bridegroom, indeed. It gave great honor and glory to Isaac. In like manner, the Holy Spirit presents Christ as a most worthy bridegroom. Christ said of the Holy Spirit, "He shall glorify me" (John 16:14). This action of the Holy Spirit helps us to discern quickly those ministries which are not of God. The apostates, as an example, are not a true ministry of God; for they do not glorify Christ. They deny such things as His virgin birth, His bodily resurrection, His sinlessness, His Deity, and His second coming. There is no glory for Christ in all of that denial. Therefore, the Spirit of God is not in those ministries; that's for sure.

He emphasized the son. We noted in our previous chapter when we examined the message of the servant, that the main person in the message was Isaac. Everything that the servant said was all related in one way or another to Isaac. The emphasis was not on the servant! He mentioned himself but only to enhance the message about Isaac. We need to ponder this truth today in view of the great emphasis on the Holy Spirit by the charismatics. Beware of movements in which the emphasis is on the Holy Spirit. A favorite song of the charismatics, "Sweet Holy Spirit," has a catchy tune; but it is theologically immoral. How awful to think of Rebekah swooning over the servant and calling him "Sweetie." What would Abraham have thought if the servant had won the girl to himself instead of to Isaac? The way many in the charismatic movement treat the Holy Spirit does indeed depict Rebekah being sweet on the servant instead of on Isaac. The charismatic movement often gives more emphasis to the Holy Spirit than to Christ. But it certainly is not

Scriptural. If people would learn the Scriptures better, they would not be taken in by the charismatics.

He enlightened about the son. The message of the servant of Abraham was to acquaint Rebekah with Isaac. She knew nothing about him until the servant came to her at the well. But after the servant came, Rebekah began to learn much about Isaac. The Scriptures do not report it; but it does not have to report it for us to realize that on the long 500 mile trip to Canaan, the servant would inform Rebekah more about Isaac. She would want to know more about him, and he would be more than glad to tell her all about Isaac. That was his job. And when she came into Canaan and saw Isaac walking towards them, it was the servant who enlightened Rebekah about the identity of the man walking to meet them. In all of this is foreshadowed the illuminating work of the Holy Spirit. Christ said of the Holy Spirit, "He shall testify of me" (John 15:26).

4. The Supplying by the Spirit

The servant of Abraham was a great supplier for Rebekah. We see it in his giving, guiding, and guarding which all speaks of the supplying by the Holy Spirit.

His giving. As soon as Rebekah had finished watering the servant's camels, he gave her "a golden earring of half a shekel weight, and two bracelets for her hands of ten shekels weight of gold" (v. 22). Later, the servant gave more gifts to Rebekah and even to her family (v. 53). This giving shows the servant as a great gift giver and pictures well the gift-giving work of the Holy Spirit which Paul speaks of in I Corinthians 12:4–10.

His guiding. When Rebekah accepted the invitation to be Isaac's bride, she "arose . . . and followed the man [the servant of Abraham]" (v. 61); and he took her to Isaac. She did not know the way, but the servant knew the way. So wisely she followed him. He was her guide. The Holy Spirit is the guide for believers just as the servant was a guide for Rebekah. "For as many as are led by the Spirit of God, they are the sons of God" (Romans 8:14). Note Acts 8:29; 13:2,4; and 16:6,7 for illustrations of the Spirit's leading in the early church.

His guarding. The servant not only guided Rebekah to Isaac, but he also provided great protection for her on the trip. He would be greatly concerned and careful to give her the best possible protection, so he could bring her safely to Isaac. He would guard her as he guarded no other. And he was successful in his work of guarding her, for he did indeed deliver her safely to Isaac (vv. 66,67).

The security of the believer is closely related to the Holy Spirit. "In whom also after ye believed, ye were sealed with that holy Spirit of promise, which is the earnest of our inheritance until the redemption of the purchased possession, unto the praise of his glory" (Ephesians 1:13,14). "And grieve not the holy Spirit of God, whereby ye are sealed unto the day of redemption" (Ephesians 4:30). To think you can lose your salvation would suggest that the servant would lose Rebekah along the way. Such is a ludicrous thought!

It is instructive to note that those who are so involved in the charismatic movement, which embraces so much false teaching about the Holy Spirit, have trouble with the doctrine of the security of the believer. That should tell you something about the perils of the charismatic movement.

XVII.
Sunset of Life

Genesis 25:1–10

The final account in Genesis of Abraham's life covers his last thirty-five years. The account moves quickly over the thirty-five years; there are no reports of any special appearances of God to him or of any special trials from God for him. As Matthew Henry said, "All the days, even of the best and greatest saints, are not eminent days, some slide on silently."

This last account of Abraham can be considered a transitional text to take us on to the next "generations" division of the book of Genesis. Abraham's story has been recorded under the "generations of Terah" (11:27). Now Scripture is ready to take us on to the "generations of Ishmael" (25:12) and more particularly to the "generations of Isaac" (25:19). Isaac's "generations" section is much lengthier and much more important than Ishmael's, for it involves the chosen seed. Transitional texts should not be despised, for they are something like a coupler on a train car—they do not carry the freight but without them no freight would move. Transitional texts have considerable value, and the Bible student will discover good lessons in them if he is diligent about his study of the Word.

The word "generations" as it is used in Genesis means the history of something. There are ten "generations" given in the book of Genesis by which the book is divided. First is the "generations of the heavens and of the earth" (2:4). Second is the "generations of Adam" (5:1). Third is the "generations of Noah" (6:9). Fourth is the "generations of the sons of Noah" (10:1). Fifth is the "generations of Shem" (11:10). Sixth is the "generations of Terah" which is the history of Terah mainly in his son Abraham (11:27). Seventh is the "generations of Ishmael" (25:12). Eighth is the "generations of Isaac" (25:19) of which a large section of that text is about his son Jacob's experiences. Ninth is the "generations of Esau" (36:1). Tenth is the "generations of Jacob" (37:2) which is the history of Jacob chiefly in his son Joseph. These "generations" divisions of Genesis remind us again of the wonderful construction of the Scripture. Contrary to what the critics want to think and try to get us to think, the Bible is not a meaningless collection of myths thrown together haphazardly without rhyme or reason. It is a Divine book of facts put together intricately by heavenly wisdom.

From this last account of Abraham which closes out this particular "generations" section in Genesis, we will consider the supplements to his family (vv. 1–4), the specifics of his will (vv. 5, 6), and the statements about his death (vv. 7–10).

A. THE SUPPLEMENTS TO HIS FAMILY

In the last thirty-five years of his life, Abraham's family grew considerably compared to his first 140 years. For the first 140 years of his life, he had but two sons. One son Ishmael came via Hagar as a result of yielding to Sarah's unholy scheme when Abraham was 86. The second son Isaac came as a result of Divine promise and power when Abraham was 100. Now, a few years after Sarah died, Abraham's family begins to grow more than it had in the previous 140 years.

We will note the two main supplements to his family: the addition of the spouse and the addition of the sons.

1. The Addition of the Spouse

"Then again Abraham took a wife, and her name was Keturah" (v. 1). There is a cloud over this marriage to Keturah. It does not represent the highest road morally. In its day, however, it would be totally acceptable—just as the arrangement Abraham had with Hagar was acceptable to society then. But it was not the high and holy standard God originally set forth in Scripture, and it is not the standard Christ and the New Testament emphasizes. Marriage is a lifetime commitment. Only when one's partner dies is the other free to marry again (Romans 7:1–3). From that standpoint, Abraham seemingly would be free to marry after Sarah died. But Keturah was something other than another wife. In Scripture she was put in the category of a concubine (v. 6 and I Chronicles 1:32). There are three Hebrew words translated concubine in the Old Testament. The Hebrew word in our text means "a concubine without the authority and dignity of a wife; spoke commonly of a female slave, who was also usually a legal concubine" (Wilson). In verse 6 the word concubine is in the plural form because Hagar is included.

Concubines are certainly not God's plan for man! Yes, in the Old Testament there was considerable plurality of wives and a host of concubines for even some of those who are considered the great saints of God. But that, of course, does not sanction such practices for today; nor did it sanction such practice in those days. God's original plan was a one man one woman arrangement. It has never changed. Jesus Christ and the New Testament repeatedly emphasize this truth and have shown the Old Testament practices to be wrong. That God blessed some of the men of old in spite of their sin in this area is not a justification of the sin. It is only a result of God's grace, not a result of God changing the rules. But even though the Old Testament does not condemn these practices as severely as the New Testament, you will still notice many problems in the lives of the saints of the Old Testament because of their unsavory women arrangements.

2. The Addition of the Sons

"And she [Keturah] bore him Zimran, and Jokshan, and Medan, and Midian, and Ishbak, and Shuah" (v. 2). Keturah bore Abraham six sons. We will note here the health of Abraham which made it possible for him to father the sons, and the history of the sons.

The health of Abraham. Abraham had become impotent and Sarah had gone past childbearing before Isaac was born. But God miraculously restored the ability of Abraham and Sarah to have children. We learn in this text that the restoration of Abraham's virility was not a temporary restoration. It was a permanent restoration. That does not justify his situation with Keturah and the having of children via her. But it does show what a great miracle God worked in Abraham when He made it possible for him to be the father of Isaac.

God is still the God of the impossible. He Who made it possible for Abraham to bear physical fruit can do the same with men spiritually. When a sinner comes to Jesus Christ for salvation, he is transformed and made able to manifest the fruit of the Spirit which he could not do before he was saved. Another application of God's enabling power for Abraham will be found in the matter of our service for God. We may be unable in ourselves to serve God and bear fruit in service; but in whatever area God calls us to serve, He will empower us in that area. This is a blessed encouragement to anyone who senses the call of God in his life but also keenly senses his own weakness.

The history of the sons. Scripture not only gives us the names of the six sons, but it also (in verses 3 and 4) gives us the names of seven of the grandsons (Sheba, Dedan, Ephah, Epher, Hanoch, Abidah, and Eldaah) and three of the great-grandsons (Asshurim, Letushim, and Leummim) which came from this union of Abraham and Keturah. Some justify the union because it helped fulfill the Divine promise that Abraham would be a father of many nations (17:4). But these sons were not necessary to fulfill that promise. That promise was more than amply fulfilled through the promised seed of Isaac and his descendants.

Scholars have attempted to learn more about the history of the peoples and nations these sons, grandsons, and great-grandsons became; but about the best they can learn is that "these six sons so mingled with Ishmael as to be indistinguishable" (Barnhouse). There is one exception, however, to the obscurity of the sons. That is the son named Midian. The descendants of the Midianites do show up significantly in Scripture in a few places which enables us to learn more about them. We note five of the times Scripture mentions them after our text; and in each case, except the first one, the mention is associated with dishonor.

The first mention of the Midianites after our text is found in Genesis 36, the chapter which gives us the "generations" of Esau. In verse 35 of this chapter we read, "And Husham (a king over Edom) died, and Hadad the son of Bedad, who smote Midian in the field of Moab, reigned in his stead."

The second mention of the Midianites after our text is found in the history of Joseph. They were involved in the selling of Joseph by his brothers—which certainly was not an honorable deed. "Then there passed by Midianites merchantmen; and they [Joseph's brothers] drew and lifted up Joseph out of the pit, and sold Joseph to the Ishmaelites for twenty pieces of silver" (Genesis 37:28). The use of both Midianites and Ishmaelites interchangeably shows what we have already mentioned, namely, that the sons of Keturah by and large merged with the descendants of Ishmael.

The third appearance of the Midianites after our text has to do with Moses. Moses fled Egypt and went to the land of Midian (in the Sinai peninsula—one of the two main locations of the Midianites—the other location being east of the Jordan in the vicinity of the Moabites) and married a daughter of a priest of Midian (Exodus 2:15–21). The dishonor associated with this marriage is that she did not prove to be the best sort of wife, however, as later Scripture attests (Exodus 4:24–26; 18:2).

The fourth appearance of the Midianites after our text is one that forever stains their record. When Moses was leading the children of Israel towards the promised land, the Midianites, along with the Moabites, tried to get Balaam to curse the Israelites. Failing in this, they then resorted to corrupting the Israelites through their women (Numbers 23–25). This evil of the Midianites against the Israelites so upset God that He commanded Moses to "Vex the Midianites, and smite them" (Numbers 25:17), and "Avenge the children of Israel of the Midianites" (Numbers 31:2). This Moses did (Numbers 31:3–12), and he did it so well that it was several hundred years before Midian again became a problem for Israel.

The fifth appearance of the Midianites after our text is a well known one found in the book of Judges. It has to do with Gideon. The Midianites were the big enemy of Israel during Gideon's time. But Gideon, through the great miracle help of God, was able to run the Midianites out of the country and bring great destruction upon them (see author's book on Gideon).

So the history we know from Scripture about Abraham's sons via Keturah does not encourage us to think approvingly of the union of Abraham and Keturah. True, good unions sometimes have bad offspring; for Isaac and Rebekah had Esau (of course, they also had Jacob which more than counteracts the bad in Esau). However, the union of Abraham and Keturah is not reported by Scripture as having any good results. The only results recorded (the Midianites) are bad results. This fact cannot be easily dismissed when assessing the wisdom of Abraham marrying Keturah. It also is a good warning to all mankind that in marriage we cannot afford to enter into doubtful arrangements. Unless the marriage situation is unquestionably a holy situation, we need to oppose it and never enter into it.

B. THE SPECIFICS OF HIS WILL

While the marriage to Keturah is questionable, the way Abraham handled the distribution of his estate certainly is not. Abraham had a good will. He exercised great wisdom in dividing his estate amongst his children. We will note three wise things regarding the will and its administration. They are the preference for Isaac, the presents for others, and the punctuality of administration.

1. The Preference for Isaac

"And Abraham gave all that he had unto Isaac" (v. 5). Abraham would have been in trouble with God if he had done other-

Sunset of Life

wise. Back when Abraham was 99, God had told him very plainly, "My covenant will I establish with Isaac" (17:21). This was in response to Abraham's plea to God, "O, that Ishmael might live before thee!" (17:18). Ishmael was not to be the heir to the covenant, but Isaac was. This truth was later emphasized and confirmed when Ishmael was mocking Isaac. Sarah told Abraham, "Cast out this bondwoman and her son [Ishmael]; for the son of this bondwoman shall not be heir with my son, even with Isaac" (21:10). God, in confirmation of what He had said earlier about establishing His covenant with Isaac, told Abraham He agreed with Sarah (21:12). In his will, Abraham did not deviate from God's mandate; and so Isaac was given the covenant blessing and "all" that went with it.

Giving all to Isaac was also a wise thing from the standpoint of Rebekah and his best servant. Abraham's servant had told Rebekah and her family that "unto him [Isaac] hath he [Abraham] given all that he hath" (24:36). The servant knew the details of Abraham's will, and it was a good selling point in gaining a wife for Isaac. She needed to know his status, and the servant told her. For Abraham to change his mind about giving all to Isaac would not only have put him in trouble with God (where the main trouble would be), but it would have also put him in trouble with his daughter-in-law Rebekah and with his best servant.

In giving all his estate to Isaac, Abraham was simply honoring God and His Word with his will. Abraham practiced what believers should always practice in regard to their wills; that is, they should always honor God and His Word with their wills. Therefore, let not the saints of God endow the world with their estates. Let not the saints of God give their estates to people and institutions that do not honor God and the Word of God. Once in awhile, one hears about some Christian who bequeathed some state college thousands of dollars. How sick! These state colleges and universities do not honor God and His Word! They do just the opposite! With many godly ministries struggling to do more for God, these estates ought to be going to help them instead of some ungodly state school.

2. The Presents for Others

"Unto the sons of the concubines, which Abraham had, Abraham gave gifts, and sent them away from Isaac" (v. 6). Whitelaw quotes Lange in saying these gifts "doubtless established them as youthful nomads." Abraham, as their father, would be obligated by the duty of a father to do something of this nature.

Note that the giving of the presents to the other sons was accompanied by the important action of sending them away from Isaac. This was necessary, for Abraham's will gave Isaac all the land of Canaan. These other sons had no claim on Canaan and needed to be sent away. Furthermore, as we noted above regarding Ishmael, it would not be good to have his other sons with Isaac; for this could jeopardize Isaac's entire situation and produce some dangerous attitudes of greed for his possessions. In this action, "Abraham bore clear witness to the fact that the spiritual and the carnal or worldly cannot and must not be mixed . . . They could have no portion with Isaac, nor could they live where they might influence Isaac" (Barnhouse).

The way Abraham dealt with his other sons promoted peace for all concerned. That is another factor we need to consider in our wills. Wills cannot control peace for centuries, but they ought to be so ordered that they do not start an immediate war within the family. Wills should prevent as much ill-will and fighting as possible. Of course, some folk are so greedy that no matter how a will is made out, they will not be satisfied and will fuss. However, generally speaking, wills can prevent many unnecessary problems and should be set up to do just that. Abraham knew how to deal well with his estate and his family.

3. The Punctuality of Administration

Abraham wisely took care of the dividing up of his estate "while he yet lived" (v. 6). This is a good example for everyone. Had Abraham left it up to his benefactors to settle his estate, untold problems would have developed—for one thing, Isaac would doubtless have had difficulty getting what he was supposed to get of the estate. If you want your estate settled a certain way, you will have to take steps to make that happen. You cannot expect it to happen if you do nothing about it before you die. Abraham sets us a good example here of taking care of his will punctually.

It may not be necessary to make a will out when you are twenty years of age and have few, if any, possessions of value. But you do need to get your house in order in a reasonable time. Failure to get your will taken care of punctually increases the cost of settling your estate and causes others a host of unnecessary problems. As an example, if your will is not made out by the time you die, the state steps in and takes a big chunk out of your estate. That is totally disgusting, but that is the law of the state. One is repulsed by the shameless heartlessness of the people that make laws which causes the government to capitalize on the sorrows of others. But much of that can be avoided by punctually taking care of one's will.

C. THE STATEMENTS ABOUT HIS DEATH

The death of Abraham is described briefly in just a few verses. But though a brief description, it is very instructive. To learn some important truths from this description of his death, we will note his age at death and his abode after death.

1. His Age at Death

"And these are the days of the years of Abraham's life which he lived, an hundred threescore and fifteen years. Then Abraham died in a good old age, and old man, and full of years" (vv. 7,8). We will look at both the quantity of his years and the quality of his years.

The quantity of his years. Living to be 175 years old before he died, meant that when Abraham died, he had lived in the land of Canaan exactly 100 years (cp. 12:4 with our text). In that time, he saw some Divine promises about his seed fulfilled in a wonderful way—promises, which for a time, he had given up ever seeing fulfilled. But God is faithful, and so Abraham not only was given a son in Isaac, but he also saw his beloved son Isaac reach the age of 75—the age of Abraham when Abraham came to Canaan (12:4). And if that were not enough, he saw his grandsons Jacob and Esau reach the age of 15; for they were born when Isaac was 60 years old (25:26). Also, in those years, he had experienced great material prosperity and had become a great man of renown—fulfilling more promises God had made to him after he entered Canaan. The length of his years had given him much opportunity to see the vindication of the Word of God repeatedly.

It is interesting to study the various ages of the patriarchs which are given in Genesis 5 and 11. In doing so, one will be very surprised to discover that Abraham died before Shem, the son of Noah. Shem lived to be 600 years old (11:10,11). In comparing Scripture with Scripture, we discover he died 33 years after Abraham died, making Jacob and Esau 48 when Shem, the godly son of Noah, died. Eber (11:16,17), a great-grandson of Shem, also outlived Abraham. He did not die until 61 years after Abraham died.

Leupold, in commenting on the great length of age of some of the old patriarchs, such as Shem, said, "No doubt, there was a divine providence behind this matter of ages. Men like Noah and Shem were granted great length of life that, being historic personages and survivors of the flood, they might by their very presence as well as by their testimony offer warning to their godless successors." The longevity of the ancient patriarchs made it possible for Divine truth to be passed along from generation to generation with very few links over a period of several thousand years from Adam all the way to Jacob. Adam lived to Methusaleh's time, Methusaleh to Shem's days, and Shem lived to Jacob's time. Divine truth will be preserved and passed along to every generation. God will see to that! Man has no excuse for not knowing God's way.

Sunset of Life

The quality of his years. Abraham "died in a good old age, an old man, and full of years" (v. 8). God had promised that Abraham would "go to thy fathers in peace; [and] thou shalt be buried in a good old age" (15:15); and our text emphasizes the fulfillment of this Divine promise.

Barnhouse said, "The Hebrew of our text says that Abraham was satisfied with days." That is, the number of days allotted him satisfied him; so that when the time of departure came, he was ready to go. But this is not the way of the world. Maclaren said, "We have all seen godless old men cynical and sour, pleased with nothing, grumbling, or feebly complaining about everything, dissatisfied with all which life has thus far yielded them, and yet clinging desperately to it, and afraid to go." Wiersbe said, "How few people really experience joy and satisfaction when they reach old age! When they look back, it is with regret; when they look ahead, it is with fear; and when they look around it is with complaint." That was not the case with Abraham, however. His faith in God throughout his life made his death far different that those without God.

How you live determines how you will die. If we want to end life successfully, we must live life successfully. We are not talking here about success materially, but about success spiritually. You do not die in peace if you have not lived in peace with God. Balaam said, "Let me die the death of the righteous, and let my last end be like his!" (Numbers 23:10). But if you want to die like the righteous, you must live like the righteous—something Balaam failed to do and so died in shame by being slain (Numbers 31:8) by the Israelites when they attacked and defeated the Midianites at the command of the Lord. The godly can rest in the arms of Christ when they pass from this scene, but the ungodly have nothing upon which to lean when life is over. When the ungodly die, it is a terrible and horrifying start of a more terrible and horrifying eternity. There is no peace there. Abraham experienced a blessed death because he had put great faith in God and His Word. It is the only way to experience death.

2. His Abode After Death

We consider here the two abodes mentioned in reference to the death of Abraham. They are the abode of his body and the abode of his soul.

The abode of his body. "And his sons Isaac and Ishmael buried him in the cave of Machpelah, in the field of Ephron, the son of Zohar the Hittite, which is before Mamre; the field which Abraham purchased of the sons of Heth: there was Abraham buried, and Sarah, his wife" (vv. 9,10). We learned about the cave of Machpelah several chapters earlier when Abraham purchased it at the time of Sarah's death. The purchase of the cave, as we noted then, spoke of faith. It said Abraham believed God about the promise in the covenant regarding the giving of the land to his seed. It was a memorial of faith in the promises of God. It was also a memorial of the faithfulness of God. Thirty-eight years after the purchase of the cave, Isaac and Ishmael buried Abraham there; for it was the only fitting place to put his body.

Every time we read of the cave of Machpelah, it ought to remind and encourage our faith that there is more to come. Many things seem so contrary to the promises of God in this life. God promises us the land, yet we do not possess any of it, and it is possessed instead by the Canaanites who seemingly have an iron grip on the land. But God is faithful; if He has promised us the blessing, the blessing will one day be ours. And death does not end or cancel out the promise. Putting faith in God, unlike putting faith in man, is faith that death does not end it all. We have not got it all yet. We still have much more to come. We will not receive many of the blessings of faith in this life, but that does not mean we will not receive them at all. What we do not receive in this life, we shall receive in eternity. We who walk by faith in God's Word can all rest in the hope of the future of which the cave of Machpelah speaks.

The abode of his soul. When Abraham died, he "was gathered to his people" (v. 8). That statement does not refer to the fact that he was buried in the same place as Sarah. Rather that statement refers to the abode of his soul. If it referred only to the abode of the body, it would have to say he was gathered with Sarah, not with "people" plural; for Sarah was the only one in the cave at that time. In referring to the abode of the soul, this statement speaks about two important truths: it speaks about the fact of life after death, and it speaks about the location of the soul after death.

First, the fact of *life after death*. Our text makes it plain that Abraham did not cease to exist when he died. It is a great statement about life after death. When the body dies, the soul does not. It continues to exist, to live for all eternity. By the way most people live, however, you would think this life was all there is. They live for today only. They think not and care not about their future after death; a future that is for eternity. It is the height of folly to ignore the truth of life after death and to live only for this life.

Second, the *location of the soul after death*. Our text tells us where Abraham continued to live after his soul left his body. He was "gathered to his people." The soul goes to live with its kind. "His people" does not mean primarily blood relatives. Yes, many blood relatives may be present. But "his people" primarily refers to those of his kind regarding the faith. Until Jesus Christ arose from the grave, all the dead went to sheol (hades in the New Testament). There were two dwelling places in sheol. One for the believers—which was a blessed place (Luke 16:25) and was called in the New Testament "Abraham's bosom" (Luke 16:22), and one for the unbelievers—which was a terrible tormenting place of fire (Luke 16:23,24). Between the two groups, "there is a great gulf fixed" (Luke 16:26); so that the unbelievers could not escape the torments of judgment; and the believers would not experience the torments of judgment. We believe that when Christ arose, He took the righteous side of sheol with Him to heaven; and now when a saved person dies, his soul goes straight to heaven. The lost still go to the fiery place in hades.

But one day they will be taken out of hades to be judged by God, and then they will be cast into the lake of fire—their eternal abode. Hades is a temporary abode, but the lake of fire is an eternal abode. Hades is like the county jail where the accused criminals are placed. The lake of fire is like the prison where they are placed after they are sentenced.

What a blessed thing to be gathered with the redeemed. What a wonderful thing to be in the company of *only* the redeemed as Abraham was. But on the other hand, what a curse to be in the company of *only* the condemned sinner. Alexander Maclaren in referring to this text and Dante's writing said, "Men in the Dantesque circles were only made more miserable because all around them were of the same sort as, and some of them worse than, themselves. And an ordered hell, with no company for the liar but liars, and none for the thieves but thieves, and none for the impure men but the impure, and none for the godless but the godless, would be hell indeed." All men die, and all men will be gathered to the people of their kind. Abraham's faith in God put him in the gathering every soul ought to want to be in when they die.

Quotation Sources

The person listed is the author of the book which follows his name unless an asterisk (*) appears after the book title. In this case the person is a contributor to the book or is quoted in the book. Our quoting of a person does not mean we necessarily endorse all the beliefs, practices, or associations of that person.

Barnhouse, Donald Grey. *Genesis (Vol. 1)*.
Bounds, E. M. *Power Through Prayer*.
Candlish, Robert S. *Studies in Genesis*.
Cook, F. C. *The Bible Commentary (Vol. 1)*.
Henry, Matthew. *Matthew Henry's Commentary (Vol. 1)*.
Keil, C. F. *Keil and Delitzsch Commentary on the O.T. (Vol. 1)*.
Leale, T. H. *The Biblical Illustrator (Vol. 1)*.*
Leupold, H. C. *Exposition of Genesis (Vol. 1)*.
MackIntosh, C. H. *Notes on Genesis*.
McMillen, S. I. *None of These Diseases*.
Meyer, F. B. *Abraham*.
Murphy, James G. *A Commentary on the Book of Genesis*.
Parker, Joseph. *Preaching Through the Bible (Vol. 1)*.
Pink, Arthur W. *Gleanings in Genesis*.
Robertson, F. W. *The Biblical Illustrator (Vol. 1)*.*
Schechter, Dr. S. *Pamphlet entitled "Jewish Contributions to America and to the World" by Gerrit Buining*.
Simeon, Charles. *Expository Outlines on the Whole Bible (Vol. 1)*.
Spurgeon, Charles H. *The Treasury of the Bible (Old Testament, (Vol. 1)*.
Strahan, James. *Hebrew Ideals in Genesis*.
Thomas, W. H. Griffith. *Genesis: A Devotional Commentary*.
Whitelaw, Thomas. *The Pulpit Commentary (Vol. 1)*.*
Wiersbe, Warren W. *Be Obedient*.
Wilson, William. *Old Testament Word Studies*.